Legali

Editorial Advisors:
Gloria A. Aluise
Attorney at Law
Jonathan Neville
Attorney at Law
Robert A. Wyler
Attorney at Law

Authors:
Gloria A. Aluise
Attorney at Law
Daniel O. Bernstine
Attorney at Law
Roy L. Brooks
Professor of Law
Scott M. Burbank
C.P.A.
Charles N. Carnes
Professor of Law
Paul S. Dempsey
Professor of Law
Jerome A. Hoffman
Professor of Law
Mark R. Lee
Professor of Law
Jonathan Neville
Attorney at Law
Laurence C. Nolan
Professor of Law
Arpiar Saunders
Attorney at Law
Robert A. Wyler
Attorney at Law

CONSTITUTIONAL LAW

Adaptable to Thirteenth Edition* of Varat Casebook

By Jonathan Neville
Attorney at Law

*If your casebook is a newer edition, go to www.gilbertlaw.com to see if a supplement is available for this title.

THOMSON
WEST

EDITORIAL OFFICE: 1 N. Dearborn Street, Suite 650, Chicago, IL 60602
REGIONAL OFFICES: Chicago, Dallas, Los Angeles, New York, Washington, D.C.

SERIES EDITOR
Linda C. Schneider, J.D.
Attorney at Law

PRODUCTION MANAGER
Elizabeth G. Duke

FIRST PRINTING—2010

SUMMARY OF CONTENTS

TABLE OF CONTENTS AND SHORT REVIEW OUTLINE

I. THE CONSTITUTION AND THE COURTS: THE JUDICIAL FUNCTION IN CONSTITUTIONAL CASES

A. THE CONSTITUTION

1. **Introduction.** The Constitution of the United States currently consists of seven articles and 27 amendments. It was created in response to the inadequacies of the Articles of Confederation and was ratified by the nine states necessary in 1788. The Constitution separates the powers of the national government into three branches: executive, legislative, and judicial. Each branch was intended to remain independent yet subject to restraint by the other branches through a system of checks and balances. The study of Constitutional Law is essentially an examination of the sources of governmental power and the limitations imposed on its exercise. Through the system of judicial review, the United States Supreme Court has the final say in interpreting the Constitution; hence the heavy reliance on studying decisions of that Court.

2. **Significant Amendments.** The Articles of the Constitution contain important protections of individual liberty, including the writ of habeas corpus, prohibition of ex post facto laws, and the Privileges and Immunities Clause. Two groups of amendments, however, provide the majority of the civil liberties enjoyed in the United States today.

    a. **The Bill of Rights.** Many of the states included a Bill of Rights in their constitutions, but none was included in the original Constitution. Adoption of the first 10 amendments, popularly known as the Bill of Rights, was prompted largely by the concerns expressed during the state ratification conventions. These amendments did not affect state power; they were only limitations on the power of the federal government.

    b. **Civil War amendments.** The conquest over slavery in the Civil War presented serious social problems. The Thirteenth Amendment, which was ratified in 1865, provided legal support to eradicate slavery, which had been recognized in the original Constitution. In 1866, Congress enacted the Civil Rights Act to prohibit racial discrimination practiced by the states. The President vetoed the act on the ground that it was unconstitutional, and although Congress overrode the veto, the Fourteenth Amendment was proposed to overcome constitutional objections to the Civil Rights Act. It was ratified largely because Congress made ratification a condition for the rebel states to be represented in Congress. The Fifteenth Amendment prohibited denial of the right to vote for racial reasons.

B. JUDICIAL REVIEW

1. The Power of Judicial Review.

a. **Introduction.** Although there was some debate at the Constitutional Convention about the role of the judiciary in reviewing legislative acts, nothing in the Constitution gives the Supreme Court power to rule on the constitutionality of acts of Congress or state statutes, or power to review decisions of state courts. Article III merely creates the Supreme Court and extends the judicial power to "all Cases, in Law and Equity, arising under this Constitution, the Laws of the United States, and Treaties made . . . under their authority."

b. **Review of acts of Congress--**

Marbury v. Madison, 5 U.S. (1 Cranch) 137.

Facts. Marbury (P) and others were appointed justices of the peace for the District of Columbia by President Adams and confirmed by the Senate on Adams's last day in office. Their formal commissions were signed but not delivered. Madison (D), as Secretary of State, was directed by the new President (Jefferson) to withhold P's commission. P brought a writ of mandamus directly to the Supreme Court under the Judiciary Act of 1789, which established United States courts and authorized the Supreme Court to issue writs of mandamus to public officers.

Issue. Is the Supreme Court empowered to review acts of Congress and void those that it finds to be repugnant to the Constitution?

Held. Yes. P's action is discharged because the Court does not have original jurisdiction; section 13 of the Judiciary Act is unconstitutional.

- The facts demonstrate a plain case for mandamus action, and under the Judiciary Act this Court could so act.
- P claims that since the constitutional grant of jurisdiction is general and the clause assigning original jurisdiction to the Supreme Court (Article III, Section 2, Clause 2) contains no negative or restrictive words, the legislature may assign original jurisdiction to this Court in addition to that specified in the Constitution. But the clause specifies in what cases this Court is to have original jurisdiction, and that in all other cases its jurisdiction is appellate. P's contention would render the clause ineffectual, an inadmissible construction. There-

fore, the Judiciary Act's grant of original mandamus jurisdiction is unconstitutional and void.

- The grant of judicial power extends to all cases arising under the Constitution and laws of the United States. Since the Constitution is superior to any ordinary legislative act, it must govern in a case to which both apply.

- The Supremacy Clause (Article VI, Section 2) declares that the Constitution and those acts of Congress made in pursuance thereof shall be the supreme law of the land. Thus, the Court must determine when such acts are actually made in pursuance of the Constitution. The power of judicial review is implicit in the Constitution.

Comment. While the *Marbury* decision has been criticized because the Constitution did not explicitly provide for judicial review, most scholars believe that the Framers recognized the necessity of judicial power to review acts of Congress and state legislation.

---

c. Congressional power over Supreme Court jurisdiction--

Ex parte **McCardle,** 74 U.S. (7 Wall.) 506 (1869).

Facts. McCardle (D) had been imprisoned by the military government of Mississippi pursuant to the federal Reconstruction Acts and sought habeas corpus, which was denied him by the lower courts. He then appealed to the United States Supreme Court under the Congressional Act of 1867. That Act empowered federal district courts to grant habeas corpus to persons restrained in violation of the Constitution, treaty, or federal law and provided for appeals to the circuit courts and then to the Supreme Court. Since this case would have presented the Court with the opportunity of reaching the merits of the constitutionality of the Reconstruction Acts, on March 27, 1868, after the Court had heard argument but before it rendered a decision, Congress repealed the portion of the 1867 Act that allowed appeals to the Supreme Court from the circuit courts in cases of habeas corpus. Argument was then heard on the effect of the repealing act.

Issue. Does Congress have the power to limit or otherwise make exceptions to the appellate jurisdiction of the Supreme Court?

Held. Yes.

- Article III states that the Supreme Court has appellate jurisdiction, "with such Exceptions, and under such Regulations as the Congress shall make."

- Even though the appellate jurisdiction of the Court is not derived from acts of Congress but is conferred by the Constitution, it is also subject by the Constitution to the regulations and limitations that Congress shall make. The 1868 Act creates an express exception, taking away the Court's appellate jurisdiction in cases of habeas corpus arising under the 1867 Act. Thus, the Supreme Court no longer has jurisdiction in this case, and the case must be dismissed.

- However, this repealing act is limited in its scope. Only cases of habeas corpus arising under the Act of 1867 are barred from appeal. Other cases, including other habeas corpus cases arising from jurisdiction previously exercised, are not affected.

Comments.

- This case did not destroy judicial review. Appeals were still available in the district and circuit courts. Had Congress attempted to deny ***all*** appeals in habeas corpus cases, serious due process questions could have been raised. Furthermore, the 1867 statute did not totally deprive the Supreme Court of jurisdiction to decide McCardle's case. D still could have petitioned the Supreme Court for an ***original*** writ of habeas corpus.

- This case should not be broadly read as giving Congress full power to regulate and limit the Supreme Court's appellate jurisdiction in any manner it pleases. Congress may eliminate certain avenues for Supreme Court review of cases within the federal judicial power, but it cannot destroy the essential role of the Supreme Court in the constitutional scheme. Furthermore, Congress may not completely deprive the federal judiciary of power over cases within the constitutional scope of the federal judicial power. Congress must allow jurisdiction over every case within the federal judicial power to vest in some federal court. To do otherwise would deprive federal courts of the "judicial power of the United States" with which they are vested by Article III.

C. THE JURISDICTION OF FEDERAL COURTS IN CONSTITUTIONAL CASES

1. Supreme Court Review of State Court Decisions.

a. Background.

1) **History.** In the Judiciary Act of 1789, the First Congress created lower federal courts as permitted by the Constitution, but did not give them general jurisdiction in civil cases arising under federal law. The state courts were to exercise jurisdiction over such cases, and appellate review was intended to insure compliance with the

Supremacy Clause of Article IV. The Supreme Court was authorized by Congress to hear three types of cases on appeal, all of which were to be cases in which state courts rejected claims made under federal law. If a state court upheld such claims, the decision could not be reviewed.

2) **Constitutionality of the Judiciary Act--**

Martin v. Hunter's Lessee, 14 U.S. (1 Wheat.) 304 (1816).

Facts. Martin (D) was heir to the Virginia estates of Lord Fairfax, who died in England in 1781. Virginia claimed to have acquired the estates through state legislation confiscating the property of British loyalists; Virginia had subsequently conveyed title to Hunter. Hunter's lessee (P) brought an action of ejectment. D defended his title by virtue of two United States-British treaties protecting such British-owned property. The Virginia Court of Appeals sustained P's claim but was reversed by the United States Supreme Court. The Virginia court refused to comply with the reversal, and D again appealed.

Issue. Does the Supreme Court have appellate jurisdiction over the highest state courts on issues involving the federal Constitution, laws, and treaties?

Held. Yes. The Virginia court must obey the United States Supreme Court's rulings.

- The Judiciary Act of 1789, section 25, provided for review by the United States Supreme Court of final state court decisions rejecting claims under the federal Constitution and laws. The outcome of this case depends on the constitutionality of that section.
- Appellate jurisdiction is given by the Constitution to the Supreme Court in all cases where it does not have original jurisdiction, subject to congressional regulations.
- All cases involving the Constitution, laws, and treaties of the United States are included in the judicial power granted by the Constitution to the Supreme Court; hence all such cases are properly subject to that Court's appellate jurisdiction, and section 25 of the Judiciary Act is valid.
- Such power is necessary for a uniformity of decisions throughout the whole United States, upon all subjects within the purview of the Constitution.

---

3) **Current Supreme Court jurisdiction.** The Supreme Court's jurisdiction to review final judgments of the highest state court decision is set forth in 28 U.S.C. section 1257:

> [B]y writ of certiorari, where the validity of a treaty or statute of the United States is drawn into question or where the validity of a statute of any state is drawn into question on the ground of its being repugnant to the Constitution, treaties, or laws of the United States, or where any title, right, privilege, or immunity is specially set up or claimed under the Constitution or the treaties or statutes of, or any commission held or authority exercised under, the United States.

b. **Adequate and independent state ground.**

1) **Basic principle.** State courts alone determine state law. The Supreme Court's only power over state judgments is to correct them to the extent that they incorrectly adjudge federal rights. Review is limited to federal issues. Where there is an adequate and independent state ground for the state court's decision, the Court will deny review, because a reversal on federal grounds would not change the outcome and would hence be an advisory opinion. Unfortunately, it is not always possible to tell from the state court opinions whether there was an adequate and independent state ground.

2) **Rule for judging existence of adequate and independent state ground--**

Michigan v. Long, 463 U.S. 1032 (1983).

Facts. Long (D) was stopped while driving his car. The police searched the passenger compartment of D's car because they had reason to believe it contained dangerous weapons. They also conducted an inventory search of the trunk. During the searches, the police found marijuana in both places, and D was eventually convicted of possessing marijuana. The Michigan Supreme Court reversed, holding that the rationale of *Terry v. Ohio*, 392 U.S. 1 (1968), which held that a protective search for weapons without probable cause was permissible, did not apply here because the search was not conducted for protection of the police and others nearby. The opinion cited some state law, but mainly relied on federal law. The United States Supreme Court granted certiorari.

Issue. Must a state court opinion that ostensibly relies on federal law expressly state that it rests on separate, adequate, and independent state grounds to preclude United States Supreme Court review?

Held. Yes. Judgment reversed.

- Respect for the independence of state courts and refusal to give advisory opinions are the two main reasons the Supreme Court does not decide cases if there is an adequate and independent state ground for the result. The existence of such a state ground has been made on a case-by-case basis, using different approaches, none of which has proved satisfactory.

- The need for consistency in this delicate area requires adoption of the following rules:

  If the state court decision appears to rest on federal law, and the adequacy and independence of any possible state law ground is not clear from the face of the opinion, this Court will assume the state court felt bound by federal law.

  If the state court relies on federal law as persuasive but not binding, it can so indicate in the opinion and specify that the result is not compelled by the federal law.

  If the state court relies on federal law, but would have the same result under state law as well, the court can indicate clearly that the result is alternatively based on bona fide separate, adequate, and independent state grounds.

- In the present case, the Michigan court relied exclusively on federal cases to hold that the search of the passenger compartment was unconstitutional. In the absence of a plain statement of an adequate and independent state ground, this Court has jurisdiction. On the merits, we conclude that the search did not violate the Constitution.

Dissent (Stevens, J.). In this case, a state has decided to provide its citizens greater protection than is required by federal law. Because this Court cannot hear all cases, it should make sure that persons seeking to vindicate federal rights are heard; judicial restraint does not favor hearing requests by states to reverse judgments that their courts have rendered in favor of their citizens. In recent years, the Court has heard an increasing number of this type of case, which is an erroneous allocation of resources.

---

c. **The distinction between appeal and certiorari in review of state court decisions.**

1) **Statutory provisions (28 U.S.C. section 1257).** Until 1988, review of final judgments of the highest state courts was permitted in two ways:

a) ***By appeal***—whenever: (i) the validity of a federal statute or treaty was questioned and the state court's decision was against its validity; or (ii) a state statute, challenged as repugnant to the United States Constitution, laws, or treaties, was upheld.

b) ***By certiorari***—whenever the above issues arise, regardless of outcome, or where any title, right, privilege, or immunity is specially set up or claimed under the United States Constitution, laws, or treaties.

2) **Practical implications.** Review by appeal was a matter of right; *i.e.,* the Court was bound to accept and hear the appeal. Review by certiorari was entirely discretionary with the Court. Yet, under section 1257, the distinction between appeal and certiorari could depend solely on how the case is presented (*e.g.,* claiming a constitutional right vs. challenging a statute as unconstitutional).

3) **Certiorari is now only means of state court review.** In 1988, Congress eliminated the provisions for appeal of state court decisions, leaving certiorari as the only means for obtaining Supreme Court review of these decisions. Certiorari is granted only where there are special and important reasons for the Court to hear the case and no right to appeal is available. At least four Justices must vote to grant certiorari. Denial of petition for certiorari has no precedential value.

2. The Justiciability Requirement.

a. Generally. Congress has limited power to regulate Supreme Court jurisdiction. In addition, the Court has itself imposed certain limits on the exercise of federal jurisdiction to avoid nonessential interpretation of the Constitution.

1) Article III, Section 2 limits the jurisdiction of all federal courts to "cases and controversies," requiring federal courts to deal only with real and substantial disputes that affect the legal rights and obligations of parties having adverse interests and that allow specific relief through a conclusive judicial decree.

2) Justiciability is the term of art expressing this limitation placed on federal courts by the case and controversy doctrine. Justiciability is a highly flexible concept, construed narrowly by activist courts, broadly by more conservative courts.

3) The limits of justiciability also preclude rendering advisory opinions (opinions based on assumed or hypothetical facts that are not part of an existing, actual controversy), deciding moot cases (ones already resolved by subsequent developments) or collusive or friendly suits, or adjudicating purely political questions.

4) Problems of case and controversy and justiciability arise most often when a plaintiff seeks an injunction or a declaratory judgment as to the constitutionality of a statute.

b. **Standing to sue.** To invoke federal jurisdiction (have standing to sue), the claimant must show that he is actually injured by the statute or act complained of. Even if the claimant shows actual injury, the Court exercises judicial "self-governance" by determining the prudence of resolving the issues presented by the party.

1) **Basic standing rules.**

a) **Requirement of personal injury.** A claimant must show an actual injury, indicating a personal stake in the outcome so that the controversy will be presented in a truly adversary context. The claim cannot be based on an abstract or generalized injury. For example, standing to sue cannot be predicated upon an injury common to all members of the public. However, the fact that no one could prove a sufficiently concrete injury in such a case is not a reason to find standing on a lesser standard.

b) **Individual plaintiffs required--**

Warth v. Seldin, 422 U.S. 490 (1975).

Facts. Warth, other individuals, and various organizations (Ps), all of Rochester, New York, sued the adjacent town of Penfield (D) and members of its zoning, planning, and town boards in federal court for violations of the First, Ninth, and Fourteenth Amendments and of various federal statutes. Ps (individuals, low-income minorities, and organizations) claimed that D's zoning ordinance and manner of administration unconstitutionally exclude persons of low and moderate income from living in Penfield. The court of appeals affirmed the district court's dismissal for lack of standing.

Issue. Are plaintiffs with interrelated claims of unconstitutional conduct against the same defendant, which (when considered as a whole) would justify standing, properly refused standing when each individual plaintiff personally fails to allege a concrete injury?

Held. Yes. Judgment affirmed.

- ♦ The Constitution requires that each plaintiff himself suffer some threatened or actual injury resulting from the putatively illegal action by the defendant in order to have standing.

- ♦ To limit the role of the courts in resolving public disputes, the Court has held that a "generalized grievance" or harm shared equally by a large class of citizens does not warrant the exercise of jurisdiction. Also, each plaintiff must assert his own legal rights and interests, and cannot rest his claim to relief on the legal rights or interests of third parties. However, the fact that a plaintiff's harm resulted indirectly through government prohibition or restriction imposed on a third party does not in itself preclude standing if the plaintiff can establish that the asserted injury was the consequence of the defendant's actions or that prospective relief will remove the harm.

- ♦ Congress can and has created statutory legal rights, the invasion of which creates standing, but each plaintiff must still allege a distinct and palpable injury to himself.

- ♦ Here, the individual Ps have failed to allege that they suffered personal injury, or that they would be able to purchase or lease in Penfield if D's restrictive zoning practices were eliminated.

- ♦ Plaintiff associations must allege that at least one member is suffering immediate or threatened injury as a result of the challenged action, which would give the injured member standing had he brought suit himself. In addition, they must show that any dispute with D is a live, concrete dispute when the complaint is filed.

Dissent (Douglas, J.). The Court should lower the technical barrier and serve the ancient need of dispensing justice, especially here, where the zoning power is claimed to have been used to foist an un-American community model on the people. It would be a better practice to decide the question of standing only when the merits have been developed.

Dissent (Brennan, White, Marshall, JJ.). The opinion can be explained only by an indefensible hostility to the claim on the merits. Courts cannot refuse to hear a case on the merits merely because they prefer not to, and it is clear here that at least three groups of Ps have made allegations sufficient to survive a motion to dismiss for lack of standing.

---

c) **Type of permissible injuries.** In *Village of Arlington Heights v. Metropolitan Housing Development Corp., infra*, the village refused to rezone certain property; a builder of low and moderate income housing and three black individuals brought suit alleging that the denial was racially discriminatory. The Court held that the plaintiffs had standing, stating that, while many additional factors would determine whether the housing project was completed, the defendant's action was an absolute barrier. Economic injury is not the only kind of injury that can support a plaintiff's standing. The specific project involved provided that "essential dimension of specificity" that informs judicial decisionmaking. The builder had based its claim on violation of the Fourteenth Amendment; however, it has no racial identity and could not be the direct target of the defendant's alleged discrimination. Ordinarily, a party is denied standing to assert the rights of third persons. But in this case there was at least one individual plaintiff who had indicated a desire to move to the proposed project. Thus, there was a specific grievance, an "actionable causal relationship" between the defendant's actions and the plaintiffs' asserted injury, such that if judicial relief was granted, there was a "substantial probability" that the injury would be relieved.

d) **Requirement of nexus between status and claim.** The Court in early decisions determined that a federal taxpayer's interest in federal spending or appropriation measures was simply "too remote and indefinite" to allow standing for taxpayers who can establish a "nexus" between their taxpayer status and the claim sought to be adjudicated sufficient to ensure the personal stake in the outcome, which is essential to standing. [*See, e.g.*, Flast v. Cohen, 392 U.S. 83 (1968)]

e) **Requirement of cause and effect.** The injury must result from the unconstitutionality of the challenged statute or conduct, so that judicial relief may prevent or redress the injury. In *Duke Power Co. v. Carolina Environmental Study Group, Inc.*, 434 U.S. 937 (1978), the Court held that residents of proposed sites of nuclear power plants had standing to challenge the constitutionality of the federal Price-Anderson Act, which limited liability for nuclear accidents to $560 million. Standing was not based on a claim for damages in excess of the liability limitations of the challenged act but on a claim of injury from construction and operation of the plants—increased water temperature and low-level radiation emissions—which would not arise but for the liability limitations that made construction financially feasible. The Court held that an "injury in fact and a substantial likelihood that the judicial relief requested will prevent or redress the claimed injury" is enough to satisfy the case and controversy requirement, except in taxpayer's suits.

2) **Asserting rights of third parties.**

a) **Introduction.** In special circumstances, a plaintiff who has personally suffered injury may be allowed to assert the rights of third parties who were also injured by the alleged unconstitutional acts. Generally, this is permitted where the third persons in question would find it difficult (if not impossible) to vindicate their own rights, or where the injury suffered by the plaintiff adversely affects her relationship with the third parties, thereby resulting in an indirect violation of their rights.

b) **Vendor asserting rights of customer--**

Craig v. Boren, 429 U.S. 190 (1976).

Facts. Craig (P), a male, challenged an Oklahoma statute that denied beer sales to males under 21 and females under 18. A licensed vendor of beer, Whitener, joined the suit with P. They sought declaratory and injunctive relief. The district court dismissed the action, and P and Whitener appealed. After the Supreme Court noted probable jurisdiction, P reached age 21, so the controversy became moot as to him. Whitener seeks to pursue the case.

Issue. May a vendor assert the constitutional rights of her customers when a restriction on the vendor would result indirectly in the violation of the customers' rights?

Held. Yes. Judgment reversed.

- The defendants never objected to Whitener's equal protection challenge and presumed she was a proper party in interest. The Court's limitation on a party's assertion of jus tertii, or third-party standing, is a rule of self-restraint, not a constitutional mandate, and is intended to avoid decisions on speculative controversies. Since this case has proceeded this far, it would be inappropriate to remand the case.

- Whitener has established her claim to third-party standing anyway, because she has shown an injury in fact inflicted on her by the statute. The legal duties under the law are imposed directly on her as a vendor. She must comply or face sanctions. If her challenge fails, her customers' rights would be adversely affected. Vendors seeking to resist restriction of their businesses have been permitted to assert the rights of third parties who seek access to their market. The impact of the litigation on the third-party interests is material enough that Whitener must be allowed to assert those interests.

Dissent (Burger, C.J.). This case fits none of the limited exceptions to the rule that a litigant may only assert her own constitutional rights or immunities. Oklahoma males prevented from buying beer are free to assert any constitutional rights they may claim to buy beer; their rights would not be diluted if Whitener could not litigate them.

c) **State standing to sue over greenhouse gases.** In *Massachusetts v. Environmental Protection Agency*, 549 U.S. 497 (2007), the Court held that Massachusetts had standing to challenge the decision of the EPA not to regulate greenhouse gases. The majority found that the state had a stake in protecting its quasi-sovereign interests and that it faced a risk of harm that was both actual and imminent.

3) **Taxpayer and citizen standing.**

a) **Background.** In early decisions, the Court held that a federal taxpayer's interest in federal spending or appropriation measures was simply "too remote and indefinite" to allow standing to attack such measures. [Frothingham v. Mellon, 262 U.S. 447 (1922)]

b) **Modern trend.** More recently, the Court has found possible standing for taxpayers who can establish a "nexus" between their taxpayer status and the claim sought to be adjudicated sufficient to insure the personal stake in the outcome that is essential to standing. [Flast v. Cohen, *supra*] In that case, taxpayers had standing only to challenge, on Establishment Clause grounds, congressional exercises of the power to tax and spend conferred by Article I, Section 8 of the Constitution. In *United States v. Richardson*, 418 U.S. 166 (1974), the Court denied standing to a taxpayer who challenged a statute permitting the CIA to avoid public accounting of its expenditures as a violation of Article I, Section 9, clause 7. The challenged statute was not enacted under Article I, Section 8, so there was no nexus to the taxpayer's status.

c) **Public interest not enough--**

Lujan v. Defenders of Wildlife, 504 U.S. 555 (1992).

Facts. Section 7(a)(2) of the Endangered Species Act ("ESA") requires federal agencies to ensure, in consultation with the Secretary of the Interior, that any action carried out by such agency is not likely to jeopardize the continued existence of any endangered or threatened species. The Fish and Wildlife Service and National Marine Fisheries Service promulgated a joint regulation stating that section 7(a)(2) extended to actions taken in foreign nations, but the regulation was later modified to require consultations only for actions taken in the United States or on the high seas. The ESA also provided that "any person may commence a civil suit on his behalf" to enjoin a government agency who is alleged to be in violation of the Act. The Defenders of Wildlife (P) brought suit against Lujan (D), the Secretary of the Interior, seeking a declaratory judgment that the more recent regulation incorrectly interpreted the ESA. Both parties moved for summary judgment. The district court granted P's motion. The court of appeals affirmed. The Supreme Court granted certiorari.

Issue. May Congress convert the public interest in proper administration of the laws into an individual right such that all citizens may have standing to sue?

Held. No. Judgment reversed.

♦ Neither P nor any of its members had any injury in fact. P's standing, if any, depends on the validity of the "citizen-suit" provision of the ESA. The court of appeals held that this provision created a "procedural right" to interagency consultation in all persons, so that anyone can file suit to challenge D's failure to follow the allegedly correct consultative procedure, even if there is no discrete injury resulting from that failure. In effect, the court held that the injury-in-fact requirement under Article III has been satisfied by congressional conferral upon all persons of an abstract, self-contained "right" to have the Executive Branch observe the procedures required by law.

♦ Article III confers jurisdiction on the federal courts only where there is a case or controversy. This requirement is not met by a plaintiff raising only a generally available grievance about government, where the harm is only to the interest of all citizens in proper application of the Constitution and laws. Hence, a taxpayer does not have standing to challenge alleged violations of the Constitution by the Executive or Legislative branches where the violations would adversely affect only the generalized interest of all citizens in constitutional governance. The federal courts may only decide on the rights of individuals. Vindicating the public interest is the function of Congress and the President.

♦ If Congress could convert the undifferentiated public interest in an executive that complies with the law into an "individual right" to be vindicated in the courts, Congress could transfer from the President to the courts the Chief Executive's most important constitutional duty, to "take Care that the Laws be faithfully executed."

♦ The fact that Congress may not eliminate the requirement of a concrete personal injury does not preclude Congress from creating legal rights, the invasion of which creates standing.

Concurrence (Kennedy, Souter, JJ.). Congress may define injuries and articulate chains of causation that give rise to a case or controversy where none existed before, but at a minimum, Congress must identify the injury it seeks to vindicate and relate the injury to the class of persons entitled to bring suit. The citizen-suit provisions of the ESA do not establish that there is an injury in any person by virtue of any violation. The case and controversy requirement ensures both that the parties have an actual stake in the outcome and that the legal questions presented will be resolved in a concrete factual context conducive to a realistic appreciation of the consequences of judicial action. The public is entitled to know what persons invoke the judicial power, their reasons, and whether their claims are vindicated or denied.

Concurrence (Stevens, J.). P does not lack standing, but Congress did not intend section 7(a)(2) to apply to activities in foreign countries.

Dissent (Blackmun, O'Connor, JJ.). Congress granted considerable discretion to the executive branch to determine how best to attain the goals of ESA, constrained by specific procedural requirements. This does not constitute a violation of the separation of powers, nor should the separation of powers be deemed violated when Congress requires the federal courts to enforce the procedures. The citizen-suit provisions of ESA were based on the same understanding that arose from earlier cases in which the Court justified a relaxed review of congressional delegation to the executive branch because Congress provided for judicial review of the exercise of that power. [*See* Immigration & Naturalization Service v. Chadha, *infra*]

---

d) Congressional standing--

Raines v. Byrd, 521 U.S. 811 (1997).

Facts. Congress enacted the Line Item Veto Act, which allowed the President to "cancel" certain spending and tax benefit measures contained in legislation, after he had signed the legislation. Following such a cancellation, Congress could consider the President's action and render his cancellation null and void. The Act also provided that any member of Congress could bring an action in federal court for declaratory judgment and injunctive relief on the ground that any provision of the Act was unconstitutional. Raines and five other members of Congress (Ps) brought this action to have the Act declared unconstitutional. The district court found the Act unconstitutional. Byrd (D) appeals.

Issue. Do Members of Congress have standing to challenge the constitutionality of an Act of Congress if they cannot show personal injury?

Held. No. Judgment reversed.

- Federal courts have jurisdiction only over a dispute that is a case or controversy. One element of the case-or-controversy requirement is that the plaintiffs must establish that they have standing to sue. The standing requirements include an allegation of personal injury fairly traceable to the defendant's allegedly unlawful conduct and likely to be redressed by the requested relief.

- The standing requirement is especially rigorous when the merits involve the question of the constitutionality of the actions taken by one of the other two branches of the federal government.

- In *Powell v. McCormack, infra*, the Court held that a member of Congress has standing to challenge his exclusion from the House of Representatives, but in this case, Ps have not been singled out for specially unfavorable treatment as opposed to other members of Congress. Ps' claim involves an institutional injury, not a personal injury. Nor does the diminution of legislative power claimed by Ps deprive them of something to which they were personally entitled. Their claim runs with their seat in Congress. It is not personal to them.

- In *Coleman v. Miller*, 307 U.S. 433 (1939), the Court recognized standing for legislators claiming an institutional injury. In that case, the plaintiffs were members of the Kansas legislature who voted against ratification of an amendment to the federal Constitution. They had standing because as a bloc of legislators, if they had been correct on the merits, their votes not to ratify the amendment were deprived of all validity. In this case, however, Ps' votes were given full effect. They simply lost the vote. The institutional injury they allege is abstract and widely dispersed, and does not amount to a personal stake.

Concurrence (Souter, Ginsburg, JJ.). This case involves an interbranch controversy about allocating legislative and executive powers and an intrabranch controversy among segments of Congress itself. The courts should not get involved in such power contests. If a party outside the federal government had challenged the Act, there would be lesser risk in having the judiciary hear the case.

Dissent (Stevens, J.). The impairment of Ps' constitutional rights has an immediate impact on their official powers, and this should satisfy the standing requirement.

Dissent (Breyer, J.). This case presents a stronger case for standing than did *Coleman* because this case involves a lawmaking procedure that threatens the validity of many laws.

Comment. The Court found standing in *Clinton v. City of New York, infra*, on the ground that the parties had a personal injury when the President cancelled a provision that allowed the plaintiffs to defer recognition of capital gains.

---

c. **Mootness.**

1) **Introduction.** The usual rule in federal cases is that an actual controversy must exist at all stages of appellate or certiorari review, and not simply at the date the action is initiated.

a) **Capable of repetition.** However, issues involving events of short duration (pregnancy, elections, economic strikes) are not necessarily moot if the issue is "capable of repetition, yet evading review."

b) **Criminal cases.** Also, a criminal case is not moot, even though the defendant has served his sentence or paid his fine, if there are any collateral consequences of the conviction, *e.g.,* loss of civil rights, damage to reputation, etc.

2) **Admission procedures--**

DeFunis v. Odegaard, 416 U.S. 312 (1974).

Facts. DeFunis (P) applied for admission to the University of Washington Law School and was denied. He brought suit, claiming that the school's admissions procedures invidiously discriminated against him on account of his race. The trial court granted a mandatory injunction, and P was admitted. The Washington Supreme Court reversed, but Justice Douglas stayed that judgment pending final disposition of the case by the United States Supreme Court. When the Court first considered P's case, he was in the first term of his third year, and the Court requested the parties to brief the issue of mootness. Both sides contended that the case was not moot, and the case was orally argued during P's last term in school.

Issue. When mootness is not compelled by the record and there is a likelihood of repetitious litigation, must the court find mootness when it can no longer affect a party's rights by its decision?

Held. Yes. The case is moot.

- Federal courts are without power to decide questions that cannot affect the rights of litigants in the case before them, because the Constitution requires an actual case or controversy.

- Although under Washington law the case would be saved from mootness, it is a federal question that must be resolved before a federal court assumes jurisdiction.

- P is entitled to complete his legal studies regardless of the Court's decision, and never will again seek admission. Therefore, the case is not "capable of repetition, yet evading review." If necessary, the issues can be raised again by other parties, should the same event recur.

Dissent (Brennan, Douglas, White, Marshall, JJ.). The issues raised will surely return to the Court. Because avoidance of repetitious litigation serves the public interest, that inevitability counsels against mootness determinations that are, as here, not compelled by the record. The Court should not transform principles of avoidance of constitutional decisions into devices for sidestepping resolution of difficult cases.

d. **Ripeness.**

1) **In general.** The Court will decide only those issues that are "ripe" for adjudication. It will not anticipate a question of constitutional law prior to the necessity of deciding it, or pass upon issues that may or may not arise sometime in the future. These problems generally arise in suits for injunctions and declaratory judgments.

a) **Possible threats not sufficient.** In *United Public Workers v. Mitchell*, 330 U.S. 75 (1947), a group of federal government employees challenged an aspect of the Hatch Act as preventing them from exercising a constitutional right to participate in political campaigns. One plaintiff (Poole) alleged that action under the Hatch Act was being taken against him for his political activity. The Court granted Poole standing, but denied it for the other plaintiffs. It found their general objection to be an "attack on the political expediency of the Hatch Act, not a presentation of legal issues." The threat to them was merely hypothetical, while Poole's injury was concrete.

b) **The importance of a constitutional determination.** In *Adler v. Board of Education*, 342 U.S. 485 (1952), Adler and others sought a judgment declaring unconstitutional the Feinberg law, which required the discharge of teachers who belonged to allegedly subversive groups. The trial court granted a judgment on the pleadings, in effect finding that there could be no constitutional applications of the statute. The Supreme Court affirmed. The question did not turn on particular conduct of the plaintiffs but solely on the statute. In addition, the case came up through the state courts, giving the Supreme Court jurisdiction by appeal. Had the Court decided against ripeness or concreteness, it would have left undisturbed the state court determination of federal constitutional law.

c) **Unenforced statutes.** In *Poe v. Ullman*, 367 U.S. 497 (1961), the plaintiffs sought a declaratory judgment on an anti-contraception law that had not been enforced for 80 years. The Court declined to decide the case, stating that the declaratory judgment device does not permit litigants to invoke the power of the Court in advance of a necessity to do so.

d) **The concept of "concreteness."** Despite what has been said above, the concept of concreteness does not always require that an actual injury has occurred, but more than a subjective apprehension of possible future injury is required. For example, in *Younger v. Harris*, 401 U.S. 37 (1971), the plaintiffs who felt inhibited by a statute on the books, but who were in no danger of prosecution, did not show the degree of concreteness required to prevent having their action dismissed.

2) **Injunctions--**

City of Los Angeles v. Lyons, 461 U.S. 95 (1983).

Facts. Lyons (P) was injured when police officers applied a "chokehold" when they stopped him for a traffic violation. P had not offered resistance or threat. P sued the officers and their employer, the city of Los Angeles (D), in federal district court, seeking damages. One count of the complaint sought a preliminary and permanent injunction against D that would bar the use of chokeholds. The district court granted D's motion for judgment on the injunction count, but the court of appeals reversed, holding that P had standing to seek relief. On remand, the court entered a preliminary injunction, which the court of appeals affirmed. The Supreme Court granted certiorari.

Issue. Must the threat to the plaintiff be real and immediate before the federal courts may exercise jurisdiction to grant an injunction?

Held. Yes. Judgment reversed.

- Article III requires those seeking to invoke federal jurisdiction to allege an actual case or controversy. In prior cases we have held that the threat to the plaintiff must be sufficiently real and immediate to show an existing controversy. Mere hypothetical or speculative future injury is not sufficient.

- P's standing in this case depends on whether he was likely to suffer future injury from D's use of chokeholds. P alleges one instance in which such an injury occurred, but this establishes no real and immediate threat that he will again be stopped for an offense by an officer who will illegally choke him without excuse.

- To establish an actual controversy, P would have had to allege that he would have another encounter with the police and that either all of D's police officers always choke any citizen with whom they have an encounter, or that D ordered or authorized its police officers to act in such a way. The odds that P would again be subjected to an unexcused, illegal chokehold are not sufficient to justify exercise of federal equitable jurisdiction.

- Even if P's pending damages suit gives him standing to seek an injunction as a remedy for the claim arising from the one incident, he cannot claim an injunction any more than any other citizen who merely asserts that certain practices of law enforcement officers are unconstitutional.

Dissent (Marshall, Brennan, Blackmun, Stevens, JJ.). P has standing by virtue of his damages suit, which will litigate the constitutionality of D's chokehold policy. The cases relied on by the majority did not involve suits for damages. The result of this case is a new doctrine that will fragment standing inquiries. A separate showing of standing is now required for each form of relief sought. Consequently, policies that authorize persistent deprivations of constitutional rights cannot be challenged unless an individual can establish with substantial certainty that he will be injured, or injured again, in the future.

---

e. **Political questions.**

1) **Introduction.** The justiciability requirement is deemed to include a prohibition against deciding purely "political questions" that are better resolved by other government departments. The primary determinants of the existence of a political question are:

a) A "textually demonstrable" constitutional commitment of the issue to the political branches for resolution;

b) The appropriateness of attributing finality to the action of the political branches;

c) The lack of adequate standards for judicial resolution of the issue; and

d) The lack of adequate judicial remedies.

2) **Political questions vs. political cases.** There is a distinction between political questions and political cases. The Court will claim jurisdiction of political cases that require discriminatory inquiry into the precise facts and posture of the particular case.

a) **Political cases--**

Powell v. McCormack, 395 U.S. 486 (1969).

Facts. Adam Clayton Powell, Jr. (P) was duly elected to the 90th Congress, but pursuant to a House resolution was not permitted to take his seat. P sued McCormack (D) and other House officials, claiming that the House could exclude him only if he failed to meet the requirements of age, citizenship, and residence contained in Article I, Section 2 of the Constitution, which the House specifically found he had met. The district court dismissed the complaint "for want of jurisdiction of the subject matter," and the court of appeals affirmed. P appeals.

Issue. Is the federal court prevented from reviewing the congressional exclusion of a duly elected member by the prohibition against deciding political questions?

Held. No. P is entitled to a declaratory judgment that he was unlawfully excluded from the 90th Congress.

- ♦ The case is not moot despite P's admittance to the 91st Congress because he has asked for damages. The case is clearly justiciable if it is not barred as a political question.

- ♦ D contends that there is a "textually demonstrable" constitutional commitment to the House of the "adjudicatory power" to determine P's qualifications. The Court nevertheless has the duty to interpret the Constitution to determine the existence and scope of such a power, and finds that P is correct that the House is without authority to exclude any person, duly elected, who meets all the requirements for membership expressly prescribed in the Constitution. Congress can judge only the qualifications expressly set forth in the Constitution, and federal courts are not barred from reviewing congressional judgments that extend beyond these qualifications.

- ♦ D fears a potentially embarrassing confrontation between coordinate branches of the federal government as a result of judicial resolution of P's claim, and thus contends that the case presents a political question. However, the alleged conflict that such an adjudication may cause cannot justify the Court's avoiding its constitutional responsibility of interpretation.

---

b) Challenge to impeachment procedure as a political question--

---

Nixon v. United States, 506 U.S. 224 (1993).

Facts. Nixon (P), a former federal district court judge, was convicted of making false statements before a federal grand jury. He was sentenced to prison, but refused to resign from his judicial office. The United States House of Representatives adopted articles of impeachment and presented them to the Senate. The Senate appointed a committee to hold evidentiary hearings. The committee made a report to the full Senate, which gave P three hours of oral argument to supplement the committee record. The Senate voted to convict P on the impeachment articles, and P was removed from his office. P then sued, claiming the Senate's failure to participate in the evidentiary hearings as a full body violated the Senate's constitutional authority to "try" impeachments. The lower courts held that P's claim was nonjusticiable, and the Supreme Court granted certiorari.

Issue. May the courts review the procedures whereby the United States Senate tries impeachments?

Held. No. Judgment affirmed.

- A controversy is nonjusticiable when there is a "textually demonstrable constitutional commitment of the issue to a coordinate political department; or a lack of judicially discoverable and manageable standards for resolving it." [Baker v. Carr, 369 U.S. 186 (1962)]

- To apply this test, the courts must determine whether and to what extent the issue is "textually committed." In this case, Article I, Section 3, clause 6 simply provides that the "Senate shall have the sole Power to try all Impeachments." This clause clearly grants the Senate the exclusive authority to try impeachments.

- The use of the word "try" does not require a judicial trial; it is not an implied limitation on how the Senate may try impeachments. This is made clear by the inclusion of specific provisions such as the two-thirds vote requirement.

- Judicial review of the Senate's trying of impeachments would be inconsistent with the system of checks and balances. Impeachment is the legislature's only check on the judicial branch, and it would be inconsistent to give the judicial branch final reviewing authority over the legislature's use of the impeachment process. The need for finality and the difficulty of fashioning relief also demonstrate why judicial review is inappropriate in this case.

Concurrence (Stevens, J.). The Framers assigned the impeachment power to the Legislative Branch and we must respect that branch and presume it acts properly.

Concurrence (White, Blackmun, JJ.). The Court should reach the merits of P's claim. But on the merits, the Senate fulfilled its constitutional duty to "try" P. The Senate has wide discretion in specifying impeachment trial procedures, and the use of a factfinding committee is compatible with the constitutional requirement that the Senate "try" all impeachments. However, it is consistent with the Constitution that while the Senate serves as a means of controlling a largely unaccountable judiciary, judicial review insures that the Senate follow minimal procedural standards.

Concurrence (Souter, J.). Judicial review would be appropriate if the Senate were to act so as to seriously threaten the integrity of the results, such as by convicting based on a coin-toss.

---

3) **The interplay between Congress and the President in foreign affairs.** The President has special powers in foreign affairs due to the need for decisive action and a uniform policy with regard to sensitive foreign relations. Congress, however, retains certain powers over foreign affairs, including the power to declare war, appro-

priate funds, and ratify treaties. The question has arisen whether the President has unilateral authority to abrogate treaties.

a) **Termination of treaties--**

Goldwater v. Carter, 444 U.S. 996 (1979).

Facts. President Carter (D) gave notice of intention to terminate a treaty with Taiwan in order to recognize the Peking government. Senator Goldwater (P) and other senators sued to enjoin termination without a two-thirds vote of the Senate. The court of appeals sustained the President's authority to terminate. The Supreme Court granted a writ of certiorari.

Issue. Is presidential action to terminate a treaty subject to judicial review when challenged by individual senators but not the Senate as a body?

Held. No. Judgment vacated and case remanded with directions to dismiss the complaint.

Concurrence (Powell, J.). A dispute between Congress and the President is not ripe for judicial review unless and until each branch has taken action to assert its constitutional authority and thereby has reached a constitutional impasse. Since the case is not ripe, it should be dismissed. However, the case, if ripe, would be reviewable. It is not a political question because: (i) there is no "textually demonstrable constitutional commitment" of the treaty termination power to the President; (ii) there is no "lack of judicially discoverable and manageable standards," so normal principles of constitutional interpretation would apply; and (iii) no prudential limitations would prohibit consideration.

Concurrence (Rehnquist, J., Burger, C.J., Stewart, Stevens, JJ.). The case involves political questions because it involves the President's authority to conduct foreign relations. Resolution of the question should be left to the executive and legislative branches.

Dissent (Blackmun, White, JJ.). The case involves serious issues that should be briefed and considered after oral argument.

Dissent (Brennan, J.). The President has the sole authority to establish or withdraw official recognition of foreign regimes; the decision of the court of appeals should be affirmed.

II. ALLOCATION OF GOVERNMENTAL POWERS: THE NATION AND THE STATES; THE PRESIDENT, THE CONGRESS, AND THE COURTS

A. THE SCOPE OF NATIONAL POWER

1. **The Constitutional Convention.** The Framers deliberated extensively on the nature and scope of national power. Constitutional jurisprudence has focused on three major areas:

    a. The federal government's power to regulate, especially under the Necessary and Proper Clause;

    b. The extent of the limitations placed on state power to regulate and tax, especially where federal preemption may apply; and

    c. The nature and scope of governmental immunities between the states and the federal government.

2. **Sources of National Power.**

    a. **The Marshall Court.** The Supreme Court under Chief Justice Marshall addressed certain fundamental problems and derived solutions that remain controlling today. In addition to the powers enumerated in Article I, Section 8, the federal government exercises certain implied powers under the Necessary and Proper Clause (Article I, Section 8, Clause 18).

        1) **Implied powers--**

McCulloch v. Maryland, 17 U.S. (4 Wheat.) 316 (1819).

Facts. A Maryland statute imposed a tax requiring all banks chartered outside the state to print their bank notes on stamped paper if they established any branch or office within the state of Maryland. The Bank of the United States came within the statutory definition, yet issued notes on unstamped paper. Accordingly, the state of Maryland (P) brought an action for debt collection against McCulloch (D), who was cashier of the Baltimore branch of the Bank of the United States. D appeals from state court judgments in favor of P.

Issues.

(i) Does Congress have the power to incorporate a bank, making it an appendage to the federal government?

(ii) Is a state constitutionally prohibited from taxing the operations of such a bank?

Held. (i) Yes. (ii) Yes. Judgment reversed.

- The government of the Union, although limited in its powers, is supreme within its sphere of action.

- Establishing a bank and creating a corporation are not specifically included among the enumerated powers, but neither is there an exclusion of incidental or implied powers. Among the enumerated powers are those to lay and collect taxes; to borrow money; to regulate commerce, etc. The grant of such large powers implies a grant of ample means for their execution; indeed, the Necessary and Proper Clause specifically gives Congress such broad powers.

- The word "necessary" is to be understood in its common usage; *i.e.,* meaning convenient or useful. To attribute a notion of indispensability to the clause (as P would do) goes contrary to the intent of the Framers, who intentionally avoided such strict interpretation by omitting a strong prefix such as "absolutely." A broad construction provides the flexibility required of the Constitution and allows the national legislature the degree of discretion that will enable that body to perform the high duties assigned to it in the manner most beneficial to the people.

- The degree of necessity is beyond judicial review, provided the law is neither prohibited by the Constitution nor seeks to accomplish objects not entrusted to the government. Therefore, the act of incorporating the Bank of the United States is constitutional.

- The power of establishing a branch in the state of Maryland may be properly exercised by the Bank itself.

- Although the states retain a power of taxation, the Constitution may withdraw any subject from subjection to state taxation. Additionally, states may tax only subjects over which they are sovereign, and states are not sovereign over those means employed by Congress to execute its own powers. Otherwise the federal government would be dependent on the states, contrary to the intent of the Constitution.

- The states, therefore, have no power, by taxation or otherwise, to retard, impede, burden, or in any manner control the operations of valid federal laws enacted to execute federal powers. P's tax on the operations of the Bank of the United States is unconstitutional and void.

Comment. Despite this ruling, the federal government may tax banks chartered by the states. When Congress taxes "the chartered institutions of the states, they tax their constituents . . . but, when a state taxes the operations of the (federal) government . . . it acts upon institutions created . . . by the people over whom they claim no control."

---

2) Exclusive vs. concurrent powers--

Gibbons v. Ogden, 22 U.S. (9 Wheat.) 1 (1824).

Facts. Ogden (P) held an assignment of the exclusive right to run a steamboat between Elizabethtown, New Jersey, and New York City. The exclusive right to operate steamships in New York waters had been granted by the New York legislature. Gibbons (D) operated boats along P's route, claiming that his boats were duly enrolled and licensed under United States law for carrying on the coasting trade. P sought and obtained a state court injunction prohibiting D's operation. The injunction was sustained by the highest state court, and D appeals.

Issue. Is state regulation of commercial navigation that excludes federally licensed operators constitutional?

Held. No. The New York statute is void. Judgment reversed.

- P admits that Congress has the power to regulate commerce with foreign nations and among the several states, but would limit the meaning of "commerce" to traffic, buying and selling, or the interchange of commodities, and would exclude navigation. But one of the primary objects of the creation of the federal government was to grant the power over commerce, including navigation.

- The commerce power of Congress must be exercised within the territorial jurisdiction of the states, even though it cannot reach solely intrastate commerce.

- P attempts to analogize between the taxing power and the commerce power, claiming that since the taxing power is concurrent, the commerce power should be. But regulation of interstate commerce is an exclusive federal power. When a state regulates commerce with foreign nations or among the several states, it exercises the very power granted to Congress, and the analogy fails.

- State inspection laws are recognized in the Constitution but do not derive from a power to regulate commerce. They act on the subject before it becomes an article of foreign commerce.

- D has been granted, through a federal license, the privilege of employment in the coasting trade. P would restrict such trade to property transport, excluding passengers. Such a narrow interpretation would eventually "explain away the Constitution"; instead, safe and fundamental principles must be followed, and coasting trade includes transport of both property and persons for hire.

- For these reasons, the federal license must be recognized, and state laws prohibiting exercise of such licenses are void.

Concurrence (Johnson, J.). The Court need not decide whether to construe constitutional provisions liberally or strictly, but must simply discover the intent and meaning and then execute the will of those who made it. On obtaining independence, the states created disruptive commercial regulation, which was the immediate cause that led to the forming of a convention. No states repealed the former statutes, but they fell "lifeless from the statute books, for want of the sustaining power relinquished to Congress." That D based his defense on a license is irrelevant, for only Congress can regulate commerce; any state regulation is automatically void.

Comment. The Supremacy Clause (Article VI, Section 2) has been interpreted to mean that to whatever extent Congress has exercised its power, any inconsistent state laws are prohibited. Thus, in *Willson v. Black Bird Creek Marsh Co.*, 27 U.S. (2 Pet.) 245 (1829), where a state law was challenged as repugnant to Congress's power to regulate commerce, but Congress had made no applicable legislation in the area, the state law was upheld.

---

b. **Exclusive vs. concurrent powers under the Commerce Clause.**

1) **License cases.** *Gibbons* did not decide whether the grant of a power to Congress was exclusive. In *The License Cases*, 46 U.S. (5 How.) 504 (1847), the Court upheld state laws prohibiting import and sale of liquor without a license because they did not conflict with any act of Congress.

2) **Congress determines.** Congress may determine that even if it has exclusive power in a given area, local regulation is more appropriate. The courts have imaginatively permitted such delegation by considering the nature of the subject of the power rather than the nature of the power itself.

a) **National vs. local issues--**

Cooley v. Board of Wardens, 53 U.S. (12 How.) 299 (1851).

Facts. Pennsylvania passed a statute requiring vessels entering or leaving the Port of Philadelphia (P) to accept local pilots while in the Delaware River. The penalty for disobedience was one-half the pilotage fees. Cooley (D), consignee of two violating vessels, was sued under the act. P relied on a 1789 congressional statute that incorporated all then existing state laws regulating pilots and that mandated conformity with subsequently enacted state regulation, like the law in this case. D contends that Congress cannot delegate its powers in this manner. D appeals state court judgments for P.

Issue. May Congress permit the states to regulate aspects of commerce that are primarily local in nature?

Held. Yes. Judgment affirmed.

- Regulation of pilots is clearly a regulation of commerce. If Congress's power to regulate commerce is exclusive, the Act of 1789 could not confer on the states the power to regulate pilots.

- The correct approach looks to the nature of the subjects of the power rather than the nature of the power itself. Many subjects are national in nature, but some are local, like the one involved here. When a subject is national, it is best governed by one uniform system, and therefore requires exclusive legislation by Congress. But a local subject is best handled by the states, which can adapt regulation to the local peculiarities.

- The Act of 1789 manifests the understanding of Congress that the nature of this subject (pilotage of local ports) does not require its exclusive legislation. That understanding must be upheld, and the statute is constitutional.

---

3) **Basic distinction.** Despite *Cooley*, the basic distinction between federal and state powers of regulation remained the distinction between intrastate and interstate, and commerce vs. not commerce. States could regulate anything that was not "interstate commerce."

   a) **Definition of interstate commerce.** *Gibbons v. Ogden, supra,* gave "commerce" a broad definition, including "any intercourse among the states." Later decisions limited the meaning to "transportation." Thus, states could regulate insurance solicitation and sales, even if by out-of-state insurance companies [*see* Paul v. Virginia, 75 U.S. (8 Wall.) 168 (1868)], and manufacturing, even if all the output was sold out of state [*see* Kidd v. Pearson, 128 U.S. 1 (1888)].

   b) **Commencement of interstate commerce.** The question of when interstate commerce begins was essential in comparing application of state and federal regulations. In *Coe v. Town of Errol*, 116 U.S. 517 (1886), the Court held that products of a state intended for exportation and prepared for shipment are subject to state taxes like other property within the state. Once goods are started in the course of transportation to another state or are delivered to a carrier for such transport, they are under the protection of the Constitution and are subject only to national regulation. But mere intention to export is insufficient. To exempt goods from state taxation, concrete steps must be taken. Property intended for export but not yet shipped may not be taxed differently from any other like property subject to state tax.

c) **Termination of interstate commerce.** *Brown v. Maryland,* 25 U.S. (12 Wheat.) 419 (1827), set up the original package doctrine for goods from other countries, which makes foreign goods immune from state taxation until the original package is broken or the goods sold. Goods from other states were susceptible to state regulation once they "came to rest" within the state, ready for final disposal or use.

d) **Congressional acceptance of state regulation.** Congress may incorporate state regulations into the federal regulatory scheme, even where it would not be permitted to delegate its authority to the states (*e.g.,* Congress properly could forbid interstate transportation of liquor intended to be used contrary to any law of the state of destination).

c. **Judicially enforceable limits on the commerce power.** Because the federal commerce power is concurrent with state power over transactions occurring within the state, the Court has been called on many times to determine the limits of the federal power. The Court's decisions over the years reflect changing social and economic policies.

1) **Definition of "commerce."** Although *Gibbons* gave a broad definition to commerce, a series of decisions limited the definition of "commerce" to transportation. Manufacturing and production were not "commerce" and hence could not be regulated by Congress. Even under the Sherman Act, the Court dismissed a suit brought by the United States to prevent creation of a sugar monopoly under this narrow definition of "commerce." [United States v. E.C. Knight Co., 156 U.S. 1 (1895)]

2) **Regulation of railroad rates.** Early cases permitted state regulation of rates charged by railroads operating within state borders. [*See* Munn v. Illinois, 94 U.S. 113 (1877)] A later case, *Wabash, St. Louis & Pacific Railway v. Illinois*, 118 U.S. 557 (1886), held that Congress had exclusive power to regulate interstate railroad rates, including intrastate segments of an interstate journey. Ac-

cordingly, Congress created the Interstate Commerce Commission ("ICC").

d. **Expansion of the congressional commerce power after 1936.**

1) **The Court-packing plan.** President Roosevelt felt that the Supreme Court was judging the public policy of the New Deal, rather than its constitutionality. He proposed legislation to allow him to appoint an extra Justice for every Justice over age 70 who did not resign. The legislation never passed, but some observers believe that it prompted a change in the Court's analysis of New Deal legislation.

2) **The affectation doctrine.** Beginning in 1937, the Court abandoned the "geographic" and "direct vs. indirect" approaches to federal regulation under the Commerce Clause. The Court's position currently extends to Congress the power to regulate any activity, whether interstate or intrastate in nature, as long as it has any appreciable effect on interstate commerce. This approach is called the "affectation doctrine."

3) **Regulation of manufacturers.** Congress may regulate a manufacturer if the manufacturer's activity significantly affects interstate commerce. The term "affecting commerce" means burdening or obstructing commerce or the free flow of commerce, or having led or tending to lead to a labor dispute burdening or obstructing commerce or the free flow of commerce. For example, labor strife at a steel plant could conceivably cripple the entire interstate operation of the company. Thus the National Labor Relations Board may regulate union-employer collective bargaining in the steel industry. [NLRB v. Jones & Laughlin Steel Corp., 301 U.S. 1 (1937)] The holding was extended to a small clothing manufacturer in *NLRB v. Fainblatt*, 306 U.S. 601 (1939), because the ***cumulative effect*** many small producers have on interstate commerce is "appreciable."

4) **Employment conditions.** In *United States v. Darby*, 312 U.S. 100 (1941), the Supreme Court held that Congress could establish and enforce wage and hour standards for manufacture of goods for interstate commerce. This case overruled *Hammer v. Dagenhart*, 247 U.S. 251 (1918).

3. **The Modern View of Federal Power.**

a. **The commerce power.** The affectation doctrine has made the federal commerce power all-pervasive.

1) **Farm production.** In *Wickard v. Filburn*, 317 U.S. 111 (1942), Filburn objected to a marketing penalty imposed by the Secretary of Agriculture on a portion of Filburn's crop grown in excess of his allotment under the Agricultural Adjustment Act of 1938. Filburn sued to enjoin enforcement of the penalty, claiming the application of the marketing quota to him was beyond Congress's commerce power, since he used the wheat on his own farm. The Supreme Court disagreed and held that Congress may regulate individual home production and use of a major interstate commodity such as wheat based on the substantial effect of the aggregate of such activity. Even if the activity is local and not regarded as commerce, it may be reached by Congress if it exerts a "substantial economic effect on interstate commerce, and this irrespective of whether such effect is what might at some earlier time have been defined as 'direct' or 'indirect.'" Home consumption of the wheat does not detract from the economic effect of the excess crop because it substitutes for purchases on the open market. That Filburn's effect was trivial was irrelevant, because taken together with many similarly situated, it was far from trivial.

2) **Insurance.** In *United States v. South-Eastern Underwriters Association*, 322 U.S. 533 (1944), the Court overruled *Paul v. Virginia*, *supra*, and held that insurance sales are interstate commerce because the entire transaction, in light of the size of the insurance industry, has the requisite appreciable effect.

3) **Racial segregation and discrimination.**

a) **Hotel--**

Heart of Atlanta Motel v. United States, 379 U.S. 241 (1964).

Facts. The owner of Heart of Atlanta Motel (P) refused to rent rooms to black customers. P sought a declaratory judgment that Title II of the Civil Rights Act of 1964 was unconstitutional. A three-judge court sustained the Act, and P appeals.

Issue. May Congress prohibit racial discrimination by private motels that accept out-of-state business?

Held. Yes. Judgment affirmed.

- The legislative history of the Civil Rights Act contains many examples of how racial discrimination places burdens on interstate commerce, which comprehends the movement of persons through more than one state.

- Even though the operation of the motel was local, if it is interstate commerce that feels the pinch, "it does not matter how local the operation which applies the squeeze."

---

b) **Restaurant--**

Katzenbach v. McClung, 379 U.S. 294 (1964).

Facts. McClung (P), owner of a restaurant that excluded black people from its dining accommodations, challenged Title II of the Civil Rights Act. The lower court granted an injunction against enforcement by Assistant Attorney General Katzenbach (D), finding that P would lose a substantial amount of business if required to serve black customers.

Issue. May Congress use its commerce power to forbid racial discrimination by a restaurant on the sole ground that slightly under one-half of the food it serves originated outside the state?

Held. Yes. Judgment reversed.

- Although the food originating out of state had "come to rest," the line of cases holding that interstate commerce ends when goods come to rest in the state of destination applies only with reference to state taxation or regulation, not to federal regulation of commerce.

- The fact that discrimination in restaurants resulted in sales of fewer interstate goods, and that interstate travel was obstructed directly by it, shows sufficient connection between the discrimination and the movement of interstate commerce to allow federal intervention.

- Once the court finds a rational basis for finding a chosen regulatory scheme necessary to the protection of interstate commerce, the only inquiry is whether the facts fit the scheme. Here the lower court found that P serves food, a substantial portion of which has moved in interstate commerce. Hence, P is covered by the regulation.

---

4) **Limits on congressional power--**

United States v. Morrison, 529 U.S. 598 (2000).

Facts. Morrison (D) was a member of a varsity football team at Virginia Tech. D assaulted and raped Brzonkala (P), a female student, and made vulgar remarks about women. P sued D under 42 U.S.C. section 13981, the Violence Against Women Act, which provided a damage remedy for a victim of gender-motivated violence. D claimed that section 13981's civil remedy was unconstitutional. The United States intervened to defend the Act under the Commerce Clause or Section 5 of the Fourteenth Amendment. The lower courts held that Congress lacked constitutional authority to enact this civil remedy. The Supreme Court granted certiorari.

Issue. May Congress provide a federal civil remedy for a violent crime on the ground that the aggregate effect of such crimes substantially affects interstate commerce?

Held. No. Judgment affirmed.

- In *United States v. Lopez*, 514 U.S. 549 (1995), the Court held that Congress could not prohibit the possession of firearms within a school zone. The rationale was that possessing a firearm is a criminal act, not an economic one. Congress has authority to regulate interstate commerce, but it must show a substantial impact on interstate commerce of the actions it seeks to regulate or proscribe.

- In adopting the Act, Congress made findings regarding the serious impact of gender-motivated violence on victims and their families, but used a but-for causal chain to show an impact on interstate commerce from these crimes. The Court has rejected this type of reasoning, since it would allow Congress to regulate any crime as long as the aggregated impact of that crime has substantial effects on any aspect of interstate commerce. This type of reasoning could as easily be applied to family law as well.

- The Constitution distinguishes between national and local issues, and the police power is one that was clearly left to the states and denied to the federal government. Congress has no authority to regulate noneconomic, violent criminal conduct based solely on the conduct's aggregate effect in interstate commerce.

- Section 5 of the Fourteenth Amendment does allow Congress to enforce the guarantee that no state shall deprive any person of life, liberty, or property without due process or deny any person equal protection of the laws. But this applies only to state action, not private conduct. Even if there had been gender-based disparate treatment by the state in this case, it would not have permitted P's suit against D as a private party.

Concurrence (Thomas, J.). The very notion of a "substantial effects" test under the Commerce Clause is inconsistent with the Constitution. This test has led Congress to act as though there are virtually no limits to the Commerce Clause. The Court should adopt an approach more consistent with the original understanding.

Dissent (Souter, Stevens, Ginsburg, Breyer, JJ.). One difference between this case and *Lopez* is that here, Congress assembled considerable data showing the effects of violence against women on interstate commerce. This Act would have been constitutional at any time between *Wickard* and *Lopez*. The majority has revived a distinction between commercial and noncommercial conduct, which had been rejected in *Wickard*. The relative powers of the federal and state systems have changed substantially since the framing of the constitution. The Seventeenth Amendment was a major factor in this change, and the modern integrated national economy is a fact not reflected in the majority's notion of federalism.

Dissent (Breyer, Stevens, Souter, Ginsburg, JJ.). The distinction between economic and noneconomic is not easy to apply. Congress could have approached the same problem with legislation that focused on acts of violence perpetrated at public accommodations or by those who have moved in interstate commerce. The majority's approach could lead to complex rules creating fine distinctions that achieve random results.

Comment. In *Reno v. Condon*, 528 U.S. 141 (2000), the Court held that drivers' personal information gathered by state motor vehicle departments is a "thing in interstate commerce," because it is used by insurers, manufacturers, marketers, and others engaged in interstate commerce to contact drivers with customized solicitations. The Court unanimously held that Congress had authority to limit disclosure of this information by state authorities because the information was an article of interstate commerce under the Commerce Clause.

---

5) **Permissible regulation.** Despite the limitations set forth in *Lopez* and *Morrison, supra,* the Court gives broad latitude to federal regulation once the commerce power is properly invoked. For example, Congress may:

   (i) Advance interstate commerce (*e.g.,* build highways, license radio and television stations, charter a private railroad corporation such as Amtrak, etc.).

   (ii) Protect instrumentalities or shipments in interstate commerce (*e.g.,* outlaw theft from interstate shipments, destruction of aircraft in interstate flights).

   (iii) Prevent misuse of channels of interstate commerce—in effect, develop a federal police power (*e.g.,* prohibit interstate transport of stolen goods or motor vehicles, shipment of misbranded goods, etc.).

   a) **Prevent the possession, obtaining, or manufacturing of marijuana for personal medical use--**

Gonzales v. Raich, 545 U.S. 1 (2005).

Facts. California created a statutory exemption for criminal prosecution for physicians, patients, and primary caregivers who possessed or cultivated marijuana for medicinal purposes with the recommendation or approval of a physician. Angel Raich and Diane Monson (Ps) sought to use medical marijuana under the California statute. Ps sued Gonzales (D), the Attorney General, seeking injunctive and declaratory relief to prohibit enforcement of the federal Controlled Substances Act ("CSA") to the extent that it prevented them from possessing, obtaining, or manufacturing cannabis for their personal medical use. The district court denied Ps' motion for a preliminary injunction, but the court of appeals reversed this denial. The Supreme Court granted certiorari.

Issue. Does the federal commerce power include the power to prohibit local cultivation and use of marijuana that is permitted by state law?

Held. Yes. Judgment vacated.

- ♦ Ps claim that applying the CSA to the intrastate manufacture and possession of marijuana for medical purposes, pursuant to California law, exceeds the federal commerce power. However, *Wickard*, *supra*, and other cases establish that Congress can regulate purely local activities that are part of an economic "class of activities" that have a substantial effect on interstate commerce, even intrastate activity that is not itself commercial.

- ♦ A primary purpose of the CSA is to control the supply and demand of controlled substances in both legal and illegal drug markets. Just as the wheat in *Wickard* was part of the regulatory scheme even when it never left the state, marijuana grown within a state affects the interstate market. Congress has a rational basis for concluding that home-consumed marijuana can affect price and market conditions in the national market. There is a likelihood that the high demand in the interstate market will draw such marijuana into that market.

- ♦ *Lopez*, *supra*, and *Morrison*, *supra*, are distinguishable on the grounds that those cases fell outside Congress's commerce power in its entirety. The statutes in those cases did not regulate economic activity. In contrast, the CSA directly involves economic activity, including the production, distribution, and consumption of commodities for which there is an established interstate market.

Concurrence (Scalia, J.).

- ♦ The Commerce Clause unquestionably permits Congress to extinguish the interstate market in Schedule I controlled substances, including marijuana. The power to regulate interstate commerce extends to those regulations that prohibit commerce as well as those that aid, foster, and protect commerce. Congress has prohibited almost all intrastate activities related to Schedule I substances—both economic activities, such as manufacture, distribution, and possession with the intent to distribute, and noneconomic activities, such as simple possession. Although simple possession is a noneconomic activity, this is immaterial as to whether it can be prohibited as a necessary part of a larger regulation.

- ♦ It is impossible to distinguish controlled substances manufactured and distributed intrastate from controlled substances manufactured and distributed interstate. It is possible for marijuana grown at home and possessed for personal use to enter the interstate market, whether or not the possession is for medicinal use under the laws of a particular state.

Dissent (O'Connor, J., Rehnquist, C.J., Thomas, J.).

- ♦ The states' core police powers include the authority to define criminal law and protect the health, safety, and welfare of their citizens. The majority's decision today permits Congress to regulate intrastate activity without any proof that the personal cultivation, possession, and use of marijuana for medicinal purposes is economic activity or that it has a substantial effect on interstate commerce and is therefore an appropriate subject of federal regulation.

- ♦ By allowing the CSA to extinguish California's experiment without proof that Ps' activity has a substantial effect on interstate commerce, the majority holds that federal regulation of local activity is immune to Commerce Clause challenge if Congress acts with an ambitious, all-encompassing statute. Congress should not regulate noncommercial activity simply because it may have an effect on the demand for commercial goods or because it may be substituted for commercial activity. Most commercial goods or services have some sort of privately producible equivalent. *Wickard* did not hold or imply that small-scale production of commodities is always economic. And in *Lopez* and *Morrison*, this Court suggested that economic activity usually relates directly to commercial activity. The marijuana at issue in this case was never in the stream of commerce; possession is not itself a commercial activity.

- ♦ There is no evidence that homegrown medicinal marijuana users constitute, in the aggregate, a sizable enough class to have a discernable, let alone substantial, impact on the national illicit drug market.

Dissent (Thomas, J.). When Congress exceeds its power under the Commerce Clause, courts should invalidate its overreaching on a case-by-case basis. If Congress can regulate this activity, it can regulate virtually anything.

---

6) **Role of the courts.** Within the constitutional constraints suggested by *Lopez* and *Morrison*, *supra*, the federal commerce power is all-pervasive, and limitations on that power stem from political rather

than judicial considerations. The major function of the federal courts is statutory interpretation or determination of congressional intent.

b. **The taxing power (Article I, Section 8, Clause 1).** The power to tax is essential to strong government and was a major reason for drafting the Constitution.

1) **Taxation in aid of general powers.** Congress may exercise its taxing power as a means of promoting any objective that is within a power specifically granted to it by the Constitution.

2) **Taxation for purpose of regulation.** If Congress has the power to regulate the activity taxed, the tax is valid even though clearly enacted for a regulatory, rather than revenue-raising, purpose. If Congress has no power to regulate the activity taxed, the validity of the tax ultimately depends on its validity as a revenue-raising measure.

a) **Motive not considered--**

Sonzinsky v. United States, 300 U.S. 506 (1937).

Facts. Sonzinsky (D) was convicted under the National Firearms Act of 1934 for dealing in firearms without paying the specified tax. The Act imposed a tax on importers, manufacturers, dealers, and sellers of specifically defined firearms and accessories. D claimed that the tax was not a true tax but a penalty intended to suppress traffic in certain noxious types of firearms, the local regulation of which belongs to the states, not the Congress. D appeals.

Issue. Does Congress's taxing power extend to a specific tax that has the effect of regulating local transactions?

Held. Yes. Judgment affirmed.

♦ The statute contains no regulatory provisions apart from those necessary for imposition of the tax, nor are there criminal sanctions. On its face it is merely a taxing measure. Also, a regulatory effect attending a tax measure does not, by itself, invalidate the tax. Nor may the Court inquire into hidden motives for creating the tax. If the tax produces revenue (acts like a tax) and is not attended by an offensive regulation, it is within the national taxing power.

c. **The spending power.** The "general welfare" power of Article I, Section 8, is connected with the taxing and spending power. This clause can therefore be invoked only when there is an expenditure of money appropriated by Congress. For example, Congress could not pass a law under the General Welfare Clause requiring seat belts in all cars, even if this would benefit the general welfare. The rule is that Congress must tax for revenue and not merely regulatory purposes, and then it must spend for the general welfare. The spending must be for a national concern as opposed to a local one. However, the Supreme Court has given great deference to the determinations of Congress in this area.

1) Local vs. general welfare--

United States v. Butler, 297 U.S. 1 (1936).

Facts. The 1933 Agriculture Adjustment Act authorized the Secretary of Agriculture to extend benefit payments to farmers who agreed to reduce their planted acreage. Processors of the covered crops were to be taxed to provide a fund for the benefit payments. Butler (P) was receiver for a processor who had paid the tax. P brought suit to recover the tax paid on grounds that it was part of an unconstitutional program to control agricultural production. The court of appeals held the tax unconstitutional. The United States (D) appeals.

Issue. May Congress use its taxing and spending powers to operate a self-contained program regulating agricultural production?

Held. No. Judgment affirmed.

- The power of Congress to authorize expenditures of public moneys for public purposes is not limited by the direct grants of legislative power found in the Constitution, but it does have limits. Appropriations cannot be made as a means to an unconstitutional end.
- Regulation of agricultural production is not a power granted to Congress; therefore it is left to the states. Attainment of such a prohibited end may not be accomplished through the use of granted powers (here the taxing powers).
- This scheme, purportedly voluntary, in reality involves purchasing, with federal funds, submission to federal regulation of a subject reserved to the states. Because the end is invalid, it may not be accomplished indirectly through the taxing and spending power.

Dissent (Stone, Brandeis, Cardozo, JJ.). Courts are concerned only with the power to enact statutes, not the wisdom of the legislature. The depressed state of agriculture is nationwide; therefore, the Act does provide for the "general welfare." There is no coercion involved, since threat of loss, not hope of gain, which is involved here, is the essence of economic coercion. Conditioning the receipt of federal funds on certain activity does not infringe on state power.

Comment. *Butler* was one of the last of the series of cases striking down parts of the New Deal. Subsequent Commerce Clause cases indicate that the area involved in *Butler* would not now be held to be one of purely local concern.

---

2) **Inducement of states.** In *Charles C. Steward Machine Co. v. Davis*, 301 U.S. 548 (1937), the Court upheld a provision of the Social Security Act that gave an employer a credit on his federal tax if he contributed to a state plan approved by the Secretary of the Treasury. Although this had the effect of inducing the states to adopt their own plans, the Court noted that the spending was for the general welfare as determined by Congress.

3) **Deference to legislative findings.** Although the spending power is limited by the General Welfare Clause, the courts defer to the legislative findings made by Congress. For example, the old-age provisions of the Social Security Act were upheld largely by ascribing wide latitude to congressional determination of the national interest. [*See* Helvering v. Davis, 301 U.S. 619 (1937)]

4) **Expansive interpretation.** In *Buckley v. Valeo*, *infra*, the Court upheld the Presidential Election Campaign Fund, a fund which is financed by individual taxpayers checking a box on their tax returns. The Court noted that the General Welfare Clause is not a limitation upon congressional power, but a grant of power, and as such merits an expansive interpretation.

d. **War and treaty powers.**

1) **Source of powers.** Article I, Section 8 grants Congress the power to regulate commerce with foreign nations, to declare war, to raise and support the armies, and to provide and maintain a navy. Article II, Section 2 provides that the President shall be Commander-in-Chief of the Army and Navy of the United States; that he has certain powers in regard to treatymaking; that he shall receive foreign ambassadors and other public ministers and consuls, subject to Senate confirmation. In addition to these powers, the federal government as sovereign has ***exclusive*** and ***plenary powers*** in the conduct of ***foreign affairs***, equal to the right and power of the other members of the international family.

2) **War powers.** The grant of war powers to the federal government includes a broad grant of judgment and discretion so that wars might be waged effectively and successfully. These powers include:

a) **Economic controls--**

Woods v. Cloyd W. Miller Co., 333 U.S. 138 (1948).

Facts. Woods (P), United States Housing Expediter, sought to enjoin violations by Miller (D) of rent controls imposed by the Housing and Rent Act of 1947. The Act was passed under the war power to assist adjustment to the housing shortage caused by World War II. D claimed that the Act was unconstitutional. The district court agreed, finding that inauguration of "peace-in-fact" by presidential proclamation precluded further congressional action based on the war powers.

Issue. May Congress continue to regulate the economy under its war powers following cessation of hostilities?

Held. Yes. Judgment reversed.

- The war power includes the power to remedy the evils that arise from war and does not necessarily end with the cessation of hostilities. The critical housing shortage directly caused by war continued after the cessation of hostilities, and application of the Necessary and Proper Clause to the war power permits congressional action to deal with war-related problems as it sees fit.
- Although a potential for abuse from attenuated interpretations of war-caused economic effects is possible, there is no such abuse here. Congress cannot be assumed to ignore constitutional responsibilities in the future, and judicial review would be available should such abuse arise.

Concurrence (Jackson, J.). War powers do not last as long as the effects and consequences of war, nor do they exist merely because of a purely legal or technical state of war. They exist only as long as there is in actuality a state of war, with armies abroad exercising our war powers and lack of peace terms with allies and enemies. Since that is still the case in certain areas of the world, I concur in the result.

b) **Imposition of curfews.** The federal government, through the exercise of its war powers, may impose a curfew order to prevent espionage and sabotage of facilities during wartime. [*See* Hirabayashi v. United States, 320 U.S. 81 (1943)]

c) **Exclusion of civilians from certain areas.** The federal government may even exclude citizens from sensitive areas or facilities during war. [*See* Korematsu v. United States, 323 U.S. 214 (1944)] However, concededly loyal citizens may not be continually detained. [*See Ex parte* Endo, 323 U.S. 283 (1944)]

3) **Treaty power.** The President has authority to make treaties with foreign nations "by and with the advice and consent of the Senate, provided two-thirds of the Senators concur."

a) **Supremacy Clause.** The Supremacy Clause makes treaties confirmed by the Senate the supreme law of the land.

(1) **Effect on state laws.** Any state statute or constitutional provision that conflicts with a treaty provision is invalid. [*See, e.g.,* Hauenstein v. Lynham, 100 U.S. 483 (1880)—treaty providing inheritance rights for aliens prevailed over state law disqualifying aliens from inheriting]

(2) **Effect on acts of Congress.** The Supremacy Clause places treaties on an equal footing with the Constitution and acts of Congress. But because of the nature of the interests involved, treaties may be justified where legislation would not be.

(3) **Leading case--**

Missouri v. Holland, 252 U.S. 416 (1920).

Facts. The Migratory Bird Treaty Act of 1918 implemented a treaty between the United States and Great Britain and prohibited killing or interfering with migratory birds except as permitted by regulations made by the Secretary of Agriculture. The state of Missouri (P) brought suit in equity to enjoin Holland (D), a United States game warden, from enforcing the Act. P claims the Act unconstitutionally interferes with state rights and that an earlier similar act of Congress, not in pursuance to a treaty, was held invalid. The district court dismissed the action, and P appeals.

Issue. May an act of Congress implementing a United States treaty create regulations that would be unconstitutional if the act stood alone?

Held. Yes. Judgment affirmed.

- The Tenth Amendment is irrelevant, since the power to make treaties is delegated expressly to the federal government. Further, if the treaty is valid, the statute is equally so, being necessary and proper. The treaty does not contravene any prohibitory words found in the Constitution and is presumed valid.

- The important national interest here can be protected only by national action in concert with that of another nation. Such a joint effort is possible only through a treaty. Since there is no specific constitutional restriction and the national interest requires it, the treaty, and therefore its implementing statute, are valid.

- ♦ The state's interest, while sufficient to justify regulation in the absence of federal regulation, is too transitory to preempt specific national regulation, especially when the national action arises from exercise of the treaty power.

Comment. The case implies that a treaty can confer upon Congress powers in addition to those granted in Article I, subject to specific constitutional prohibitions. A subsequent case, *Geofrey v. Riggs*, 133 U.S. 258 (1890), noted that the treaty power may extend only to "proper subjects of negotiation between our government and the governments of other nations." For a case where a treaty was not upheld as the supreme law of the land due to inconsistency with a specific constitutional provision, *see Reid v. Covert*, 354 U.S. 1 (1957).

---

b) **International executive agreements and compacts.** The ever-growing complexity of foreign relationships has led to the practice of making executive agreements and compacts covering minor, everyday matters (such as sales of American products to foreign nations) that would not justify a formal treaty.

(1) These executive agreements are the sole responsibility of the President, and do not require the "advice and consent" of the Senate.

(2) Nonetheless, such agreements and compacts have a status and dignity "similar" to treaties, and prevail over any inconsistent state law. [United States v. Belmont, 301 U.S. 324 (1937); United States v. Pink, 315 U.S. 203 (1942)]

e. **The property power.** Article IV, Section 3 provides in part that Congress shall have power "to dispose of and make all needful rules and regulations respecting the territory or other property belonging to the United States."

1) **Broadly interpreted.** This power is broadly interpreted. The implied power to appropriately dispose of federal property has provided a basis for ruling that the government may compete with private utilities. [*See* Ashwander v. Tennessee Valley Authority, 297 U.S. 288 (1936)—Congress could sell electric power from a dam it constructed; if the government had the power to create a facility, it had the power to take any benefits flowing from the facility and dispose of same as it saw fit] Furthermore, Congress has proprietary power in addition to its legislative power.

2) **Protection of wildlife--**

Kleppe v. New Mexico, 426 U.S. 529 (1976).

Facts. The Wild Free-Roaming Horses and Burros Act protected wild horses and burros on United States public lands. A New Mexico rancher complained to the Bureau of Land Management ("BLM") that wild burros were interfering with his cattle operation on BLM land, but the BLM refused to remove them. The rancher went to the state Livestock Board (D), which removed the burros and sold them. Kleppe (P), a BLM administrator, brought this action to recover the burros. The district court held the Act unconstitutional, and P appeals.

Issue. Does the Property Clause permit Congress to regulate and protect unclaimed but offensive wildlife living on federal lands located within state boundaries?

Held. Yes. Judgment reversed.

♦ The Property Clause gives Congress power to "make all needful Rules and Regulations respecting the . . . Property" of the United States. D would give a restrictive application of the clause, but such interpretation is unwarranted. The clause gives Congress broad power to determine what are "needful" rules "respecting" public lands. Congress, as both proprietor and legislator over the public domain, has complete power over it, including power to regulate and protect the wildlife living there.

f. **Other federal powers.**

1) **Fiscal powers.** To provide for the same currency, having a uniform legal value in all the states, the federal government was granted exclusive power to regulate the value of money. Such regulation may be enforced even on contracts previously entered into by private parties. [*See* Norman v. Baltimore & Ohio Railroad, 294 U.S. 240 (1935)]

2) **Naturalization.** Congress has exclusive power to establish rules of naturalization.

3) **Regulation of aliens.** The authority of Congress over admission, exclusion, and deportation of aliens is plenary. In *Kleindienst v. Mandel,* 408 U.S. 753 (1972), the Court held that if there is a bona fide reason for excluding an alien, citizens have no standing to complain that such exclusion interferes with their First Amend-

ment rights (*i.e.,* to "receive information and ideas" from the excluded alien).

4) **Regulation of commerce with the Indian tribes.** The federal commerce power permits regulation of trade with the Indian tribes, even to the extent of regulating the activities of non-Indians on privately owned land where such activities affect Indian tribe commerce. And Congress may delegate this power to the Indian tribes. [*See* United States v. Mazurie, 419 U.S. 544 (1975)]

B. STATE SOVEREIGNTY AND FEDERAL REGULATION

1. Intergovernmental Immunity: Regulation.

a. **Federal immunity.** Except as authorized by Congress, the instrumentalities and agents of the federal government are immune from state regulation insofar as the regulation might interfere with their efficiency in performing their functions for the federal government.

b. **Regulation of the state by federal government.**

1) **Basic principles.** The federal government has the same power to regulate the conduct and activities of a state and its agents as it has to regulate private organizations and their agents, subject to the procedural safeguards inherent in the federal system.

2) **Minimum wage laws.** In 1974, Congress passed amendments to the Fair Labor Standards Act that extended minimum wage and maximum hour provisions to almost all state and local government employees. The Supreme Court held that Congress could not impose the minimum wage and maximum hour regulations on states in their role as employers. [National League of Cities v. Usery, 426 U.S. 833 (1976)] The Court found that even though the amendments were within the scope of congressional power under the Commerce Clause, there are constitutional limits on Congress's powers to override state sovereignty. This was the first decision in 40 years to hold a federal law unconstitutional for exceeding the commerce power, and it has since been overruled.

3) ***National League of Cities* overruled--**

Garcia v. San Antonio Metropolitan Transit Authority, 469 U.S. 528 (1985).

Facts. The San Antonio Metropolitan Transit Authority (D), a public mass transit authority, received substantial federal financial assistance. In 1974, Congress extended the minimum wage and overtime provisions of the Fair Labor Standards Act ("FLSA") to mass transit employees and virtually all state and local government employees. After *National League of Cities, supra,* was decided, D told its employees that the FLSA no longer applied to them. In 1979, however, the United States Department of Labor determined that D's activity was not immune from FLSA. Garcia (P) sued D for overtime pay under FLSA. In a separate action, D sought a declaratory judgment that it was exempt from FLSA. The district court granted D's motion and denied P's cross-motion for partial summary judgment. P appeals.

Issue. May Congress enforce minimum wage and overtime requirements against a local government's mass transit authority?

Held. Yes. Judgment reversed.

- If D is exempt from FLSA, it must be because of its status as a governmental agency, for if it were a private enterprise, Congress could clearly apply FLSA under the commerce power.

- Under the four-part test of *Hodel v. Virginia Surface Mining & Reclamation Association, Inc.,* 452 U.S. 264 (1981), the third requirement—that the federal statute impair traditional governmental functions—is involved here. This requirement has produced confusion and a variety of interpretations, with no clear constitutional distinction between what is and what is not a "traditional governmental function."

- The problem with these standards is that they ignore the principle of federalism, which allows states to experiment with ways to solve problems. Thus, there are no "traditional," "integral," or "necessary" government functions that should be more carefully protected than other government functions. Just as the "governmental/proprietary function" distinction used in cases involving state immunity from federal taxation eventually was discarded as unworkable, so the "traditional governmental function" analysis must be discarded.

- The constitutional structure does impose limits on the commerce power. But the sovereignty of the states is limited by the Constitution itself, through the Supremacy Clause, the Fourteenth Amendment, and Article I, Section 10. The states have influence over Congress through equal representation in the Senate. State sovereign interests are more properly protected by procedural safeguards inherent in the structure of the federal system than by judicially created limitations on federal power. The limit on the commerce power is one of process, not result.

- Nothing in the FLSA, as applied to D, destroys state sovereignty or violates any constitutional provision.

- The states have been able to protect themselves. They receive significant federal aid. They are exempt from the operation of many federal statutes.

Dissent (Powell, J., Burger, C.J., Rehnquist, O'Connor, JJ.).

- The *National League of Cities* rationale has been followed in several cases. Departure from the doctrine of stare decisis requires special justification; the majority has undermined the stability of judicial decisions by so suddenly overruling *National League of Cities.*

- Under the majority's opinion, the Tenth Amendment is nothing more than meaningless rhetoric when Congress exercises its commerce power. The Court cites no authority for its view that the role of the states in the federal system depends on the grace of elected federal officials rather than on the Constitution as interpreted by this Court.

- *National League of Cities* adopted a familiar type of balancing test that requires weighing the respective interests of the states and federal government. Under the Tenth Amendment, the states' role is a matter of constitutional law, not of legislative grace. The Court holds that federal political officials, invoking the Commerce Clause, are the sole judges of the limits of their own power. Federal overreaching under the Commerce Clause undermines the constitutionally mandated balance of power between the states and the federal government.

- The Court's view ignores the understanding of federalism that has long been accepted. Congress is not free under the Commerce Clause to assume a state's traditional sovereign power, and to do so without judicial review. This relegates the states to precisely the trivial role feared by opponents of the Constitution.

Dissent (Rehnquist, J.). The judgment should be affirmed under Justice Powell's approach, Justice Blackmun's concurrence in *National League*, or Justice O'Connor's approach. I am confident that the principle will, in time, command the support of a majority of this Court.

Dissent (O'Connor, Powell, Rehnquist, JJ.). The essence of federalism is that the states, as states, have legitimate interests that the national government is bound to respect even though its laws are supreme. It is not enough that the end be legitimate—the means to that end chosen by Congress must not contravene the spirit of the Constitution. The proper resolution of this conflict is to weigh state autonomy as a factor in the balance when interpreting the means by which Congress can regulate the states as states. A state is different from a private citizen. Regardless of difficulty, the Court must reconcile these concerns.

---

4) Limit on congressional regulatory authority--

New York v. United States, 505 U.S. 144 (1992).

Facts. Low level radioactive waste is generated in substantial quantities by various industries, including the medical and research industries, but in 1979 the only three United States disposal sites for radioactive waste were in Nevada, Washington, and South Carolina. Each of these states objected to accepting wastes from other states, and in 1980, Congress enacted the Low-Level Radioactive Waste Policy Amendments Act. The Act authorized states to enter into regional compacts that, once ratified by Congress, could after 1985 restrict the use of their disposal facilities to waste generated within member states. By 1985, only three approved regional compacts had operational disposal facilities—the ones existing in 1979. Thirty-one states (the unsited states) were not members of these compacts. Congress amended the Act in 1985, based on a proposal submitted by the National Governors' Association, whereby sited states agreed to accept waste for seven more years, collecting a graduated surcharge for waste from unsited states, and unsited states agreed not to rely on sited states after 1992. A portion of the surcharges would be collected by the Secretary of Energy, who in turn would pay them to unsited states that comply with a series of deadlines for joining a regional compact or creating their own disposal sites. States that failed to meet the deadlines could lose access to disposal sites. Finally, any state or regional compact that was unable to dispose of all waste generated within its borders by 1996 would, upon the request of the waste generator, take title to the waste and be liable for all damages incurred by such generator as a consequence of the state's failure to take possession of the waste once notified that it is available. New York (P) did not join a regional compact, but did enact legislation providing for the siting and financing of a disposal facility. The two target counties objected and joined P in suing the United States (D), seeking a declaratory judgment that the Act violates the Tenth Amendment. The district court dismissed the complaint. The court of appeals affirmed, and the Supreme Court granted certiorari.

Issue. May Congress direct the states to regulate in a particular field or a particular way, using them as implements of regulation?

Held. No. Judgment reversed in part.

- The power of Congress to legislate so as to impact state autonomy has been analyzed both by inquiring whether Congress has the power under Article I to so act, and by determining whether Congress has invaded the province of state sovereignty reserved by the Tenth Amendment. But these inquiries may be mirror images, because if a power is delegated to Congress, the Tenth Amendment expressly disclaims any reservation of power to the states, and if a power is an attribute of state sovereignty reserved by the Tenth Amendment, it is necessarily one not conferred on Congress. The Tenth Amendment merely states the truism that all is retained by the states that has not been surrendered to the federal government; yet it requires the courts to determine whether an incident of state sovereignty is protected by a limitation on an Article I power.

- P claims that Congress exceeded its powers not by regulating radioactive waste, which is interstate in character and thus falls within the Commerce Clause, but by directing the states to regulate in this field in a particular way. The Court has long recognized that Congress cannot directly compel the states to enact and enforce a federal regulatory program. A key difference between the Constitution and the Articles of Confederation is that under the Constitution, the federal government can exercise its legislative authority directly over individuals rather than over states.

- Congress may create incentives for states to adopt a legislative program consistent with federal interests, however. Congress has done so by attaching conditions on the receipt of federal funds and by offering states the option of regulating private activity in interstate commerce according to federal standards or having state law preempted by federal regulation. Such incentives do not compel state action. This preserves the accountability of both federal and state officials to their respective constituencies.

- The Act in this case creates three sets of incentives. First, the surcharge provisions provide for imposition by sited states of surcharges that are partially remitted to the federal government and paid out to states that meet specified milestones. The burden on interstate commerce is within Congress's Commerce Clause authority, and the payments are within its Spending Clause authority.

- The second set of incentives allows states with disposal sites to gradually increase the cost of access to the sites and then deny access altogether to waste generated in states that do not meet federal guidelines. This gives nonsited states the choice of complying with federal standards for self-sufficiency or becoming subject to federal regulation that allows sited states to deny access to their disposal sites. The affected states are not thereby compelled by Congress to regulate; the incentives are a conditional exercise of Congress's commerce power, which is permissible.

- The third set of incentives requires states that do not regulate according to federal standards to take title to and possession of the waste generated within their borders and become liable for all damages waste generators suffer as a result of the states' failure to do so promptly. But the Constitution would not permit Congress to simply transfer radioactive waste from generators to state governments, or force states to become liable for generators' damages, either of which would "commandeer" state governments into the service of federal regulatory purposes. And Congress cannot require state governments to implement federal legislation. Since neither "option" is constitutional, a choice between them is not permissible either. This "take title" provision is severable from the rest of the Act, however.

- No matter how great the federal interest, the Constitution does not give Congress authority to require the states to regulate. Congress must legislate directly, not by conscripting state governments. State officials cannot give Congress this authority by consenting to the federal statute.

- ♦ Ps claim that the first two incentives violate the Guarantee Clause, but neither incentive denied any state a republican form of government.

Concurrence and dissent (White, Blackmun, Stevens, JJ.). The Act is a result of the efforts of state governments seeking to achieve a state-based remedy for the waste problem. It is essentially a congressional sanction of interstate compromises, not federal preemption or intervention. New York in particular should be estopped from asserting the unconstitutionality of the Act after the state has derived substantial benefits under the Act. The Court's opinion that the "take title" provision is unconstitutional does not preclude Congress from adopting a similar measure through its powers under the Spending or Commerce Clauses. Ironically, the Court gives Congress fewer incentives to defer to the wishes of state officials in achieving local solutions to local problems, all in the name of promoting federalism.

Concurrence and dissent (Stevens, J.). The Constitution enhanced the power of the federal government, and there is no history to suggest that the federal government may not impose its will upon the states as it did under the Articles of Confederation.

---

5) Limit on congressional power to use state officers directly--

Printz v. United States, 521 U.S. 898 (1997).

Facts. The federal Brady Handgun Act required the United States Attorney General to create a national system to instantly check the background of prospective handgun purchasers. Pending establishment of the national system, the Act also required the chief law enforcement officer ("CLEO") of each local jurisdiction to conduct the background checks. Printz (P) and another sheriff challenged the statute under *New York v. United States, supra.* The lower courts upheld the statute. The Supreme Court granted certiorari.

Issue. May Congress compel state officers directly to enforce a federal regulatory program?

Held. No. Judgment reversed.

- ♦ There is no constitutional text that addresses the issue of congressional action compelling state officers to execute federal laws.
- ♦ Historical practice has required state judges to enforce federal prescriptions. But courts commonly apply the law of other sovereigns. The Full Faith and Credit Clause requires state courts to enforce obligations arising in other states.

This practice does not mean that Congress can impress the state executive into its service. Other historical texts refer to the ability of the federal government to use state officers to execute federal laws, but none imply that this can be done without the consent of the states.

- ♦ The structure of the Constitution gives Congress the power to regulate individuals, but not states. The separation of the federal and state governments is one of the Constitution's structural protections of liberty. The power of the federal government would be augmented immeasurably if it could impress into its service the state police officers.

- ♦ Federal control of state officers would also affect the balance of powers among the three branches. The President is responsible for executing the laws, but the Brady Act transfers this responsibility to the CLEOs in the 50 states, without Presidential control.

- ♦ Under *New York,* Congress cannot compel the states to enact or enforce a federal regulatory program. Congress cannot circumvent that prohibition by conscripting the states' officers directly. Such a practice would be fundamentally incompatible with the constitutional system of dual sovereignty.

Concurrence (O'Connor, J.). Nothing in this holding precludes Congress from imposing purely ministerial reporting requirements. But the provisions that directly compel state officials to administer a federal regulatory program are contrary to the Constitution.

Concurrence (Thomas, J.). The Commerce Clause power does not extend to regulation of wholly intrastate, point-of-sale transactions. Without that power, Congress cannot force state law enforcement officers to administer and enforce such regulations. Even if Congress did have authority to regulate intrastate transactions that substantially affect interstate commerce, the Second Amendment right to keep and bear arms might be implicated by these regulations.

Dissent (Stevens, Souter, Ginsburg, Breyer, JJ.). The Commerce Clause itself supports the regulation of commerce in handguns by the Brady Act. Nothing in the Constitution would allow a local police officer to ignore a command contained in a federal statute enacted pursuant to an express delegation of power such as the Commerce Clause. The basic difference between the Articles of Confederation and the Constitution was the ability of the federal government to govern individuals directly. If the statute were directed at private individuals with relevant information instead of at public officials, it would present no structural problem. Allowing the Brady Act to impose this duty on state officers is less burdensome to state power than to require the government to create a vast national bureaucracy to implement the policy.

Dissent (Souter, J.). The Federalist Papers would support the federal government's position in this case, although Congress should not be allowed to require administrative support without also paying fair value for it.

Dissent (Breyer, Stevens, JJ.). There is no need to set forth an absolute, inflexible rule in this case. Federal systems in Europe, for example, provide that constituent states implement many of the laws enacted by the central "federal" body.

Comment. In *Reno v. Condon, supra*, the Court held that Congress can restrict the ability of state motor vehicle departments to disclose drivers' personal information without the drivers' consent. The rationale was that the law regulated state activities, not state regulation of private parties.

---

2. **Constitutional Cases Brought in Federal Courts.**

   a. **Federal court jurisdiction to enforce federal rights.** Following the Civil War, Congress began using the lower federal courts as the primary means of enforcing the newly created federal rights against state governments. Furthermore, federal officials may be sued in federal court for denials of constitutional rights.

   b. **The Eleventh Amendment and federal suits against state officials.**

      1) **History.** The Eleventh Amendment was adopted in response to early Supreme Court decisions that permitted a state to be sued by citizens of another state or country, despite disclaimers by many of the Framers that the federal judiciary would have such power. It provides:

         > The Judicial power of the United States shall not be construed to extend to any suit in law or equity, commenced or prosecuted against one of the United States by Citizens of another State, or by Citizens or Subjects of any Foreign State.

      2) **Judicial interpretation.** The Eleventh Amendment has been interpreted also to prevent suits by citizens of the state sued; therefore, no state may be sued in federal court without its consent by any private individual. [Hans v. Louisiana, 134 U.S. 1 (1890)]

      3) **Action to enjoin violation of federal rights.** In *Ex parte Young*, 209 U.S. 123 (1908), the Court held that the Eleventh Amendment did not bar federal court action to enjoin a state officer from enforcing a state law claimed to violate the federal Constitution. The rationale was that if an officer of the state seeks to enforce an unconstitutional statute, he must do so without the authority of the state, and so acts as a private individual. The Eleventh Amend-

ment does not apply because the state is not taking the action once the officer is stripped of his official capacity.

4) **Suits for retroactive relief.** The "stripping" doctrine of *Ex parte Young* is sufficient to enable private parties suing in federal court to force officials to comply with federal statutes. However, it does not extend to actions for retroactive relief if the plaintiff seeks payment of state funds for past violations of state law. [Edelman v. Jordan, 415 U.S. 651 (1974)]

5) **Injunctive relief against state officials based on state law--**

Pennhurst State School & Hospital v. Halderman, 456 U.S. 89 (1984).

Facts. Halderman and others (Ps) brought suit in federal district court against the Pennhurst State School and Hospital (D), claiming the conditions at D violated Ps' federal and state rights. The district court issued a remedial order and the court of appeals affirmed, based on a federal act that it held entitled Ps to habilitation in the least restrictive environment. The United States Supreme Court reversed, holding that the federal statute did not create substantive rights. On remand, the court of appeals again affirmed, this time on the basis that the state law required the state to adopt the "least restrictive environment" approach. The Supreme Court granted certiorari.

Issue. May a federal court award injunctive relief against state officials on the basis of state law?

Held. No. Judgment reversed.

- The Eleventh Amendment was intended to make it clear that sovereign immunity limits the Article III grant of judicial authority. Although a sovereign's immunity can be waived, the state's consent to be sued must be unequivocally expressed. Federal courts should be reluctant to infer that a state's immunity from suit has been waived.

- The basic rule that an unconsenting state is immune from suits brought in federal courts by her own citizens as well as by citizens of another state is subject to an exception: A suit challenging the constitutionality of a state official's action is not one against the state. This is the rule of *Ex parte Young, supra.* Ironically, in such cases the unconstitutional conduct is state action for Fourteenth Amendment purposes but not for Eleventh Amendment purposes. This theory has not received an expansive interpretation, however.

- The need to vindicate federal rights that underlies the *Young* doctrine must be accommodated to state sovereign immunity. But when the case rests on an allegation that a state official has violated state law, there are no competing interests. The federal court's involvement does not vindicate any federal law, but instead intrudes on state sovereignty by telling state officials how to comply with state law. This result conflicts with the concept of federalism.

- Ps also claim that the federal court could hear the state claim under pendent jurisdiction. This judge-made doctrine inferred from the general language of Article III cannot be used to displace the explicit limitation on federal jurisdiction contained in the Eleventh Amendment. Even if this results in bifurcation of claims, the policy favoring pendent jurisdiction cannot override the Eleventh Amendment's limitation on the authority of the federal judiciary to adjudicate claims against a state.

Dissent (Brennan, J.). The Eleventh Amendment bars federal court suits against states only by citizens of other states. Also, since D's conduct was prohibited by state law, the protections of sovereign immunity do not apply.

Dissent (Stevens, Brennan, Marshall, Blackmun, JJ.). As a result of the majority opinion, federal courts will be required to decide federal constitutional questions despite the availability of state law grounds for decision, contrary to the policy favoring judicial restraint. The Court eliminates a simple rule, that conduct exceeding the scope of an official's lawful discretion is not conduct the sovereign has authorized and hence is subject to injunction.

---

6) Limitation on federally created cause of action against a state--

Seminole Tribe of Florida v. Florida, 517 U.S. 44 (1996).

Facts. The Seminole Tribe of Florida (P) sought to conduct certain gambling activities in the state of Florida (D). The Indian Gaming Regulatory Act allowed such activities only in conformance with a valid compact between P and D. The Act also requires states to negotiate in good faith with an Indian tribe toward forming such a compact, and authorizes a tribe to sue a state in federal court to compel negotiations. When D refused to negotiate a compact with P, P sued in federal court. D moved to dismiss. The district court denied D's motion on the ground that Congress acted under the Indian Commerce Clause in the Constitution [Art. I, §10, cl. 3]. The court of appeals reversed under the Eleventh Amendment, and the Supreme Court granted certiorari.

Issue. Does the Eleventh Amendment prevent Congress from authorizing suits by Indian tribes against states for prospective injunctive relief to enforce legislation enacted pursuant to the Indian Commerce Clause?

Held. Yes. Judgment affirmed.

- Under the Eleventh Amendment, the federal judicial power does not extend to a suit against a state brought by citizens of another state or by subjects of a foreign state. The amendment reflects the principles that each state is a sovereign entity and that a sovereignty is not amenable to the suit of an individual without its consent.

- Congress may abrogate the states' sovereign immunity where it unequivocally intends to do so and it acts pursuant to a valid exercise of power. The language of the Indian Gaming Regulatory Act clearly expresses the intention to abrogate state immunity. But the Court has traditionally found only one provision to give Congress power to abrogate state immunity—the Fourteenth Amendment.

- In *Pennsylvania v. Union Gas Co.*, 491 U.S. 1 (1989), the Court held that Congress could abrogate state sovereign immunity under the Commerce Clause because otherwise Congress could not effectively regulate interstate commerce. However, the case was decided by a plurality with no expressed rationale agreed upon by a majority. The plurality's rationale deviated sharply from precedent and is hereby overruled.

- Because Congress could not abrogate D's sovereign immunity, P lacked jurisdiction and the suit must be dismissed. P seeks nevertheless to apply the principle of *Ex parte Young, supra*, on the theory that D's refusal to negotiate under the Act is a continuing violation of federal law. But the enforcement method created by the Act—a suit against the state—would have been superfluous if the Act could have been enforced under *Ex parte Young*.

Dissent (Stevens, J.). The overruling of *Union Gas* may have far reaching consequences. But the Act in this case involved suits by citizens of the state being sued, which are not barred by the Eleventh Amendment.

Dissent (Souter, Ginsburg, Breyer, JJ.). The plain statement rule, by itself, sufficiently protects the states "from undue federal encroachment upon their traditional immunity from suit." The fact that Congress was granting states additional regulatory powers over Indian Tribes as part of the abrogation of sovereign immunity shows that the political safeguards of federalism are working.

---

c. **Nonconstitutional limits on federal court treatment of state law.**

1) **Abstention.** When a party challenges a state law in federal court, there may be an interpretation issue if the state law is ambiguous or has never been interpreted. In such situations, federal courts have normally retained jurisdiction pending a separate state court suit brought to resolve the state law issue. This doctrine was adopted

in a 1941 Supreme Court case; after *Pennhurst, supra,* it applies when the constitutionality of a challenged state law depends upon its meaning, but not when the state law issue is whether the challenged official action violated state law.

2) **Federal court injunctions of state proceedings.** There is no requirement that a plaintiff exhaust administrative remedies before bringing suit in federal court to enjoin state officials from enforcing unconstitutional acts. Under 28 U.S.C. section 2283, federal courts are prevented from enjoining state court proceedings except as authorized by Congress. The Court has held that suits under 42 U.S.C. section 1983 are exempt from this restriction; because most suits to enjoin enforcement of unconstitutional state action are brought under section 1983, such injunctions are permitted. However, federal courts are still restricted by principles of equity, comity, and federalism from enjoining already pending state action in certain situations.

C. THE SCOPE OF STATE POWER

1. **Basic Principles of Regulatory Authority.** The Commerce Clause clearly gives Congress power to regulate interstate commerce. A significant question was whether the states retained any power to regulate interstate commerce. The Supreme Court has determined that Congress has preemptive regulatory power under the Commerce Clause, and that the clause also forbids some, but not all, state regulation even when Congress has not acted. The basic rule now is that if a state statute (i) directly regulates or discriminates against interstate commerce or (ii) has the effect of favoring in-state economic interests over out-of-state interests, it is invalid. If the state statute only indirectly affects interstate commerce and regulates fairly, it may be upheld as long as (i) the state's interest is legitimate and (ii) the burden on interstate commerce does not clearly exceed the local benefits.

2. **Basic Principles of Taxation Authority.** The Constitution does not expressly recognize or reject state power to tax interstate commerce, so a particular tax on interstate commerce must be carefully examined to determine its true nature and effect. Although interstate commerce "must pay its own way," a state's interest in securing revenue must be balanced against the strong national interest in (i) protecting the free flow of commerce from state to state and (ii) preventing state regulation through taxation of any area of commerce that is properly subject only to uniform national regulation.

    a. **Due process and equal protection.** Due process and equal protection concerns require that the benefits and protection afforded by the taxing state have a sufficient relationship to the subject matter taxed so that the subject matter may be deemed to have a tax situs or nexus in the taxing state.

b. **Commerce Clause problems.** Clearly, state taxes that formally discriminate against interstate or foreign commerce are not permitted. A long line of cases deals with the various issues raised by the numerous types of taxes states have imposed on such commerce. The details of such tax law are beyond the scope of this outline, but a brief familiarity with the issues involved is important. The Supreme Court adopted a four-part test for analysis of such issues.

c. **Four-part test.** A state tax levied on an interstate business for "the privilege of doing business" within the state is not per se unconstitutional. [Complete Auto Transit, Inc. v. Brady, 430 U.S. 274 (1977)] The relevant considerations are:

1) Is the activity sufficiently connected to the state to justify a tax?

2) Is the tax fairly related to benefits provided by the state to the taxpayer?

3) Does the tax discriminate against interstate commerce?

4) Is the tax fairly apportioned?

d. **Use tax.** States typically impose a use tax on goods purchased outside the state for goods used in the state. The amount of the tax is usually equal to the amount of the state's sales tax, and typically a credit against the use tax is granted for the amount of any sales tax paid to another state on the purchase. For this reason, a use tax does not favor local business; it merely attempts to treat out-of-state purchases the same way as in-state purchases.

e. **Use of tax credits to discriminate against interstate commerce--**

New Energy Co. of Indiana v. Limbach, 486 U.S. 269 (1988).

Facts. Despite the environmental advantages of ethanol, it is more expensive than gasoline and was not widely used until Congress exempted it from federal motor fuel excise taxes. To promote production of ethanol in Ohio, the state of Ohio granted a tax credit against the state fuels sales tax for ethanol, but only if the ethanol was produced in Ohio or in a state that granted similar tax advantages to Ohio-produced ethanol. The New Energy Company of Indiana (P) manufactured ethanol in Indiana, a state that repealed its ethanol tax exemption in favor of a direct subsidy to Indiana ethanol producers. As a result, P's ethanol was not eligible for the Ohio tax credit when sold in Ohio. P challenged the law in Ohio courts, but lost. P appeals.

Issue. May a state grant a sales tax credit limited to products produced in the taxing state or in other states that grant similar tax advantages to products produced in the taxing state?

Held. No. Judgment reversed.

- The Commerce Clause prevents states from engaging in economic protectionism, and state statutes that discriminate against interstate commerce are unconstitutional unless demonstrably justified by a valid factor unrelated to economic protectionism. On its face, the Ohio tax credit appears discriminatory.
- D claims that by making the credit available to producers in other states that provide a credit, Ohio has actually promoted interstate commerce by encouraging the adoption of similar tax advantages. However, such reciprocity requirements are based on a threat of economic isolation and cannot be upheld.
- Even though the Ohio statute does not prohibit the transport of out-of-state ethanol into Ohio for sale, it imposes a significant commercial disadvantage on such ethanol. Such an economic barrier violates the Commerce Clause. It does not matter that the practical effect of the law is limited, or that Indiana's subsidy program has the effect of conferring a commercial advantage over out-of-state producers. The Commerce Clause prohibits state action giving its residents an economic advantage only in connection with the state's regulation of interstate commerce. The subsidy program does not involve regulation of interstate commerce.
- D claims two justifications for the discriminatory tax credit: (i) health and (ii) commerce. While the use of ethanol may constitute a health benefit over the use of gasoline, there is no evidence that ethanol produced in a non-tax credit state is less healthful. Health is thus no more than an accidental side benefit of the tax credit. The commerce justification relies on the supposition that if more states granted tax subsidies, commerce in ethanol would increase, but the tax credit is aimed at favorable treatment for Ohio ethanol, not at increasing ethanol subsidies in general.

---

f. **Protectionism.** In *Wyoming v. Oklahoma*, 502 U.S. 437 (1992), the Court invalidated an Oklahoma statute that required Oklahoma electric generating plants to use Oklahoma mined coal for at least 10% of their coal requirements. This preference for domestic coal was protectionist and discriminatory; even though it applied only to a small part of the market, the extent of the discrimination is not a determining factor under the Commerce Clause.

3. **State Regulation of Transportation Under the Commerce Clause.**

a. **Basic principles.** Where Congress has not enacted legislation regarding the subject matter of commerce, the states may regulate local transactions even though they affect interstate commerce—subject, however, to certain limitations. To be constitutional, state regulation must conform to all of the following:

1) **Nondiscriminatory.** The state regulation must not discriminate against interstate commerce so as to "substantially impede" the free flow of commerce across state lines.

2) **Uniform national regulation not required.** The subject matter must not be one that inherently requires uniform, national regulation.

3) **Balance of interests favors the state.** The state interest underlying the regulation must not be outweighed by the burden on interstate commerce—*i.e.,* the "balance of interests" favors the state over national interests.

b. **Controlling competition.** While state interests in protecting public health and welfare are given considerable weight, a state's interest in controlling competition is not. For example, in *Buck v. Kuykendall*, 267 U.S. 307 (1925), the Court struck down a Washington law that required refusal of a common carrier's application for a certificate to use Washington's highways if the territory was already being adequately served.

c. **Public safety and welfare interest.** A state's interest in the public safety and welfare (where it is the predominant interest) may justify obstruction of interstate commerce. In *Bradley v. Public Utilities Commission*, 289 U.S. 92 (1933), the Court allowed Ohio to regulate interstate carriers primarily to promote safety, even though the indirect result was obstruction of interstate commerce. There, Ohio's denial of an application to become an interstate carrier was to promote safety, and the test used was undue highway congestion. This was a proper state action. *Buck* did not apply because the state in that case acted primarily to restrict competition, not primarily to promote safety. Similarly in *South Carolina State Highway Department v. Barnwell Brothers*, 303 U.S. 177 (1938), South Carolina was permitted to impose highly restrictive width and weight limitations nondiscriminately on interstate carriers that had the effect of seriously impeding interstate travel.

d. **Traditional state regulation.** Where the subject matter is traditionally subject to local regulation, the Court is more likely to allow state regulation.

e. **The state interest must be clearly advanced.** The challenged regulation must clearly promote a valid state interest to be upheld. In *Southern Pacific Co. v. Arizona*, 325 U.S. 761 (1945), the Court found that the Arizona Train Limit Law, which imposed restrictions on the number of cars permitted on any train operating within the state (14 passenger cars or 70 freight cars), unconstitutionally burdened interstate commerce. In balancing the effect of a state regulation on interstate commerce against the state's safety and welfare interests, the Court will consider the efficacy of the regulation in furthering the state's interests. Constitutional doctrine mandates that the Court, not the state legislature, is the final arbiter of competing state and national interests under the Commerce Clause. In *Southern Pacific*, the Court found that the serious impediment of state car limitations on interstate commerce indicated the need for uniform national legislation on the subject. Congress's inaction was interpreted as intending that there be no restrictions on car numbers. Further, upon a review of the record, the Court found that the total effect of the law as a safety measure in reducing accidents and casualties was so slight or problematic that it did not outweigh the national interest in keeping interstate commerce free from interferences. Justices Black and Douglas dissented. Note that *Barnwell Brothers*, *supra*, is distinguishable from *Southern Pacific* because it dealt with state highways, which are of more local concern than railroads, and because in that case the record supported the state's safety findings.

f. **Burden of proof when interstate commerce is burdened.** When the challenged regulation significantly burdens interstate commerce, the state must meet a heavy burden of justification based on its interests.

   1) **Degree of proof required.** State standards out of line with other states are not per se unconstitutional, but to be upheld, there must be a strong showing of a compelling safety consideration. Even though the Court generally defers to legislative policy decisions, it cannot uphold such decisions in light of severe interstate commerce burdens without a clear showing as to safety effects. [Bibb v. Navajo Freight Lines, Inc., 359 U.S. 520 (1959)] In *Bibb*, the Court invalidated an Illinois statute requiring that all trucks operating within the state be equipped with contour rear fender mudguards, which were illegal in another state. The statute prohibited the conventional mudguards allowed in 45 states. The Court found that there, unlike earlier cases, including *Barnwell Brothers*, *supra*, the statute imposed a standard that conflicted with another state's standard. The record demonstrated that the result was a substantial burden on interstate commerce that surpassed the permissible limits even for safety regulations.

2) **State's safety claim must be supported by proof--**

Kassel v. Consolidated Freightways Corp., 450 U.S. 662 (1981).

Facts. Consolidated Freightways Corporation (P) challenged an Iowa statute that, like Wisconsin's law in *Raymond Motor Transportation, Inc. v. Rice*, 434 U.S. 429 (1978), prohibited the use of 65-foot double trailers on Iowa highways, with certain specified exceptions. Kassel (D), an Iowa official, defended the law as a reasonable safety measure in light of the *Raymond* case. The lower courts held the law unconstitutional as seriously impeding interstate commerce while providing slight, if any, safety. D appeals.

Issue. May the courts examine evidence to determine whether a state's purported interest in safety is real and substantial enough to justify applying its police power to burden interstate commerce?

Held. Yes. Judgment affirmed.

- ♦ A state cannot avoid a Commerce Clause attack merely by invoking public health or safety arguments. The courts are required to balance the state's safety interest against the federal interest in free interstate commerce. Despite the "special deference" usually accorded to state highway safety regulations and D's serious effort to support the safety rationale, the record here is no more favorable to D than was Wisconsin's evidence in *Raymond.* P has demonstrated that D's law substantially burdens interstate commerce. Therefore, D's law is unconstitutional.

Concurrence (Brennan, Marshall, JJ.). D's law is unconstitutional under *Raymond* since it is protectionist. The plurality and the dissent insist on considering the legislative purposes advanced by D's lawyers. Separation of powers, however, requires that we defer to the elected lawmakers' judgment, not that we defer to the arguments of lawyers. D's statute exists because the governor of Iowa vetoed legislation that would have permitted 65-foot doubles, giving an essentially protectionist rationale for his action. This is an improper purpose. Safety became a purpose for the law only in retrospect, to defeat P's challenge.

Dissent (Rehnquist, J., Burger, C.J., Stewart, J.). Both the plurality and concurring opinions have intruded on the fundamental right of the states to pass laws to secure the safety of their citizens. D's law is rationally related to its safety objectives. We are essentially reweighing the state legislature's policy choice, and are forcing D to lower its safety standards merely because its sister states' standards are lower.

4. State Regulation of Production and Trade Under the Commerce Clause.

a. **Restrictions on imports.**

1) **Quarantine and inspection laws.** Quarantine and inspection laws enacted to protect public health are upheld as long as they do not discriminate against or unreasonably burden interstate commerce. [*See* Hannibal & St. Joseph Railroad Co. v. Husen, 95 U.S. 465 (1877)] A local statute requiring that cattle or meats imported from other states be certified as free from disease by the state of origin has been upheld. The burden on interstate commerce caused by supplying such a certificate was outweighed by the public health objectives of the state law. [Mintz v. Baldwin, 289 U.S. 346 (1933)]

2) **Economic restrictions.** Economic barriers to imported goods are invalid if their purpose is to protect local business against out-of-state competition. For example, to prevent ruinous competition among local producers and ensure public supplies of a commodity "affected with a public interest," states are generally authorized to license, bond, and regulate the prices paid to local milk producers. However, a state law forbidding local sale of milk produced outside the state if purchased at lower than the minimum prices set locally is invalid, since it discriminates against the out-of-state milk producers. [Baldwin v. G.A.F. Seelig, Inc., 294 U.S. 511 (1935)]

3) **Less burdensome alternatives--**

Dean Milk Co. v. City of Madison, 340 U.S. 349 (1951).

Facts. An ordinance by the city of Madison, Wisconsin (D) prohibited (i) the sale of pasteurized milk unless processed at an approved plant within a five-mile radius of downtown Madison, and (ii) the sale, importation, receipt, or storage of milk for sale in Madison unless originating at a farm inspected by Madison officials, who were also relieved from inspecting any farms further than five miles from the city center. Dean Milk Company (P), an interstate milk processor and dealer, was denied a license to sell its products in Madison solely because P's plants were more than five miles away. P challenged the ordinance, but the state courts upheld it. P appeals.

Issue. May a local statute, having a valid purpose but discriminating against interstate commerce, be upheld if there are nondiscriminatory yet effective alternatives?

Held. No. Judgment vacated and case remanded.

♦ No federal legislation pertains to the issue, nor does D contend that Congress has authorized the regulation. But the enactment clearly does have a valid purpose and is thus within the scope of local power to regulate.

- However, the effect of the regulation is discrimination against interstate commerce, which contravenes the Commerce Clause. Local statutes cannot erect such barriers to interstate commerce even to further valid health and welfare objectives if reasonable nondiscriminatory alternatives are available to protect these local interests. The record discloses at least two such alternatives that would further the legitimate local interests in health and safety (*e.g.*, United States Public Health Service inspections and out-of-town ratings and inspections).

- Permitting D to enforce a nonessential and discriminatory regulation would invite a multiplication of preferential trade areas destructive of the very purpose of the Commerce Clause.

Dissent (Black, Douglas, Minton, JJ.). There is no showing that P was unable to process its milk within the five-mile radius. Local determination of the best method of sanitary control should not be overruled by the Court. To do so elevates the right to traffic in commerce for profit above the power of the people to guard the purity of their daily diet of milk.

---

4) **Reciprocity agreements.** Reciprocity agreements between states respecting the sale of products do not automatically violate the Commerce Clause. But a mandatory reciprocity requirement forbidding sale of products from another state unless that state reciprocates is invalid, unless there is a substantial state interest involved (*e.g.,* health or welfare), that cannot be achieved by some alternative means.

5) **Environmental protection favoring local industry--**

Minnesota v. Clover Leaf Creamery Co., 449 U.S. 456 (1981).

Facts. Minnesota (D) banned the retail sale of milk in plastic nonreturnable, nonrefillable containers. Clover Leaf Creamery Company (P) successfully challenged D's law in the state courts under the Equal Protection and Commerce Clauses. D appeals.

Issue. May a state enact a statute that does not on its face discriminate against interstate commerce but that does cause a shift in an industry from a predominant out-of-state location to a predominant in-state location?

Held. Yes. Judgment reversed.

- Applying the familiar rational basis test, D's law is certainly rationally related to its conservation interests and does not deny equal protection.

- D's ban applies to all plastic container manufacturers. While most of these are located out of state and production of the raw material for nonplastic containers is a major state industry, there is no discrimination against interstate commerce as such. There is an incidental burden on interstate commerce, but it is not "clearly excessive" in light of D's legitimate purposes in imposing the ban.

Concurrence and dissent (Powell, J.). I agree that the statute survives the equal protection challenge, but I would remand for the Commerce Clause issue.

Dissent (Stevens, J.). Federal courts are bound to respect the interpretation of state law announced by the highest judicial tribunal in that state. The factual conclusions drawn by the Minnesota courts are clearly supported by the record, and the Minnesota Supreme Court applied the proper rule of federal law to the equal protection issue. Thus it is our duty to affirm that judgment.

---

6) Subsidies instead of regulation--

West Lynn Creamery, Inc. v. Healy, 512 U.S. 186 (1994).

Facts. Massachusetts adopted a milk pricing order that required every milk dealer in the state to make a monthly "premium payment" based on the amount of its sales. The funds generated by these payments were distributed to Massachusetts dairy farmers in proportion to their respective contributions to the state's total milk production. West Lynn Creamery, Inc. (P) challenged the milk order in state court. The lower courts upheld the milk order, and the United States Supreme Court granted certiorari.

Issue. May a state impose a tax on all sales of a particular product in order to subsidize in-state producers of that product?

Held. No. Judgment reversed.

- The clearest examples of laws that discriminate against interstate commerce are protective tariffs or customs duties, which tax imported goods only and thereby make goods more expensive. Such a duty both raises revenue and benefits local producers at the expense of out-of-state producers.

- The purpose for the milk order is to allow higher-cost in-state producers to compete with lower-cost producers in other states. The effect of the milk pricing order is to make milk that is produced in other states more expensive.

- Even though the pricing order is imposed on milk produced in state as well as milk produced out of state, its effect on in-state producers is more than offset by the subsidy. Consequently, it functions like a protective tariff or customs duty.

- The state may properly tax all milk dealers, and it may also subsidize in-state farmers (although the constitutionality of subsidies has never been squarely addressed). However, the combination of a tax and subsidy is "more dangerous to interstate commerce than either part alone." The combination impairs the state's political process because those instate interests who would otherwise oppose the tax are mollified by the subsidy.

- The fact that the taxes are paid by in-state businesses and consumers is irrelevant. The impact of the order is to divert market share to dairy farmers in Massachusetts, which hurts out-of-state farmers.

Concurrence (Scalia, Thomas, JJ.). Nearly all subsidies, whether funded by taxes imposed on out-of-state products, in-state revenues, etc., "neutralize advantages possessed by out-of-state enterprises." Standing alone, this effect does not render a subsidy scheme unconstitutional. A state may subsidize its own industry provided that the subsidies are funded through nondiscriminatory taxes, the proceeds of which go into a general revenue fund rather than back to those in-state persons burdened by the tax.

Dissent (Rehnquist, C.J., Blackmun, J.). The political reality is that there are other groups, namely milk dealers and consumers, who could still oppose the tax even if the dairy farmers choose not to. No precedent justifies applying the negative Commerce Clause against a subsidy funded from a lawful, neutral tax.

Comment. Both the majority and dissent (in the full opinion) cited *Bacchus Imports, Ltd. v. Dias, infra.* That case involved a Hawaii liquor tax with exemptions for fruit wine manufactured in Hawaii and for a brandy distilled from a plant indigenous to Hawaii. The tax exemption was deemed a protective tariff. While the majority in *West Lynn Creamery* thought insignificant the fact that the Massachusetts milk order did not help those who paid the tax (the milk dealers), as compared to the Hawaii tax exemption, which directly helped in-state producers, the dissenters thought that was an important difference that justified upholding the Massachusetts tax.

---

b. Keeping business in the state. One way to develop a state's economy is to require businesses to operate within the state. The Commerce Clause prohibits such legislation if it burdens interstate commerce and is not necessary to promote a valid state purpose.

1) Inspections. Although having a valid "public health" purpose, a state law requiring local inspection of slaughterhouses prior to slaughter of livestock destined for local consumption has been held unconstitutional because it discriminates against out-of-state slaughterhouses (*i.e.,* it prevents importation of sound meats from animals slaughtered in other states). [*See* Minnesota v. Barber, 136 U.S. 313 (1890)]

2) **Protection of reputation.** State laws enacted to protect local, publicly owned natural resources are traditionally a proper exercise of the state's "police power" and will usually be upheld by the Court—*i.e.,* the Court tends to "balance the interests" in favor of such regulations. However, a state may not prohibit local fruit growers from exporting their crops to another state for packaging. The state's interest in maintaining its reputation for "quality" fruit does not justify requiring state growers to package their crops locally. This would impose too great a burden on local growers whose packing facilities are in neighboring states, and this burden would inevitably be passed on to interstate commerce. [Pike v. Bruce Church, Inc., 397 U.S. 137 (1970)]

c. **Keeping resources within the state.**

1) **Statutes banning export.** Under the Commerce Clause, some state laws restricting the export of local products have been upheld: a statute banning shipment of immature citrus fruits was upheld as a reasonable measure for the protection of the state's reputation for quality citrus in out-of-state markets. [Sligh v. Kirkwood, 237 U.S. 52 (1915)] But if the statute's primary purpose or effect is to discriminate against out-of-state commerce rather than to conserve the local resource, it is invalid. [*See* Pennsylvania v. West Virginia, 262 U.S. 553 (1923)—West Virginia required that pipeline companies transporting natural gas produced in the state satisfy the needs of all West Virginia customers, which substantially restricted supplies to out-of-state users; *see also* Hughes v. Oklahoma, *infra*]

2) **Attempt to use health and safety powers--**

H.P. Hood & Sons v. DuMond, 336 U.S. 525 (1949).

Facts. New York law required milk handlers to obtain a license prior to opening any new receiving depot. H.P. Hood & Sons (P), interstate milk handlers, were denied such a license by DuMond (D), a state officer, who found that the requested license would "tend to aid destructive competition in a market already adequately served," thus violating New York law. P challenges the law.

Issue. May a state use its power to protect the health and safety of its people as a means to suppress interstate competition?

Held. No. Judgment reversed.

- Although states may impose even burdensome regulations in the interests of local health and safety, their attempts to advance their own purely commercial interests by curtailing the movement of articles of interstate commerce are impermissible. Therefore, a state may not use its admitted powers to protect the health and safety of its people as a basis for suppressing competition. Because this statute has the prohibited effect, it is void.

Dissent (Black, Murphy, JJ.). The result of this decision is to leave large areas of local business activity free from not only state regulation but any regulation, since Congress cannot be expected to pass uniform national legislation capable of adjustment and application to all local phases of interstate commerce.

---

3) Attempt to preserve landfill space--

Philadelphia v. New Jersey, 437 U.S. 617 (1978).

Facts. New Jersey (D) passed a law prohibiting importation into the state of solid or liquid wastes to protect the public health, safety, and welfare from the consequences of excessive landfill developments. Philadelphia and other cities, as well as New Jersey landfill operators, (Ps) challenged the law under the Commerce Clause. The New Jersey Supreme Court upheld the law; Ps appeal.

Issue. May a state prohibit importation of environmentally destructive substances solely because of their source of origin?

Held. No. Judgment reversed.

- D's reason for passing the law may be legitimate, but the evils of protectionism can reside in the legislative means as well as legislative ends sought. D's ultimate purpose may not be achieved by discriminating against out-of-state items solely because of their origin; D has failed to show any other valid reason for its discrimination.

- D's statute requires out-of-state commercial interests to carry the burden of conserving D's remaining landfill space in an attempt to isolate itself from a problem shared by all. Protection against such trade barriers serves the interest of all states, and may even work to the advantage of New Jersey in the future.

- D claims that this statute resembles quarantine laws, which are exceptions to these general rules. But quarantine laws merely prevent traffic in noxious articles, regardless of their origin. D claims no harm from the very movement of waste into its borders, and concedes that when the harm is felt (upon disposal), there is no basis to distinguish out-of-state wastes from domestic wastes.

Dissent (Rehnquist, J., Burger, C.J.). D's law essentially prohibits importation of items that could endanger its population, and should be upheld. The Court implies that the challenged laws must be invalidated because domestic waste may be used in the state's landfills. This fact ought not require D to exacerbate its problems by accepting out-of-state waste.

4) Attempt to preserve natural wildlife--

Hughes v. Oklahoma, 441 U.S. 322 (1979).

Facts. An Oklahoma statute prohibited shipment of natural minnows for sale outside the state. Hughes (D), a licensed commercial minnow operator in Texas, transported a load of natural minnows from Oklahoma to Texas, and was convicted of violating the statute. He challenged the statute as an unconstitutional burden on interstate commerce, but the state courts upheld the conviction on the authority of *Geer v. Connecticut*, 161 U.S. 519 (1896). D appeals.

Issue. May a state prohibit, as a conservation measure, transportation beyond its borders of natural wildlife captured within the state?

Held. No. Judgment reversed.

- *Geer* was an early case, virtually identical to this one, which upheld a similar state regulation on the theory that Connecticut, as representative for its citizens, "owned" game captured within its boundaries and could therefore retain it. *Geer* is now expressly overruled, and state regulation of wild animals must be considered pursuant to the same test that applies to regulation of other natural resources.

- The basic test requires consideration of: (i) whether the regulation actually discriminates against interstate commerce; (ii) whether it serves a legitimate local purpose; and, if so, (iii) whether alternative, less discriminatory means would be as effective. P's statute obviously discriminates against interstate commerce. Although conservation is a legitimate purpose, other more effective yet nondiscriminatory means are available. For example, P could limit the manner of natural minnow use within the state, or could limit the permitted "catch" by both residents and nonresidents to ensure conservation. Therefore, the statute is invalid.

Dissent (Rehnquist, J., Burger, C.J.). The statute is not discriminatory, since no persons, whether residents or not, may export the natural minnows. The flow of interstate commerce is not affected, since there is no restriction on exports of hatchery minnows. The minimal burden resulting from requiring D to purchase hatchery rather than natural minnows is more than outweighed by P's interest in conservation.

5) **Attempt to protect integrity of local natural wildlife against imports.** In *Maine v. Taylor*, 477 U.S. 131 (1986), the Court upheld a Maine statute prohibiting the importation of live baitfish because of the adverse biological consequences of nonnative species and parasites. Justice Stevens dissented. He believed that Maine was clearly discriminating against out-of-state baitfish and should have the burden of proof to support its ban.

d. **Retaining state-owned resources.**

1) **Introduction.** States may enter the marketplace as participants in order to further state policies. For example, in *Hughes v. Alexandria Scrap Corp.*, 426 U.S. 794 (1976), the Court permitted Maryland to impose more exacting documentation requirements on out-of-state junk car processors than it imposed on in-state processors. The documentation was required to receive a "bounty" from the state of Maryland, which made specified payments for each junk car registered in Maryland; the junk cars were then recycled. The purpose was to improve the environment in the state. The Court reasoned that Maryland did not attempt to prohibit the flow of junk cars, but merely entered the market to bid up the value of Maryland junk cars. The state was a market participant, not a market regulator, so the Commerce Clause was not applicable.

2) **Restricting exports of goods manufactured by the state--**

Reeves, Inc. v. Stake, 447 U.S. 429 (1980).

Facts. In 1919, South Dakota began building a cement plant in response to regional cement shortages. By the 1970s, about 40% of the plant's output was sold to out-of-state buyers. Reeves (P), a Wyoming cement distributor, bought 95% of its cement from the South Dakota plant. In 1978, however, the plant was unable to meet all orders and the State Cement Commission, represented by Stake (D), "reaffirmed its policy of supplying all South Dakota customers first," with any remaining volume allocated on a first-come, first-served basis. P suffered losses and sued D, seeking injunctive relief. The district court enjoined D's practice, but the court of appeals reversed. The Supreme Court granted certiorari.

Issue. May a state that itself produces cement restrict sales to its residents in a time of shortage?

Held. Yes. Judgment affirmed.

- The basic distinction articulated in *Alexandria Scrap, supra*, between states as market participants and states as market regulators, makes good sense and sound law. The Constitution sets no limits on state power to operate freely in the free market. This is especially true where, as here, the state has acted as a sovereign in meeting the needs of its residents.

- ♦ The fact that South Dakota made sales to P does not distinguish the case from one in which a state offered cement only to domestic buyers from the start.

- ♦ The state preference for resident buyers is not protectionist but merely a means of serving its citizens. Nor is a natural resource at stake, so there is no danger of resource hoarding.

Dissent (Powell, Brennan, White, Stevens, JJ.). D's policy represents precisely the kind of economic protectionism that the Commerce Clause was intended to prevent. We agree that South Dakota could allocate cement to meet its public needs, but when it acts as a market participant to benefit private citizens, the effect is the same as if the state legislature had imposed the policy on private cement producers. Although a private business could properly exclude out-of-state customers, when a state adopts such a policy, it violates the Commerce Clause.

---

3) Preference for local labor on city construction projects--

---

White v. Massachusetts Council of Construction Employers, 460 U.S. 204 (1983).

Facts. White (D), the mayor of Boston, required that all city-funded construction projects be performed by a work force consisting of at least half bona fide residents of Boston. The Massachusetts Council of Construction Employers (P) successfully challenged the scheme in the state supreme court on the theory that it violated the Commerce Clause. The Supreme Court granted certiorari.

Issue. Is a local government exempt from Commerce Clause restraints if it enters a market as a participant, even if the participation has a significant impact on out-of-state residents?

Held. Yes. Judgment reversed.

- ♦ The basic rule is that when a state or local government enters the market as a participant, it is not subject to the restraint of the Commerce Clause. The only necessary inquiry is whether the program constitutes direct participation in the market. D's program here is clearly direct participation as far as its use of its own funds is concerned. The impact, if any, on out-of-state residents is thus irrelevant.

- Much of the funds spent by D for construction are federal funds that D merely administers. But such funds are provided by Congress. When state or local government action is specifically authorized by Congress, it is not subject to the Commerce Clause even if it interferes with interstate commerce. The purposes of the federal program are harmonious with D's use of the funds, and D's type of parochial favoritism is permitted by the applicable federal regulations.

---

4) **Post-sale obligations imposed by the state selling its resources.** In *South-Central Timber Development v. Wunnicke*, 467 U.S. 82 (1984), the state of Alaska had offered to sell its timber but only with a contractual requirement that it be processed within the state before being exported. In return, the price for the timber was significantly reduced. South-Central Timber Development, which normally sold unprocessed logs to Japan, sought an injunction in federal court, claiming that the requirement violated the negative implications of the Commerce Clause. The Supreme Court found that the fact that the state acted through a contract was not enough to exempt the restrictions from the Commerce Clause under the market-participant doctrine. The market-participant doctrine must be limited to allowing a state to impose burdens on commerce within the market in which it participates. Alaska went too far by imposing conditions that had a substantial regulatory effect outside of the market it had entered. Thus its program did not fall within the market-participant exception. In *New Energy Co. of Indiana v. Limbach*, *supra*, the Court invalidated an Ohio tax scheme that provided a fuel sales tax rebate for ethanol sold if the ethanol was produced in Ohio. Assuming that the tax scheme was discriminatory, Ohio claimed it was covered by the market participant doctrine. The Court held that Ohio was not a market participant and distinguished *Alexandria Scrap*, *supra*, in which Maryland acted in the place of a private buyer of auto hulks.

e. **Restrictions on entry of business into state--**

Lewis v. BT Investment Managers, Inc., 447 U.S. 27 (1980).

Facts. BT Investment Managers, Inc. (P) was an investment management subsidiary owned by a New York bank holding company. It was organized to operate in Florida, but after P filed an application with the Federal Reserve Board for approval, the Florida legislature passed a statute intended to prevent P from getting approval. The statute prohibits ownership of local investment or trust businesses by firms possessing two characteristics: (i) a certain kind of business organization and purpose, whether as a bank, trust company, or bank holding company; and (ii) location of principal operations outside Florida. P was denied approval solely because of the statute and sued Lewis (D), the Florida Comptroller, for declaratory and injunctive relief. The district court granted declaratory relief, and D appeals.

Issue. May a state restrict business activity by distinguishing between those entities having their principal operations out of state and those operating principally in state?

Held. No. Judgment affirmed.

- ♦ Economic protectionism is per se invalid. Regulation that incidentally affects interstate commerce is permissible if it advances a legitimate local public interest. The principal focus of inquiry is the practical operation of the statute.
- ♦ Banking and related financial activities are of both local and interstate interest. The same interstate attributes that permit Congress to regulate banking also support constitutional limitations on state powers. Thus, Commerce Clause principles apply.
- ♦ This statute differs from the one in *Exxon v. Governor of Maryland*, 437 U.S. 117 (1978), since out-of-state characteristics are determinative. In *Exxon*, the state law prohibited producers of petroleum products from operating retail service stations, without regard to whether the producers were located within Maryland. The statute here discriminates among affected businesses according to the extent of their contacts with the local economy. Therefore, it is an impermissible burden on interstate commerce.

---

f. **Corporate anti-takeover statutes.**

1) **Balancing approach.** In *Edgar v. MITE Corp.*, 457 U.S. 624 (1982), the Court overturned an anti-takeover statute on the ground that the substantial burden it imposed on interstate commerce outweighed the putative local benefits of the statute. The statute required a 20-day preregistration of takeover offers, during which period the target company, but not the offeror, could communicate with shareholders. There was no indication that the statute had a protectionist purpose or effect.

2) **Neutral statute--**

CTS Corp. v. Dynamics Corp. of America, 481 U.S. 69 (1987).

Facts. Indiana adopted an anti-takeover statute that applied to any Indiana public corporation, defined as a corporation with at least 100 shareholders, headquarters or substantial assets in Indiana, and 10,000 resident shareholders or 10% of its shares owned by residents or 10% of its shareholders as residents. Under the statute, an entity that acquires control shares in a public corporation would not acquire voting rights unless the shareholders approved. Dynamics Corporation of America (P), which already owned almost 10% of the stock of CTS Corporation (D), announced a tender offer for another 7.5%. The same day, P filed a securities action against D. D then elected to be governed by the provisions of the anti-takeover statute. P amended its suit to claim that the anti-takeover statute violated the Commerce Clause. The district court held that the statute violated the Commerce Clause. The court of appeals affirmed, and D appeals.

Issue. May a state adopt an anti-takeover statute that has the effect of making it more difficult for out-of-state entities to take control over a state's corporations?

Held. Yes. Judgment reversed.

- The principal focus of the Commerce Clause is to prevent state discrimination against interstate commerce. Indiana's statute does not discriminate against interstate commerce because it applies equally to domiciliaries of Indiana who make tender offers as well as to nondomiciliaries. It does not matter that, as P claims, most tender offers are made by out-of-state entities.

- The Commerce Clause is also concerned with statutes that subject interstate commerce to inconsistent activities, such as the railroad regulations in *Southern Pacific Co. v. Arizona, supra*. However, Indiana's statute does not present such a problem because it applies only to corporations that the state has created, and no other state can regulate the voting rights of an Indiana corporation.

- The court of appeals held the statute unconstitutional because it could hinder tender offers. However, a corporation's very existence and attributes are a product of state law. Every state regulates the governance of corporations created by state law, and every such regulation has some effect on interstate commerce, especially when shareholders live in other states. It is common for states to require supermajority votes to approve mergers, for example, and to provide for dissenting shareholders' rights.

- Indiana's statute does not prevent purchasers from acquiring control, but does impose regulatory procedures to protect shareholders of Indiana corporations by letting them decide whether a change in management would be desirable. This is a response to the threat of coercive tender offers, a threat Indiana could deem serious.

- D claims Indiana has no legitimate interest in protecting out-of-state shareholders, but it does have an interest in protecting shareholders of Indiana corporations, whether they are Indiana residents or not.

Concurrence (Scalia, J.). The Court need only determine that the statute neither discriminates against interstate commerce nor creates inconsistent regulation. It is inappropriate for the courts to go further and determine whether the burden on commerce imposed by a state statute is excessive in relation to the local benefits.

Dissent (White, Blackmun, Stevens, JJ.). Indiana's statute substantially burdens the interstate market in corporate ownership and will have a greater impact as other states adopt similar statutes.

Comment. This case represents an apparent retreat from the balancing approach used in *Pike* and subsequent cases. Justice Scalia, concurring in *Bendix Autolite Corp. v. Midwesco Enterprises, Inc.*, 486 U.S. 888 (1988), expressly repudiated the balancing approach. Under his approach, a state statute would be invalid only if it accords discriminatory treatment to interstate commerce in a respect not required to achieve a lawful state purpose; it would be up to Congress, not the courts, to determine whether the purpose is not significant enough to justify the burden on commerce.

---

5. **Other Constitutional Restrictions on State Regulatory Power.**

   a. **Article IV, Section 2: The Privileges and Immunities Clause (Comity Clause).**

      1) **Basic rule.** This clause states that "[t]he Citizens of each State shall be entitled to all Privileges and Immunities of Citizens in the several states." This prohibits discrimination by a state against noncitizens (or nonresidents) of the state with respect to "essential activities" or "basic rights," unless justified by a substantial reason. To justify an exception, the state must show that the nonresidents are a peculiar source of the evil sought to be avoided, and that the discrimination bears a substantial relation to the problem. Thus, there is a two-part test for assessing possible violations of this clause. If the state's discriminatory scheme is overbroad, it will not withstand scrutiny under this clause.

      2) **Protection of basic activities.** The clause protects activities such as pursuit of a livelihood, the transfer of property, access to the state's courts, etc. [Toomer v. Witsell, 334 U.S. 385 (1948)] The Court has held that sport hunting is not an essential activity, so that a state may discriminate against nonresidents in this area. [Baldwin v. Montana Fish & Game Commission, 436 U.S. 371 (1978)]

      3) **Application to municipalities--**

United Building and Construction Trades Council of Camden County and Vicinity v. Mayor and Council of the City of Camden, 465 U.S. 208 (1984).

Facts. The city of Camden (D) adopted an ordinance requiring that at least 40% of the employees of contractors and subcontractors working on city construction projects be Camden residents. The United Building and Construction Trades Council (P) challenged the ordinance as violating the Privileges and Immunities Clause. After the state treasurer approved the ordinance in administrative proceedings, the state supreme court upheld it, holding that the clause does not apply to discrimination on the basis of municipal residency. P appeals.

Issue. Does the Privileges and Immunities Clause apply to municipalities that require contractors to hire the municipality's own residents to work on the municipality's construction projects?

Held. Yes. Judgment reversed and case remanded.

- A municipality derives its authority from the state. If the state cannot discriminate in this manner, neither can a political subdivision of the state. Nor is the ordinance immune from attack because it discriminates against some in-state residents as well as out-of-state citizens. The former have the opportunity to directly change state law through the state legislature; the latter do not.

- P must first show that the ordinance burdens a privilege and immunity protected by the clause. The opportunity to seek employment is a fundamental privilege protected by the clause.

- The Privileges and Immunities Clause does not preclude discrimination against out-of-state residents if there is a substantial reason for the difference in treatment. Although D alleges several such reasons—including increasing unemployment in the city, declining population, and a depleted tax base—no trial has been held and no findings of fact have been made. The case must be remanded.

Dissent (Blackmun, J.). With no historical or textual support, the Court has expanded the scope of the clause to prohibit laws that discriminate among state residents on the basis of municipal residence. This is substantially different from discrimination on the basis of state citizenship. The protection afforded by the disadvantaged state resident's power to change state law also protects the interests of nonresidents, so the political impotency of nonresidents that the clause was designed to cure does not exist here.

Comment. At some length the Court distinguished the *White* case, *supra*, by describing the different purposes of the Commerce Clause and the Privileges and Immunities Clause. The former acts as an implied restraint on state power to regulate interstate commerce, so when a state acts as a market participant, no Commerce Clause problem arises. The latter clause directly restrains state action so as to promote interstate harmony. Even if a state acts as a market participant, its actions must not violate the restraints of the Privileges and Immunities Clause; hence, the analysis applied to this case.

4) Admission on motion of nonresident attorneys--

Supreme Court of Virginia v. Friedman, 487 U.S. 59 (1988).

Facts. The Supreme Court of Virginia (D) adopted a rule that permitted admission on motion of attorneys who have been licensed for at least five years and are admitted to a jurisdiction that gives reciprocal admission to Virginia attorneys. The applicant must be a permanent resident of Virginia and intend to practice full time as a member of the Virginia bar. Friedman (P) was a resident of Virginia for nine years, but she worked in Washington, D.C. She then took a job in Virginia, but one month later moved to Maryland. Five months later, she applied for admission on motion despite her change of residence. D denied P's request. P sued in federal court, claiming that the residency requirement violated the Privileges and Immunities Clause. The district court agreed, and the court of appeals affirmed. D appeals.

Issue. May a state condition admission to its bar without taking the bar exam on the applicant's residency in the state?

Held. No. Judgment affirmed.

- The Privileges and Immunities Clause was intended to place the citizens of each state on the same footing with citizens of other states with respect to the privileges of citizenship in those other states. A two-step analysis applies to privileges and immunities claims: (i) Is the restricted activity sufficiently basic to the livelihood of the nation as to merit protection? If so, (ii) is the restriction closely related to the advancement of a substantial state interest so that it is justifiable despite the deprivation of a protected privilege?

- Under *Supreme Court of New Hampshire v. Piper*, 470 U.S. 274 (1985), it is clear that a nonresident who takes and passes a bar exam has an interest protected by the Privileges and Immunities Clause. D claims that this rule does not apply to P because (i) its rule does not prevent P from taking the bar exam and being admitted under *Piper*, and (ii) since D could require all applicants to pass the bar, P does not have a protected right to admission on motion.

- D's claims are invalid because they ignore the principle that citizens of one state are guaranteed the privilege of doing business in another state on terms of substantial equality with the citizens of the latter state. Practicing law is sufficiently basic to the livelihood of the nation as to merit protection. It does not matter that P is not totally excluded from practicing law in Virginia; she may not do so on the same basis as Virginia residents.

- Because D's rule affects a protected privilege, D's justifications must be evaluated. D claims that the residency requirement will ensure that motion admittees, who otherwise have made no investment such as preparing for and taking a bar exam, will have the same commitment to service and familiarity with Virginia law that examinees would have. However, it cannot be said that nonresidents are less likely to respect the bar than are residents. P herself works full time in Virginia, and her residence in Maryland is essentially irrelevant to her participation in the Virginia bar. Most nonresident motion admittees would be similar to P because of the full-time practice requirement.

Dissent (Rehnquist, C.J., Scalia, J.). *Piper* was incorrectly decided, and so is this case. The effect of this opinion may be to eliminate Virginia's provision for admission on motion, which was a partial step toward accommodating practicing attorneys who move to Virginia and should be encouraged rather than penalized.

---

b. The Twenty-First Amendment.

1) **Introduction.** The Twenty-First Amendment prohibits "the transportation or importation into any state for delivery or use therein of intoxicating liquors in violation of local laws." This amendment has been held to give the states broader regulatory power in this area than over any other type of interstate commerce. States have substantial control over whether to permit importation or sale of liquor and how to structure its distribution. However, federal intervention still prevails in certain instances.

2) **Excise tax exemptions for local liquor not permitted--**

Bacchus Imports, Ltd. v. Dias, 468 U.S. 263 (1984).

Facts. The state of Hawaii imposed a 20% excise tax on wholesale liquor sales. However, sales of two specified locally produced alcoholic beverages were exempt from the excise tax. Bacchus Imports, Ltd. (P), a liquor importer, challenged the tax by seeking a refund of taxes paid. The state courts upheld the tax and P appeals.

Issue. May a state exempt locally produced alcoholic beverages from an excise tax that applies to all imported liquor?

Held. No. Judgment reversed.

- The Commerce Clause prohibits state-imposed taxes that discriminate against interstate commerce. The evidence does not support a conclusion that the local liquor does not compete with nonexempt liquor. It is clear that the legislature acted to protect the local producers. This discriminatory purpose and effect violate the Commerce Clause.

- ♦ The Twenty-First Amendment did not entirely remove state regulation of liquor from Commerce Clause constraints. The amendment was not intended to allow states to erect barriers to competition in order to favor local liquor industries. The amendment authorizes states to protect against the problems caused by unrestricted liquor traffic, but does not permit mere economic protectionism. Because the exemption here does not promote any clear concerns of the Twenty-First Amendment, yet violates a clear Commerce Clause doctrine, it cannot be sustained.

Dissent (Stevens, Rehnquist, O'Connor, JJ.). The amendment expressly authorizes the type of action taken by Hawaii. The state could prohibit all imported liquor, thus creating a local monopoly. If it has such power, there is no justification for prohibiting it from exercising a lesser form of discrimination.

Comment. New York State required that liquor distillers selling to New York wholesalers file a price schedule before the 25th day of each month for the second following month, and required that the price be no higher than the lowest price the distiller charges wholesalers anywhere in the United States. Some distillers offered volume promotional discounts to wholesalers. New York prohibited such payments, considering them as discounts. Other states that regulated prices did not treat the payments as discounts. The New York requirement was held to be a regulation of out-of-state transactions in violation of the Commerce Clause because once a distiller posted its price in New York, it could not change its prices anywhere else in the United States during the relevant month. By applying a unique treatment to volume discounts, New York also forced distillers to abandon the practice in states where it is legal. One state may not project its legislation into other states. [Brown-Forman Distillers Corp. v. New York State Liquor Authority, 476 U.S. 573 (1986)]

---

3) Federal preemption of advertising rules--

Capital Cities Cable, Inc. v. Crisp, 467 U.S. 691 (1984).

Facts. Oklahoma required all cable TV operators in the state to delete all advertisements for alcoholic beverages contained in the out-of-state signals they retransmitted by cable to subscribers. Capital Cities Cable, Inc. (P) challenged the law, but the Tenth Circuit upheld it. P appeals.

Issue. May a state prohibit intrastate advertisement of liquor if the advertisement is transmitted through interstate means that are exclusively regulated by the federal government?

Held. No. Judgment reversed.

- The states have broad power to regulate the importation and use of intoxicating liquor within their borders, but they may not ignore their obligations under other provisions of the Constitution. When a state has not attempted directly to regulate the sale or use of liquor within its borders, a conflicting exercise of federal authority may prevail.

- The basic test consists of determining whether the interests implicated by the state regulation are so closely related to the powers reserved by the Twenty-First Amendment that the regulation may prevail even if it directly conflicts with express federal policies.

- Here, there is a strong federal policy to regulate cable TV, and such regulation has preempted state regulation in the area. On the other hand, Oklahoma's restriction on advertising is very limited. The state permits many other forms of advertising of liquor. Its selective approach suggests that the interests it asserts are not substantial. Hence, the state's interests are not of the same stature as the federal interest in regulating cable TV. The state law is prohibited by the Supremacy Clause.

---

6. **The Supremacy Clause.** Congress may prohibit or preempt state regulation of any part of interstate commerce, either specifically or by implication. This is the effect of the Supremacy Clause.

   a. **Background.** The Supreme Court originally interpreted the Supremacy Clause to mean that once Congress regulated in an area, Congress had "occupied the field" and states could not regulate in that field. The modern trend is to require a fairly direct conflict between the state and federal regulation.

   b. **Dual-impact state statute--**

Gade v. National Solid Wastes Management Association, 505 U.S. 88 (1992).

Facts. Pursuant to the federal Occupational Safety and Health Act Association ("OSH Act"), the Occupational Safety and Health Administration ("OSHA") promulgated regulations on hazardous waste operations, including worker training requirements. Subsequently, the state of Illinois adopted a statute that required hazardous waste workers to be licensed by the state, and required as a prerequisite for a license certain training within the state and a minimum amount of prior experience. The National Solid Wastes Management Association (P) sued Gade (D), a state official, to enjoin enforcement of the Illinois licensing acts on the ground that they were preempted by the federal OSH Act. The district court denied relief, except for the requirement that the training take place within Illinois. The court of appeals affirmed in part and reversed in part. The Supreme Court granted certiorari.

Issue. Does a federal law preempt a state law where both promote safety for workers and the general public if the state law is specifically directed at regulation of workers also covered by the federal law?

Held. Yes. Judgment affirmed.

- D claims the OSH Act does not preempt nonconflicting state regulations. Preemption depends on the intent of Congress. In section 18 of the OSH Act, Congress specified that the Act does not preempt state laws regarding occupational safety or health issues with respect to which no federal standard is in effect (18(a)). It also gave the states the option of preempting federal regulations entirely by submitting to the Secretary of Labor a state plan for development of standards. If approved, the state may assume responsibility for enforcement of the standards (18(b)). If approval is ever withdrawn, the state plan ceases to be in effect (18(f)). For the first two years after passage of the Act, the Secretary may allow the state to continue to enforce its own standards (18(h)). This statutory scheme shows an intent to preempt any state law or regulation that establishes a standard on an issue covered by an OSHA standard, unless the Secretary approves the state plan.

- Preemption may be either express or implied (by either field or conflict preemption). Field preemption arises where the scheme of federal regulation is so pervasive that there is no room for state supplementation. Conflict preemption arises where compliance with both federal and state regulations is a physical impossibility, or where the state law creates an obstacle to accomplishment of the federal purpose.

- In this case, a nonapproved state regulation that applies concurrently with a federal regulation would conflict with the federal purpose of subjecting employers and employees to only one set of regulations, whether federal or federally approved state. The fact that both D's laws and the OSHA regulations are designed to promote worker safety does not rule out preemption, because the state law still interferes with the methods by which the federal law was designed to reach the objective.

- D also claims that the state law should not be preempted because it has a broader purpose than just worker safety; *i.e.,* the safety of the general public. A conflicting state law does not avoid preemption merely by having dual or multiple impacts. In the absence of the Secretary's approval, the OSH Act preempts all state law that constitutes, in a direct, clear and substantial way, regulation of worker health and safety.

Concurrence (Kennedy, J.). This case involves express preemption, not implied preemption. State power is not to be preempted unless Congress clearly intends to do so;

the courts should not engage in extensive inquiry into whether a state statute is in tension with federal objectives, because Congress, not the courts, preempts state law. Preemption due to conflicts with the purposes of a federal Act should arise only when the state laws impose prohibitions or obligations that directly contradict Congress's primary objectives. Potential tensions would not constitute such actual conflict. However, in this case, the most reasonable inference from section 18, which permits states to obtain approval of a plan, is that a state may not enforce standards without such approval. The Court should look no further than this language.

Dissent (Souter, Blackmun, Stevens, Thomas, JJ.). The key in preemption cases is congressional intent. Such intent must be determined starting with the presumption that Congress did not intend to displace state law, so that if a statute can be read sensibly not to have a preemptive effect, no preemption may be inferred. In this case, each provision of the OSH Act may be read consistently with the others without any implication of preemptive intent. Section 18 can reasonably be read to rule out field preemption, so that preemption arises only when there is an actual conflict between the state and federal regulation such that both cannot be complied with. Section 18(b) does not preempt state law; instead, it provides a mechanism for state law to preempt federal law. Section 18(h) allows the Secretary to permit the state to enforce state regulations that would otherwise have been preempted for actual conflict with federal regulations pending approval of the state plan, avoiding the confusion of requiring employers and employees to comply first with a state regulation, then a federal regulation, then a state regulation again.

Comment. The plurality noted that a law of general applicability, such as a traffic or fire safety law, that regulates the conduct of workers and nonworkers alike and does not conflict with OSHA standards would not be deemed to be preempted, because it would not be an "occupational" standard and would regulate workers as members of the public instead of as workers.

D. SEPARATION OF POWERS

1. The President's Role in Policymaking.

a. Legislating.

1) **General rules.** Although Congress has the primary legislative power, the President may propose legislation and must approve every act of Congress before it can become effective (unless Congress overrules the President's veto). The President may not assume any other legislative power.

2) **Limit on exercising legislative power--**

Youngstown Sheet & Tube Co. v. Sawyer (The Steel Seizure Case), 343 U.S. 579 (1952).

Facts. The steel workers, after prolonged negotiations, went on a nationwide strike during the Korean War. Citing the serious national interest in steel production, President Truman ordered Sawyer (D), Commerce Secretary, to seize the steel mills and keep them running. Youngstown Sheet and Tube Company (P) challenged the seizure as unconstitutional and unauthorized by Congress. Congress had earlier passed the Taft-Hartley Act, giving the President authority to seek an injunction against such strikes, but had rejected an amendment to permit government seizures to avoid serious shutdowns. The district court issued a preliminary injunction against D, which was stayed by the court of appeals. The United States Supreme Court granted certiorari.

Issue. May the President, acting under the aggregate of his constitutional powers, exercise a lawmaking power independent of Congress to protect serious national interests?

Held. No. Judgment affirmed.

- The President's power to issue the order must stem either from an act of Congress or from the Constitution itself. Congress clearly gave no such power; in fact, it specifically rejected the means used by D.

- The President's authority as Commander-in-Chief does not warrant the seizure, as it is too far removed from the "theater of war." His general executive powers are inapplicable, since there is no relevant law to execute. The order does not direct that a congressional policy be executed in a manner prescribed by Congress but that a presidential policy be executed in a manner prescribed by the President. Such presidential usurpation of the lawmaking power is unauthorized and invalid.

Concurrence (Jackson, J.).

- There are three categories of circumstances in which the President may act.

    (i) He may act pursuant to the authorization of Congress. This situation gives him maximum authority because he acts under the powers granted to him by the Constitution plus all the authority delegated by Congress.

    (ii) The President may act on the strength of his independent powers, absent any authorization by Congress.

    (iii) He may act in ways contrary to the expressed will of Congress. In such a situation, his power is at its lowest ebb.

- This case clearly falls under the third category, and the President's action can be sustained only if it was entirely within his constitutional domain and beyond control of Congress. However, this action was not within his constitutional domain. The President cannot use his powers as Commander-in-Chief or his powers to control the nation's foreign policy to enlarge his mastery over the internal affairs of the nation.

Concurrence (Clark, J.). The President must follow the procedures laid down by Congress.

Dissent (Vinson, C.J., Reed, Minton, JJ.). The President has a duty to execute the legislative programs of supporting the armed forces in Korea. The President's action was an effective means of performing his duty, and was clearly temporary and subject to congressional direction.

---

b. **International relations.**

1) **General rules.** Most federal power to conduct foreign affairs is given to the executive branch. The President makes treaties and appoints ambassadors, with the approval of the Senate. The President is the Commander-in-Chief of the armed forces. The President may also enter into executive agreements in conducting foreign policy.

2) **Executive orders.** In *Dames & Moore v. Regan*, 453 U.S. 654 (1981), the Court held that the President, in response to a national emergency, may suspend claims that are outstanding in American courts. The President had agreed to terminate all legal proceedings in United States courts against Iran in order to secure the release of American hostages. The Court held the executive order valid in light of congressional authorization of such an agreement and the existence of an alternative forum for resolution of the claims.

c. **National defense.**

1) **General rules.** Although the United States Constitution specifies that the President is the Commander-in-Chief of both the Army and Navy, the Constitution provides that only Congress has the power to initiate or declare war. The interplay of these powers was not made clear in the United States Constitution.

2) **Institution of blockade--**

The Prize Cases, 67 U.S. (2 Black) 635 (1863).

Facts. During a blockade of southern ports instituted by President Lincoln, Union ships seized vessels and cargoes of foreign neutrals, which were then condemned by federal court order. The ship and cargo owners appeal.

Issue. May the President, acting without a congressional declaration of war, institute a blockade of southern ports that neutrals are bound to respect?

Held. Yes. Decrees of condemnation affirmed.

- ♦ The law of nations requires that a war must exist de facto to legitimate the capture of a neutral vessel or property on the high seas. Congress had not declared a war, but had earlier authorized the President to call out the militia and use military force to resist invasion and suppress insurrection against the government of a state or of the United States. He need not wait for special legislative authority to respond to such challenges.

- ♦ The determination of the extent of an armed challenge to the United States rests with the President. His proclamation of blockade is, itself, adequate evidence to the Court that a state of war existed that demanded the use of such force as the President deems necessary.

- ♦ The legislature subsequently ratified the President's actions.

Dissent (Nelson, J., Taney, C.J., Catron, Clifford, JJ.). Congress alone can determine whether war exists or should be declared, and until it has acted, there can be no penalty of confiscation for the acts of others with whom the owner had no concern. The congressional ratification of the seizures is invalid as an ex post facto law.

---

3) Military activity in Vietnam--

Mora v. McNamara, 389 U.S. 934 (1967).

Facts. Mora (P) and others were drafted and ordered to a replacement station for shipment to Vietnam. They sought declaratory and injunctive relief against McNamara (D), Secretary of Defense, on grounds that such military action was illegal. The lower courts dismissed the case. P petitions for a writ of certiorari.

Issue. Is the military activity in Vietnam a "war" such that the Executive may constitutionally order participation?

Held. Certiorari denied.

Dissent (Stewart, Douglas, JJ.). The case touches extremely important questions that ought to be faced.

Dissent (Douglas, Stewart, JJ.). The dispute over the proper relationship between the Executive and Legislative branches in the initiation and conduct of war, reflected in *The Prize Cases*, *supra*, has not been adequately resolved.

---

4) **Executive detention of enemy combatants.** The Constitution does not contain any general "state of emergency" exception to its provisions that would suspend constitutional rights in the event of a national emergency. The Fifth Amendment does relax the requirement for a grand jury indictment for military cases in actual service in time of war or public danger. The United States Supreme Court has held that the constitutional protections apply even in time of war, such as in *Youngstown Sheet & Tube Co. v. Sawyer, supra.* In *Ex Parte Milligan*, 71 U.S. 2 (1866), the Court held that President Lincoln could not suspend the writ of habeas corpus during the Civil War and could not try civilians in military tribunals. In 1948, Congress enacted the Non-Detention Act, 18 U.S.C. section 4001(a), which provides that no citizen shall be imprisoned or otherwise detained by the United States except pursuant to an Act of Congress.

   a) **Enemy combatants in military tribunals.** In *Ex Parte Quirin*, 317 U.S. 1 (1942), the Court held that the Constitution gives the President the power to wage war once Congress declares it. Congress provided that military tribunals have jurisdiction to try offenders against the law of war. The law of war distinguishes between armed forces and unlawful combatants. Lawful combatants are subject to capture and detention as prisoners of war, but unlawful combatants are not entitled to status as prisoners of war. They may be subject to trial and punishment by military tribunals. It does not matter whether an enemy belligerent is a United States citizen. The Constitution does not extend the right to trial by jury to the cases of alien or citizen offenders against the law of war otherwise triable by military tribunals.

   b) **Joint resolution authorizing the use of military force.** In response to the attack on September 11, 2001, Congress passed a joint resolution titled "Authorization for Use of Military Force" ("AUMF") that gave the President broad authority to use force against nations, organizations, or persons that the President determines aided the terrorist attacks. No particular enemy was defined. President Bush committed the United States military to combat in Afghanistan and Iraq and detained alleged enemy combatants inside the United States and at Guantanamo Bay, Cuba.

c) **Detention of enemy combatants at Guantanamo Bay.** The United States military captured several hundred foreign fighters in Afghanistan and held them as "enemy combatants" at Guantanamo Bay, a territory leased by the United States from Cuba since 1903. Under the lease, the territory remains under the "ultimate sovereignty" of Cuba. Some of the prisoners sought writs of habeas corpus in the federal district court for the District of Columbia. In *Rasul v. Bush*, 542 U.S. 466 (2004), the Court held that federal judges do have jurisdiction to consider such habeas petitions from Guantanamo detainees. The Court reasoned that although technically Cuba has sovereignty over the territory, under the lease, the United States exercises "complete jurisdiction and control" over the base and may continue to exercise such control permanently if it chooses. As such, Guantanamo Bay is in every practical respect a territory of the United States. Another consideration is the indefinite status of the detention and the lack of any legal procedure to determine the detainees' status. The dissenters argued that the decision extends the habeas statute to aliens beyond the sovereign territory of the United States to anywhere in the world and that Congress could have changed the habeas jurisdiction of federal judges if it wanted to.

d) **Detention of United States citizens--**

Hamdi v. Rumsfeld, 542 U.S. 507 (2004).

Facts. Hamdi (P), a Louisiana-born Saudi-American, was captured in an active combat zone abroad, detained by the United States military as an "enemy combatant," and held in a naval brig in Virginia. P sought habeas corpus relief against Rumsfeld (D), Secretary of Defense, in federal court in Virginia, claiming that the Non-Detention Act of 1948 barred indefinite detention. The Fourth Circuit held that P was not entitled to habeas relief, despite being a United States citizen, because of military needs. The court held that the Authorization for Use of Military Force ("AUMF") satisfied the requirement in the Non-Detention Act for an Act of Congress authorizing detention. P appeals.

Issue. Does the President have the authority to detain citizens who qualify as "enemy combatants" for an indefinite period of time with no opportunity for an impartial hearing?

Held. No. Judgment vacated and case remanded.

- D claims that the Executive has plenary authority to detain pursuant to Article II, but that question need not be addressed because Congress authorized detention through the AUMF. The detention of individuals falling into the limited category of combatants, for the duration of the particular conflict in which they were captured, is a fundamental incident of war and falls within the AUMF.

- There is no reason that the government cannot hold one of its own citizens as an enemy combatant. *Quirin, supra*, held that citizenship does not preclude detention for the duration of hostilities.

- P claims that Congress did not authorize indefinite detention. He also claims that he faces the prospect of perpetual detention, because the "war on terror" is an unconventional war that does not fit within normal law-of-war principles. While indefinite detention is not authorized by Congress, there are active combat operations in Afghanistan against Taliban combatants, and the United States may lawfully detain Taliban combatants during these hostilities.

- Although the AUMF did authorize the detention of combatants such as P in the narrow circumstances of this case, the writ of habeas corpus remains available to every person detained within the United States. The writ has not been suspended. P may properly seek a habeas determination on the issue of whether he falls within the category of hostile forces subject to detention. Due process demands that a citizen held in the United States as an enemy combatant be given a meaningful opportunity to contest the factual basis for that detention before a neutral decisionmaker.

- To satisfy the minimum requirements for such a hearing, the citizen-detainee must receive notice of the factual basis for his classification and a fair opportunity to rebut the government's factual assertions before a neutral decisionmaker. Evidentiary standards may be relaxed so that the government may use hearsay to support the classification. There may be a rebuttable presumption in favor of the government's evidence.

Concurrence and dissent (Souter, Ginsburg, JJ.). To the extent that the plurality rejects the government's proposed limit on the exercise of habeas jurisdiction, it is correct. However, the plurality goes too far when it agrees that P can be detained if his designation as an enemy combatant is correct. The AUMF does not refer to detention, so it cannot provide a basis for P's detention. The government has failed to justify holding P in the absence of an Act of Congress, criminal charges, a showing that P's detention conforms to the law of war, or a showing that section 4001(a) is unconstitutional. Without a showing of something more, P should be released. In a moment of genuine emergency, the President can detain a citizen if there is a reason to fear he is an imminent threat to the safety of the Nation and its people, but such emergency power must be limited by the emergency. P has been held for over two years, so that exception does not apply here.

Dissent (Scalia, Stevens, JJ.). A citizen who wages war against the United States may be prosecuted for treason, but unless Congress suspends the usual protections under the Suspension Clause, a citizen cannot be detained without charge. The lower court decision should be reversed. The traditional treatment of enemy aliens that includes detention until the cessation of hostilities does not apply to American citizens. The criminal law process is the only means for punishing and incapacitating traitors. Unless the writ of habeas corpus is suspended, a citizen is entitled either to a criminal trial or a judicial decree requiring his release. The AUMF is not a suspension of the writ. The Court's opinion establishes a procedure that makes P's detention legal, but that is an incorrect application of the writ.

Dissent (Thomas, J.). The detention of P falls within the government's war powers, and the courts have no expertise or capacity to second-guess the decision to detain P. The President has constitutional authority to protect the national security and has broad discretion to exercise that authority. The courts should not interfere in these matters. Due process requires only a good-faith executive determination.

Comment. In *Rumsfeld v. Padilla*, 542 U.S. 426 (2004), Padilla, a United States citizen, was first held in criminal custody in New York as a material witness in connection with a federal grand jury investigation of the September 11th terrorist attacks. Padilla was later transferred to a naval brig in South Carolina for indefinite detention after being declared an "enemy combatant" by the President. Padilla challenged his detention. The Second Circuit held that the President did not have authority to detain Padilla under section 4001(a). The Supreme Court remanded, holding that Padilla should have filed his habeas petition in South Carolina where he was confined by the time the petition was filed. Justice Stevens, joined by three other Justices, wanted to reach the merits of the case. Justice Stevens asserted that the Non-Detention Act prohibited, and the AUMF did not authorize, Padilla's protracted, incommunicado detention. He said that the detention for purposes of interrogation was like the Star Chamber and that it was a violation of due process.

---

e) Habeas corpus for aliens--

Boumediene v. Bush, 128 S. Ct. 2229 (2008).

Facts. Boumediene and other aliens designated as enemy combatants (Ps) were detained at the United States Naval Station at Guantanamo Bay, Cuba. Ps sought writs of habeas corpus in the United States District Court for the District of Columbia. The district court dismissed the cases for lack of jurisdiction because Guantanamo Bay is outside the sovereign territory of the United States. The Court of Appeals affirmed. In *Rasul v. Bush, supra*, the Supreme Court reversed, holding that statutory habeas corpus jurisdiction extended to Guantanamo. While Ps' appeals were pending, Congress passed the Detainee Treatment Act of 2005 ("DTA"), which provided, in part, that federal courts did not have jurisdiction to consider writs of habeas corpus from aliens detained in Guantanamo Bay. In *Hamdan v. Rumsfeld*, 548 U.S. 557 (2006), the Court held that that provision of the DTA did not apply to Ps, whose cases were pending when the DTA was adopted. Congress then passed the Military Commissions Act of 2006 ("MCA"). The court of appeals concluded that the MCA stripped all federal courts of jurisdiction to hear Ps' habeas corpus applications and that Ps were not entitled to habeas corpus. The Supreme Court granted certiorari.

Issue. Are alien detainees designated as enemy combatants and held by United States forces outside the United States in Guantanamo Bay entitled to habeas corpus?

Held. Yes. Judgment reversed.

- Under the Authorization for Use of Military Force ("AUMF"), Congress authorized the President to use all necessary and appropriate force against anyone who participated in the September 11 attacks, as well as against any organizations or persons who harbored such individuals, in order to prevent future acts of international terrorism against the United States. In *Hamdi v. Rumsfeld, supra*, the Court held that detention of individuals who fought against the United States in Afghanistan was an authorized use of such necessary and appropriate force. The Department of Defense ordered detention of Ps pursuant to the AUMF. No P is a citizen of a nation now at war with the United States, and each P claims not to be a member of al Qaeda.

- The MCA denied the federal courts jurisdiction to hear Ps' habeas corpus petitions pending at the time the MCA was enacted.

- The privilege of habeas corpus was included in the Constitution before the Bill of Rights, reflecting the importance the Framers placed on the writ to secure freedom from unlawful restraint. The Framers specified in the Suspension Clause that the writ could not be suspended except, when in cases of rebellion or invasion, the public safety may require it.

- The Suspension Clause ensures that, except during periods of formal suspension, the judiciary has the writ to maintain the "delicate balance of governance" that safeguards liberty. The Clause protects the rights of the detained by affirming the duty and authority of the judiciary to question the legality of the prisoner's custody. The separation of powers doctrine, and the history that influenced its design, inform the reach and purpose of the Suspension Clause.

- The government claims that, according to English history, the writ ran only to those territories over which the king was sovereign, but Ps claim that jurisdiction followed the king's officers. There is no controlling case law on this point. The government points out that the United States does not claim sovereignty over Guantanamo Bay, a leased territory over which Cuba retains ultimate sovereignty. Even so, the United States does maintain de facto sovereignty there. The Constitution does not necessarily stop where de jure sovereignty ends.

- The reach of the Suspension Clause depends on three factors: (i) the citizenship and status of the detainee and the adequacy of the process through which that status determination was made; (ii) the nature of the sites where apprehension and then detention took place; and (iii) the practical obstacles inherent in resolving the prisoner's entitlement to the writ.

- Here, Ps' status is a matter of dispute. Ps deny they are enemy combatants. They have been afforded some process in CSRT proceedings to determine their status, but there has been no trial by military commission for violations of the laws of war. The procedural protections afforded to the detainees in the CSRT hearings fall short of the procedures and adversarial mechanisms that would eliminate the need for habeas corpus review. The detainee is assigned a "Personal Representative" to assist him during CSRT proceedings, but this representative is not the detainee's lawyer. The government's evidence is accorded a presumption of validity. The detainee is allowed to present "reasonably available" evidence, but his ability to rebut the government's evidence against him is limited because of his confinement and his lack of counsel. And although the detainee can seek review of his status determination in the court of appeals, that review process cannot cure all of the deficiencies in the CSRT proceedings.

- Regarding the second factor, the sites of Ps' apprehension and detention are technically outside the sovereign territory of the United States. Although this is a factor that weighs against finding they have rights under the Suspension Clause, Guantanamo Bay is not a transient possession, in every practical sense it is not abroad, and it is within the constant jurisdiction of the United States.

- As to the third factor, habeas corpus proceedings may require expenditure of funds by the government and may divert the attention of military personnel from other important tasks. However, compliance with any judicial process requires some expenditure of resources. And the government has offered no credible arguments that the military mission at Guantanamo would be compromised if habeas corpus courts had jurisdiction to hear Ps' claims.

- Ps have been detained by executive order for the duration of a conflict that, if measured from September 11, 2001, to the present, is already among the longest wars in American history. And Ps are being held in a territory that, while technically not part of the United States, is under the complete and total control of the United States Government.

- We hold that the Suspension Clause has full effect at Guantanamo Bay. The MCA does not purport to be a formal suspension of the writ, and the government has not argued that it is. Therefore, Ps are entitled to the privilege of habeas corpus.

- The government claims that the review process under the DTA is an adequate substitute procedure for habeas corpus. Key elements of habeas corpus include the prisoner's meaningful opportunity to demonstrate he is being held pursuant to the erroneous application or interpretation of relevant law. The habeas court must have the power to order the conditional release of an individual unlawfully detained. The necessary scope of habeas review depends in part on the rigor of any prior proceedings for procedural adequacy. When a person is detained by executive order, rather than after being tried and convicted in a court, the need for collateral review is crucial.

- There is considerable risk of error in the findings of fact in the CSRT proceedings. There are constraints upon the detainee's ability to rebut the factual basis for the government's assertion that he is an enemy combatant, and he may not be aware of the most critical allegations that the government relied on to order his detention. And although the detainee can confront witnesses who testify during the CSRT proceedings, there are no limits on the admission of hearsay evidence.

- The court that conducts the habeas proceeding must have the means to correct errors that occurred during the CSRT proceedings, the authority to assess the sufficiency of the government's evidence against the detainee, and the authority to admit and consider relevant exculpatory evidence that was not introduced during the earlier proceeding. But the DTA's "Scope of Review" provision confines the role of the court of appeals to reviewing whether the CSRT followed the "standards and procedures" issued by the Department of Defense and assessing whether those "standards and procedures" are lawful. One of these standards is a rebuttable presumption in favor of the government's evidence. Furthermore, the DTA does not provide an opportunity for the detainee to present relevant exculpatory evidence that was discovered after the CSRT proceedings concluded.

- The underlying detention proceedings lack the necessary adversarial character, and the detainee cannot be held responsible for all deficiencies in the record. The DTA review process is, on its face, an inadequate substitute for habeas corpus. Thus, the MCA effects an unconstitutional suspension of the writ of habeas corpus.

- Some of the detainees here have been held for six years without the judicial oversight that habeas corpus or an adequate substitute demands. To require them to complete DTA review before proceeding with their habeas corpus actions would be to require additional months, if not years, of delay. The first DTA review applications were filed over a year ago, but no decisions on the merits have been issued. Ps are entitled to a prompt habeas corpus hearing. However, both the DTA and the CSRT process remain intact, and the courts should give the Executive reasonable time to determine the status of other detainees before entertaining their habeas corpus petitions.

Dissent (Roberts, C.J., Scalia, Thomas, Alito, JJ.). The processes established by Congress and the President were the result of considerable investigation and debate and provided the most generous set of procedural protections ever afforded aliens detained by the United States as enemy combatants. The majority has replaced this review system with a set of shapeless procedures to be defined by the courts in the future. The established review system protects whatever rights Ps may possess; there is no need for additional process. The majority cannot explain what rights Ps have that cannot be vindicated through the DTA system.

Dissent (Scalia, J., Roberts, C.J., Thomas, Alito, JJ.).

- The majority has conferred a constitutional right to habeas corpus on alien enemies detained abroad by the United States military in the course of an ongoing war. The writ of habeas corpus has never been applied in favor of aliens abroad and should not be now. The Court's decision will make the war harder on us and will cause more Americans to be killed. At least 30 of those prisoners who have been released from Guantanamo Bay have returned to the battlefield. We owe great deference to Congress's view that a law it has passed is constitutional, especially in the area of foreign and military affairs.
- The Court asserts that because "the writ of habeas corpus is itself an indispensable mechanism for monitoring the separation of powers," the test of its extraterritorial reach "must not be subject to manipulation by those whose power it is designed to restrain." But "manipulation" of the territorial reach of the writ by the Court poses as much a threat to the proper separation of powers as "manipulation" by the Executive.
- The Court's decision breaks a chain of precedent that prohibits judicial inquiry into detentions of aliens abroad absent statutory authorization, and it requires that our military commanders attempt the impossible task of proving to a civilian court, under whatever standards this Court devises in the future, that evidence supports the confinement of each and every enemy prisoner.

---

d. Legislative veto.

1) **Introduction.** Article I, Section 7 provides that "Every Bill which shall have passed the House of Representatives and the Senate, shall, before it become a Law, be presented to the President of the United States; If he approves he shall sign it, but if not he shall return it, with his Objections to the House in which it shall have originated, who shall . . . proceed to reconsider it. If after such Reconsideration two thirds of that House shall agree to pass the Bill . . . and if approved by two thirds of [the other] House, it shall become a Law." This clause requires the President to approve or disapprove a complete law. For years, Presidents have requested a line item veto that would allow them to veto portions of statutes, leaving the balance intact. When Congress did enact a line item

veto, the constitutionality of the statute was immediately challenged.

2) **Line item veto--**

Clinton v. City of New York, 524 U.S. 417 (1998).

Facts. In *Raines v. Byrd*, 521 U.S. 811 (1997), the Court held that members of Congress do not have standing to challenge the Line Item Veto Act because they lacked a sufficiently concrete injury. The Act allowed the President, after making specific determinations, to cancel three types of provisions that have already been signed into law, including any item of new direct spending or any limited tax benefit. The cancellation becomes effective when Congress receives noticc from the President, but Congress may render the cancellation void by passing a disapproval bill. Shortly after the *Raines* decision, President Clinton (D) applied the Act to cancel sections of two separate statutes, one that waived the federal government's right to recoupment of up to $2.6 billion in taxes from the state of New York and another that gave tax preferences to certain food refiners and processors. These provisions fell within the criteria set forth in the Act, and Congress did not pass a disapproval bill. The city of New York and others (Ps) sued, claiming the cancellations were unconstitutional. The district court consolidated the suits, found that Ps had standing, and held that the Act was unconstitutional. D appeals.

Issue. May Congress grant the President a line item veto that allows the President to cancel legislation after it is duly enacted and signed?

Held. No. Judgment affirmed.

♦ Article I, Section 7 allows the President to return a bill to Congress. This action takes place before a bill becomes law. By contrast, the cancellation provision in the Act occurs after the bill becomes law. A constitutional return applies to the entire bill, but a cancellation under the Act applies only to a part of a bill. These are constitutionally significant differences.

♦ The Constitution expressly permits the return of a bill, but it is silent regarding unilateral Presidential action that either repeals or amends parts of a duly enacted statute. Constitutional silence on a matter as important as Presidential action regarding statutes must be construed as an express prohibition on such actions. Presidents may either approve all parts of a bill or reject it completely.

♦ D claims that a cancellation is not actually an amendment or a repeal. In *Field v. Clark*, 143 U.S. 649 (1892), the Court allowed a Tariff Act that gave the President authority to suspend certain products' exemptions from import duties upon making certain findings. Such a suspension power differs from a cancellation power because exercise of the suspension power depended on conditions that did not exist when the Tariff Act was passed, because the President had a duty to suspend under specified circumstances, and because when the President did suspend the duties, he was executing congressional policy. A cancellation under the Act has none of these factors that justified upholding the suspension power. For example, the President can cancel a portion of a statute for his own policy reasons, independent of Congress. Congress cannot so alter the constitutional provisions without a constitutional amendment.

- ♦ The President has a traditional power to decline to spend appropriated funds. But never before this Act has Congress given the President the unilateral power to change the text of duly enacted statutes. The line item veto procedures are simply not allowed under Article I, Section 7.

Concurrence (Kennedy, J.). The Act threatens the liberties of individual citizens because liberty is always at stake when one or more branches of government seeks to transgress the separation of powers.

Dissent (Breyer, O'Connor, Scalia, JJ.). The Court appears to conclude that a cancellation is the equivalent of a repeal or amendment of a law, but it is not. A cancellation under the Act leaves the statutes as they were literally written, intact. In canceling a law under the Act, the President follows the law. He neither repeals nor amends anything. Congress has granted a contingent power to deny effect to certain statutory language in many other statutes. Finally, the Act does not violate the separation of powers because Congress retains the power both to disapprove a cancellation and to include in any bill a provision that says the act will not apply.

Concurrence and dissent (Scalia, O'Connor, Breyer, JJ.). The tax benefit Ps do not have standing, although the New York Ps do. On the merits, the Court fails to observe that the Act applies only after the requirements of the Presentment Clause have been satisfied. This means that the Court's problem focuses on the President's power to prevent certain parts of duly enacted statutes to have full force and effect. Yet there is no difference between Congress allowing the President to cancel a spending item and allowing money to be spent on a particular item at the President's discretion. The latter approach has been allowed throughout history. If the Act had allowed the President to decline to spend any item of spending in the budget bills, it would have been constitutional. The Act uses a technically different approach, but it does not violate Article I, Section 7, and the doctrine of unconstitutional delegation is not a doctrine of technicalities.

---

2. Power of Congress to Interfere with the Executive Branch.

a. The legislative veto.

1) **Introduction.** Congress has occasionally included provisions in legislation that leave it some power to override executive action

taken pursuant to the legislation. This device, called the "legislative veto," has been praised for bringing greater efficiency to the government, but it presents important questions about the separation of powers among the branches of government.

2) **Rejection--**

Immigration & Naturalization Service v. Chadha, 462 U.S. 919 (1983).

Facts. Chadha (P) was an East Indian who lawfully entered the United States on a nonimmigrant student visa. After his visa expired, the Immigration and Naturalization Service (D) held a deportation hearing. The immigration judge suspended P's deportation and sent a report to Congress as required by section 244(c)(1) of the Immigration and Naturalization Act. Section 244(c)(2) provided that either house of Congress could veto a suspension of deportation. The House of Representatives adopted a unilateral resolution opposing P's permanent residence, and P was ordered deported. P sought review in the Ninth Circuit, which held section 244(c)(2) unconstitutional. The Supreme Court granted certiorari.

Issue. May Congress employ the legislative veto device to oversee delegations of its constitutional authority to the executive branch?

Held. No. Judgment affirmed.

- Although this case has political ramifications, it is primarily a constitutional challenge that presents a bona fide controversy, properly subject to judicial action.

- Article I of the Constitution vests all legislative powers in both houses of Congress. Every bill or resolution must be passed by both houses and approved by the President (or his veto overridden) before it takes effect. These provisions are intended to secure liberty through separation of powers. The bicameral nature of Congress similarly ensures careful consideration of all legislation.

- The action taken by the House in this case was essentially legislative in purpose and effect. The legislative veto replaced the constitutional procedure of enacting legislation requiring P's deportation (a private bill). Yet the Constitution enumerates only four instances in which either house may act alone—impeachment, trial after impeachment, ratification of treaties, and confirmation of presidential appointments. The legislative veto is not enumerated.

- Although the legislative veto may be efficient, efficiency is not the overriding value behind the Constitution. Separation of powers, as set up by the Constitution, may not be eroded for convenience. Therefore, the legislative veto is unconstitutional. Once Congress delegates authority, it must abide by that delegation until it legislatively alters or revokes it.

Concurrence (Powell, J.). There is no need to invalidate every legislative veto. This one is an unconstitutional exercise of the judicial function by the House because it decided the specific rights of P.

Dissent (White, J.). The legislative veto is a valid response to the dilemma of choosing between no delegation (and hence no lawmaking because of the vast amount of regulation necessary under our system) and abdication of the lawmaking function to the executive branch and administrative agencies. The legislative veto has been included in nearly 200 statutes, accepted by presidents for 50 years, and allows resolution of major constitutional and policy differences between Congress and the President. Because the underlying legislation is properly enacted, and because the Constitution does not prohibit it, the legislative veto is constitutional.

Dissent (Rehnquist, White, JJ.). Section 244(c)(2) is not severable from the rest of the Act, so the judgment below should be reversed.

Comment. Subsequent to *Chadha*, the Court held that Congress can delegate the power to establish sentencing guidelines for criminal cases to a sentencing commission located in the federal courts and made up, in part, of federal judges, as long as the tasks delegated do not undermine the integrity of the judiciary or usurp the powers of the other branches. [Mistretta v. United States, 488 U.S. 361 (1989)]

---

b. The appointment power and the office of independent counsel--

---

Morrison v. Olson, 487 U.S. 654 (1988).

Facts. The Ethics in Government Act of 1978, 28 U.S.C. sections 591 *et seq.*, provided for the appointment of an "independent counsel" to investigate and prosecute specified government officials for violations of federal criminal law. Under the Act, the Attorney General conducts a preliminary investigation of possible violations, and then reports to the Special Division, a court created by the Act. If the Attorney General determines that there are reasonable grounds to believe further investigation or a prosecution is warranted, she applies for appointment of independent counsel. The Special Division then appoints such counsel and defines the counsel's prosecutorial jurisdiction. The independent prosecutor is required to comply with Department of Justice policies to the extent possible. The Attorney General may remove an independent prosecutor for cause; otherwise, the counsel's tenure expires on completion of the specified investigations or prosecutions. The counsel notifies the Attorney General of the completion; alternatively, the Special Division may find the task completed. Certain congressional committees have oversight jurisdiction regarding the independent counsel's conduct. Pursuant to this Act, the Special Division appointed Morrison (D) to investigate allegations that Olson (P), an assistant attorney general, had lied in testimony to Congress. D obtained a grand jury subpoena against P. P moved to quash the subpoenas, claiming that D had no authority to proceed because the Act was unconstitutional. The trial court upheld the Act, but the court of appeals reversed. D appeals.

Issue. May Congress provide for the judicial appointment of independent counsel for purposes of investigating and prosecuting federal criminal offenses?

Held. Yes. Judgment reversed.

- Under the Appointments Clause, there are two classes of officers: (i) principal officers, who are selected by the President with the advice and consent of the Senate; and (ii) inferior officers whom Congress may allow to be appointed by the President alone, by the heads of departments, or by the Judiciary. Thus, if D is a principal officer, the Act violates the Constitution.

- The difference between principal and inferior officers is not always clear. It requires consideration of several factors.

    D may be removed by a higher executive branch official, despite having independent powers.

    D's authority is limited to performing specified, limited duties. D has no policymaking authority and must comply with Department of Justice policies.

    D's office is limited in jurisdiction to the terms of the appointment. It is also limited in tenure; it does not extend beyond the completion of the specific task given.

    Evaluation of these factors leads to the conclusion that an independent counsel is an inferior officer. However, P claims that Congress may not provide that an officer of one branch be appointed by officers of another branch.

- The clause itself does not forbid interbranch appointments, but instead gives Congress discretion to determine the propriety of vesting the appointment of executive officials in the courts. The limitation on this power is where it implicates the separation of powers or impairs the constitutional functions assigned to one of the branches. The very reason for the Act was to remove the appointment power from the executive branch, and the judicial branch is the most logical alternative. By making members of the Special Division ineligible to participate in any matters relating to an independent counsel they have appointed, Congress has protected the separation of powers.

- Article III limits the judicial power to cases and controversies. However, if the Appointments Clause gives Congress the power to authorize the courts to appoint officials such as an independent counsel, which it does, the appointment power is a source of authority independent of Article III. The additional powers granted to the Special Division, such as defining the counsel's authority and tenure of office, are incidental to the exercise of the appointment power itself.

- ♦ The Special Division also has power to terminate an independent counsel's office, which is an administrative power. This power must be narrowly construed to avoid constitutional problems. It is thus limited to removing an independent counsel who has served her purpose but does not acknowledge that fact and remains on the payroll.

- ♦ P also asserts a separation of powers problem because the Attorney General can remove an independent counsel only by showing "good cause." In *Bowsher v. Synar*, 478 U.S. 714 (1986), for example, Congress could not involve itself in the removal of an executive officer. Under the Act in this case, however, Congress did not acquire a removal power over executive officials beyond its power of impeachment and conviction.

- ♦ The Attorney General retains the removal power, subject to the good cause requirement. But the Constitution does not give the President unbridled discretion to remove officials of independent agencies. Prior cases have distinguished purely executive officials from quasi-legislative and quasi-judicial officials, but this is an inappropriate distinction for analyzing removal powers. The proper question is whether the removal restrictions impede the President's ability to perform his constitutional duty. Because the independent counsel has a limited function, and because the Attorney General has removal authority for good cause, the good cause restriction does not unconstitutionally impede the President.

- ♦ The second separation of powers issue is based on interference with the role of the executive branch. However, the Act does not permit either congressional or judicial usurpation of executive functions. It also leaves the executive branch with the ability to supervise the counsel's prosecutorial powers.

Dissent (Scalia, J.). The power to conduct a criminal prosecution is a purely executive power, and the Act deprives the President of the exclusive control over the exercise of that power. It does not matter how much the Act reduces presidential control; the Act violates the separation of powers doctrine. In addition, P's appointment could only be constitutional if she is an "inferior" officer, but she is not inferior because she is not subordinate to another officer. The final infirmity of the Act is that it improperly imposes restrictions on the removal of the independent counsel.

---

c. **Impeachment.** Article II, Section 4 permits removal from office of all civil officers of the United States by impeachment and conviction. The device has been used sparingly.

3. Executive and Legislative Immunities.

a. **Executive immunities.** The courts have recognized an executive privilege against the disclosure of presidential communications made in the exercise of the executive power, based on the doctrine of separation of powers and the inherent need to protect the confidentiality of high-level communications, but there are limitations to this power.

1) **Need for evidence in criminal trial--**

United States v. Nixon, 418 U.S. 683 (1974).

Facts. The special prosecutor, acting for the United States (P) in the Watergate investigation, sought and received a subpoena ordering President Nixon (D) to produce various tapes and other records relating to presidential conversations and meetings, despite D's motion to quash and motions to expunge and for protective orders. D appealed, and the Supreme Court granted certiorari.

Issue. Does executive immunity give the President an absolute, unqualified general privilege of immunity from judicial process under all circumstances?

Held. No. Judgment affirmed.

- D contends that the case is merely an intra-branch dispute between officers of the executive branch and thus lacks the requisite justiciability. However, the special prosecutor has been given special authority to pursue the criminal prosecution and has standing to bring this action in the courts.

- The doctrine of separation of powers does not preclude judicial review of a President's claim of privilege, because it is the duty of the courts to say what the law is with respect to that claim of privilege, even if the judicial interpretation varies from the President's.

- The President's need for and the public interest in the confidentiality of presidential communications is accorded great deference. But absent a need to protect military, diplomatic, or sensitive national security secrets, in camera inspection of presidential communications will not significantly diminish the interest in confidentiality. Legitimate judicial needs may therefore outweigh a blanket presidential privilege.

- Application of a balancing test to the interests involved results in affirmation of the district court's order. P sought the subpoena to ensure fair and complete presentation of evidence in a criminal proceeding, pursuant to the fundamental demands of due process. The generalized assertion of privilege must yield to the demonstrated, specific need for evidence in a pending criminal trial.

2) No immunity for unofficial conduct--

Clinton v. Jones, 520 U.S. 681 (1997).

Facts. Clinton (D) was elected President in 1992 and re-elected in 1996. In 1991, D was the Governor of Arkansas. In 1994, Jones (P) filed suit in federal court claiming that D had made sexual advances toward her in 1991, when P was an employee of the state of Arkansas. P sought actual and punitive damages for D's alleged deprivation of her constitutional rights and for state claims. The allegations were unrelated to any of D's official duties as President and preceded his election. D filed a motion to dismiss on grounds of Presidential immunity. The trial court denied D's motion but ordered the trial stayed until the end of D's Presidency on the ground that the public interest in avoiding litigation that might hamper the President outweighed any demonstrated need for an immediate trial. The court of appeals reversed the postponement of the trial, which it considered to be the functional equivalent of a grant of temporary immunity. The Supreme Court granted certiorari.

Issue. Must a claim by a private citizen against the President of the United States, based on actions allegedly taken before his term began, be deferred until the expiration of the President's term of office?

Held. No. Judgment affirmed.

- ♦ Certain public servants, including prosecutors, legislators, and judges, have immunity from suits for money damages arising out of their official acts, because this serves the public interest in allowing such officials to perform their designated functions effectively, without fear of personal liability for a particular decision. This rationale does not support immunity for unofficial conduct, however.

- ♦ There is no precedent to support D's position that he should have immunity for unofficial acts purely because of the identity of his office. The President is not above the laws, but is amenable to them in his private character as a citizen, and in his public character by impeachment.

- ♦ Despite the importance of the office of the President, whatever the outcome of this case, it will not curtail the scope of the official powers of the Executive Branch. The fact that a federal court's actions in this case may significantly burden the President's time and attention does not establish a constitutional violation. Courts have the authority to determine whether a President's official actions are within the law. Presidents are subject to judicial process in other areas, such as in complying with a subpoena. The separation of powers doctrine does not require federal courts to stay all private actions against the President until he leaves office.

- The district court did not grant immunity, but it did grant a stay until after D leaves office. This was an abuse of discretion because it did not take into account P's interest in bringing the case to trial. Such a long delay would increase the risk of prejudice to P resulting from the loss of evidence, impaired memory, or perhaps even the death of a party. If greater protection of the President becomes necessary, Congress can provide appropriate legislation.

Concurrence (Breyer, J.). While there should be no automatic temporary immunity, the courts cannot unduly interfere with the President's performance of his duties.

Comment. The Court explained that the result might be different if the case were being heard in a state forum, where federalism might apply, and noted that it did not address the question of whether a court could compel the attendance of the President at any specific time or place.

III. GOVERNMENT AND THE INDIVIDUAL: THE PROTECTION OF LIBERTY AND PROPERTY UNDER THE DUE PROCESS AND EQUAL PROTECTION CLAUSES

A. THE BILL OF RIGHTS, THE CIVIL WAR AMENDMENTS, AND THEIR INTERRELATIONSHIP

1. The Pre-Civil War Background.

a. **Introduction.** The Contract Clause (Article I, Section 10), which prohibits the impairment of the obligation of contracts, and the Privileges and Immunities Clause (Article IV, Section 2) were the major restraints on state regulation found in the original United States Constitution. The Bill of Rights, as originally adopted, protected the individual and the state only from actions of the federal government.

b. **Bill of Rights not applied to states--**

Barron v. Mayor of Baltimore, 32 U.S. (7 Pet.) 243 (1833).

Facts. Barron (P) sued the Mayor and City Council of Baltimore (Ds) for permitting street construction that had the effect of depositing silt in front of his wharf, making it inaccessible. P obtained a verdict for $45,000, which was reversed by the state court. P appeals on the ground that his property was not granted proper protection under the Fifth Amendment (*i.e.,* there was a "taking" without compensation).

Issue. Does the Bill of Rights accord citizens of the United States protection from state government actions?

Held. No. Case dismissed.

♦ The limitations on government power expressed in the federal Constitution are applicable only to the government created by that instrument. Had the Framers intended them to be limitations on the powers of the state governments, they would have expressed that intention. Any limits on state powers can only be found in the respective state constitutions. For this reason, the Court has no jurisdiction and must dismiss the case.

2. Initial Narrow Interpretation of the Thirteenth and Fourteenth Amendments--

Slaughter-House Cases, 83 U.S. (16 Wall.) 36 (1872).

Facts. New Orleans butchers (Ps) challenged a state law granting a state corporation the exclusive right to operate facilities in New Orleans for the landing, keeping, and slaughter of livestock. Ps' only means of practicing their trade was to pay fees to the state corporation and work at the corporation plant. The state courts upheld the statute. Ps appeal, based on the following constitutional objections: (i) the statute created an involuntary servitude forbidden by the Thirteenth Amendment; (ii) it abridged the privileges and immunities of citizens of the United States; (iii) it denied Ps the equal protection of the laws; and (iv) it deprived Ps of their property without due process of law, all in violation of the Fourteenth Amendment.

Issue. Do the Civil War amendments grant United States citizens broad protection from the actions of state governments?

Held. No. Judgment affirmed.

- Interpretation of the meaning of the Civil War amendments must reflect their historical setting. Therefore, the meaning of "involuntary servitude" in the Thirteenth Amendment is restricted to personal servitude, not a servitude attached to property as Ps claimed.

- The Fourteenth Amendment clearly distinguishes between citizenship of the states and citizenship of the United States. Only those privileges and immunities of ***United States citizens*** are protected by the Fourteenth Amendment; privileges and immunities of state citizens on which Ps rely here are unaffected, and rest for their security and protection in the power of the several states as recognized in Article IV. The United States Constitution does not control the power of the state governments over the rights of their own citizens except to require that a state grant equal rights to its own citizens and citizens of other states within its jurisdiction. Therefore, Ps have no privilege or immunity as citizens of the United States that is infringed by the state law.

- The Equal Protection Clause of the Fourteenth Amendment was intended primarily to prevent state discrimination against blacks, although Congress may extend its scope to other areas. But Ps have not claimed a denial of equal justice in the state courts and therefore have no reason to have a remedy under the Equal Protection Clause.

- The restraint imposed by Louisiana on the exercise of Ps' trade simply cannot be held, consistent with prior interpretations, to be a deprivation of property within the meaning of that provision.

Dissent (Field, J., Chase, C.J., Swayne, Bradley, JJ.). These amendments were intended to protect the citizens of the United States against the deprivation of their common rights by state legislation. The majority holding as to the Privileges and Immunities Clause would add no more protection than existed prior to adoption of the amendment, making it meaningless. A distinguishing privilege of citizens of the United States is equality of right to the lawful pursuits of life throughout the whole country. To permit a state to interfere with such a basic privilege is to ignore the true purpose of the Fourteenth Amendment.

---

3. **Effect on Citizenship.**

   a. **Introduction.** The constitutional basis for federal and state citizenship is found in Section 1 of the Fourteenth Amendment, which provides that "all persons born or ***naturalized*** in the United States, and subject to the jurisdiction thereof, are citizens of the United States and of the State wherein they reside" (emphasis added).

      1) The power of naturalization is vested exclusively in Congress. [Holmgren v. United States, 217 U.S. 509 (1910)]

      2) Congress has enacted detailed laws regarding immigration and naturalization. [8 U.S.C. §1401]

      3) The rights of native-born and naturalized citizens are of the same dignity and are coextensive (except that only a native-born citizen can be elected President). Hence, a statute that attempts to discriminate between the two classes of citizenship is unconstitutional. *Schneider v. Rusk*, 377 U.S. 163 (1964), held unconstitutional a statute that deprived naturalized citizens of their citizenship if they resumed foreign residence.

   b. **Loss of citizenship.** Under the Fourteenth Amendment, Congress does ***not*** have the power to take away the citizenship of native-born or naturalized citizens without their consent. *Afroyim v. Rusk*, 387 U.S. 253 (1967), held unconstitutional a statute that provided for loss of citizenship for voting in a foreign election. In *Vance v. Terrazas*, 444 U.S. 252 (1980), the Court upheld a rebuttable presumption that, when a statutory expatriation act is proved, the act is voluntary, but the government must still prove that the act was performed with the necessary intent to relinquish citizenship.

      1) But Congress does have power to revoke the citizenship of persons who have become citizens in some other manner; *e.g.,* by being born abroad to an American parent. *Rogers v. Bellei*, 401

U.S. 815 (1971), upheld a statute that provided that a person who becomes a citizen by reason of having been born abroad to an American parent loses his citizenship unless he resides continuously in the United States for five years between ages 14 and 28.

2) And statutes that provide for revocation of naturalization on appropriate grounds have also been upheld. *Schneiderman v. United States*, 320 U.S. 118 (1945), concerned a naturalized citizen guilty of fraud in swearing allegiance.

4. **Application of the Bill of Rights to the States.** Although the *Slaughter-House Cases, supra,* held that the Bill of Rights might not be "privileges and immunities of national citizenship," they are certainly so fundamental as to be protected against state abridgment through the Fourteenth Amendment Due Process Clause. This clause thus came to be relied on as the basis for the protection of personal rights against arbitrary state action.

a. **Total incorporation rejected.** It has been argued that the Fourteenth Amendment Due Process Clause incorporates all of the Bill of Rights in toto, but this view has been consistently rejected by the Court. [*See* Adamson v. California, 332 U.S. 46 (1947)] In *Adamson*, the Court decided that due process did not require reversal of a state criminal conviction where the prosecution had commented on the defendant's refusal to testify, although such a comment would be reversible error at the federal level because of the Fifth Amendment. Justices Black and Douglas dissented, arguing that the original purpose of the Fourteenth Amendment was to incorporate fully all of the Bill of Rights guarantees. They argued that failure to incorporate those specific guarantees would leave citizens without assured rights and would at the same time grant the Court an unauthorized broad power to expand or contract the scope of due process virtually at will. They also indicated a preference for selective incorporation over no incorporation at all.

b. **Doctrine of selective incorporation.** Instead, the Court has held that the limitations contained in the Bill of Rights restrict the states only on a selective basis. In essence, this means that the Bill of Rights is incorporated by the Fourteenth Amendment Due Process Clause only to the extent that the Court is convinced on a case-by-case basis that the protections and rights in question are so essential to fundamental principles of due process of law as to be preserved against both federal and state action. [Bloom v. Illinois, 391 U.S. 194 (1968)]

c. **Double jeopardy provision not incorporated--**

Palko v. Connecticut, 302 U.S. 319 (1937).

Facts. Palko (P) was indicted for first degree murder and convicted of second degree murder. The state of Connecticut (D), based on a state statute permitting appeals by the prosecution, appealed the sentence and won a reversal and an order for a new trial. P was convicted of first degree murder in the second trial and now challenges the Connecticut statute as a violation of the Fourteenth Amendment Due Process Clause, since it placed him in double jeopardy (a violation of the Fifth Amendment if P had been tried in a federal court for a federal crime).

Issue. Does the Fourteenth Amendment prevent a state from enacting a statute permitting double jeopardy?

Held. No. Judgment affirmed.

- While it is true that the Fifth Amendment prohibits federal retrial against the will of a defendant once convicted, no such protection extends to a prosecution by a state. P would apply all of the protections of the original Bill of Rights to state action, but there is no such general rule. Some immunities, such as those found in the First Amendment, have been extended to state action, but solely because of their indispensability to the concept of ordered liberty. Absorption of any of the Bill of Rights by the Fourteenth Amendment Due Process Clause is due solely to the belief that neither liberty nor justice would exist without them.

- The double jeopardy provision is not such an essential privilege—some would even say it is a mischief rather than a benefit. P has not claimed any lack of due process of law other than the Fifth Amendment claim, so his conviction is sustained.

---

d. Right to trial by jury incorporated--

Duncan v. Louisiana, 391 U.S. 145 (1968).

Facts. Duncan (D) was convicted of simple battery, a misdemeanor in Louisiana punishable by up to two years' imprisonment and a $300 fine. D was fined $150 and sentenced to serve only 60 days. D was refused a trial by jury under a Louisiana law, which he then challenged, but the state supreme court refused review. D appeals.

Issue. May a state that provides trial by jury for all "felonies" try charges of simple battery to the court alone?

Held. No. Judgment reversed and case remanded.

- The right of trial by jury in serious criminal cases is fundamental to the American scheme of justice and qualifies for protection under the Due Process Clause against violation by the states. The authorized penalty is of major relevance in determining whether a particular crime is serious; the possibility of two years' imprisonment clearly indicates a serious offense, so it is within due process protection. The Sixth Amendment guarantee of a right to jury trial is hereby applicable through the Fourteenth Amendment to state criminal cases, which, if tried in a federal court, would be covered.

Concurrence (Black, Douglas, JJ.). The Court ought to make an absolute incorporation into the Fourteenth Amendment of all of the Bill of Rights, but since the selective process adopted by the majority will eventually reach the same result, I concur. The Court ought to avoid the due process approach of Justices Fortas and Harlan, which would give due process an impermanent meaning subject to varying judges' predilections and understandings of what is best for the country.

Concurrence (Fortas, J.). A correct due process view would require that the states accord the right to jury trial in prosecution for offenses that are not petty.

Dissent (Harlan, Stewart, JJ.). The first section of the Fourteenth Amendment was meant neither to incorporate, nor to be limited to, the specific guarantees of the first eight amendments. The true intention was to ensure due process, based on a gradual process of judicial inclusion and exclusion. The Court errs in focusing on the simple incorporation question. Examination of the true merits reveals that D has not been denied any element of fundamental procedural fairness. States should be free to experiment with alternatives (fair procedures that may prove more effective).

B. THE DUE PROCESS, CONTRACT, AND JUST COMPENSATION CLAUSES AND THE REVIEW OF THE REASONABLENESS OF LEGISLATION

1. Business Regulation.

a. The due process limitation.

1) **The rise of substantive due process.** Originally, due process remained an assurance of fair procedures. Then the Court began to examine the substantive reasonableness of state legislation (substantive due process). The Court invalidated several state laws that were not "fair and appropriate" in the Court's judgment. [*See, e.g.*, Allgeyer v. Louisiana, 165 U.S. 578 (1897)—invalidating state law that rendered certain types of contracts unenforceable; Adkins v. Children's Hospital, 261 U.S. 525 (1923)—invalidating federal minimum wage law applicable only to the District of Columbia]

a) **The pivotal case--**

Lochner v. New York, 198 U.S. 45 (1905).

Facts. Lochner (D) was convicted of permitting an employee to work for him more than the statutory maximum of 60 hours per week. D challenged the law as a violation of the liberty to contract protected by the Fourteenth Amendment.

Issue. May a state generally prohibit private agreements to work more than a specified number of hours?

Held. No. Judgment reversed.

- ♦ The general right to contract in business is clearly part of the individual liberty protected by the Fourteenth Amendment. However, the right to hold both property and liberty are subject to such reasonable conditions as may be imposed by a government pursuant to its police powers.
- ♦ An earlier law restricting the work hours in certain dangerous occupations was upheld. The law challenged here, however, has no reference whatever to the health, safety, morals, or welfare of the public. The state claims an interest in the individual worker's health, but this goes too far; the individual's liberty must impose some restraint on the police power.
- ♦ This is not a substitution of the Court's judgment for the legislature's but merely a determination of whether the attempted regulation is within the state's police power.

Dissent (Harlan, White, Day, JJ.). There is room for debate about the validity of the state's interest in preventing more than 10 hours' work per day. Excessive work could impair the ability of workers to serve the state and provide for their dependents. The Court should not go further than to determine that such reasons for the law exist.

Dissent (Holmes, J.). Many comparably restrictive uses of the police power have been upheld by the Court. The United States Constitution was not intended to embody a particular economic view, but was framed to permit expression of dominant opinions, *i.e.*, that the laws freely reflect the people's choices. The law is not clearly unrelated to public health and ought to be upheld.

2) **The shift away from use of due process to invalidate economic legislation.** Eventually the Court changed its approach and began to presume the validity of state legislation, refusing to substitute its opinion on the merits or desirability of the legislation for that of the state legislature that enacted it. [*See, e.g.*, Phelps-Dodge v.

NLRB, 313 U.S. 177 (1941)—upholding statutes regulating collective bargaining and preventing discrimination against organized labor]

a) **No area outside power of state to regulate--**

Nebbia v. New York, 291 U.S. 502 (1934).

Facts. New York (P) passed a law establishing minimum and maximum retail prices for milk. The purpose was to aid the dairy industry, which was in a desperate situation because the prices received by farmers for milk were below the cost of production. Nebbia (D), a retail grocer, sold milk below the minimum price and was convicted of violating the statute. D challenged the statute as a violation of due process.

Issue. May a state strictly control retail prices, even if such control inhibits the use of private property and the making of contracts?

Held. Yes. Judgment affirmed.

- As long as the Court finds the law to have a reasonable relationship to a proper legislative purpose, to be neither arbitrary nor discriminatory, and to have means chosen that are reasonably related to the ends sought, due process is not offended.
- No area is outside the province of state regulation for police power purposes, including the direct regulation of prices.

Comment. In *West Coast Hotel Co. v. Parrish*, 300 U.S. 379 (1937), the Court overruled *Adkins v. Children's Hospital*, *supra*, permitting a state to impose a minimum wage. The Court held that the liberty to contract is subject to the restraints of due process, which comprehends reasonable regulation adopted in the interests of the community. The employees' lack of bargaining power makes "liberty to contract" meaningless without minimum protection by the state.

---

b) **Federal commerce power--**

United States v. Carolene Products Co., 304 U.S. 144 (1938).

Facts. Carolene Products Company (D) was indicted for shipping a milk substitute product prohibited by the Federal Filled Milk Act. D challenged the law by demurrer and won. The United States (P) appeals.

Issue. May Congress prohibit interstate shipment of food products that it deems injurious to the public health?

Held. Yes. Judgment reversed.

- The statute clearly falls within the commerce power. Congress has authority to protect the public from fraudulent substitutions. Its decision to prohibit interstate shipment rather than merely requiring true labels is within its judgment and, being reasonable, is not reviewable. The fact that other food substitutes are not so regulated is irrelevant; a legislature may hit an abuse it has found, even though it has failed to strike another.

- D challenged the statute by demurrer, and Congress clearly had adequate evidence to support its legislative findings to uphold the statute on its face. Of course D would be able to show factual arguments in another proceeding, but deference to the legislative determinations is strong.

Comment. Footnote 4 of the opinion sets forth principles regarding this varying presumption of constitutionality. It noted that the scope of the presumption may be narrower when the legislation appears on its face to be within a specific prohibition of the Constitution, such as those of the Bill of Rights. Another area that may invoke a narrower presumption is when the legislation may restrict the political process that could lead to repeal of undesirable legislation. The third general area is legislation directed at particular religions or minorities.

---

c) Deference to state legislature--

Williamson v. Lee Optical of Oklahoma, Inc., 348 U.S. 483 (1955).

Facts. Lee Optical of Oklahoma (P) challenged a state law that, among other things: (i) forbade an optician from fitting or duplicating lenses, even replacements, without a prescription from an ophthalmologist or optometrist; (ii) prohibited advertising of eyeglass frames; and (iii) prohibited optometrists from working in a general retail establishment. The district court held these three parts of the act invalid under the Due Process Clause of the Fourteenth Amendment. Williamson (D), a state official, appeals.

Issue. Does the Fourteenth Amendment prohibit all state business regulation that is not essential and directly related to the harm it intends to cure?

Held. No. Judgment reversed.

- Although the law may exact a needless, wasteful requirement in many cases, the legislature, not the courts, must balance the advantages and disadvantages of a new requirement. There is ample reason for the legislative means adopted to correct an actual evil.

- The law need not be in every respect logically consistent with its aims to be constitutional. The Court will not strike down state laws regulating business and industrial conditions merely because they may be unwise, improvident, or out of harmony with a particular school of thought. The people as voters, not the courts, are the protection against legislative abuse.

d) **Prohibitory vs. regulatory state laws--**

Ferguson v. Skrupa, 372 U.S. 726 (1963).

Facts. Kansas prohibited the business of "debt adjusting" except as incident to "the lawful practice of law" in Kansas. Skrupa (P), who was engaged in the business of debt adjusting, challenged the law as an unconstitutional prohibition of a "useful" business not "inherently immoral or dangerous to public welfare." The district court held for P; Ferguson (D), the state attorney general, appeals.

Issue. May the Court review economic legislation on grounds that it is prohibitory instead of regulatory?

Held. No. Judgment reversed.

- It is not within the province of courts to draw on their own views as to the morality, legitimacy, and usefulness of a particular business to decide whether a statute bears too heavily on that business and so violates due process.

- We refuse to sit as a superlegislature. We are neither willing nor able to draw lines by calling a law "prohibitory" or "regulatory." P must seek relief in the legislature, not the courts.

b. **The Contract Clause contribution.** Article I, Section 10 provides that "No State shall . . . pass any . . . Law impairing the Obligation of Contracts."

1) **Definitions.**

a) A law that "impairs" is one that substantially invalidates, releases, or extinguishes the obligations of a contract, or that derogates substantial contractual rights. [Home Building & Loan Association v. Blaisdell, 290 U.S. 398 (1934)]

b) Obligation connotes not only the terms of the contract but also the legal rules that are in force when the contract is made and that enter into and comprise a part of the agreement—*i.e.,* it is presumed that the contracting parties adopt the terms of their bargain in reliance on the law in effect at the time the agreement is reached.

c) Contracts include both public agreements (*i.e.,* those entered into by a state either as a sovereign or in its proprietary capacity) and private bargains (*i.e.,* those entered into between persons). It includes both executed agreements and executory agreements. [Fletcher v. Peck, 10 U.S. (6 Cranch.) 87 (1810)—land grant case; Dartmouth College v. Woodward, 17 U.S. (4 Wheat.) 518 (1819)—college charter case]

2) **Limitations on protection afforded to public contracts.** Subsequent impairments of public contracts are subject to the same limitations of reasonableness, necessity, and important public interest as private contracts. However, public contracts involve the legislature's own self-interest, so its judgment as to reasonableness and necessity is given no deference.

a) **State obligations--**

United States Trust Co. of New York v. New Jersey, 431 U.S. 1 (1977).

Facts. New York and New Jersey (Ds) formed by compact the New York and New Jersey Port Authority. In 1962, both states passed statutes prohibiting financing of railroad deficits with revenue pledged to pay the authority's bond, with minor exceptions. In 1974, the states retroactively repealed the 1962 covenant to permit greater subsidizing of mass transit. United States Trust Company of New York (P), trustee and holder of authority bonds, challenged the 1974 repealing act as violative of the Contract Clause. The state courts upheld the repeal, and P appeals.

Issue. May a state impair the obligation of its own contract based on its own determination of reasonableness and necessity?

Held. No. Judgment reversed.

♦ The Contract Clause does not require state adherence to a contract that surrenders an essential attribute of its sovereignty. The contract here is purely financial and does not compromise the state's sovereignty. But impairment of Ds' duties is therefore constitutional only if it is reasonable and necessary.

♦ Allowing a state to reduce its financial obligations whenever it wanted to spend the money for what it regarded as an important public purpose would negate all Contract Clause protection. For this reason, complete deference to legislative assessments of reasonableness and necessity is inappropriate, and the Court must examine independently the possibility of less severe alternatives. Based on the existence of less drastic alternatives, we find Ds' repealing act excessively harmful to P's contractual interests; it therefore cannot be upheld.

Concurrence (Burger, C.J.). Note that the Court does not hold that any particular "less drastic modification" would pass constitutional muster.

Dissent (Brennan, White, Marshall, JJ.). Elevation of the Contract Clause to the status of regulation of the municipal bond market at the heavy price of frustration of sound legislative policymaking is unwise and unnecessary. P's realistic economic interests are adequately protected by the political processes and the bond marketplace itself. The Court ought not restrict the legislature's responsiveness to changing public needs by preventing adoption of measures not plainly unreasonable and arbitrary. Ds' proper legislative decision ought to be upheld.

---

3) **Limitations on protection afforded to private contracts.**

a) **Introduction.** Not all "impairments" of contracts are deemed unconstitutional. Thus, although the Contract Clause prevents state destruction of all rights or all enforcement of existing contracts, the rights and responsibilities in a private contract can be modified by legislation that: (i) serves an important and legitimate public interest; (ii) is necessary for the achievement of that public interest; and (iii) is a reasonable impairment of the contract.

b) **Private obligations--**

Allied Structural Steel Co. v. Spannaus, 438 U.S. 234 (1978).

Facts. Allied Structural Steel Company (P) established a pension plan pursuant to IRS regulations that provided that qualifying employees would acquire pension rights but gave no assurance that any employee would not be dismissed at any time. P began to close one of its offices in Minnesota. A few months earlier, Minnesota had passed a law that subjected employers to a "pension funding charge" on termination of a pension plan or closing of a Minnesota office. The law had the effect of making several of P's otherwise unqualified employees pension obligees, resulting in a charge of $185,000. P sued Spannaus, a Minnesota official, for injunctive and declaratory relief. The federal district court held the Act valid. P appeals, claiming violation of the Contract Clause.

Issue. Does the Contract Clause preclude state legislation that significantly expands duties created by private contract?

Held. Yes. Judgment reversed.

- The Contract Clause is not an absolute prohibition against any impairment of contracts. It does not operate to obliterate state police power, but it does limit a state's ability to abridge existing contractual relationships. The first issue is whether the state law has substantially impaired a contractual relationship. The challenged law nullifies express terms of P's contractual obligations and imposes a completely unexpected liability in potentially disabling amounts. Such severe impairment may be condoned only if justified by the need for the law.

- To survive a Contract Clause challenge, a state statute must: (i) deal with a broad, generalized economic or social problem; (ii) operate in an area already subject to state regulation when the contract was made; (iii) effect a merely temporary alteration of contractual relationships; or (iv) apply to a broad class of persons. The Minnesota law fails to meet any of these criteria and cannot be upheld. It is not necessary to hold that the impairment is "without moderation or reason or is in a spirit of oppression."

Dissent (Brennan, White, Marshall, JJ.). The Contract Clause is simply an adjunct to the currency provisions of Articles I and X, and was intended only to prevent alteration of contracts that relieved one party of the duty to pay a debt. To "impair" a contract is not to add duties but to take away duties. Creation of a previously nonexisting duty, as the Minnesota law does, is not an impairment of a contract but a valid exercise of the state's police power. The effect of the Court's adoption of these vague testing criteria, which are arguably satisfied by the statute in any case, is to invite judicial discretion to protect property interests that happen to appeal to them.

---

c. **The contribution of the Just Compensation Clause of the Fifth Amendment.**

1) **Introduction.** The Fifth Amendment provides that private property shall not be taken for public use without just compensation. This clause has produced significant amounts of litigation.

2) **Complete destruction of property value--**

Lucas v. South Carolina Coastal Council, 505 U.S. 1003 (1992).

Facts. Lucas (P) purchased two residential lots for $975,000, intending to build single-family homes. Two years later, South Carolina enacted the Beachfront Management Act, which required P to obtain a permit from the South Carolina Coastal Council (D) before changing the use of his land. This effectively barred P from building homes on the land. P sued and the trial court found that he was entitled to compensation because his property was now valueless. The South Carolina Supreme Court reversed, and the Supreme Court granted certiorari.

Issue. Must the government compensate a private landowner if the government's regulation prohibits all economically productive or beneficial uses of the land?

Held. Yes. Judgment reversed.

- In *Pennsylvania Coal Co. v. Mahon*, 260 U.S. 393 (1922), the Court held that the Takings Clause extended beyond direct appropriations of property to regulations that go "too far." There are at least two categories of regulatory action that are compensable: (i) physical invasions, such as requiring landlords to allow television cable companies to put cable in their apartment buildings [*see* Loretto v. Teleprompter Manhattan CATV Corp., 458 U.S. 419 (1982)]; and (ii) denial of all economically beneficial or productive use of land.

- The functional basis for allowing the government, without making compensation, to affect property values through regulation is the recognition that the government could not operate if it had to pay for every change in the law that affected property values, but this basis does not apply where the government deprives a landowner of all economically beneficial uses. Such regulation really presses the private property into a form of public service under the guise of mitigating serious public harm.

- P claims that the finding that his property has been rendered valueless requires compensation, regardless of the reason for the regulation. Prior opinions held that harmful or noxious uses of property may be proscribed by government regulation without compensation, but this really means that land-use regulation does not effect a taking if it "substantially advances legitimate state interests." But D cannot take land without compensation merely by reciting a noxious-use or benefit-conferring rationale. D could avoid paying compensation only if the nature of P's estate shows that the proscribed use interests were not part of his title to begin with; *i.e.*, that his bundle of rights did not include an expectation that the state would eliminate all economically valuable use.

- Confiscatory regulations cannot be newly legislated without compensation; they must inhere in the title itself, in the restrictions that background principles of the state's law of property and nuisance already place on land ownership. The fact that a particular use has long been engaged in by similarly situated owners, or that other landowners similarly situated are permitted to continue the use denied to P, demonstrate a lack of any common law prohibition on the use. In this case, it is unlikely that common law principles would have prevented P from building a house on the land, but this must be determined on remand.

Concurrence (Kennedy, J.). When a regulation deprives the property of all value, whether it is a taking depends on whether the deprivation is contrary to reasonable, investment-backed expectations. The state supreme court erred in not evaluating P's reasonable expectations. And D did not act until after the property had been zoned for residential development and other parcels had been built on, so that the remaining lots have to bear the entire burden of the regulation.

Dissent (Blackmun, J.). The state may prevent any use of property it finds to be harmful to its citizens, and a state statute is entitled to a presumption of constitutionality. The record supports D's assessment that the building restriction is necessary to protect people and property, and the Court had departed from traditional rules by creating a new scheme for regulations that eliminate all economic value.

Dissent (Stevens, J.). The Court's new categorical rule is arbitrary since it distinguishes between a landowner whose property is diminished in value 95% and recovers nothing, and a landowner whose property is diminished in value 100% and recovers its full value. The reliance on a common law exception prevents the states from developing the common law in response to new learning, such as the significance of endangered species and wetlands.

---

3) **Challenge against regulation in place when property was purchased.** The Supreme Court has held that a property owner can challenge a regulatory taking even when the restriction was in place when he purchased the property. *Palazzolo v. Rhode Island*, 533 U.S. 606 (2001).

4) **Temporary restriction.** *Tahoe-Sierra Preservation Council, Inc. v. Tahoe Regional Planning Agency*, 535 U.S. 302 (2002), involved a temporary moratorium on development. The Court held that the question whether a temporary moratorium was a taking depended on the particular circumstances of the case. In some circumstances, it might be a per se taking under *Lucas*; in others, it would require case-by-case evaluation under *Penn Central Transportation Co. v. New York City*, 438 U.S. 104 (1978). The duration of the restriction is one of several factors for the courts to consider. The dissent noted that the moratoria in the case had lasted six years, a duration long enough to constitute a per se taking under *Lucas*.

5) **Proportionality requirement--**

Dolan v. City of Tigard, 512 U.S. 374 (1994).

Facts. Dolan (P) owned a plumbing and electric supply store in the city of Tigard (D). P's store was on a 1.67-acre lot that bordered the Fanno Creek and was therefore in the floodplain. P applied to D for a permit to double the size of her store and pave a parking lot. D's planning commission granted P's application, subject to D's Community Development Code ("CDC"). The CDC requires property owners to comply with a 15% open space and landscaping requirement as well as to dedicate land for a pedestrian/bicycle pathway. The total dedication was 10% of P's property for the pathway and for drainage improvements on the floodplain. P sought variances, but D refused, finding that the pedestrian/bicycle pathway might offset some of the traffic on area streets, and that the required floodplain dedication was related to P's plan to intensify development, which would likely increase storm water flow into the creek. P challenged the dedication requirements, but the state courts upheld them. The Supreme Court granted certiorari.

Issue. May a city condition the approval of a building permit on the dedication of a portion of the property for public purposes?

Held. No. Judgment reversed.

- The Takings Clause of the Fifth Amendment was intended to prevent the government from forcing some people alone to bear public burdens that should be borne by the public as a whole. If D had simply required P to dedicate her land for public use, a taking clearly would have occurred. However, land use regulation does not constitute a taking if it "substantially advances legitimate state interests and does not deny an owner economically viable use of his land." In this case, D's requirements are adjudicative in nature because they apply only to P's land, as opposed to common zoning requirements that are legislative in nature and apply to entire areas. D's requirements also do not merely limit P's use of the land, but constitute an actual conveyance of property.

- The two-part test for takings cases requires (i) a determination as to whether an "essential nexus" exists between the legitimate state interest and the conditions imposed; and (ii) a sufficient degree of connection between the conditions and the projected impact of the proposed development.

- D's interests in preventing flooding and reducing traffic congestion are legitimate public purposes.

- A variety of approaches have been adopted by courts to find the required degree of connection between the regulation and the proposed development. The best approach is an intermediate one that requires the city to show a "reasonable relationship" between the required dedication of land and the expected impact of the proposed development. However, the term is confusingly similar to the term "rational basis," so instead we will use the term "rough proportionality." This requires D to "make some sort of individualized determination that the required dedication is related both in nature and extent to the impact of the proposed development."

- In this case, D could have satisfied its floodplain interests by simply requiring P to leave 15% of the property as open space. D never explained why a public greenway, rather than a private one, was required for flood control. D's permanent recreational easement would destroy P's right to exclude others from her property and control access to her store. D has failed to show the required reasonable relationship between the floodplain easement and P's proposed new building. D has also failed to quantify its findings that purportedly support the dedication for the pedestrian/bicycle pathway.

Dissent (Stevens, Blackmun, Ginsburg, JJ.). Prior cases have held that a restriction on the right to exclude others is permissible unless it unreasonably impairs the value or use of the property. P has shown no adverse impact on the value of her property. The Court should merely determine whether the required nexus is present and avoid considerations of proportionality. The Court also loses sight of the fact that P has suffered no "taking." She merely challenges the terms D is offering in exchange for her building permit. As long as the government can show that the conditions it imposes in a land-use permit are rational, impartial, and conducive to fulfilling the aims of a valid land-use plan, the courts should apply a strong presumption of validity.

Dissent (Souter, J.). If as the Court determined there is no relation between flood control and the permanent recreational easement, it is not because of lack of proportionality but because of no rational connection, which is simply the *Nollan v. California Coastal Commission*, 483 U.S. 825 (1987), nexus analysis. But *Nollan* has not been properly applied here, because the Court has placed the burden of proving a relationship on D, contrary to the normal rule that the government in these cases is presumed to have acted in a constitutional manner.

---

6) **Remedies for de facto regulatory taking (inverse condemnation).** The Court, in *First English Evangelical Lutheran Church of Glendale v. County of Los Angeles*, 482 U.S. 304 (1987), determined when land use regulation was so burdensome to a landowner as to constitute a taking. Mere invalidation of the regulation is an insufficient remedy. A state must also pay damages for the temporary taking in effect before invalidation of the regulation.

2. **Personal Liberties.**

a. **Introduction.** Although substantive due process no longer imposes any serious restraints on economic regulations, the Court has revived the notion as a means of protecting certain fundamental personal rights not specifically enumerated in the United States Constitution, including the right of privacy.

1) **Source.** The right of privacy is nowhere mentioned in the Constitution. Nevertheless, in a series of cases, the Court has recognized that a right of personal privacy, or at least a guarantee of certain areas or zones of privacy, ***is*** constitutionally protected. The Court has had trouble, however, in articulating the constitutional source of such protection.

a) At least for search and seizure purposes, the right of privacy has been rooted in the Fourth and Fifth Amendments. [Katz v. United States, 389 U.S. 347 (1967)]

b) In cases involving freedom of expression, it has been deemed inherent in the First Amendment. [Stanley v. Georgia, 394 U.S. 557 (1969)]

c) In cases involving marital rights, some justices have pegged the right in the Ninth Amendment ("The enumeration of certain rights shall not be construed to deny or disparage others retained by the people"), while other justices felt it was within the "penumbras" (shades) of the Bill of Rights. [*See* Griswold v. Connecticut, below]

2) **Marital rights within the Bill of Rights--**

Griswold v. Connecticut, 381 U.S. 479 (1965).

Facts. Griswold (D) and an associate were convicted as accessories to the crime of using contraceptives in violation of a Connecticut (P) statute prohibiting all such use. The conviction was upheld in all the state courts, and D appeals.

Issue. Does a constitutional right of privacy exist that prohibits states from making use of contraceptives by a married couple a crime?

Held. Yes. Conviction reversed.

- The specific guarantees in the Bill of Rights have penumbras, or peripheral rights, that make the specific rights more secure. The existence of a right of privacy has been noted in earlier cases, and ought to especially protect the marriage relationship. The statute is overbroad and thus void.

Concurrence (Goldberg, J., Warren, C.J., Brennan, J.). The Ninth Amendment expressly recognizes fundamental personal rights not specifically mentioned in the United States Constitution. Privacy in the marital relation is clearly one of these basic personal rights "retained by the people."

Concurrence (Harlan, J.). The Due Process Clause independently requires rejection of the Connecticut statute without reference to the Bill of Rights.

Concurrence (White, J.). Application of the law to married couples deprives them of "liberty" without due process of law.

Dissent (Black, Stewart, JJ.). While the law is offensive, it is not prohibited by any specific constitutional provision and therefore must be upheld. Constitutional amendments, not judge-made alterations, are the correct means of modernizing the Constitution.

Dissent (Stewart, Black, JJ.). The law is silly since it is obviously unenforceable, but there is no general right of privacy found in the Constitution, so we cannot hold that it violates the Constitution.

Comment. More recently, the Court has simply held that the right of personal privacy is implicit in the concept of "liberty" within the protection of the Fourteenth Amendment Due Process Clause—*i.e.,* personal privacy is one of those basic human rights that are of "fundamental" importance in our society. [*See* Roe v. Wade, *infra*]

---

b. **Family relationships.**

1) **Basic rule.** The right of personal choice in matters of marriage and the bearing and raising of children is protected from undue governmental intrusion in a variety of contexts and is so fundamental to society that it is afforded protection under the Due Process Clause. Hence, any regulation of familial rights must be justified by a compelling state interest and must be narrowly drawn so as to protect only the legitimate state interest at stake.

2) **Housing--**

Moore v. City of East Cleveland, 431 U.S. 494 (1977).

Facts. Moore (D) lived with her son and two grandsons, who were cousins. The city of East Cleveland (P) filed a criminal charge against D because her living arrangement violated a city ordinance restricting occupancy of a dwelling unit to members of a single family, defined by certain categories, none of which included D's arrangement. D moved to dismiss, but her motion was overruled and she was convicted. The state courts upheld the conviction, and D appeals.

Issue. May a local ordinance restrict occupation of dwelling units to certain categories of related individuals, excluding other categories of related individuals?

Held. No. Judgment reversed.

♦ The state court based its decision on *Village of Belle Terre v. Boraas*, 416 U.S. 1 (1974), but that case involved restrictions only on unrelated individuals. When the government intrudes on choices of family living arrangements, the legitimacy of the governmental interests and the effectiveness of the regulations must be carefully examined. This statute cannot stand such scrutiny, since it only marginally, if at all, works to reduce overcrowding and traffic problems.

♦ P contends that a constitutional right to live together extends only to the nuclear family. Such legislative classifications are appropriate limits on substantive due process only if they reflect respect for and recognition of the basic values that underlie our society. The extended family has a strong tradition in our history, and the United States Constitution prohibits P from forcing all its people to live in certain narrowly defined family patterns.

Concurrence (Brennan, Marshall, JJ.). The extended family is not merely a historical tradition but remains a vital tenet of our society, especially among ethnic and racial minority groups.

Concurrence (Stevens, J.). The ordinance exceeds the constitutional scope of the zoning power in seeking to exclude an owner's relatives from possibly sharing her residence.

Dissent (Stewart, Rehnquist, JJ.). The constitutionally protected freedom of association relates to promotion of speech, assembly, the press, or religion, not to an interest in the gratification, convenience, and economy of sharing the same residence. D's interest in sharing the dwelling cannot be equated with the fundamental decisions to marry and to bear and raise children, which the majority has done. P's line drawing is no more onerous than other lines that have been upheld in earlier cases.

Dissent (White, J.). The Court ought not expand the substantive content of the Due Process Clause in order to strike down what it considers unfavorable legislation. The issue is whether there is actual deprivation of life, liberty, or property. The Due Process Clause should not be used to protect any right or privilege that the Court deems deeply rooted in the country's tradition from all but the most important state regulatory interests.

---

3) The fundamental right to marry--

Zablocki v. Redhail, 434 U.S. 374 (1978).

Facts. Redhail (P), a Wisconsin resident, was denied a marriage license for failure to comply with a Wisconsin statute requiring that an applicant who has a support obligation for a child not in his custody prove that the child is not a public charge and that he has complied with the support obligation. P challenged the statute and obtained declaratory and injunctive relief. Zablocki (D), the county clerk, appeals.

Issue. May a state protect the welfare of out-of-custody children by denying a marriage license to persons not fulfilling their support obligations to such children?

Held. No. Judgment affirmed.

♦ Marriage is a fundamental right, and significant interference with its exercise cannot be upheld unless closely tailored to effectuate sufficiently important state interests. Assuming the state's interests of protecting out-of-custody children and motivating applicants to fulfill prior support obligations are valid, the means used by the state unnecessarily impinge on the right to marry.

- ♦ The state's procedure relies on a collection device rationale that is inappropriate. The state has numerous other effective means for exacting compliance with support obligations that do not restrict the right to marry. In addition, the statute tends to impair an applicant's ability to improve his financial situation and thus improve his ability to meet prior support obligations.

Concurrence (Stewart, J.). The problem here is not discriminatory classifications but unwarranted encroachment on liberty protected by the Due Process Clause. The equal protection doctrine as applied here is no more than substantive due process by another name.

Concurrence (Powell, J.). The Court's rationale intrudes too broadly into the state's traditional power to regulate the marriage relation. This statute is improper only because it fails to provide for those without means to comply with child-support obligations.

Concurrence (Stevens, J.). This discrimination between the rich and the poor is irrational and cannot withstand Equal Protection scrutiny.

Dissent (Rehnquist, J.). Under the Equal Protection Clause, the statute need pass only the rational basis test, and under the Due Process Clause, the statute need only bear a rational relation to a constitutionally permissible objective. This is a permissible exercise of the state's power to assure the support of children.

---

4) Constitutional preference for husband over natural father--

Michael H. v. Gerald D., 491 U.S. 110 (1989).

Facts. Gerald D. (D) was married to Carole D., an international model. While they were married, Carole had an adulterous affair with Michael H. (P), a neighbor. Carole gave birth to Victoria D., and D was listed as her father. During the ensuing three years, Carole had flings with other men as well as P. A blood test showed a 98% probability that P was the father of Victoria. Finally, P filed for visitation rights. D moved for summary judgment on the ground that under the California Evidence Code, there were no triable issues of fact because the law provides that the issue of a wife cohabiting with her husband, who is not impotent or sterile, is conclusively presumed to be a child of the marriage. The presumption may be rebutted by blood tests, but only if a motion is made within two years of the child's birth by one of the marriage partners. The court granted D's motion. The appellate courts affirmed, and P appeals.

Issue. Does a purported natural father have a constitutional right to challenge the presumption of paternity of a child born in wedlock to another man's wife?

Held. No. Judgment affirmed.

- P claims that he has a constitutionally protected liberty interest in his relationship with Victoria. Such a liberty interest must be both fundamental and traditionally protected by our society.

- The relationship between persons in the situation of P and Victoria has not been treated as a protected family unit under the historical practices of our society. To the contrary, our traditions have protected the marital family.

- Even if P had standing to challenge the marital child's legitimacy, he is seeking more; P wants parental prerogatives. But no states award substantive parental rights to the natural father of a child conceived within and born into an extant marital union that wishes to embrace the child. To provide protection to P as an adulterous natural father is to deny protection to D as a marital father. The people of California have chosen between these two.

Concurrence (O'Connor, Kennedy, JJ.). I agree with all of Justice Scalia's opinion except footnote 6.

Concurrence (Stevens, J.). Even assuming P's relationship with Victoria is entitled to constitutional protection, California already affords him a right to seek custody in the best interests of the child. The trial court found that it was not in the best interests of Victoria for P to have visitation.

Dissent (Brennan, Marshall, Blackmun, JJ.). The concept of liberty is not limited to "tradition," which by itself can be as malleable and elusive as "liberty."

Dissent (White, Brennan, JJ.). An unwed father who has demonstrated a sufficient commitment to his paternity by way of personal, financial, or custodial responsibilities has a protected liberty interest that cannot be denied without due process of law.

Comment. The majority opinion, written by Justice Scalia, included a footnote 6 that described a method of historical analysis to be used to identify liberty interests protected by the Due Process Clause. Only two Justices fully endorsed this footnote.

---

c. **Privacy and personal autonomy.** Regardless of its source, the right to privacy is regarded as a "fundamental" right for equal protection and due process purposes, which means that regulation in these areas can only be justified by a "compelling state interest."

1) **Interests protected.** The right of privacy protects two kinds of interests: (i) the individual interest in avoiding disclosure of personal matters; and (ii) the interest in independently making certain kinds of important decisions.

2) **Contraceptives.** In *Eisenstadt v. Baird*, 405 U.S. 438 (1972), the Court held that the decision whether to use contraceptives was one of individual privacy, and hence that the right belonged to single as well as married persons. In *Carey v. Population Services International*, 431 U.S. 678 (1977), the Court held that a state could not prohibit distribution of nonmedical contraceptives to adults except through licensed pharmacists, nor prohibit sales of such contraceptives to persons under age 16 who did not have approval of a licensed physician.

3) **Abortion.** A woman's decision as to whether to terminate her pregnancy is within her constitutionally protected right of privacy, and cannot be made subject to parental or spousal consent. [Planned Parenthood v. Danforth, 428 U.S. 52 (1976)] However, at some point during a pregnancy, the state's interest in protecting the mother's life and in protecting prenatal life become sufficiently "compelling" to justify state regulation of abortion.

4) **Current constitutional rule on abortion--**

Roe v. Wade, 410 U.S. 113 (1973).

Facts. Roe (P), unmarried and pregnant, sought declaratory and injunctive relief against Wade (D), a county district attorney, to prevent enforcement of Texas criminal abortion statutes. The district court invalidated the statutes.

Issue. May a state constitutionally make it a crime to procure an abortion except to save the mother's life?

Held. No. Judgment affirmed.

- P claims a constitutional right to terminate her pregnancy, based on the Fourteenth Amendment concept of personal "liberty," the Bill of Rights penumbras, and the Ninth Amendment. D claims a state interest in regulating medical procedures to ensure patient safety and in protecting prenatal life.

- The right of privacy generally relates to marriage, procreation, and contraception, and includes the abortion decision, but is not without restraint based on the state's compelling interests. The state's interest in prenatal life cannot be based on the fetus's right to life, for a fetus cannot be considered a "person" in the constitutional sense. Unborn children have never been recognized in any area of the law as persons in the whole sense. However, the pregnant woman cannot be isolated in her privacy. The state may decide that at some time another interest, that of the health of the mother or that of potential human life, becomes significantly involved. The woman's right of privacy must be measured accordingly.

- The state's interest in the health of the mother becomes "compelling" at approximately the end of the first trimester, prior to which mortality in abortion is less than mortality in normal childbirth. Only from this point forward may the state regulate the abortion procedure as needed to preserve and protect maternal health.

- The state's interest in potential life becomes "compelling" at viability. A state interested in protecting fetal life after viability may proscribe abortion except when necessary to preserve the life or health of the mother.

- The Texas statute challenged here is overbroad and cannot be upheld.

Dissent (Rehnquist, J.). An abortion is not "private" in the ordinary use of this word. The Court seems to define "privacy" as a claim of liberty from unwanted state regulation of consensual transactions, protected by the Fourteenth Amendment. But that liberty is not guaranteed absolutely against deprivation, only against deprivation without due process of law. The traditional test is whether the law has a rational relation to a valid state objective, but this test could not justify the Court's outcome. Instead, the Court adopts the "compelling state interest test," which is more appropriate to a legislative judgment than to a judicial one. The Court's conclusions are more like judicial legislation than determination of the intent of the drafters of the Fourteenth Amendment. Furthermore, the fact that most states have had restrictions on abortion for over a century indicates that the asserted right to an abortion is not so universally accepted as P claims.

Concurrence (Burger, C.J.). The Texas statute was overbroad in not permitting legal exceptions for rape and incest.

Concurrence (Douglas, J.). The present statute has struck the balance between the woman's and the state's interest wholly in favor of the latter. It is overbroad.

Dissent (White, Rehnquist, JJ.). There is nothing in the language or history of the Constitution to support the Court's judgment. The Court apparently values the convenience of the pregnant mother more than the continued existence and development of the life or potential life that she carries. This issue should be left with the people and to the political processes the people have devised to govern their affairs.

Comment. The Court has held that a state law may require notice be given to an unemancipated minor's parents prior to her undergoing an abortion. A compelling state interest is present when the minor is a dependent, there is no emergency, and notifying the parents is in the child's best interest. [H.L. v. Matheson, 450 U.S. 398 (1981)]

5) **Regulation of abortion.**

a) **Permissible state regulation--**

Planned Parenthood of Southeastern Pennsylvania v. Casey, 505 U.S. 833 (1992).

Facts. Pennsylvania adopted an Abortion Control Act that required that a woman seeking an abortion must be given certain information at least 24 hours before the abortion; that the woman give informed consent prior to the abortion; that, if a minor, the woman obtain the informed consent of her parents unless a judicial bypass option is followed; that, if married, the woman certify that she informed her husband; and that facilities providing abortion services must make certain reports about each abortion, including the woman's age, gestational age, type of abortion procedure, medical conditions and results, and the weight of the aborted fetus. Compliance with the requirements is not required in certain medical emergencies. Planned Parenthood of Southeastern Pennsylvania (P) challenged the Act on its face by suing Casey (D), the Governor. The district court held all the provisions unconstitutional, but the court of appeals upheld everything except the husband notification requirement. The Supreme Court granted certiorari.

Issue. May a state impose notification and consent requirements as prerequisites for obtaining an abortion?

Held. Yes. Judgment reversed in part.

- The three parts of the essential *Roe v. Wade, supra,* holding are reaffirmed. These are: (i) the woman's right to have an abortion before viability without undue state interference; (ii) the state's power to restrict abortions after fetal viability, so long as there are exceptions to protect a woman's life or health; and (iii) the state's legitimate interests from the outset of the pregnancy in protecting the health of the woman and the life of the fetus that may become a child.

- Substantive due process claims require courts to exercise reasoned judgment, and the Court must define the liberty of all, not mandate a moral code. The Constitution has been interpreted to protect personal decisions regarding marriage, procreation, and contraception. Defining one's own concept of existence, meaning, and the mystery of human life is at the heart of liberty. At the same time, abortion has consequences for persons other than the woman who is pregnant.

- *Roe* should be upheld under the principle of stare decisis because it has not proved unworkable, because people have relied on the availability of abortion, because under *Roe* women have been better able to participate equally in the economic and social life of the country, because no evolution of legal principle has left *Roe*'s doctrinal footings weaker than they were in 1973 when the decision was announced, and because there have been no changed circumstances or new factual understandings. Even if *Roe* is wrong, the error involves only the strength of the state interest in fetal protection, not the liberty of women. Overruling *Roe* simply because of a change in philosophical disposition would undermine the Court's legitimacy.

- ♦ Although *Roe* has been criticized for drawing lines, the Court must draw specific rules from the general standards in the Constitution. The trimester approach was not part of the essential holding in *Roe* and it both misconceived the nature of the pregnant woman's interest and undervalued the state's interest in potential life. It is therefore overruled and replaced with a line drawn only at viability. Under this approach, a law that serves a valid purpose not designed to strike at the right of abortion itself may be sustained even if it makes it more difficult or more expensive to obtain an abortion, unless the law imposes an undue burden on a woman's ability to make an abortion decision. Thus, the state may further its interest in potential life but cannot place a substantial obstacle in the path of a woman's choice.

- ♦ The state may adopt health regulations to promote the health or safety of a woman seeking an abortion. It may not prohibit any woman from making the ultimate decision to terminate her pregnancy before viability. After viability, the state may promote its interest in the potentiality of human life by regulating and even proscribing abortion except where it is necessary to preserve the life or health of the mother.

- ♦ With regard to the specific provisions of D's Act, the definition of medical emergency does not impose an undue burden on a woman's abortion right. The informed consent requirement is also permissible because it furthers the legitimate purpose of reducing the risk that a woman may elect an abortion, only to discover later, with devastating psychological consequences, that her decision was not fully informed. The 24-hour waiting period does not impose substantial obstacles, and it is not unreasonable to conclude that important decisions will be more informed and deliberate if they follow some period of reflection. The exception for cases in which a physician reasonably believes that furnishing the information would have a severely adverse effect on the woman's physical or mental health accommodates the interest in allowing physicians to exercise their medical judgment.

- ♦ The spousal notification requirement does impose an undue burden on a woman's choice to undergo an abortion and cannot be sustained. In well-functioning marriages, the spouses discuss important intimate decisions such as whether to bear a child, and the notification requirement adds nothing in such situations. However, millions of women are the victims of physical and psychological abuse from their husbands, and requiring spousal notification in these situations can be tantamount to preventing the woman from getting an abortion. The husband's interest in the life of the child his wife is carrying does not permit the state to empower him with a veto over the abortion decision. Men do not have the kind of dominion over their wives that parents have over their children.

- ♦ The parental consent provision has been sustained before, and provided there is an adequate judicial bypass procedure, its constitutionality is reaffirmed. The recordkeeping and reporting requirements are also permissible, with the exception of whether the spouse was notified of the abortion.

Concurrence and dissent (Stevens, J.). The Court properly follows the principle that a developing organism that is not yet a "person" does not have a "right to life." The state's interest in protecting potential life is not grounded in the Constitution, but reflects humanitarian and pragmatic concerns, including the offense taken by a large segment of the population at the number of abortions performed in this country and third-trimester abortions specifically. But the woman's interest in liberty is constitutional; the Constitution would be violated as much by a requirement that all women undergo abortion as by an absolute ban on abortions. The 24-hour delay requirement should not be upheld because it presumes that the abortion decision is wrong and must be reconsidered. The state may properly require physicians to inform women of the nature and risks of the abortion procedure and the medical risks of carrying to term, but it should not be allowed to require that the woman be provided with materials designed to persuade her to choose not to undergo the abortion.

Concurrence and dissent (Blackmun, J.). The Court's decision preserves the liberty of women that is one vote away from being extinguished. The Court also leaves open the possibility that the regulations it now approves may in the future be shown to impose an unconstitutional burden.

Concurrence and dissent (Rehnquist, C.J., White, Scalia, Thomas, JJ.). *Roe* was wrongly decided, and it can and should be overruled consistently with the traditional approach to stare decisis in constitutional cases. Stare decisis is not a reason to retain *Roe*; the Court's legitimacy is enhanced by faithful interpretation of the Constitution. The Court's revised "undue burden" standard is an unjustified constitutional compromise that allows the Court to closely scrutinize all types of abortion regulations despite the lack of any constitutional authority to do so. The new "undue burden" approach is still an imposition on the states by the Court of a complex abortion code. Abortion involves the purposeful termination of potential life and is thus different in kind from the other areas of privacy recognized by the court, including marriage, procreation, and contraception. Prohibitions on abortion have been part of the law of many of the states since before the Fourteenth Amendment was adopted; there is no deeply rooted tradition of unrestricted abortion in our history that justifies characterizing the right as "fundamental." A woman's interest in having an abortion is a form of liberty protected by the Due Process Clause, but states may regulate abortion procedures in ways rationally related to a legitimate state interest. D's act should be upheld in its entirety.

Concurrence and dissent (Scalia, J., Rehnquist, C.J., White, Thomas, JJ.). The states may permit abortion-on-demand, but the Constitution does not require them to do so.

It is a legislative decision. The issue is not whether the right to an abortion is an absolute liberty or whether it is an important liberty to many women, but whether it is a liberty protected by the Constitution. It is not, because the Constitution says nothing about it and because longstanding traditions of American society have permitted it to be prohibited. Under the rational basis test, D's statute should be upheld. Instead, the Court perpetuates the premise of *Roe*, which is a value judgment, not a legal matter. The "undue burden" standard lacks meaningful content, and may be summed up by concluding that a state may regulate abortion only in such a way as to not reduce significantly its incidence. *Roe* nourished the deeply divisive issue of abortion by elevating it to the national level, where it is much more difficult to resolve than it was at the state level. Political compromise is now impossible, and *Roe* has been a major factor in selecting Justices to the Court. The Court should not be concerned with predicting public perceptions but should do what is legally right by asking whether *Roe* was correctly decided and whether it has succeeded in producing a settled body of law. The answer to both questions is no, and *Roe* should therefore be overruled. The Court's reliance on value judgments instead of interpreting text has created political pressure directed to the Court, whereby various groups of people demonstrate to protest that the Court has not implemented the respective group's values.

---

b) Ban on partial birth abortion upheld--

Gonzales v. Carhart, 550 U.S. 124 (2007).

Facts. Most of the 1.3 million abortions performed annually in the United States occur during the first trimester. Of the remaining 10% to 15%, most occur in the second trimester, usually by a procedure called "dilation and evacuation" or "D & E." The doctor grabs the fetus in the womb and tears it apart, removing it piece by piece. In a variation of D & E, called "intact D & E" or "partial birth abortion," the fetus is extracted intact or largely intact. In *Stenberg v. Carhart*, 530 U.S. 914 (2000), the Court struck down a Nebraska statute that: prohibited partial birth abortions, did not distinguish between partial birth abortions and D & Es, and lacked an exception for the preservation of the health of the woman. In response to *Stenberg*, Congress enacted the Partial-Birth Abortion Ban Act. Carhart and other abortion doctors (Ps) challenged the constitutionality of the Act on its face. The lower courts held the Act unconstitutional. The Supreme Court granted certiorari.

Issue. May Congress prohibit a specific form of abortion as long as it does not impose a substantial obstacle to late-term, but previability, abortions?

Held. Yes. Judgment reversed.

♦ Before viability, a state may not prohibit any woman from making the ultimate decision to terminate her pregnancy and may not impose an undue burden on this right. Regulations may not present a substantial obstacle to a woman's exercise of the right to choose.

- Ps argue that the Act is void for vagueness because its scope is indefinite. In the alternative, Ps argue that the Act's language bars all D & Es. They suggest that the Act imposes an undue burden, because D & E is the most common second-trimester abortion method.

- The Act is not void for vagueness and does not impose an undue burden. The Act punishes knowingly performing a partial birth abortion. To fall within the Act, the doctor performing the abortion must vaginally deliver a living fetus. The Act's definition of partial birth abortion requires the fetus to be delivered until, in the case of a head-first presentation, the entire fetal head is outside the body of the mother, or, in the case of breech presentation, any part of the fetal trunk past the navel is outside the body of the mother. The doctor must perform an overt act that kills the partially delivered living fetus.

- As a facial matter, the Act does not impose an undue burden. It does not prohibit the D & E procedure in which the fetus is removed in parts; it adopts the phrase "delivers a living fetus," instead of "delivering . . . a living unborn child, or a substantial portion thereof"; its language expresses the usual meaning of "deliver" when used in connection with "fetus," which is the extraction of an entire fetus, rather than removal of fetal pieces; it identifies specific anatomical landmarks to which the fetus must be partially delivered; and the interpretation of the Act so that it does not prohibit standard D & E is the most reasonable reading and understanding of its terms.

- Ps contend that D & Es could sometimes result in the delivery of a living fetus beyond the Act's anatomical landmarks. Thus, they assert that any D & E has the potential to violate the Act and that a doctor will not know beforehand whether the abortion will proceed in a prohibited manner. However, the Act's intent requirements preclude liability from attaching to an accidental intact D & E.

- The Act does not on its face impose a substantial obstacle to a woman's exercise of the right to choose. The Act prohibits a method of abortion in which a fetus is killed just inches before completion of the birth process. Congress was concerned about the hardening of society to the humanity of newborns and to all vulnerable and innocent human life. Congress was also concerned with the effects on the medical community and on its reputation caused by the practice of partial-birth abortion.

- *Casey*, *supra*, held that the government may use its authority to show profound respect for the life within the woman. The state's regulatory interest in protecting the life of the fetus that may become a child cannot be set aside by interpreting *Casey*'s additional requirement of a health exception into an unrestricted right for a doctor to choose whatever abortion method he prefers. The state may bar certain procedures in furtherance of its legitimate interests in regulating the medical profession in order to promote respect for life.

- The Act's ban on abortions that involve partial delivery of a living fetus furthers the government's objectives. The Act expresses respect for the dignity of human life. Congress determined that partial birth abortion has a disturbingly similarity to the killing of a newborn infant. The Act draws a bright line between abortion and infanticide.

- A woman's decision to have an abortion is fraught with emotional consequences, and some doctors may prefer not to disclose details of the means that will be used. However, this lack of information concerning the way in which the fetus will be killed is of legitimate concern to the state, which has an interest in ensuring that such a serious decision is well informed.

- It is argued that the standard D & E is as brutal, if not more, than the intact D & E. However, it was reasonable for Congress to think that partial birth abortion, more than the standard D & E, undermines the public's perception of the appropriate role of a physician during the delivery process.

- There is medical uncertainty as to whether the Act creates significant health risks for women. The evidence presented demonstrates that both sides have medical support for their position. The Court has traditionally given state and federal legislatures wide discretion to pass legislation in areas where there is medical and scientific uncertainty. This Act is not invalid on its face because of uncertainty over whether the barred procedure is ever necessary to preserve a woman's health, since there are other abortion procedures that are considered to be safe alternatives.

- Although the Act is not invalid on its face, it may be challenged on an as-applied basis.

Concurrence (Thomas, Scalia, JJ.). The Court's opinion accurately applies current jurisprudence. However, the Court's abortion jurisprudence has no basis in the Constitution.

Dissent (Ginsburg, Stevens, Souter, Breyer, JJ.).

- The majority opinion does not take *Casey* and *Stenberg* seriously. Instead, it encourages federal intervention to ban a procedure that medical experts find necessary and proper in certain cases. It blurs the line between previability and postviability abortions, and does not include an exception for a woman's health. Instead, it bans intact D & E, which provides safety benefits over D & E by dismemberment.

- In *Stenberg*, we expressly held that a statute banning intact D & E was unconstitutional, in part because it lacked a health exception. We made clear that as long as "substantial medical authority supports the proposition that banning a particular abortion procedure could endanger women's health," a health exception is required.

- ♦ Congress claimed that there was no credible medical evidence that partial birth abortions are safer than other abortion procedures. But during the district court trials, many accomplished and experienced medical experts explained that, in certain circumstances and for women with certain medical conditions, intact D & E is safer than alternative procedures and is necessary to protect women's health. Each of the district courts to consider the issue rejected Congress's findings as unreasonable and not supported by the evidence.

- ♦ The notion that the Act furthers any legitimate governmental interest is irrational. The Act does not save a single fetus from destruction; it merely requires doctors to use a brutal and more risky method. The Court is simply chipping away at the right to abortion.

---

6) Liberty interest in homosexual conduct--

Lawrence v. Texas, 539 U.S. 558 (2003).

Facts. Police officers responding to a reported weapons disturbance entered an apartment where Lawrence (D) resided. The officers found D and another man engaging in a sexual act. D was arrested and convicted of "deviate sexual intercourse with a member of the same sex." D claimed the statute was unconstitutional under the Due Process Clause of the Fourteenth Amendment. The Texas state courts upheld the statute. The Supreme Court granted certiorari.

Issue. May a state criminalize private and consensual sexual activity between two adults of the same sex?

Held. No. Judgment reversed and case remanded.

- ♦ In *Bowers v. Hardwick,* 478 U.S. 186 (1986), the Court held that there was no fundamental right for homosexuals to engage in sodomy, so the Constitution did not prevent the states from making such activity illegal. This framing of the issue, however, limited the claim to the right to engage in certain sexual conduct. In reality, criminal statutes prohibiting certain sexual activity have more far-reaching consequences because they control a personal relationship that is within the liberty of persons to choose without being punished as criminals.

- ♦ The *Bowers* Court based its decision in part on proscriptions against homosexual conduct that have ancient roots. The historical premises relied on by the court, however, have been reevaluated by scholars. The concept of the homosexual as being in a distinct category did not actually emerge until the late 19th century. Before that, sodomy laws were designed to prohibit non-procreative sexual activity, regardless of gender. Laws against same-sex couples were not enacted until the last third of the 20th century.

- The *Bowers* Court did note that societies have condemned homosexual conduct as immoral for many centuries. While many people may consider this a moral issue, the legal issue is whether the majority may use the power of the state to enforce these views on the whole society through the operation of the criminal law.

- In recent years, society has recognized that liberty gives substantial protection to adults in deciding how to conduct their private sex lives. The European Convention on Human Rights has been interpreted to preclude laws against consensual homosexual conduct in Europe, for example. Since the *Bowers* decision, 12 states have abandoned their laws against sodomy, and the remaining 13 states have a pattern of non-enforcement against consenting adults acting in private.

- *Romer v. Evans*, *infra*, recognized that class-based legislation directed at homosexuals violates the Equal Protection Clause. This undermines the central holding of *Bowers* because the continued validity of *Bowers* demeans the lives of homosexual persons.

- The erosion of *Bowers* under *Romer*, the invalidity of many of the premises upon which *Bowers* was based, and the substantial criticism of *Bowers* by the states and the European Court of Human Rights suggest that *Bowers* should be overruled. Despite the importance of stare decisis, it is time to recognize that *Bowers* was incorrectly decided and it is hereby overruled.

Concurrence (O'Connor, J.). I do not join the Court in overruling *Bowers*, but I agree that the Texas statute here is unconstitutional under the Equal Protection Clause instead of the Due Process Clause. The Texas statute prohibits sodomy between homosexual partners, but not between opposite-sex partners. This makes homosexuals unequal in the eyes of the law. The Court need not decide whether a sodomy law violates the substantive component of the Due Process Clause. As long as the Equal Protection Clause requires a sodomy law to apply equally to the private consensual conduct of homosexuals and heterosexuals alike, the democratic process would soon dispense with such a law.

Dissent (Scalia, J., Rehnquist, C.J., Thomas, J.). The Court has strongly rejected overruling *Roe v. Wade* out of stare decisis concerns, but the very conditions the Court finds applicable to *Bowers* also apply to *Roe*. The Court now allows us to overrule precedent if: (i) its foundations have been "eroded" by subsequent decisions; (ii) it has been subject to substantial and continuing criticism; and (iii) it has not induced individual or societal reliance that counsels against overturning. The Court's reasoning in this case calls into question laws against bigamy, prostitution, adultery, and related conduct. Until today, only fundamental rights qualify for heightened scrutiny protection, and all others may be abridged if the law is rationally related to a legitimate state interest. Homosexual sodomy is not such a fundamental right. The Court today effectively decrees the end of all morals legislation by holding that majoritarian sexual morality is not even a legitimate state interest.

Dissent (Thomas, J.). The Texas law is uncommonly silly and a waste of law enforcement resources, but there is no constitutional right of privacy that invalidates such laws.

Comment. The *Lawrence* opinion is the first Supreme Court majority opinion to cite an authority from European law as a factor in the decision. The Court took judicial notice of the laws in Europe, apparently concluding that it was useful to determine the extent of the governmental interest in proscribing such conduct.

---

7) **Assisted suicide.** In most states, patients may refuse even lifesaving medical treatment, or accept pain medication that can hasten death, but it is a crime to aid another to commit or attempt suicide. Many physicians assert that the assisted suicide ban prevents them from providing lethal medication for mentally competent, terminally ill patients who are suffering great pain and desire a doctor's help in taking their own lives, although it would be consistent with the standards of their medical practices to provide this type of service.

   a) **Due process analysis--**

Washington v. Glucksberg, 521 U.S. 702 (1997).

Facts. Washington (D) enacted a statute that prohibited assisting suicide. Glucksberg and other physicians (Ps) occasionally treated terminally ill, suffering patients and would assist these patients in ending their lives if not for D's ban on assisted suicide. Ps brought suit seeking a declaration that the statute violates the Fourteenth Amendment, because Ps' patients have a liberty interest in a personal choice to commit physician-assisted suicide. The district court held the statute unconstitutional. The court of appeals initially reversed, but after an en banc hearing, affirmed the district court. The Supreme Court granted certiorari.

Issue. Is there a constitutional right to assistance in committing suicide?

Held. No. Judgment reversed.

- It is a crime to assist a suicide in almost every state, and almost every western democracy. This reflects the states' commitment to protect and preserve all human life. For over 700 years, the Anglo-American common-law tradition has punished both suicide and assisting suicide.

- In modern times, the states' bans on assisted suicide have been reexamined and mostly reaffirmed. There have been modifications to reflect current medical technology, which can prolong life. For example, states permit "living wills," surrogate health-care decisionmaking, and withdrawal or refusal of life-sustaining medical treatment. However, the states continue to prohibit assisted suicide. D's voters rejected a ballot initiative that would have permitted a form of physician-assisted suicide.

- The Court has previously applied the Due Process Clause so as to protect the right to marry, have children, educate one's children, enjoy marital privacy, use contraception, and have abortions. Under *Cruzan v. Director, Missouri Department of Health*, 497 U.S. 261 (1990), the Clause protects the traditional right to refuse unwanted lifesaving medical treatment. However, the extension of constitutional protection to an asserted right or liberty interest is only appropriate for those areas that are rooted in the nation's history and tradition, and even then only when there is a careful description of the asserted fundamental liberty interest.

- To recognize the right asserted by Ps, the Court would have to reverse centuries of legal doctrine and practice, including the policy choices of almost every state. In contrast, the right to refuse medication recognized in *Cruzan* reflected a long legal tradition. Forced medication was a battery at common law.

- Given that the right to assisted suicide is not a fundamental liberty interest, the Constitution still requires that D's ban be rationally related to legitimate government interests. That is satisfied here, where D has an interest in the preservation of human life, an interest in protecting the integrity and ethics of the medical profession, an interest in protecting vulnerable groups, and an interest in not opening the door to euthanasia, both voluntary and involuntary.

Concurrence (O'Connor, J.). There is no generalized right to "commit suicide." A terminal patient who suffers great pain may obtain medication to alleviate that suffering, even to the point of hastening death. The state's interest in protecting those who are not truly competent or facing imminent death is sufficiently weighty to justify a prohibition against physician-assisted suicide. The democratic process will strike the proper balance in this area.

Concurrence (Stevens, J.). The value to others of a person's life is far too precious to allow the individual to claim a constitutional entitlement to complete autonomy in making a decision to end that life. But there may be situations where the individual's interest in choosing how to die might be paramount.

Concurrence (Souter, J.). The appropriate test would be to determine whether D's statute sets up an arbitrary imposition or a purposeless restraint contrary to the Due Process Clause. Substantive due process analysis requires a court to assess the relative weights of the contending interests. Statutes must give way when the legislation's justifying principle is so far from being commensurate with the individual interest as to be arbitrary or pointless. This case involves the right of a narrow class to help others in a narrow class under a set of limited circumstances. Ps note that D has largely repudiated the common law of suicide by decriminalizing suicide. A right to physician assistance in committing suicide is analogous to the right to physician assistance in abortion. D already allows doctors to administer pain relief medication that may hasten death. D could address its legitimate interests through a regulatory system.

Concurrence (Ginsburg, J.). I concur for substantially the same reasons as Justice O'Connor.

Concurrence (Breyer, J.). Justice O'Connor's approach is persuasive. There may be a right to die with dignity, or a right to personal control over the manner of death, professional medical assistance, and the avoidance of unnecessary and severe physical suffering. Changes in medical technology may affect these types of cases in the future.

---

3. The Second Amendment and the Scope of an Enumerated Right--

District of Columbia v. Heller, 128 S. Ct. 2783 (2008).

Facts. The District of Columbia (D) prohibited residents from possessing handguns and required residents to keep their lawfully owned firearms, such as registered long guns, unloaded and disassembled or bound by a trigger lock, unless they were located in a place of business or were being used for lawful recreational activities. Heller (P) applied for a registration certificate for a handgun to keep at home, but D refused to issue the certificate. P challenged D's refusal as a violation of his Second Amendment rights. The district court dismissed P's suit, but the court of appeals reversed. The Supreme Court granted certiorari.

Issue. May the District of Columbia prohibit the possession of usable handguns in the home?

Held. No. Judgment affirmed.

- D claims that the Second Amendment only protects the right to possess and carry a firearm in connection with militia service. P claims that the right extends to possession unconnected with militia service and for traditionally lawful purposes, including self-defense inside one's home.

- The Second Amendment refers to the "right of the people," which means individual, not collective, rights. The word "arms" means weapons not specifically designed for military use and not employed in a military capacity. To "keep arms" means to possess arms. The term "bear arms" has included carrying weapons outside of an organized militia. Historical experience in England left Englishmen wary of concentrated military forces run by the state, and the right to bear arms was considered a fundamental right of Englishmen.

- The Framers debated whether the right to keep and bear arms needed to be codified in the Constitution; Congress had not been granted power to abridge the ancient right of individuals to keep and bear arms. However, the Second Amendment was included to help secure the ideal of a citizen militia, which might be necessary to oppose an oppressive military force if the constitutional order broke down.

- Almost all interpreters of the Second Amendment in the century after its enactment interpreted the amendment as we do, and no precedents foreclose this interpretation. *United States v. Miller*, 307 U.S. 174 (1939), upheld the conviction of two men for transporting an unregistered short-barreled shotgun in interstate commerce, but that case involved the type of weapon. *Miller* stands for the proposition that the Second Amendment right extends only to certain types of weapons and does not protect weapons not typically possessed by law-abiding citizens for lawful purposes.

- D's law totally bans handgun possession in the home and requires that any lawful firearm in the home be rendered inoperable. The inherent right of self-defense is central to the Second Amendment right, but the handgun ban prohibits an entire class of arms that has been overwhelmingly chosen by Americans for self-defense, and it applies to the home, where the need for self-defense is most acute. Under any of the standards of scrutiny that we have applied to enumerated constitutional rights, the ban would fail constitutional muster.

Dissent (Stevens, Souter, Ginsburg, Breyer, JJ.). The Second Amendment does not protect the right to use a gun for any purpose, such as robbing a bank. It clearly protects the right to use weapons for certain military purposes, but the question is what non-military purposes are protected. The amendment was adopted to protect state militias because of concerns raised during the ratification of the Constitution that the power of Congress to disarm the state militias and create a national army posed a threat to the sovereignty of the states. The amendment does not refer to any civilian uses of weapons. Until today, legislatures have been allowed to regulate the civilian use and misuse of firearms as long as they do not interfere with the preservation of a well-regulated militia.

Dissent (Breyer, Stevens, Souter, Ginsburg, JJ.). The Second Amendment protects interests related to militia, not to self-defense. Its protection is not absolute in any case. D's regulation in this case is a permissible legislative response to a serious problem in high-crime urban areas. D's decision is supported by empirical fact, and legislators, not judges, have primary responsibility for drawing policy conclusions from empirical fact. Because important interests lie on both sides of the constitutional equation, rational-basis review or strict scrutiny are not appropriate. Instead, an interest-balancing inquiry should be applied. There are no less restrictive alternatives that D could have adopted to further its compelling life-preserving and public safety interests. The law concerns only one class of weapons, and the area that falls within its scope is totally urban. The majority does not give an adequate replacement for the law it is striking down, and the decision could throw into doubt the constitutionality of gun laws throughout the United States

---

C. THE EQUAL PROTECTION CLAUSE AND THE REVIEW OF THE REASONABLENESS OF LEGISLATION

1. **Scope.** Most economic and social regulations are reviewed under the traditional equal protection test, based on the existence of a rational basis for the regulation.

    a. The first requirement that must be established under the traditional test is that any statutory classification be "rational," or based on factors (economic, social, historical, geographic, etc.) that justify disparate treatment. This requirement is generally satisfied as long as the classifications are not patently arbitrary.

    b. The second requirement is that the classification (the disparate treatment) rationally promote a proper governmental purpose.

    c. Assuming that the classification drawn in the statute meets the first two requirements, it is also required that all persons affected by the classification be treated equally.

2. **Regulatory Legislation.**

    a. **Safety regulation--**

Railway Express Agency v. New York, 336 U.S. 106 (1949).

Facts. The city of New York (P) passed a traffic regulation that prohibited advertising on vehicles except for "business notices upon business delivery vehicles," or in other owner-advertising. Railway Express Agency (D), a nationwide express business, sold the space on its trucks for advertising by other businesses, and was convicted for violation of P's regulation. The trial court found a reasonable basis for the regulation and upheld the conviction. D appeals.

Issue. May a local business regulation make distinctions based on practical considerations but that are theoretically discriminatory?

Held. Yes. Judgment affirmed.

- D's equal protection argument is based on the allegedly irrational distinction between allowing owner-advertising but banning advertising-for-hire. However, P may have concluded that the former type of advertising is less distracting and possibly necessary for business.

- Equal protection questions are answered by such practical considerations based on experience rather than by purely theoretical inconsistencies.

Concurrence (Jackson, J.). The Equal Protection Clause is properly invoked as the best measure to assure just laws.

Comment. *See also Williamson v. Lee Optical Co. of Oklahoma, supra.*

---

b. **Scope of review--**

FCC v. Beach Communications, Inc., 508 U.S. 307 (1993).

Facts. Under the Cable Act, facilities that serve one or more buildings under common ownership or management are exempt from regulation if they do not use public rights-of-way, while facilities that serve separately owned and managed buildings are not exempt from regulation. The FCC (D), which administers the Cable Act, interpreted the term "cable system" to apply to satellite master antenna television ("SMATV") facilities. Beach Communications, Inc. (P) challenged the interpretation and its application to its SMATV system. The court of appeals held that the Cable Act violated the equal protection element of the Fifth Amendment, and D appeals.

Issue. Is a scope-of-coverage provision in a regulation constitutional so long as it has a rational basis?

Held. Yes. Judgment reversed.

- In areas of social and economic policy, a statutory classification that neither proceeds along suspect lines nor infringes fundamental constitutional rights must be upheld against an equal protection challenge if there is any reasonably conceivable state of facts that could provide a rational basis for the classification.

- On rational-basis review, a classification has a strong presumption of validity. The courts are not to judge the wisdom, fairness, or logic of legislative choices, and where the legislature must engage in a process of line-drawing, such as the class of persons subject to a regulatory requirement, the precise placement of the line is a legislative, not a judicial, consideration.

- The scope-of-coverage provision in this case is the type of line-drawing that must be done to regulate the field. As long as there is any sufficient rationale, the provision must be upheld.

- There are two possible bases for the common-ownership distinction, either of which is sufficient. First, common ownership was previously thought to be indicative of those systems for which the costs of regulation would outweigh the benefits to consumers. Subscriber influence over an SMATV system serving multiple buildings under common ownership could have greater bargaining power with the cable owner because all the subscribers could negotiate with one voice through the common owner. Second, the potential for monopoly power where there is common ownership is less than where there are multiple owners and subsequent satellite owners cannot effectively compete with a first operator.

Concurrence (Stevens, J.). It is reasonable to presume that Congress was motivated by an interest in allowing property owners to exercise freedom in the use of their own property.

Comment. In *Heller v. Doe*, 509 U.S. 312 (1993), the Court held that a state may require a lower standard of proof for involuntary commitment of the mentally retarded (clear and convincing evidence) than for involuntary commitment of the mentally ill (proof beyond a reasonable doubt). Among several rationales given by the state was that mental retardation is easier to diagnose than is mental illness. The Court held that each of the rationales given by the state, standing on its own, would suffice to establish a rational basis for the different burdens of proof.

---

3. **Suspect Classifications.** All classifications based on suspect criteria are subject to the strict equal protection standard of review. The traditional indicators of a suspect class are that the class: (i) is determined by characteristics that are solely an accident of birth; or (ii) has been subjected to such a history of purposefully unequal treatment, or relegated to a position of such political powerlessness, as to command extraordinary protection from the majority.

   a. **Classifications detrimental to racial minorities.**

      1) **Generally.** Race is a class that includes the traditional indicators of a suspect class, and the Court is extremely sensitive to improper racial classifications.

      2) **Interracial marriage--**

Loving v. Virginia, 388 U.S. 1 (1967).

Facts. Loving (D), a white man, married a black woman in violation of a Virginia (P) antimiscegenation statute and was convicted. The state courts upheld the conviction. D appeals, claiming that the statute violated the Equal Protection and Due Process Clauses of the Fourteenth Amendment.

Issue. May a state prevent marriages between persons solely because they are of different races?

Held. No. Judgment reversed.

- The state claims that equal protection is afforded when any penalties due to interracial elements of an offense are applied equally to members of both races. However, equal protection means more than mere "equal application." The Court must consider whether statutory classifications constitute arbitrary and invidious discrimination.

- Racial classifications, especially in criminal statutes, are subject to the most rigid scrutiny and must be essential to the accomplishment of some permissible state objective to be permitted. The state has failed to show any legitimate overriding purpose for the distinction between one-race and interracial marriages other than invidious racial discrimination, and the statute cannot be upheld.

Concurrence (Stewart, J.). It is impossible for a state law that makes the criminality of an act depend on the race of the actor to be constitutional.

---

3) **Private bias cannot be used in making child custody determination--**

Palmore v. Sidoti, 466 U.S. 429 (1984).

Facts. Upon her divorce from Sidoti (P), Palmore (D) was awarded custody of the couple's three-year-old daughter. Subsequently D, who was white, began cohabiting with a black man. P petitioned for custody based on changed circumstances. Although D later married the man with whom she was living, the court determined that the best interests of the child required that P obtain custody of her. The court stated that the child would suffer from social stigmatization because of the racially mixed household. The state appellate court affirmed, and the Supreme Court granted certiorari.

Issue. May a court divest a natural mother of the custody of her child because of her remarriage to a person of a different race?

Held. No. Judgment reversed.

- The state court did not make findings that D was unfit to continue having custody of her child. Its only rationale for changing custody was the racial consideration.

- Although the state has a high duty to protect the interests of minor children, and racial prejudices may subject D's daughter to pressures and stresses she would not face if her stepfather were of the same race as D, such private biases are not permissible considerations under the Constitution. Private biases may be beyond the reach of the law, but the law cannot give them effect.

Comment. Despite the strict scrutiny applied to racial classifications, the Court did uphold overt racial discrimination in *Korematsu v. United States, supra.* Korematsu was convicted of remaining in a "military area" in violation of an Army command during World War II that all persons of Japanese ancestry be excluded from certain areas for national defense reasons. The Court reasoned that military authorities had determined that the existence of Japanese sympathizers was a threat and that espionage and sabotage must be deterred at great cost. Under war emergency, nothing less than exclusion of the entire group would solve the problem of guarding against disloyalty. The Court viewed the case as involving military necessity, not racial antagonism.

---

b. Racial segregation in schools and other public facilities.

1) State-mandated racial segregation.

a) Separate but equal doctrine--

Plessy v. Ferguson, 163 U.S. 537 (1896).

Facts. Plessy (P), who was seven-eighths white and one-eighth black, refused to comply with a demand that he sit in the black railway carriage rather than the one for whites, and was convicted of violation of a state statute providing for separate railway carriages for the white and black races. P challenges the law, which was upheld in the lower courts.

Issue. May a state require that separate railway carriages be provided for black citizens and white citizens?

Held. Yes. Judgment affirmed.

- The law does not imply the inferiority of either race to the other. The only proper restraint on the exercise of state police power is that it be reasonable and intended for the promotion of the general good.

- The state legislature may properly have concluded that the law would preserve the public peace and good order. It certainly is no more obnoxious to the Fourteenth Amendment than laws requiring separate schools, which are universally accepted.

- Legislation cannot overcome social prejudices; the attempt to do so can only result in accentuating difficulties. The United States Constitution can act to equate civil and political rights of the two races, but cannot affect social standing.

Dissent (Harlan, J.). No legislature or court may properly regard the race of citizens where civil rights are involved. Every citizen, regardless of color, has a right to occupy the public transportation of his choice; governmental infringement of that right is unconstitutional. Our United States Constitution is color-blind, and neither knows nor tolerates classes among citizens. Any evils resulting from commingling of the races are less than those resulting from curtailment of civil rights upon the basis of race.

---

b) Repudiation of the doctrine--

Brown v. Board of Education (Brown I), 347 U.S. 483 (1954).

Facts. Brown (P) and other black schoolchildren (the opinion consolidates appeals from four states) were denied admission to schools attended by white children under laws requiring or permitting segregation based on race. P challenged the law but was denied relief under the "separate but equal" doctrine. (In the Delaware case, the plaintiff was admitted solely because the white school was superior; *i.e.,* separate was not equal.) P appeals.

Issue. May children be segregated in essentially "equal" public schools solely on the basis of race?

Held. No. Judgments vacated and reargument on the issue of appropriate relief ordered.

- The circumstances surrounding adoption of the Fourteenth Amendment are not conclusive to its determination, especially here, where public education, which barely existed then, is at issue. The effect of segregation on public education in its current setting is therefore determinative.

- Granted that black and white schools are substantially "equal" in tangible factors, there yet exists an invidious effect when black and white children are segregated. Namely, segregation creates a feeling of inferiority that may significantly affect a child's motivation to learn; separate educational facilities are therefore inherently unequal, and their maintenance by government authority denies equal protection of the law.

---

c) **Application to federal government--**

Bolling v. Sharpe, 347 U.S. 497 (1954).

Facts. Bolling (P), a black person, was denied admission to a white school in Washington, D.C., to which the Fourteenth Amendment was inapplicable. P challenged the segregation under the Due Process Clause of the Fifth Amendment. The district court dismissed P's complaint, and P appeals.

Issue. Does the concept of due process preclude federal segregation of public schools?

Held. Yes. Judgment vacated and reargument ordered.

- While "equal protection" and "due process" are not interchangeable phrases, they are not mutually exclusive. Discrimination may be so unjustifiable as to deny due process. Liberty under law is a broad concept and includes school attendance. It cannot be restricted except for a proper governmental objective. Since segregation is unrelated to any such proper objective, it results in an arbitrary deprivation of P's liberty in violation of the Due Process Clause.

---

2) **Judicial remedies for racially segregated schools in the South.**

a) **General principles.** The Court has adopted a bifurcated approach to school segregation problems. "De facto" segregation is nondeliberate segregation. If an official segregative policy existed as of 1954, there could not be de facto segregation in the system. Thus, in the South, most systems were characterized by "de jure" or deliberate segregation. The Court faced three alternatives in fashioning guidelines for remedying segregation:

(1) Only prohibit activity that results in segregation; *i.e.*, require desegregation only (emphasis on process);

(2) Hold that any racially imbalanced school system is by itself a violation; *i.e.*, require integration (emphasis on results); or

(3) Hold that, once de jure segregation is shown (process), integration is required (results). This is the approach applied today by the Court.

b) **Implementation of desegregation--**

Brown v. Board of Education (Brown II), 349 U.S. 294 (1955).

Facts. *See Brown v. Board of Education* (*Brown I*) above. The Court initially permitted gradual integration of public schools in recognition of the difficulties inherent in school desegregation. This opinion addresses the relief granted in *Brown I.*

Issue. In what manner is relief to be accorded?

Held.

- The full implementation of the constitutional principles requires solution of various local school problems, to be solved by school authorities and reviewed by the courts to assure good faith compliance.
- The cases are remanded to the lower courts, who are to be guided by equitable principles in fashioning decrees. The competing interests involve Ps' rights to admission at the earliest date and the need for systematic, effective, and orderly removal of obstacles to full integration.

c) **District courts empowered to remedy desegregation of local schools--**

Swann v. Charlotte-Mecklenburg Board of Education, 402 U.S. 1 (1971).

Facts. The Board of Education (D) had a long history of maintaining a dual set of schools in a single system in order to perpetuate discrimination in spite of *Brown I, supra*. Swann (P) brought suit to force desegregation. The district court ordered D to establish a plan, which it did, but the court rejected it and instead adopted a plan created by a court-appointed master. The United States Supreme Court granted certiorari to review the district court's implementation order.

Issue. Are district courts justified in ordering compliance with their own desegregation plans when the local school authorities fail to desegregate voluntarily?

Held. Yes. Judgment affirmed.

- The objective of the federal courts from *Brown I* to the present is to eliminate all vestiges of state-imposed segregation in the public schools. Judicial authority to remedy violations expands when local authority defaults.

- The central problems, which involve student assignment, are separated into four categories. The first category is the extent to which racial quotas may be used to correct a segregated system. A remedial plan is judged by its effectiveness. Awareness of the racial composition of a school system is a useful starting point in shaping an effective remedy, and limited use of mathematical ratios is permissible. The guiding principle is that no pupil should be excluded from any school on account of race, but every school need not always reflect the racial composition of the school system as a whole.

- The remaining categories are elimination of one-race schools, remedial altering of attendance zones, and transportation of students in order to dismantle the dual school system. Demographic factors may result in virtually or completely one-race schools; these are not certain indications of imposed segregation. However, gerrymandering of school districts and attendance zones and provision for optional transfer of students to other schools is useful, and, to be effective, must grant free transportation and assurance of a place in the desired school.

---

3) **Judicial remedies for northern schools.**

a) **All minorities.** In determining whether a school is "segregated," the courts must consider the number of all minority groups (not just blacks) who have suffered unequal treatment in education. [Keyes v. School District No. 1, 413 U.S. 189 (1973)]

b) **Presumption.** A finding that school authorities intentionally segregated—or delayed integrating—any significant portion of the school district creates a presumption that the entire school district is being operated on a segregated basis. This is because of the "substantial reciprocal effect" that segregation of some schools may have on others. [Keyes v. School District No. 1, *supra*]

(1) This presumption is not rebutted or satisfactorily explained merely by showing that the board had adopted a "neighborhood school policy" (assigning students to the schools closest to their homes), even though such policy on its face appears to be racially neutral.

(2) But the presumption may be rebutted by a showing that because of natural geographic boundaries, the school district is in fact divided into clearly unrelated areas, which require separate treatment. But the burden of proving this is on the school board.

c) **Systemwide impact.** In *Columbus Board of Education v. Penick*, 443 U.S. 499 (1979), and *Dayton Board of Education v. Brinkman (Dayton II)*, 443 U.S. 526 (1979), the Court affirmed a court of appeals decision that found that, since the school districts had been intentionally segregated in 1954 and had therefore been under obligation to disestablish the dual system, their failure to do so permitted the courts to require a systemwide desegregation plan. The failure to desegregate after 1954, by itself, was found to be a policy having a systemwide impact.

d) **Extent of remedies.** Permissible judicial remedies include designating the location of new schools and abandonment of old schools so as not to perpetuate segregation; gerrymandering school districts and attendance zones, even if the result is that the new districts and zones are neither compact nor contiguous; and assigning students, faculty, and staff to schools in ratios substantially the same as in the community.

e) **Limits on remedies.** A federal court may not order busing of students between or among school districts to remedy de jure segregation in only one of the districts, unless discriminatory acts of one school district have been a substantial cause of interdistrict segregation; *e.g.,* the district boundaries were drawn so as to foster such segregation, or one district had engaged in racial discrimination that caused the segregation to exist in the other district. [Milliken v. Bradley, 418 U.S. 717 (1974)] The impact is that federal courts cannot achieve desegregation of urban schools by ordering the children bused to suburban school districts (and vice versa) as long as the suburban school districts had nothing to do with causing the segregation in the city school district (*i.e.,* no interdistrict remedies).

4) **Classification of students by race in making school assignments--**

Parents Involved in Community Schools v. Seattle School District.
(See *infra*

---

c. **Gender.** Although early decisions dealt with sex-based classifications under the traditional equal protection tests, more recent cases have judged sex-based classifications under a higher standard, but not so high a test as would apply to the inherently suspect classes. The Court will uphold government action based on such classifications if it is substantially related to an important government interest.

1) **Estate administration; rational basis standard applied--**

Reed v. Reed,

Facts. Reed, a minor, died intestate after his adoptive parents separated. Each of the parents sought to administer his estate. The probate court ordered that Mr. Reed (D) be appointed administrator, because a state statute required that when equally entitled persons claimed to administer, males must be preferred to females. Mrs. Reed (P) challenged the law, which was upheld by the Idaho Supreme Court. P appeals.

Issue. May a state prefer one sex over the other in determining who will administer an estate?

Held. No. Judgment reversed.

- Idaho does not forbid females from administering estates, but provides for different treatment of applicants to administer solely on the basis of sex. Such a classification is subject to scrutiny under the Equal Protection Clause, and may stand only if it bears a rational relationship to a valid state objective.
- The only objectives given by the state involve reducing the probate workload and avoiding intrafamily controversy, neither of which is relevant to a classification based on sex. Therefore, the state statute is invalid.

---

2) **Military benefits; strict scrutiny applied--**

Frontiero v. Richardson,

Facts. Frontiero (P), a female officer in the Air Force, sought to claim her husband as a "dependent" in order to receive the additional benefits attached to such a claim. Male members of the armed forces could claim wives as dependents without any showing, but women in the service had to show that their spouses were actually dependent on them for over one-half of their support. P claimed that the distinction violated the Due Process Clause. The district court upheld the statutes making the distinction, and P appeals.

Issue. May the military require that servicewomen and not servicemen make a showing that their spouses are actually dependent before claiming them as "dependents"?

Held. No. Judgment reversed.

- ♦ Classifications based on sex are included among those that are inherently suspect and therefore subject to close judicial scrutiny.
- ♦ This statute cannot withstand such scrutiny. Its sole justification lies in administrative convenience, which, though important in some circumstances, is hardly a significant governmental interest closely and reasonably related to the classification. The statutes involve arbitrary discrimination and deny due process.

Concurrence (Stewart, J.). The statute works an invidious discrimination and the outcome is correct.

Dissent (Rehnquist, J.). The lower court's reasoning was correct.

Concurrence (Powell, J., Burger, C.J., Blackmun, J.). The statutes are unconstitutional under *Reed v. Reed, supra.* There is no need to go further and characterize sex as a suspect classification. To do so unnecessarily preempts the prescribed constitutional processes of amending the Constitution, which at this time is dealing with this very issue in the guise of the Equal Rights Amendment.

---

3) Liquor regulation; intermediate standard applied--

Craig v. Boren,

Facts. Craig (P), a male, challenged an Oklahoma statute that denied beer sales to males under 21 and females under 18. The three-judge district court dismissed P's action, and P appeals.

Issue. May a state properly impose gender-based differentials in regulating sales of alcoholic drinks?

Held. No. Judgment reversed.

- ♦ Classifications by gender must serve important governmental objectives and must be substantially related to the achievement of those objectives to withstand constitutional challenge.
- ♦ The state objective—the enhancement of traffic safety—is clearly important. However, the relation between this objective and the challenged statute is based on statistical evidence fraught with shortcomings and is inadequate to show

that sex represents a legitimate, accurate proxy for the regulation of drinking and driving. Failure to show a substantial relation between the gender-based classification and achievement of the state's objectives requires that the statute be invalidated as unconstitutional.

- ♦ The operation of the Twenty-First Amendment, limited as it is when applied outside Commerce Clause issues, does not alter application of the equal protection standards that govern here.

Concurrence (Blackmun, J.). The Twenty-First Amendment does not save the statute.

Concurrence (Powell, J.). The Court has added confusion to the appropriate standard for equal protection analysis. The statistics do tend to support the state's view, but are inadequate to support the classification.

Concurrence (Stewart, J.). The Equal Protection Clause requires only one standard—that every state govern impartially. The classification here is not totally irrational, but is unacceptable because it has little relation to traffic safety (it prohibits only sales, not consumption) and it punishes all males for the abuses of only 2% of their class.

Dissent (Burger, C.J.). The majority of the Court has not found the state's means to be totally irrational, so we ought not strike down the statute.

Dissent (Rehnquist, J.).

- ♦ Men challenging a gender-based statute unfavorable to themselves should not be able to invoke a more stringent standard of review than normally pertains to most other types of classifications, since men, as a group, have not suffered the type of prior discrimination that has always supported a standard of special scrutiny. Nor is the interest involved—beer purchasing—"fundamental" in the constitutional sense of invoking strict scrutiny.

- ♦ The Court has added a new standard to the norm of "rational basis" and the "compelling state interest" required where a "suspect classification" is involved—that of the "important governmental objectives" and "substantial relation to achievement of those objectives." This new standard is not needed and invites judicial confusion and interference into the proper roles of the legislature.

- ♦ The correct standard here is the rational basis test, under which a classification is invalid only if it rests on grounds wholly irrelevant to the achievement of the state's objective. The state has shown sufficient evidence to show a rational basis, and the statute should be upheld.

---

4) **Pregnancy.** A state law that excluded from state disability insurance benefits "disabilities arising from normal pregnancy and child-

birth" has been upheld. This provision did not violate equal protection because it furthered the state policy of making the disability insurance program self-supporting by excluding certain physical conditions from coverage thereunder. The fact that this particular condition (pregnancy) happens to only one sex does not render the exclusion invalid. [Geduldig v. Aiello, 417 U.S. 484 (1974)] In *General Electric Co. v. Gilbert*, 429 U.S. 125 (1976), the Court upheld a private disability insurance contract that excluded pregnancy disabilities, relying on *Geduldig*.

5) **Rape statutes--**

Michael M. v. Superior Court,

Facts. California's statutory rape law makes men alone criminally liable for the act of sexual intercourse with a minor. Michael M. (D) was prosecuted under the statute and challenged it as an unlawful discrimination on the basis of gender. The California Supreme Court upheld the law, and D appeals.

Issue. May a state's statutory rape law permit prosecution only against members of one sex?

Held. Yes. Judgment affirmed.

- A legislature may not make overbroad generalizations based on sex that are entirely unrelated to any differences between men and women or that demean the ability or social status of the affected class. However, legislation may realistically reflect the fact that the sexes are not similarly situated in certain circumstances.

- The asserted purpose of the statute is to prevent illegitimate pregnancy and its attendant social harms, a valid state purpose. The question is whether a state may attack the problem directly by prohibiting a male from having sexual intercourse with a minor female. We hold that such a statute is sufficiently related to the state's objectives to pass constitutional muster.

- D claims the statute is underinclusive since a gender-neutral statute would serve the state's goal equally well. We do not sit to redraw constitutionally permissible lines, and even if we were so inclined, we cannot say that a gender-neutral statute, attended by increased enforcement difficulties, would be equally effective.

Concurrence (Stewart, J.). Equal protection prohibits classifications of similarly situated people on the basis of the immutable characteristics with which they were born. Males and females are not similarly situated with respect to the problems addressed by this statute, so the classification does not deny equal protection.

Concurrence (Blackmun, J.). This statute is a sufficiently reasoned and constitutional effort to control the problem at its inception. It does not implicate the serious questions arising when the state seeks to regulate a woman's dealing with pregnancy once it has become a reality.

Dissent (Brennan, White, Marshall, JJ.). While the desirability of achieving the state's asserted statutory goal is unquestionable, this statute is not substantially related to success. California has failed to prove that its gender-based law is more successful than would be a gender-neutral law.

Dissent (Stevens, J.). The validity of a total ban is not an adequate justification for a selective prohibition. A rule that authorizes punishment of only one of two equally guilty wrongdoers violates the essence of the constitutional requirement that the sovereign must govern impartially.

---

6) **Draft registration.** In *Rostker v. Goldberg*, 453 U.S. 57 (1981), the Court held that Congress may restrict draft registration to males. The purpose of registration was to prepare for a draft of combat troops. Women were not eligible for combat. Thus, the exemption of women from registration was not only sufficiently but also closely related to Congress's purpose in authorizing registration. Since men and women were not similarly situated with respect to combat, the classification challenged did not violate the United States Constitution.

7) **All female school.** In *Mississippi University for Women v. Hogan*, *infra*, the Court invalidated a state statute that prevented males from enrolling in a state-supported nursing school. The state had failed to meet its burden of showing an "exceedingly persuasive justification" for the gender-based classification.

8) **Peremptory challenges.** In *J.E.B. v. Alabama ex rel. T.B.,* 511 U.S. 127 (1994), the Court held that gender, like race, was an unconstitutional proxy for juror competence and impartiality. This means that peremptory challenges to potential jurors may not be exercised on the basis of gender, just as they may not be used on the basis of race under *Batson v. Kentucky*, 476 U.S. 79 (1986).

9) **Separate program for women not sufficient--**

United States v. Virginia,

Facts. Virginia (D) operated the Virginia Military Institute ("VMI") as part of its system of public institutions of higher learning. VMI was a single-sex school with the goal of producing citizen-soldiers through pervasive training, including the adversative method that instills physical and mental discipline. The method included requirements that cadets wear uniforms, eat together in the mess hall, participate in drills, and live in spartan barracks with constant surveillance and no privacy. The United States (P) sued D to force acceptance of females into VMI. The district court found for D. The court of appeals reversed, giving D the options of admitting women to VMI, establishing a parallel institution for females, or abandoning state support. On remand, D chose the parallel program option. The courts upheld this choice. The Supreme Court granted certiorari.

Issue. Where a state-sponsored single-sex school denies equal protection, may the state offer a parallel program for the opposite sex while retaining the single-sex status of the school?

Held. No. Judgment reversed.

- To defend gender-based actions, D must demonstrate an "exceedingly persuasive justification" for that action. D claims that single-sex education provides important educational benefits that justify VMI's policy. While such pedagogical benefits may exist, D has not shown that VMI was established, or has been maintained, in order to diversify educational opportunities within the state.

- D also asserts that the adversative method could not be made available to women without modification. But the necessary modifications, such as arranging housing and physical training programs for the women, would not affect the goal or methodology. So long as some women have the will and capacity to participate, D cannot constitutionally deny the program to all women. Thus, D has shown no exceedingly persuasive justification.

- Establishment of a comparable school for women would not remedy the constitutional problem. D's separate program does not include the rigorous military training found at VMI. D claims that the methodological differences between the institutions are based on "real" differences between men and women, but again this is based on estimates of what is appropriate for most women. Such generalizations fail to recognize that some women do well under the adversative method and want to attend VMI. D's alternative program for women is simply not the equal of VMI.

Concurrence (Rehnquist, C.J.). If D had made a genuine effort to devote comparable public resources to a facility for women, it may have avoided an equal protection violation. Its facility fails as a remedy because it is simply not the institution VMI is.

Dissent (Scalia, J.). VMI existed for over 150 years. The tradition of having government-funded military schools for men has not been unconstitutional over those years. Changes such as the one the Court imposes should be brought about through democratic means, not by the courts. The Court now holds that a sex-based classification is invalid unless it relates to characteristics that hold true in every instance. In so doing, it has executed a *de facto* abandonment of the intermediate scrutiny that should be applied to gender-based classifications. The facts in this case show that D's real options were an adversative method that excludes women or no adversative method at all. The courts below found that VMI would be fundamentally changed if it admitted women.

---

d. **The relevance of discriminatory impact in finding a discriminatory purpose.**

1) **General rule.** Laws or other official actions that are racially neutral on their face and that rationally serve a permissible government end do not violate equal protection simply because they have a racially discriminatory impact (*i.e.,* affect minorities more adversely than whites). A violation requires that the government action have a discriminatory purpose (intentional or deliberate discrimination).

2) **Qualification test--**

Washington v. Davis,

Facts. Davis (P), a black police officer, and other interested blacks challenged the promotion policies and recruiting practices of the District of Columbia Police Department. P filed for partial summary judgment on the recruiting question, specifically challenging a qualification test that allegedly discriminated against blacks in violation of the Fifth Amendment Due Process Clause. The district court denied P's motions, and the court of appeals reversed. Washington (D) appeals.

Issue. Does a qualification test that has not been established as a reliable measure of job performance and that fails a higher percentage of blacks than whites violate the Fifth Amendment Due Process Clause?

Held. No. Judgment reversed.

- A disproportionate impact on different races resulting from a general qualification test does not, by itself and independent of any discriminatory purpose, establish a constitutional violation. Government action is not unconstitutional solely because it has a racially disproportionate impact; there must be a racially discriminatory purpose to justify invalidation. The purpose need not be express, but it must exist, whether on the face of the statute or in its application.

- When a disproportionate racial impact is proved, the government must show that the law is neutral on its face and serves proper governmental ends, but the burden is not high. The test involved here has a reasonable relation to the need for competent police officers. Additionally, D has made affirmative efforts to recruit black officers, indicating a lack of intent to discriminate.

♦ Even though the test was not shown to relate directly to eventual job performance, it is closely related to the requirements of the training program for new recruits.

Concurrence (Stevens, J.). The link between discriminatory purpose and impact is not bright and not determinative since dramatic discriminatory impact is unacceptable.

---

3) **Inference of discriminatory purpose raised by showing of discriminatory impact.** In *Village of Arlington Heights v. Metropolitan Housing Development Corp.,* 429 U.S. 252 (1977), the Supreme Court held that without proof of improper intent, a mere showing of disproportionate impact on a racial minority is inadequate to the constitutional question. In that case, the plaintiff applied for rezoning in order to build units for low-income tenants, many of whom would be racial minorities. When the city denied the application pursuant to standard procedures, the plaintiff sued, claiming the denial was racially discriminatory. The Supreme Court found for the city and reaffirmed the *Davis* requirement that governmental action having a racially disproportionate impact must also have a discriminatory purpose to justify judicial invalidation. The challenged action need not rest solely on such a racially discriminatory purpose; it is enough to show that such a purpose was a motivating factor in the decision.

4) **Two-step analysis.** In *Personnel Administrator of Massachusetts v. Feeney*, 442 U.S. 256 (1979), the Court upheld a veterans preference law, although 98% of the veterans were male. The Court articulated a two-step analysis of facially neutral statutes alleged to have a discriminatory impact. First, is the statute indeed neutral? Second, if it is, does the adverse impact reflect invidious discrimination? Here, the statute was truly neutral, and the intent was not to discriminate against women but to assist veterans, male and female.

5) **Assumption about behavior.** In *Castaneda v. Partida*, 430 U.S. 482 (1977), the Court determined that on a showing of invidious discrimination in the makeup of a grand jury, it is not enough for the state to prove that the governing majority in the local government was of the same race as the race allegedly discriminated

against. Such a rebuttal relies on the assumption that human beings would not discriminate against their own kind. Instead, the Court required rebuttal consisting of evidence about how the people selecting grand jurors operated and why they did so in that manner.

6) **Subjective evidence--**

Rogers v. Lodge,

Facts. Lodge and other black citizens of Burke County, Georgia, (Ps) brought suit against Rogers and four other county commissioners (Ds), challenging Ds' system of at-large elections. The majority of the county population was black, but because the white population was older, a slight majority of the voting population was white. About 38% of the registered voters were black. Commissioners were elected by majority vote, in runoff elections if necessary. No black had ever been elected to the commission. The trial court found that the election system was racially neutral when adopted but was being maintained for invidious purposes, and ordered that the county be divided into five districts for purposes of electing commissioners. The court of appeals affirmed, and D appeals.

Issue. May sociological evidence be used to prove a discriminatory intent behind an at-large voting system?

Held. Yes. Judgment affirmed.

- At-large voting systems are not per se unconstitutional, although they tend to minimize the voting strength of minority groups by allowing the political majority to elect all representatives of the district. To prove a violation of the Equal Protection Clause, Ps must trace the invidious quality of the law to a racially discriminatory purpose. This requires inquiry into the available circumstantial and direct evidence of intent.

- In *Mobile v. Bolden*, 446 U.S. 55 (1980), the Court held that the presence of a discriminatory effect is insufficient; there must be a finding of discriminatory purpose. This case differs from *Mobile* because the district court below considered the relevant proof and concluded that Ds' scheme is being maintained for invidious purposes. It did not stop at finding the existence of discriminatory effect.

- The evidence of bloc voting along racial lines and the fact that no black has ever been elected to the commission are themselves insufficient to prove intentional discrimination. However, the trial court also considered the impact of past discrimination, which resulted in low black voter registration and absence of blacks in various governmental positions. Ds' voting scheme has served to maintain the status quo.

- ♦ There is no reason to overturn the district court's order to use single-member districts.

Dissent (Powell, Rehnquist, JJ.). The largely sociological evidence relied on by the Court is the same type of evidence that was insufficient in *Mobile*. Under the majority opinion, the district courts must assess at-large voting systems free from any standards. They must make subjective inquiries into the motivations of local officials in structuring local governments. Courts should instead focus on objective factors that are direct, reliable, and unambiguous indicia of discriminatory intent.

---

e. **Affirmative action, quotas, and gender and race preferences.**

1) **Introduction.** Attempts to remedy adverse effects of past discrimination have resulted in various means, such as affirmative action, quotas, and minority preferences, which in effect discriminate in favor of minorities. Such means do not violate equal protection if they fall within certain constitutional parameters.

2) **Classifications advantaging females.**

a) **Economic--**

Kahn v. Shevin,

Facts. Kahn (P), a widower, applied for a Florida property tax exemption available to widows, but his application was denied. He brought suit for a declaratory judgment that restricting the exemption to widows denied him equal protection. The Florida Supreme Court upheld the law, and P appeals.

Issue. May a state restrict certain tax benefits to one gender?

Held. Yes. Judgment affirmed.

- ♦ Past discrimination has resulted in a generally less favorable economic position for women, especially for widows. Since Florida's differing treatment of widows and widowers has a fair and substantial relation to the object of the legislation, it is permissible.

- ♦ The reason for the classification is more than mere administrative convenience. It is based on the state policy of cushioning the financial impact of spousal loss on the typically more needy sex. States have more freedom in making classifications for tax purposes, as long as there is a reasonable distinction.

Dissent (Brennan, Marshall, JJ.). Females, having been discriminated against, properly deserve remedial measures to correct prior economic imbalances. However, this statute is overbroad. The state has not borne its burden of proving that its compelling interest could not be achieved by a more precisely tailored statute or by use of equally feasible, less drastic means.

Dissent (White, J.). The discrimination here is invidious and requires more justification than the state has offered. The state assists some widows who do not actually need help, yet excludes widowers who may need it. The only true justification is administrative efficiency, which we have previously said is insufficient.

Comment. The Court has upheld a Social Security Act formula entitling women wage earners to greater benefits than males. The Court recognized reduction of the disparity in economic condition between men and women, caused by the long history of discrimination against women, as an important governmental objective. [Califano v. Webster, 430 U.S. 313 (1977)] The Court has also held a state law requiring husbands, but not wives, to pay alimony invalid. [Orr v. Orr, 440 U.S. 268 (1979)]

---

b) Education--

Mississippi University for Women v. Hogan,

Facts. The Mississippi University for Women (D) was a state school that excluded males. D established a school of nursing. Hogan (P), a male registered nurse, applied for admission to D, the only state school in the city, to obtain a degree. P was denied admission but was allowed to audit classes. P sued in federal court, claiming that D violated the Equal Protection Clause. The district court denied preliminary injunctive relief, but the court of appeals reversed. The Supreme Court granted certiorari.

Issue. May a state exclude males from enrolling in a state-supported professional nursing school?

Held. No. Judgment affirmed.

- Because D's policy discriminates on the basis of gender, it is subject to equal protection scrutiny. D must show that the classification serves important governmental objectives and that the discriminatory means employed are substantially related to the achievement of those objectives.

- D claims that its policy compensates for discrimination against women and is educational affirmative action. While a compensatory purpose may justify an otherwise discriminatory classification in some situations, this argument is unpersuasive with respect to the nursing school. Women have earned the large majority of nursing degrees in the state, and in the nation as a whole. The actual effect of D's policy is to perpetuate the stereotypical view of nursing as a woman's job.

♦ D has also failed to show that the classification is substantially and directly related to its compensatory objective. D allows men to audit classes and to participate in continuing education classes. Women must not, therefore, be adversely affected by the presence of men.

Dissent (Burger, C.J.). The opinion is limited to professional nursing schools.

Dissent (Blackmun, J.). The Equal Protection Clause does not require needless conformity. There is no need to forbid a state from offering a choice to some people while not depriving others of an alternative choice.

Dissent (Powell, Rehnquist, JJ.). Women's colleges have been an element of diversity that has enriched American life. The majority errs by assuming that the equal protection standard is appropriate here, where the intent was to expand women's choices. P's only real claim is that the colleges open to him are located at inconvenient distances, and that he has a right to attend a college in his home city.

---

3) Classifications advantaging social minorities.

a) Background. In the 1970s, responding to social trends, some schools and employers began voluntary use of racial criteria to benefit racial minorities.

(1) ***Bakke.*** The Court evaluated the constitutionality of a voluntary affirmative action program in *Regents of the University of California v. Bakke*, 438 U.S. 265 (1978). The Regents had established a special admissions program for the Medical School of the University of California at Davis that reserved 16 out of 100 places in the first-year class for minorities. Bakke, a white applicant, was denied admission for two consecutive years. He sued to be included in the special admissions program. The Court held that a state school could use race as a factor in its admissions process, but that the specific program in this case was unlawful. There was no majority opinion. Four Justices held that the program was unconstitutional and that the states cannot consider race as a factor, even for a "benign" preference for minorities. Four Justices held that the program was not unconstitutional and that the states can consider race as a factor. Justice Powell agreed that the program was unconstitutional because it set aside seats specifically for minorities, but he also concluded that the states can constitutionally consider race as a factor in pursuit of a goal of assembling a diverse student body.

(2) ***Fullilove.*** Congress included a Minority Business Enterprise provision in the Public Works Employment Act of 1977, which denied applications for grants to receive public funding if the application did not include assurances that at least 10% of the grant would be spent with minority-owned businesses. In *Fullilove v. Klutznick*, 448 U.S. 448 (1980), the Court upheld the statute by finding that it was narrowly tailored to the achievement of the goal of remedying the present effects of past discrimination.

(3) ***Wygant.*** In *Wygant v. Jackson Board of Education*, 476 U.S. 267 (1986), the Court considered a collective bargaining agreement that limited the percentage of minority personnel laid off to the percentage of minorities employed at the time of the layoff. The effect was to protect recently-hired minority teachers at the expense of more senior white teachers. The Court held that the provision was unconstitutional because it was not related to specific prior discrimination by the government unit involved and did not necessarily bear a relationship to the harm caused by prior discriminatory hiring practices.

b) Rejection of state and local set-aside programs absent evidence of direct discrimination--

City of Richmond v. J.A. Croson Co.,

Facts. Citing the authority of the opinion in *Fullilove v. Klutznick*, *supra*, the city of Richmond (P) required prime contractors on city projects to set aside at least 30% of its subcontracts to minority business enterprises, using the *Fullilove* definition of minority group members. The program was adopted based on evidence that minority businesses had received a significantly lower percentage of contracts (.67%) than the percentage of minorities living in the city (50%). However, there was no evidence of racial discrimination on P's part or on the part of any of P's prime contractors. P brought suit against J.A. Croson Company (D) to enforce the rule. The district court found for P. The court of appeals reversed, and P appeals.

Issue. May a city adopt a set-aside program favoring minority-owned contractors on city projects when there is no evidence of direct discrimination on the part of the city or its prime contractors?

Held. No. Judgment affirmed.

- ♦ P notes that under *Fullilove*, Congress was not required to make specific findings of discrimination to engage in race-conscious relief. P asserts that if the federal government could do this, a city such as P can as well. However, unlike the states and their subdivisions, such as P, Congress has a specific constitutional mandate to enforce the Fourteenth Amendment.

- ♦ To enable states to use racial classifications merely by reciting a benign or compensatory purpose would be to give them the full power of Congress under Section 5 of the Fourteenth Amendment, and to insulate their actions from judicial scrutiny under Section 1. However, the objective of the Fourteenth Amendment was to limit the states' use of race as a criterion for legislative action and to empower the federal courts to enforce those limitations.

- ♦ Under the Equal Protection Clause, a state or its subdivisions may eradicate the effects of private discrimination within its own legislative jurisdiction, but this requires that the discrimination be identified with the particularity required by the Fourteenth Amendment. P would have to show that it had become a "passive participant" in a system of racial exclusion practiced by elements of the local construction industry, but it failed to do so.

- ♦ The Equal Protection Clause protects individual persons; P's plan denied certain citizens the opportunity to compete for a fixed percentage of public contracts based solely on their race, and thereby implicates the personal rights of the excluded persons. Such race-based regulations are subject to strict scrutiny, regardless of the race of those burdened or benefited by the classification. [Wygant v. Jackson Board of Education, *supra*]

- ♦ P's factual predicate for its plan consists of a generalized assertion that there has been past discrimination in the "construction industry," attributable to a series of racial as well as nonracial factors. P can do no more than speculate as to how many minority firms would exist absent past discrimination. It cannot show how many minority members are qualified to act as contractors, or how many minority members are eligible for membership in contractors' associations. All P can show is that minority businesses received less than 1% of prime contracts, even though its minority population is 50%, but statistical generalizations cannot substitute for evidence of discrimination. Permitting a racial classification on such generalizations would enable local governments to create a patchwork of racial preferences without ascertainable limit on size or duration.

- P's plan covers Spanish-speaking, Oriental, Indian, Eskimo, and Aleut persons, against whom there is no evidence of discrimination in P's construction industry. This suggests that P's purpose was not to remedy past discrimination.

- A court cannot assess whether P's plan is narrowly tailored to remedy prior discrimination because it is not linked to identified discrimination. There is no indication that P considered race-neutral means to increase minority participation in the construction industry. The quota's only goal appears to be racial balancing. But unlike the plan upheld in *Fullilove*, P's plan does not provide for a waiver of the set-aside provision where the minority contractor's higher price was not attributable to the effects of past discrimination. P evaluates bids on a case-by-case basis, and can investigate the need for remedial action in particular cases as appropriate; P cannot use broad statistical requirements simply to minimize the administrative burdens of remedying specific prior discrimination.

Concurrence (Stevens, J.). Unlike the plan in *Wygant*, which was intended to improve education by assuring an integrated faculty, P's plan has no objective to increase efficient performance of its construction contracts. P's plan was formulated by a legislative body; instead of a court, which is better equipped to identify past wrongdoers and to fashion appropriate remedies. P's plan does not address the specific characteristics of the racial groups involved; it relies merely on a stereotypical analysis that cannot be condoned under the Equal Protection Clause.

Concurrence (Kennedy, J.). The driving force of the Equal Protection Clause is the moral imperative of racial neutrality. Justice Scalia's proposed rule of automatic invalidity would reduce caseloads but is a break from our precedents. The majority's strict scrutiny standard will generally accomplish the same objective while being consistent with our precedents.

Concurrence (Scalia, J.). There are no situations in which state and local governments may discriminate on the basis of race (except a social emergency, such as a prison race riot, or when necessary to undo the effects of their own unlawful racial classifications), because a solution to past discrimination that consists of aggravating present discrimination is no solution. The federal government is uniquely capable of dealing with past racial discrimination because racial discrimination finds more ready expression at the state and local levels than it does at the federal level. P's plan is an example of local racial classification; it directly benefits the dominant political group, which is also the dominant racial group. P is free to give a contracting preference to identified victims of discrimination, but this could apply to whites as well as blacks; it would be race-neutral. Remedies must address discrimination against individuals; a past injustice to a black man cannot be compensated for by discriminating against a white man.

Dissent (Marshall, Brennan, Blackmun, JJ.). P's plan was patterned after, and is indistinguishable from, the *Fullilove* plan. The majority is unpersuaded by P's factual findings, but it should not second-guess the judgment of the former capital of the Confederacy, which found that its local construction industry did not deviate from the national pattern Congress found as set forth in *Fullilove*. P has a compelling interest other than remedying past discrimination; it has an interest in preventing its own spending decision from furthering racial discrimination. P's plan is substantially related to these interests and is appropriately limited to five years in duration, has a waiver provision, and has a minimal impact on innocent third parties, since it only affects 3% of overall contracting in P's area. The majority also for the first time introduces strict scrutiny of race-conscious remedial remedies as if racial discrimination and its vestiges have been eradicated in the United States. It also imposes a difficult factual standard of proof of a prima facie case of a constitutional or statutory violation before states and localities can act to remedy racial discrimination. This decision marks a full-scale retreat from the Court's long-standing solicitude to race-conscious remedial efforts.

Comment. The plurality, which stated that race-based regulations are subject to strict scrutiny in all cases, noted that while Justice Marshall's approach would apply a relaxed standard of review to race-conscious classifications designed to further remedial goals, in this case the majority of P's city council, and about half of P's population, were black. Under this view, if the level of scrutiny varied according to the ability of different groups to defend their interests in the representative process, the plurality argued that heightened scrutiny would be appropriate in this case because the classification was to the advantage of the racial group that had a political majority. Justice Marshall noted that numerical inferiority is but one of several factors to be considered.

---

c) Strict scrutiny of affirmative action--

Adarand Constructors, Inc. v. Pena,

Facts. Adarand Constructors, Inc. (P) submitted the low bid for a guardrail subcontract on a federal road project. The prime contract's terms provided for additional compensation if subcontractors were hired who were certified as small businesses controlled by "socially and economically disadvantaged individuals." P's competitor, Gonzales Construction Company, certified as such a business and received the subcontract, although its bid was higher than P's. Under federal law, general contractors must presume that "socially and economically disadvantaged individuals" include specified racial minorities. P sued Pena (D), Secretary of Transportation, claiming he was deprived of property without due process of law under the Fifth Amendment. The court of appeals upheld the law, and P appeals.

Issue. Is the federal government's use of race-based classifications subject to strict scrutiny even for affirmative action?

Held. Yes. Judgment reversed and case remanded.

- The Fifth Amendment protects against arbitrary treatment by the federal government, but it does not guarantee equal treatment.

- In *Croson, supra*, the Court held that the Fourteenth Amendment requires strict scrutiny of all race-based action by state and local governments. Thus, any person, of whatever race, has the right to demand that the government justify any racial classification subjecting that person to unequal treatment under the strictest judicial scrutiny.

- In *Metro Broadcasting, Inc. v. FCC*, 497 U.S. 549 (1990), the Court held that "benign" racial classifications required only intermediate scrutiny. This holding undermined the basic principle that the Fifth and Fourteenth Amendments protect persons, not groups. Group classifications must be subject to detailed inquiry to assure that the personal right to equal protection has not been infringed. Therefore, it is inconsistent to treat "benign" racial classifications differently from other types of racial classifications, and all racial classifications shall now be subject to strict scrutiny.

- This holding does not preclude the government from acting in response to the lingering effects of racial discrimination. When race-based action is necessary to further a compelling interest, it is permitted as long as it satisfies the "narrow tailoring" test of strict scrutiny.

Concurrence (Scalia, J.). There can never be a compelling interest in discriminating on the basis of race to compensate for past racial discrimination in the opposite direction. Under the Constitution, there can be neither a creditor nor a debtor race.

Concurrence (Thomas, J.). The government may not make distinctions on the basis of race, whether the objectives are to oppress a race or to help a race. Affirmative action programs undermine the moral basis of the equal protection principle and arouse resentment by those not benefited. The targeted minorities are stamped with a badge of inferiority and are prompted to develop dependencies or an attitude that they are "entitled" to preferences.

Dissent (Stevens, Ginsburg, JJ.). There is a clear distinction between policies designed to oppress minorities and policies designed to eradicate racial subordination.

Dissent (Souter, Ginsburg, Breyer, JJ.). Stare decisis compels the application of *Fullilove, supra*, to this case. Although *Fullilove* was not doctrinally consistent, its holding has been generally accepted.

Dissent (Ginsburg, Breyer, JJ.). The judiciary should defer to Congress, as the political branches are better suited to respond to changing conditions.

Comment. *See Miller v. Johnson*, *infra*, regarding the use of race in redistricting plans for Congress.

---

d) **Post-*Bakke* university admissions policies**. In response to *Bakke*, state schools modified their admissions policies to avoid racial quotas. This did not eliminate the use of race as a factor in deciding whether to admit individual students, however. The Supreme Court has recognized that diversity is a legitimate basis for considering race, but not if the admissions policy is in effect a quota.

(1) **Race as a factor for law school admission--**

Grutter v. Bollinger

Facts. Grutter (P), who was white, applied for admission to the University of Michigan Law School. P had a 3.8 grade point average and an LSAT score of 161. P was denied admission. P sued Bollinger (D), the President of the University, and other officials, claiming that their admissions policy discriminated against her on the basis of race. D's admissions policy sought to achieve diversity in the student body and therefore enrolled a "critical mass" of minority students, including African-Americans, Hispanics, and Native Americans. The district court found that D's use of race as a factor in admissions decisions was unlawful, but the court of appeals reversed. The Supreme Court granted certiorari.

Issue. Does a state university have a compelling state interest in obtaining the educational benefits that flow from a diverse student body, sufficient to justify the use of race as a factor in admissions criteria?

Held. Yes. Judgment affirmed.

- Under the Equal Protection Clause, a racial classification must survive strict scrutiny review. Justice Powell's decision in *Bakke* recognized that student body diversity is a compelling state interest that can justify the use of race in university admissions.
- The Court has never held that only remedial objectives can provide a basis for consideration of race. D in this case was not seeking to remedy past discrimination, but was seeking diversity in its student body, which D considers essential to its educational mission.
- Given the important purpose of public education and the expansive freedoms of speech and thought associated with the university environment, universities have a special niche under the Constitution. D's consideration of race is not

simply to assure racial balancing, which is patently unconstitutional, but instead focuses on the educational benefits that diversity produces. In addition, law schools are the training ground for a large number of civil leaders. To cultivate a set of leaders that the citizens deem legitimate, the path to leadership must be open to talented and qualified individuals of every race and ethnicity.

- D's admissions policy is narrowly tailored to further the compelling state interest. There is no quota. Admissions decisions are based on individual considerations. Race is considered as a "plus" factor during consideration of each individual candidate. Race is not the defining feature of an application. There are many other diversity considerations, including living or traveling abroad, speaking other languages, etc. At the same time, D's program does not unduly burden individuals who are not members of the favored racial and ethnic groups.

- D's race-conscious admissions program must be limited in time, however. In 25 years, racial preferences will likely be unnecessary to further the diversity interest.

Concurrence (Ginsburg, Breyer, JJ.). Minority students still encounter inadequate and unequal educational opportunities, which hopefully will be remedied within the next generation.

Dissent (Renhquist, C.J., Scalia, Kennedy, Thomas, JJ.). D's admissions program is not narrowly tailored to the interest D asserts. Over five years, D has admitted 91 to 108 African-Americans to achieve "critical mass," so that members of that race would not feel isolated or like spokespersons for their race. During the same time, D admitted 13 to 19 Native Americans and between 47 and 56 Hispanics. D offers no explanation why fewer Hispanics and Native Americans are needed to achieve "critical mass." It turns out that the percentage of students admitted in each of these groups corresponds very closely to the percentage of applicants who were in the same groups. This is the type of racial balancing that is not permissible.

Dissent (Kennedy, J.). Justice Powell's approach in *Bakke* is the correct approach to this case. A university admissions program may take account of race as one nonpredominant factor in a system that considers each applicant as an individual, but the program must satisfy strict scrutiny. The Majority here has distorted the strict scrutiny test. D's pursuit of critical mass has mutated into the equivalent of a quota. To be constitutional, a university's compelling interest in a diverse student body must be achieved while safeguarding individual assessment throughout the process.

Concurrence and dissent (Scalia, Thomas, JJ.). The Court invites further litigation about the scope of a "good faith effort" and the extent of the permissible "critical mass." The government should simply not discriminate on the basis of race.

Concurrence and dissent (Thomas, Scalia, JJ.). Minorities can achieve in every avenue of American life without the meddling of university administrators. The Court has deferred to D in an unprecedented way that is inconsistent with the concept of "strict scrutiny." "Selective" admissions should not be protected by the Constitution. If D wants to use the LSAT test, on which D knows blacks perform poorly, D should not also be allowed to "correct" for black underperformance by using racial discrimination. Racial classifications are per se harmful and are not necessary to remedy general societal ills. The Court is correct in holding that racial discrimination that does not help a university to enroll a "critical mass" of underrepresented minority students is unconstitutional. However, the Court should not uphold discrimination even to achieve the critical mass.

---

(2) Race as a preferential factor for undergraduate admission--

Gratz v. Bollinger,

Facts. Gratz (P) and other Caucasian students were denied admission to the University of Michigan as undergraduates. They sued Bollinger (D), the University President, claiming that D's policy of including race as a factor in making admissions decisions was unconstitutional. Under D's policy, an applicant needed 100 points to guarantee admission. Applicants who were African-American, Hispanic, or Native American automatically received 20 points. The district court certified Ps as a class and granted Ps summary judgment on the basis that D's policy was the equivalent of a quota. While the case was under appeal, the Sixth Circuit decided *Grutter*, *supra*. The Supreme Court granted certiorari in both cases, even though the Sixth Circuit had not rendered a judgment in *Gratz*.

Issue. May an undergraduate university automatically confer 20 points, out of the 100 needed to guarantee admission, to every applicant who is a member of a specified race?

Held. No. Judgment affirmed.

- D's policy grants preferences to every minority applicant, solely on the basis of race. This policy is not narrowly tailored to achieve the interest in educational diversity that D claims as justification.

- Under Justice Powell's *Bakke* opinion, each applicant should be assessed as an individual. No single characteristic automatically ensures a specific and identifiable contribution to a university's diversity. D's policy does not include such individualized consideration.

- Although D's policy may be easier to administer than an individualized consideration process, administrative challenges cannot make constitutional an otherwise problematic system.

Concurrence (O'Connor, J.). D's policy relies on a selection index to assign every underrepresented minority applicant the same automatic 20-point bonus without consideration of the background, experiences, or qualities of each individual applicant. D's policy is in sharp contrast to the law school admissions program in *Grutter*, which did allow admissions officers to make individualized judgments.

Concurrence (Thomas, J.). Any use of racial discrimination in higher education admissions is prohibited by the Equal Protection Clause.

Concurrence (Breyer, J.) While I concur with the judgment, I agree with Justice Ginsburg that the government may distinguish between policies of inclusion and exclusion.

Dissent (Souter, J.). D's policy is closer to *Grutter* than to what *Bakke* prohibits. There is no quota, and the 20 points does not convert race into a decisive factor comparable to reserving minority places as prohibited by *Bakke*.

Dissent (Ginsburg, Souter, JJ.). D's policy was designed to help achieve equality in light of the history of discrimination against these minorities. D has not limited or decreased enrollment by any particular racial or ethnic group, and it has not reserved places on the basis of race.

---

(3) Race as a factor in K-12 school assignments--

Parents Involved in Community Schools v. Seattle School District,

Facts. The Seattle school district and the Jefferson County school district (Ds) voluntarily adopted student assignment plans that used race as a factor in determining which public school certain children could attend. The Seattle school district classified children as "white" or "nonwhite," and used its plan to allocate slots in oversubscribed high schools. The Jefferson County school district classified children as "black" or "other," and used its plan to make certain elementary school assignments. Both school districts sought to maintain a racial balance within a predetermined range based on the racial composition of the school district as a whole. Seattle used a series of tiebreakers when its schools were oversubscribed by students. The first tiebreaker was whether the student had a sibling at the school. The second tiebreaker was based on race. If an oversubscribed school was not within 10 percentage points of the district's overall white/nonwhite racial balance, it selected students who would bring the school into balance. Seattle had never operated segregated schools. Although the Jefferson County district had maintained a segregated school system in the past, it achieved unitary status in 2000. Still, in 2001, the county adopted a voluntary assignment plan that required nonmagnet schools to maintain black enrollment between 15% and 50%. Parents whose children were denied assignments to desired schools solely because of race (Ps) sued, contending that the plans denied equal protection. The appellate courts upheld the plans. The Supreme Court granted certiorari.

Issue. May a public school that has not operated legally segregated schools or that has been found to have achieved unitary status choose to classify students by race and rely upon that classification in making school assignments?

Held. No. Judgment reversed and case remanded.

- Government action that distributes benefits or burdens on the basis of individual racial classification is subject to strict scrutiny. Thus, Ds' use of racial classifications in this case must be narrowly tailored to achieve a compelling government interest.

- In the school context, one compelling interest is remedying the effects of past intentional discrimination, but that interest does not apply to either D in this case. The other compelling interest is diversity in higher education, as upheld in *Grutter*. But *Grutter* approved the use of racial classifications as part of a broader assessment of diversity, not merely as an effort to achieve racial balance. And since *Grutter* applied to higher education, it does not govern cases involving Ds.

- In this case, Ds' plans are directed only to racial balance and are not narrowly tailored to achieve educational and social benefits that allegedly flow from racial diversity. The plans are tied solely to racial demographics. However, Ds offer no evidence that the level of racial diversity needed to achieve the asserted educational benefits coincides with the racial demographics of the school districts.

- Ds claim that they have to use these classifications to achieve their stated ends, but in fact they have used the racial classifications to shift only a small number of students. This suggests that the racial classifications are not really necessary. They failed to show that they considered methods other than explicit racial classifications.

- Both parties have debated the *Brown* case, but the plaintiffs in *Brown* asserted that "[t]he Fourteenth Amendment prevents states from according differential treatment to American children on the basis of their color or race." The way to stop discrimination on the basis of race is to stop discrimination on the basis of race.

Concurrence (Thomas, J.). Racial imbalance is not segregation, and the remediation of segregation should not be placed on the same plane as the remediation of racial imbalance. Also, contrary to the dissent's assertion, it has not been shown that coerced racial mixing has any educational benefits or that black achievement depends on integration. Most of the dissent's criticisms of today's decision can be traced to its rejection of the fact that our Constitution is color-blind.

Concurrence in part (Kennedy, J.).

- The government has a legitimate interest in ensuring that all people have equal opportunity regardless of race. School districts cannot ignore the problem of de facto resegregation. To the extent the plurality opinion suggests that the Constitution mandates that state and local school authorities must accept the status quo of racial isolation in schools, it is mistaken.

- State and local authorities should be able to consider the racial makeup of schools and adopt general policies to encourage a diverse student body. However, the small number of students affected by Ds' plans suggests that they could have achieved their stated ends through different means, without treating students differently based solely on race. There are dangers presented by individual classifications based on racial typologies; this can cause new divisiveness.

Dissent (Stevens, J.). *Brown* applied to situations in which only black children were told where to go; white children were not striving to get into black schools.

Dissent (Breyer, Stevens, Souter, Ginsburg, JJ.).

- Because of the evident risk of a return to school systems that are resegregated, many school districts have maintained or extended their integration efforts. Seattle and Louisville are typical of the numerous districts that have devised various plans, often with race-conscious elements, to eradicate earlier school segregation, bring about integration, or prevent de facto resegregation.

- There is a compelling interest in promoting or preserving racial integration of public schools. The three essential elements to the interest at stake are: (i) an interest in setting right the consequences of prior conditions of segregation; (ii) an interest in overcoming the adverse educational effects of highly segregated schools; and (iii) an interest in producing an educational environment that reflects the pluralistic society in which our children will live. Ds' plans are narrowly tailored to achieve their compelling goals.

---

f. **Classifications disadvantaging aliens.** Although Congress has plenary power over admission or exclusion of aliens, state laws discriminating against aliens once admitted are inherently suspect.

1) **State welfare--**

Graham v. Richardson,

Facts. Richardson (P), a resident alien for 13 years, was denied welfare benefits under an Arizona law requiring 15 years of United States residence before an alien could be eligible for welfare benefits. P's case was joined with a similar Pennsylvania case. The respective states appeal district court decisions that the statutes violated the Equal Protection Clause.

Issue. May a state classify potential welfare recipients on the basis of alienage or term of residency?

Held. No. Judgment affirmed.

- The states claim a "special public interest" in favoring their own citizens over aliens in distributing limited welfare benefits. The contemporary validity of that doctrine is in doubt owing to its reliance on the now discarded right/privilege notion. Additionally, an alien as well as a citizen is a "person" for equal protection purposes, and the saving of welfare costs cannot justify an otherwise invidious classification of persons.

- These state statutes also interfere with federal power. Congress forbids entry of indigent aliens, but has not restricted aliens who become indigent after entering the United States. The state statutes would also deny other specific congressional protection of aliens and would amount to an improper assumption of a right to deny entrance and abode within the state. For these reasons, states may not deny welfare benefits to aliens regardless of the term of residency.

Comment. States likewise cannot exclude aliens from all civil service jobs [Sugarman v. Dougall, 413 U.S. 634 (1973)], nor may they prescribe citizenship as a requirement for the practice of law [*In re* Griffiths, 413 U.S. 717 (1973)], nor may they deny financial assistance for higher education to aliens who were eligible to become citizens but chose not to.

2) **Notary public--**

Bernal v. Fainter,

Facts. Bernal (P), a resident alien, worked as a paralegal. P applied to become a notary public, but Texas law required that a notary public be a United States citizen. P challenged the requirement in federal court. The district court found for P, but the court of appeals reversed. P appeals.

Issue. May a state include citizenship as an essential qualification for becoming a notary public?

Held. No. Judgment reversed.

- ♦ State law discrimination against aliens is subject to strict judicial scrutiny; the law must advance a compelling state interest by the least restrictive means available. For example, states cannot prohibit aliens from admission to the state bar, or from the practice of civil engineering.

- ♦ The "political function" exception has been created to allow states to exclude aliens from positions intimately related to the process of democratic self-government. The exception permits states to limit the right to govern to those who are full-fledged members of the political community. Under this exception, states may require police and probation officers to be citizens, and may require aliens to declare their intent to become citizens before teaching in public schools. The exception applies if a two-part test is satisfied: (i) the classification must be specific, neither overinclusive nor underinclusive; and (ii) the classification must be applied only to those public officers who participate directly in the formulation, execution, or review of broad public policy and hence perform functions that go right to the heart of representative government.

- ♦ A notary's duties, though important, do not go to the heart of representative government. They are essentially clerical and ministerial. If the political function exception does not apply to attorneys, it should not apply to notaries public. The state's justifications for the discrimination—that notaries should be familiar with state law and available to testify to acts they have performed—are not shown by the evidence to be compelling. The state requires no proficiency tests of notary applicants, and has not shown that the unavailability of notaries' testimony presents a real problem.

---

3) **Federal regulation--**

Mathews v. Diaz,

Facts. Diaz (P) and other aliens were lawful resident aliens, all over 65 years old, who had been denied participation in Medicare because they had not met federal prerequisites of five-year continuous residence and admission for permanent residence. The district court held the requirements unconstitutional. Mathews (D), representing the United States, appeals.

Issue. May Congress condition an alien's Medicare eligibility on certain residency requirements?

Held. Yes. Judgment reversed.

- ♦ That aliens are not entitled to all the advantages of citizenship is clear. Congress has broad power over naturalization and immigration that cannot be applied to citizens. All aliens need not be placed within a single legal class; Congress properly may distinguish among aliens based on pertinent characteristics.

- ♦ The federal government's flexibility in foreign affairs must not be unnecessarily restricted. Clearly, it is reasonable for Congress to make an alien's eligibility depend on the character and duration of his residency. P merely claims that Congress has drawn the line in the wrong place, but the Court will not substitute its judgment, especially in this area.

- ♦ Rather than proving P's contention, *Graham, supra,* further supports this holding, as it recognizes a difference between state and federal regulation concerning aliens. The federal government clearly has authority to classify aliens; such classifications apply equally throughout the nation.

Comment. When a benefit as important as federal employment is involved, any determination that national interests justify a denial to aliens must be made by Congress or the President—not an administrative agency with a limited range of concerns. [Hampton v. Mow Sun Wong, 426 U.S. 88 (1976)—refusal to employ aliens by the Civil Service Commission denied "liberty" without due process]

---

g. **Nonmarital children.**

1) **Basic rule.** Whether the impact of legislation on nonmarital children requires equal protection analysis depends on whom the legislation was intended to affect and whether its effect is sufficient to treat it as discrimination against nonmarital children.

2) **Proof of paternity for inheritance.** In *Lalli v. Lalli*, 439 U.S. 259 (1978), the Court held that a state may require a certain form of proof of paternity before allowing nonmarital, but not marital, children to inherit from their fathers by intestate succession. The majority reasoned that the state has a legitimate interest in providing for the just and orderly disposition of property at death. The Court found that particular problems of proof arise when an alleged heir is born out of wedlock and that spurious claims could be difficult to expose.

3) **Proof of paternity for child support.** In *Clark v. Jeter*, 486 U.S. 456 (1988), the Court held that a state could not impose a requirement that illegitimate children bring paternity suits within six years of birth in order to receive child support. Legitimate children had no such time limit on their right to seek child support.

h. Discrimination against the mentally retarded--

Cleburne v. Cleburne Living Center, Inc.,

Facts. Under a city zoning ordinance, group homes for the mentally retarded may operate only with a special permit that requires the signatures of property owners within 200 feet of the property to be used. The applicants were unable to obtain the required signatures in a residential neighborhood. The lower courts held the ordinance unconstitutional, and the Supreme Court granted certiorari.

Issue. Is mental retardation a suspect class for equal protection analysis?

Held. No. Judgment affirmed on other grounds.

- ♦ Generally, under the Equal Protection Clause, legislation is presumed valid and will be upheld if the classification drawn by the statute is rationally related to a legitimate state interest. Certain types of classifications are subject to strict scrutiny, others to heightened scrutiny.

- ♦ The court of appeals held that mental retardation is a quasi-suspect classification. However, the legislature has a legitimate interest in providing for the various problems of the mentally retarded, and courts are ill-equipped to make substantive judgment about legislative decisions in this area. Legislatures have addressed the problems of the mentally retarded and need the flexibility of the rational basis test to be effective.

- ♦ Under the rational basis test, however, the ordinance is defective. It does not apply to nursing homes for the aged or convalescents, apartment houses, sanitariums, or boarding houses. Nothing in the record explains how the permit requirement for only facilities for the mentally retarded is rationally related to any governmental purpose.

Concurrence (Stevens, J., Burger, C.J.). The mentally retarded have historically been subject to unfair mistreatment. This ordinance reflects the irrational fears of neighboring property owners, not a concern for the welfare of the mentally retarded.

Concurrence and dissent (Marshall, Brennan, Blackmun, JJ.). The Court has created a "second order" rational basis review. Normally under the rational basis test, the legislature does not have to address all ills at once. Thus, zoning plans based on fears of proximity to a high school, location in a floodplain, and crowded living conditions or increased congestion are perfectly valid, even if applied one step at a time. However, the class of mentally retarded persons deserves heightened scrutiny, and the Court reaches the correct result.

i. **Discrimination against homosexuals.**

1) **Special status--**

Romer v. Evans,

Facts. Colorado voters adopted an amendment to the Colorado Constitution that prohibited all legislative, executive, or judicial action at any level of state or local government designed to confer a protected status upon, or to allow claims of discrimination by, any person based on homosexual, lesbian, or bisexual orientation. Evans (P) initiated litigation to have the amendment declared unconstitutional. The Colorado Supreme Court held that the amendment was subject to strict scrutiny because it infringed the fundamental right of homosexuals to participate in the political process, and, after remand to the trial court, held the amendment unconstitutional. The Supreme Court granted certiorari.

Issue. May a state prohibit governmental action that confers a protected status upon, or allows claims of discrimination by, any person based on homosexual, lesbian, or bisexual orientation?

Held. No. Judgment affirmed.

- ♦ D claims that the amendment simply puts homosexuals in the same position as all other persons; *i.e.,* it does no more than deny homosexuals special rights. However, the actual effect of the amendment is to put homosexuals in a solitary class with respect to transactions and relations in both the private and governmental spheres. It imposes a special disability upon these persons by forbidding them to seek or enjoy the safeguards against discrimination that other groups can enjoy.

- ♦ To reconcile the Equal Protection Clause with the reality that most legislation creates classes, the Court has held that legislation that neither burdens a fundamental right nor targets a suspect class will be upheld so long as the classification bears a rational relation to some legitimate end. The amendment in this case has the peculiar property of imposing a broad and undifferentiated disability on a single named group, and its breadth is so discontinuous with the purported reasons for it that it cannot be explained by anything but animus toward homosexuals. As such, it lacks a rational relationship to legitimate state interests.

- ♦ Animus toward a politically unpopular group cannot constitute a legitimate state interest. The interest asserted by D is respect for other citizens' freedom of association, such as the liberties of employers or landlords who oppose homosexuality. But the breadth of the amendment is so far removed from these justifications that they cannot reasonably be deemed the true legitimate purpose of the amendment.

Dissent (Scalia, J., Rehnquist, C.J., Thomas, J.). This amendment is a modest attempt to preserve traditional sexual mores against the efforts of a politically powerful minority to revise those mores through the use of the laws. The majority has made the Court accept the proposition that opposition to homosexuality is as reprehensible as racial or religious bias. But the Constitution says nothing about the subject, and the resolution of such public values should be left to the democratic processes, not the courts. The only denial of equal treatment articulated by the Court is that homosexuals may not obtain preferential treatment without modifying the state constitution. Furthermore, there was a legitimate rational basis for the amendment. In *Bowers v. Hardwick*, *supra*, the Court held that the Constitution does not prohibit making homosexual conduct a crime. If a state may make homosexual conduct criminal, it should be allowed to enact laws disfavoring homosexual conduct; and, if so, it should certainly be allowed to adopt a provision that does not even disfavor homosexual conduct but merely prohibits special protections for homosexuals. The animus toward homosexuals—moral disapproval of homosexual conduct—is the same "animus" that for centuries led to criminalization of homosexual conduct. Congress itself required the states of Arizona, New Mexico, Oklahoma, and Utah to adopt, as a condition of statehood, a ban against polygamy. The Court has approved this criminalization of polygamy; thus the Court has today concluded that the perceived social harm of polygamy is a legitimate concern of government, and the perceived social harm of homosexuality is not. The amendment is simply designed to prevent piecemeal deterioration of the sexual morality favored by a majority of Coloradans, and should be upheld.

---

2) **Protection of sexual privacy--**

Lawrence v. Texas. *See* *supra*

4. **Personal Liberties.**

a. **The right to marry--**

Zablocki v. Redhail. *See* *supra*

b. **Voting and elections.**

1) **Introduction.** Several constitutional provisions relate to voting and elections. Consider whether equal protection analysis adds anything to the outcome of cases controlled by other constitutional provisions.

a) **Fourteenth Amendment.**

"Section 1. . . . No State shall . . . deny to any person within its jurisdiction the equal protection of the laws."

"Section 5. The Congress shall have power to enforce, by appropriate legislation, the provisions of this article."

b) **Fifteenth Amendment.**

"Section 1. The right of citizens of the United States to vote shall not be denied or abridged by the United States or by any State on account of race, color, or previous condition of servitude."

"Section 2. The Congress shall have power to enforce this article by appropriate legislation."

c) **Nineteenth Amendment.** "The right of citizens of the United States to vote shall not be denied or abridged by the United States or by any State on account of sex."

d) **Twenty-Fourth Amendment.** "The right of citizens of the United States to vote in any primary or other election for President or Vice President, for electors for President or Vice President, or for Senator or Representative in Congress, shall not be denied or abridged by the United States or any State by reason of failure to pay any poll tax or other tax."

e) **Twenty-Sixth Amendment.** "The right of citizens of the United States, who are eighteen years of age or older, to vote shall not be denied or abridged by the United States or by any State on account of age."

2) **Legislative districting.**

a) **Federal vs. state apportionment.** In federal elections, representation must reflect the total population as precisely as possible. More flexibility is permitted in apportionment of state legislatures, but grossly disproportionate districts are not allowed. State apportionment may not be used to further discrimination, but numerical deviations resulting from political considerations may be allowed.

b) **State apportionment--**

Reynolds v. Sims,

Facts. Sims (P) and others challenged the apportionment of the Alabama legislature, which was based on the 1900 federal census and thus seriously discriminated against voters who lived in areas whose population has grown disproportionately in the intervening years. The district court ordered temporary reapportionment. Reynolds (D) and other state officials appeal.

Issue. Must a state apportion its legislative districts on the basis of population?

Held. Yes. Judgment affirmed.

- The right to vote is essential to a democratic society, and is denied by abasement or dilution of a citizen's vote just as effectively as by wholly prohibiting the free exercise of the franchise. The fundamental principle of representative government is one of equal representation for equal numbers of people, regardless of race, sex, economic status, or place of residence within a state.

- The Equal Protection Clause guarantees the opportunity for equal participation by all voters in the election of state legislators. Therefore, votes cannot be weighed differently on the basis of where voters happen to reside. This applies whether the state legislature is unicameral or bicameral.

- The federal Congress cannot be taken as a guide for state legislative district apportionment because it arose from unique historical circumstances and represents a union of sovereigns. Political subdivisions or states never have been sovereign entities in that sense.

- Each state district must contain as nearly an equal population as possible, although precision, being impossible, is not required. Substantial equality of population must be the overriding objective. States need not perpetually update their apportionment plans, but there must be a reasonable plan for periodic readjustment.

Comment. In some cases, states may justify otherwise unacceptable deviations in state legislative districts on the basis of maintaining the integrity of political subdivisions. [Mahan v. Howell, 410 U.S. 315 (1973)] A state may consider political factors as well as census data in creating its legislative districts. [Gaffney v. Cummings, 412 U.S. 735 (1973)] The very essence of districting is to produce a more "politically fair" result than elections at large, in which the winning party would take all legislative seats. Political considerations are inseparable from districting and apportionment. The danger arises from manipulation intended to minimize or eliminate the political strength of any group or party.

---

c) Population equality required--

Karcher v. Daggett,

Facts. The New Jersey legislature reapportioned the state's congressional districts. The districts were described as "bizarre" configurations that disregarded geographical compactness and county boundaries. Each district did not have the same population. The largest district, with a population of 527,472, had only 3,674 people more than the smallest, which was less than a 1% deviation. The state legislature had available other plans with much smaller population deviations, one with a maximum population difference of only 2,375. Once the reapportionment plan was enacted, a group of congressmen and others (Ps) challenged it under Article 1, Section 2 of the Constitution. The district court held the plan unconstitutional, and Ds appeal.

Issue. Must a congressional apportionment plan represent a good faith effort to achieve population equality to be upheld, even if the population of the largest district is less than 1% greater than the population of the smallest district?

Held. Yes. Judgment affirmed.

- The Constitution establishes a high standard of justice and common sense for apportionment of congressional districts. Exact mathematical equality may be impossible, but districts must be apportioned to achieve population equality as nearly as is practicable.

- Ps must prove that the population differences among districts could have been reduced or eliminated by a good faith effort to equalize them. If Ps succeed, the state must prove that each significant variance between districts was necessary to achieve some legitimate objective.

- Ds claim that because the population deviation is smaller than the predictable census errors, the existing plan should be regarded per se as the product of good faith efforts to equalize population. However, the only standard that fulfills the Constitution's ideal of equal representation is total population equality. Equality must therefore be the standard in assessing congressional district apportionment plans.

- Because Ps have satisfied their burden of showing that the population differences could have been reduced, the state must justify the differences. There are several legislative policies that, if consistently applied, might justify some variance. These include making districts compact, respecting municipal boundaries, preserving the cores of prior districts, and avoiding contests between incumbents. Ds here have not been able to justify the population deviations in their plan, however.

Concurrence (Stevens, J.). Ps also claimed that the shapes of the districts demonstrated that the plan was the product of political gerrymandering, which is unconstitutional. The Equal Protection Clause requires every state to govern impartially, so that gerrymandering against any cognizable group of voters is unconstitutional. Inquiry into the process that led to the adoption of this plan reveals that the legislative majority selected it out of overt partisanship. Consideration of the shapes of the districts should be a factor, as well as the mathematical equality of the populations residing therein.

Dissent (White, J., Burger, C.J., Powell, Rehnquist, JJ.). The Court unreasonably insists on unattainable perfection in equalizing congressional districts. Under the Court's ruling, any variance between districts must be considered significant. It would be better to use the approach adopted for dealing with state legislative apportionment, whereby certain small deviations do not constitute a prima facie constitutional violation.

Dissent (Powell, J.). Gerrymandering presents a greater threat to equal representation than does failure to attain equal populations based on inexact census figures. Constitutional challenges to partisan gerrymandering should be heard, but this issue was not addressed by the district court, so we should not reach it here.

---

d) Race as a primary factor in reapportioning districts--

Miller v. Johnson,

Facts. Twenty-seven percent of Georgia's population is black. The 1990 census gave Georgia an 11th congressional district. Previously, the state had one majority-black district. After two redistricting plans were rejected by the United States Attorney General, the state legislature adopted one that included three majority-minority districts. One of the plans used narrow corridors to connect two cities containing black neighborhoods. Miller and others (Ps) challenged the reapportionment. The district court held that race was the predominant, overriding factor in designing the plan and granted relief. Johnson (D) appeals.

Issue. May a state use race as the primary factor in designing reapportionment districts?

Held. No. Judgment affirmed.

- The claim in *Shaw v. Reno,* 509 U.S. 630 (1993), was not a vote dilution claim, but an equal protection claim based on allegations that the state has used race as a basis for separating voters into districts. A state may not separate its citizens into different voting districts on the basis of race any more than it may separate them on the basis of race on its parks, buses, golf courses, etc.
- *Shaw* does not require that the challenged district be bizarre on its face. Shape

is merely circumstantial evidence of intent to use race for its own sake. The state may not apply the stereotype that persons of the same or a particular race share a single political interest.

- The distinction between being aware of racial considerations and being motivated by them can be difficult to make, and federal courts must be careful not to improperly intrude upon districting legislation. Thus, a plaintiff has the burden to show that race was the predominant factor motivating the legislature's decision to place a significant number of voters within or outside a particular district. This means showing that the traditional race-neutral districting principles such as compactness, contiguity, etc., were subordinated to racial considerations.

- The state's claim that it had a compelling interest in complying with the Attorney General's requirements is not acceptable to the extent that the Attorney General required more than is required by the Voting Rights Act. In this case, the Attorney General's objective was to maximize majority-black districts, which is not required by federal law. The Attorney General used the Voting Rights Act to demand the very kind of racial stereotyping forbidden by the Fourteenth Amendment.

Concurrence (O'Connor, J.). The Court's threshold standard allows judicial review only in extreme instances where the legislature subordinates traditional race-neutral districting principles to racial considerations.

Dissent (Stevens, J.). Ps' standing in this case depends on the unacceptable premise that voters of a particular race share the same political interests and prefer the same candidates for office.

Dissent (Ginsburg, Stevens, Breyer, Souter, JJ.). The *Shaw* plan was not a problem because race was a factor, but because nonracial factors were virtually excluded. In this case, race did not overwhelm the other factors. The plan in this case did group people according to ethnicity, but that is a common factor for districting plans.

---

e) Private citizen challenge to redistricting--

Vieth v. Jubelirer

Facts. The 2000 census resulted in a decrease of Pennsylvania's Congressional delegation from 21 Representatives to 19. Consequently, the Pennsylvania General Assembly, represented in this case by Jubelirer (D), the President of the Pennsylvania Senate, drew a map with new election districts. Vieth (P) and other Democratic voters challenged the redistricting, claiming that it was an unconstitutional political gerrymander. The U.S. District Court dismissed Ps' claim. Ps appeal.

Issue. May a private citizen challenge a state legislature's redistricting plan in federal court?

Held. No. Judgment affirmed.

- In *Davis v. Bandemer*, 478 U.S. 109 (1986), the Court held that a political party has equal protection rights that can be violated by an improper legislative apportionment plan. *Bandemer* should be overruled because political gerrymandering claims are nonjusticiable; there are no judicially discernible and manageable standards for adjudicating such claims.

- Political gerrymanders existed before the Constitution was framed, and the Constitution provides a remedy for potential problems by giving Congress power to "make or alter" federal election districts drawn by state legislatures. *Bandemer* extended that control to the courts through the Equal Protection Clause, but nothing in the Constitution establishes a judicially enforceable limit on the political considerations that the state legislatures and Congress may use in districting.

- Eighteen years of experience with the *Bandemer* ruling has left the courts without any judiciable standards to apply. After considering several *Bandemer* claims, the lower courts have consistently refused judicial intervention even under *Bandemer*. There is no reason to retain *Bandemer*.

- Ps rely on *Miller v. Johnson, supra*, where the test involves a challenge to the particular district in which the plaintiffs lived, based on the predominant intent of the gerrymandering. The predominant motivation test is useless when applied to a statewide redistricting. Even if the challenged redistricting produces disproportional representation, there is no constitutional right to proportional representation.

- Three of the dissents in this case propose different standards for adjudicating political gerrymandering claims, each with serious unresolved problems.

- Justice Kennedy concurs in the judgment on the ground that there are no existing manageable standards for measuring whether apolitical gerrymander burdens the representational rights of a party's voters. While he would have the courts continue to adjudicate such claims because such a standard may one day be discovered, this disposition is not legally available. The Court can affirm because political districting presents a nonjusticiable question or because the correct standard has not been met, but not because the Court does not know what the correct standard is.

Concurrence (Kennedy, J.). If a limited and precise rationale were found to correct an established violation of the Constitution in some redistricting cases, an injured party should have the possibility of judicial relief. For a gerrymander to violate the Constitution, Ps would have to show that the political classifications used were applied in an invidious manner or in a way unrelated to any legitimate legislative objective. So far, there are no agreed-upon substantive principles of fairness to apply to districting cases. If the courts refuse to consider claims of partisan gerrymandering, the use of sophisticated computer technology could permit abusive partisan favoritism.

Dissent (Stevens, J.). Five members of the Court believe political gerrymandering claims are justiciable, although for different reasons. Equal justice requires the state to govern impartially. It cannot do this if partisanship is the legislature's sole motivation, forsaking all neutral principles. Here, Ps have alleged that D's redistricting plan was created "solely" to effectuate the interests of Republicans, which, at least with respect to Ps' own district, violates equal protection principles.

Dissent (Souter, Ginsburg, JJ.). Too much partisan competition is unconstitutional. The question is, how much is too much? To have a case, a plaintiff would have to show: (i) his membership in a cohesive political group or party; (ii) deviations in his district indicating a disregard for traditional districting principles; (iii) specific correlations between that disregard and the distribution of the population of his group; (iv) a hypothetical district that deviates less from traditional districting principles; and (v) intentional action by defendants to adversely affect his group. After a plaintiff makes out a prima facie case, defendants would be required to justify their decision by referring to objectives other than pure partisan advantage.

Dissent (Breyer, J.). Normally, the legislature does not abuse the process when drawing districting lines. However, the Constitution does not allow the use of purely political boundary-drawing factors in an unjustified way so as to entrench a minority in power. The use of computerized mapping makes this potential danger more possible than before, and the courts may need to intervene to prevent the harm to basic democratic principles.

---

3) Voter qualifications--

Harper v. Virginia State Board of Elections,

Facts. Harper (P) and other Virginia residents brought suit to have Virginia's poll tax declared unconstitutional. The district court, under *Breedlove v. Suttles*, 302 U.S. 277 (1937), dismissed P's complaint. P appeals.

Issue. May a state exact a poll tax as a condition for exercise of the right to vote?

Held. No. Judgment reversed.

- Once the franchise is granted to the electorate, lines may not be drawn that are inconsistent with the Equal Protection Clause of the Fourteenth Amendment.

- Lines drawn by voter affluence or by the payment of any fee violate equal protection. Undoubtedly, states may impose reasonable voter qualifications, but these must pass careful scrutiny, since the franchise preserves other basic civil and political rights. Wealth or payment of a fee is an irrelevant factor in measuring a voter's qualifications. Notions of what constitutes equal treatment for purposes of the Equal Protection Clause do change. *Breedlove* is overruled.

Dissent (Black, J.). The Court has ignored the original meaning of the Constitution and has instead given the Equal Protection Clause a new meaning according to the Court's idea of a better governmental policy. Such changes are unjustifiable; they should be made only through the proper amendment procedure.

Dissent (Harlan, Stewart, JJ.). The decision to abolish state poll taxes for state elections ought to be made by the states, not the Supreme Court.

Comment. State residence requirements have been held to violate the Equal Protection Clause because they divide voters into two classes—old and new residents—and discriminate against the latter. [*See* Dunn v. Blumstein, 405 U.S. 330 (1972)—using the burden on the right to travel, as well as the burden on the right to vote, to invalidate such state residence requirements] However, the Court has recognized the need for some registration requirements, and upheld a 50-day residency and registration requirement where necessary to prepare voters' lists, etc. [*See* Marston v. Lewis, 410 U.S. 679 (1973)]

---

4) **Filing fees.** A state has a legitimate interest in requiring candidates to pay a filing fee to get their names on the ballots; *e.g.,* to keep the ballot within manageable and understandable limits and to defray the administrative costs of an election. However, such goals cannot be pursued at the expense of excluding serious candidates from access to the ballot (no "compelling state interest"). [Lubin v. Panish, 415 U.S. 709 (1974)]

   a) Thus, a state law that required filing fees of up to $8,900 to get a candidate's name on the primary election ballot was held invalid as discriminatory against candidates of modest means and the voters who supported them. The state was required to find other alternative means to defray its election expenses and limit the ballot size. [Bullock v. Carter, 405 U.S. 134 (1972)]

b) Moreover, it has been held that ***any*** filing fee requirement violates the Equal Protection Clause insofar as an ***indigent*** candidate is concerned, where the state fails to provide an alternative means for ballot access.

c. **Travel and interstate migration.**

1) **Introduction.** A citizen has a constitutional right to travel freely from state to state. State durational residence requirements that would impair this right must be justified by a "compelling" state interest, at least where they affect the citizen's right to receive some vital government benefit or service. However, states may apply a requirement of residency at the time of (and during) receipt of governmental benefits, subject only to the "traditional" test. [*See, e.g.,* McCarthy v. Philadelphia Civil Service Commission, 424 U.S. 645 (1976)—requiring personal residence at place of governmental employment does not violate the right to travel]

2) **State welfare--**

Shapiro v. Thompson,

Facts. The Thompsons (Ps) were denied welfare benefits solely because they had not been residents of Connecticut for a full year before their application. Two similar cases were joined before the United States Supreme Court. In all three instances, the district courts found that the state's denial of benefits to otherwise eligible residents of less than one year constituted an invidious discrimination denying the plaintiffs equal protection of the laws. Shapiro (D), representing Connecticut, appeals.

Issue. May a state create a one-year residency requirement as a condition for receiving state welfare assistance?

Held. No. Judgment affirmed.

- D argues that the statute preserves the fiscal integrity of state public assistance programs, which it clearly does, but only by discouraging the influx of poor families needing assistance. However, a state purpose of inhibiting immigration by needy persons is constitutionally impermissible as a burden on the right to travel. Any law whose sole purpose is the chilling of the exercise of constitutional rights is invalid. D's argument that the statute intends to discourage immigration of needy people seeking solely to obtain larger benefits does not save it from this constitutional defect since, in such circumstances, it still infringes on those persons' right to travel.

- States may not withhold welfare benefits from short-term residents who have contributed through taxes any more than they may restrict state services such as fire and police protection to long-term residents.

- Because the classification here touches on a fundamental constitutional right, it must be judged under the strict standard of whether it promotes a compelling state interest. D's assertion that other administrative objectives are served by the one-year requirement falls short of satisfying this standard. D claims the statutes are approved by federal legislation. Even if true, it is the state statutes, by themselves, which must be examined for constitutional defects. Congress cannot authorize the states to violate the Equal Protection Clause.

- The state statutes violate the Equal Protection Clause and are invalid—the District of Columbia provision is invalid under the Due Process Clause of the Fifth Amendment.

Concurrence (Stewart, J.). The Court has simply recognized and protected an established constitutional right.

Dissent (Warren, C.J., Black, J.). Congress has the power both to impose minimal nationwide residence requirements and to authorize the states to do so. Since the states here acted pursuant to congressional authorization, the statutes should be upheld.

Dissent (Harlan, J.). The "compelling interest" doctrine constitutes an increasingly significant exception to the rule that a statute does not deny equal protection if it is rationally related to a legitimate government interest.

---

3) **Voting.** State residence requirements have been held to violate the Equal Protection Clause because they divide voters into two classes—old and new residents—and discriminate against the latter. *See Dunn v. Blumstein*, 405 U.S. 330 (1972), which used the burden on the right to travel, as well as the burden on the right to vote, to invalidate such state residence requirements. However, the Court has recognized the need for some registration requirements, and has upheld a 50-day residency and registration requirement where necessary to prepare voters' lists, etc. [*See* Marston v. Lewis, 410 U.S. 679 (1973)]

4) **Medical care.** Medical care is a basic necessity of life, and thus to deny such care to a nonresident would penalize an immigrant for exercising the right to travel. Thus a state may not require a year's residence before providing even nonemergency medical care to

an indigent. [Memorial Hospital v. Maricopa County, 415 U.S. 250 (1974)]

5) **Domestic relations--**

Sosna v. Iowa,

Facts. Sosna (P) moved from New York to Iowa with her children and within two months petitioned for a dissolution of her marriage. The Iowa court dismissed P's petition for lack of jurisdiction, since P had not met Iowa's (D's) one-year residency requirement for invoking its divorce jurisdiction. The district court upheld the requirement, and D appeals.

Issue. May a state include a durational residency requirement as part of its regulation of domestic relations?

Held. Yes. Judgment affirmed.

- Domestic relations have long been regarded as a virtually exclusive province of the states. Most states do, in fact, impose durational residency requirements for divorce. D's requirement may reasonably be justified on grounds other than purely budgetary considerations or administrative convenience, which were involved in *Shapiro* and *Maricopa County*, *supra*.

- D might recognize the significant consequences of divorce and insist on more than a minimal attachment to the state. Additionally, D might seek to avoid interfering with another state's interests and might seek to minimize the susceptibility of its own divorce decrees to collateral attack. Nor does the statute create a permanent and irrebuttable presumption of nonresidence.

Dissent (White, J.). The case is moot and should not be decided.

Dissent (Marshall, Brennan, JJ.). The Court has ignored the test established by *Shapiro* and instead used an ad hoc balancing test. Application of the *Shapiro* test compels reversal here. If the waiting period is essentially a penalty (interferes with a necessity), it is unconstitutional.

6) **Duration of residency and distribution of state resource income--**

Zobel v. Williams,

Facts. Alaska enacted a statute by which dividends from the state's permanent fund derived from mineral royalties would be distributed to the state's adult residents depending on how long they were residents of the state. Each resident would receive one dividend unit for each year of residence. Zobel (P), a relatively recent Alaska resident, challenged the statute on equal protection grounds. The Alaska courts upheld the plan, and P appeals.

Issue. May a state distribute income derived from its natural resources to the citizens of the state in amounts depending on the length of the individual citizen's residence?

Held. No. Judgment reversed.

- ♦ The Equal Protection Clause applies whenever a state distributes benefits unequally. The asserted state purposes here are: (i) a financial incentive for citizens to maintain residence in Alaska; (ii) incentive for prudent management of the fund; and (iii) recognition of the contributions made by citizens over the years.

- ♦ The first two purposes are not rationally related to the distinctions made. The third is not a legitimate state purpose. Governmental services and benefits may not be apportioned according to past taxes or other contributions of the citizens involved, nor may a state favor established residents over new residents. Therefore, the statute denied equal protection.

Concurrence (Brennan, Marshall, Blackmun, Powell, JJ.). Any distinctions must be based upon relevant characteristics. The length of residence does not necessarily reflect the value of contributions made to the state.

Concurrence (O'Connor, J.). A state may recognize past contributions of its citizens. However, it must comply with the protections of the Privileges and Immunities Clause.

Dissent (Rehnquist, J.). This distribution scheme is essentially economic regulation; equal protection is not involved. The state is merely dividing its resources among its citizens.

7) Irrelevance of historical fact of residence--

Attorney General of New York v. Soto-Lopez,

Facts. Soto-Lopez (P) was a veteran of the United States Army and a long-time resident of New York, but he had been a resident of Puerto Rico when he joined the Army. P passed the New York City civil service exam and applied for a veteran's preference, but under New York law the preference applied only to veterans who were New York residents when they joined the service. Accordingly, P was denied the preference. P sued, and the New York attorney general (D) intervened. The district court dismissed the complaint, but the court of appeals reversed, holding that the prior residence requirement violated the Equal Protection Clause and the right to travel. D appeals.

Issue. May a state provide civil service employment preference only to veterans who were residents of the state when they entered the military?

Held. No. Judgment affirmed.

- ♦ The freedom to travel among the states, although not explicitly provided for in the Constitution, has long been recognized as a basic constitutional liberty. A state impairs this right when it uses any classification that serves to penalize the exercise of the right to travel.

- ♦ The creation of different classes of residents also implicates the Equal Protection Clause, and the state must show a compelling justification if it burdens the right to migrate. The basic rule is that the right to migrate protects some residents of a state from being treated differently from other residents simply because of the timing of their migration.

- ♦ In this case, P was denied a significant benefit granted to all veterans similarly situated, the only exception being their state of residence when they entered the military. This can make the difference in obtaining civil service employment and constitutes a burden on the right to migrate. D must show its classification is necessary to accomplish a compelling state interest.

- ♦ D claims four interests: (i) encouraging New York residents to join the military; (ii) compensating residents for their service; (iii) inducing veterans to return to New York after their service; and (iv) employing experienced public servants. However, none of these interests justifies the exclusion of applicants who were not New York residents when they joined the military.

Concurrence (Burger, C.J.). The judgment should be affirmed under the Equal Protection Clause as construed by *Zobel, supra*, without reaching the right to travel.

Concurrence (White, J.). The classification is irrational and cannot pass equal protection analysis; the right to travel is not sufficiently implicated to be discussed.

Dissent (O'Connor, Rehnquist, Stevens, JJ.). This case should be evaluated under the Privileges and Immunities Clause. New York has merely recognized the contribution and sacrifice of its citizens, which is a valid state interest, and has not infringed on any constitutionally protected individual interest, including the right to settle in another state under the Privileges and Immunities Clause. The law does not prevent P from moving to New York, and it does not place him at a disadvantage vis-a-vis most other New York residents. It in no way penalizes P for moving to New York.

8) **Reconsideration of *Shapiro*--**

Saenz v. Roe,

Facts. In response to high welfare benefit payments, California began limiting welfare benefits, for the first 12 months of a new citizen's residency in the state, to the level received by the individual in his previous state of residence. This change was apparently permitted by Congress in a statute titled Temporary Assistance to Needy Families ("TANF"). Roe and others (Ps) challenged the California statute. The lower courts held the California statute unconstitutional. The Supreme Court granted certiorari.

Issue. May a state limit the welfare benefits of new citizens to the amount the new citizen would have received in his previous state of residency?

Held. No. Judgment affirmed.

- D claims that, unlike the law in *Shapiro, supra,* the California statute here does not penalize the right of travel because new arrivals are not ineligible for benefits.

- The right to travel includes at least three components:

  (i) The right to enter and leave another state;

  (ii) The right to be treated as a welcome visitor; and

  (iii) The right to elect to become a permanent resident and to be treated like other citizens of the new state.

- The statute in this case does not directly impair the right to free interstate movement. As for visitor status, there are some situations in which a noncitizen may be treated differently from a citizen, such as in tuition fees for a state university. But this case involves the third aspect of the right to travel, since Ps became residents of the state.

- The Privileges and Immunities Clause of the Fourteenth Amendment protects the third element of the right to travel. Under that Clause, a United States citizen can become a citizen of any state by a bona fide residence therein, with the same rights as other citizens of that state. The right to travel includes the citizen's right to be treated equally in the new state of residence, so the discriminatory classification is itself a penalty. The Citizenship Clause expressly equates citizenship with residence, and does not allow for degrees of citizenship based on length of residence. California has created a hierarchy of subclasses based on the original state from which the immigrants came. Yet neither the duration of Ps' California residence, nor the identity of their prior states of residence, has any relevance to their need for benefits.

- D claims that the statute will save the state approximately $11 million per year, but the state's legitimate interest in saving money does not justify discrimination among equally eligible citizens.

Dissent (Rehnquist, C.J., Thomas, J.). The right to travel is distinct from the right to become a citizen. In fact, Ps had to stop traveling to become citizens of California. The Court has confused the right to travel with the right to enjoy the privileges of citizenship. The Court has ignored the state's need to assure that only persons who establish a bona fide residence receive the benefits provided to current residents of the state. States cannot determine an individual's subjective intent, so the Court has allowed states to impose durational residence requirements to test intention. States can impose a residence requirement prior to granting the right to educational benefits, the right to terminate a marriage, or the right to vote in primary elections, and they should be able to do the same for welfare benefits.

Dissent (Thomas, J., Rehnquist, C.J.). The Court's reliance on the Privileges and Immunities Clause is surprising because that Clause has been drained of meaning. The Court should consider how the Clause relates to equal protection and substantive due process.

Comments.

- The Court noted that Congress approved durational residence requirements, but held that Congress cannot authorize the states to violate the Fourteenth Amendment. The Citizenship Clause is a limitation on the powers of the federal government as well as the state governments.

- In *Williams v. Vermont*, 472 U.S. 14 (1985), the Court disallowed a Vermont statute that exempted Vermont residents from the state motor vehicle use tax when they purchased a vehicle in another reciprocating state, but did not allow the same exemption to nonresidents who did the same thing before becoming Vermont residents. The Court found no relevant difference between the two classes that would justify the disparate treatment.

---

9) Disadvantage to nonresidents--

Metropolitan Life Insurance Co. v. Ward,

Facts. The state of Alabama imposed a gross premium tax of 1% on all types of insurance premiums collected by its domestic insurance companies, but out-of-state companies were required to pay a 3% tax on life insurance premiums and 4% on other types of insurance premiums. Metropolitan Life Insurance Company (P) challenged the tax provision as a violation of the Equal Protection Clause. The trial court upheld the statute because it encouraged the formation of new insurance companies in Alabama and encouraged capital investment by out-of-state companies in Alabama. The appellate court affirmed in part but remanded for an evidentiary hearing as to whether the law was rationally related to the legitimate state purpose. P, having waived its right to an evidentiary hearing, appeals.

Issue. May a state impose a higher tax on out-of-state insurance companies than it imposes on in-state companies?

Held. No. Judgment reversed.

- ♦ It is clear that while a state may have some authority to exclude foreign corporations from doing business within its boundaries, it may not impose more onerous taxes on such corporations than those imposed on domestic corporations unless the discrimination bears a rational relation to a legitimate state purpose. P has waived the rational relation requirement in this case, so the only issue is whether D's asserted purposes are legitimate.

- ♦ D claims that encouraging the formation of new domestic insurance companies is a legitimate state purpose that should survive equal protection scrutiny. However, D's reliance on other cases involving state efforts to promote interstate business is misplaced, because D's law discriminates solely to promote domestic industry. This is the very type of action the Equal Protection Clause was designed to prevent.

- ♦ D argues that because the insurance industry is exempt from Commerce Clause restrictions by the McCarran-Ferguson Act, it is inappropriate to apply Commerce Clause analysis using equal protection language. However, D ignores the significant difference between the two clauses. A legitimate state interest is upheld under the Commerce Clause if it outweighs the burden it imposes on interstate commerce, but under the Equal Protection Clause, it is upheld if it is rationally related to that purpose. One protects interstate commerce, the other protects persons against unconstitutional state discrimination. At any rate, promoting domestic business by discriminating against nonresident competitors is not a legitimate state purpose.

- ♦ D's second purpose was to encourage investment in Alabama assets. This is not a legitimate state purpose to be promoted by discrimination. Domestic insurers benefit from the lower tax regardless of whether they invest, and nonresident companies cannot benefit from the lower tax even if they do invest.

Dissent (O'Connor, Brennan, Marshall, Rehnquist, JJ.). P relies on the Equal Protection Clause because it is not a citizen for privileges and immunities purposes and cannot assert the Commerce Clause. Equal protection challenges to local economic regulation bear a heavy burden, and tax classifications normally merit strong judicial deference. The majority has avoided the proper two-step analysis and determined that

D's objectives are improper because the means used is discriminatory taxation; this despite the fact that Congress itself has legitimated these objectives. Instead, the classification should be upheld because it bears a rational relationship to a legitimate purpose, the only proper equal protection consideration.

---

d. **Economically disadvantaged persons.**

1) **Access to the courts by the poor.**

a) **The concept of poverty.** Poverty is a relative concept and must be measured by reference to the particular need or service under consideration.

(1) **Right to counsel.** The criterion here is the lack of financial ability to hire a lawyer.

(2) **Other problems.** Poverty problems may also arise with respect to any number of other services—finances for an adequate pretrial investigation or for hiring expert witnesses, etc.

b) **Criminal cases.**

(1) **Right to a record on appeal.** In *Griffin v. Illinois*, 351 U.S. 12 (1956), the United States Supreme Court relied on equal protection to hold that, in a state prosecution where no appeal was possible without a transcript from the trial court, the state must provide indigent defendants a free transcript in all felony criminal cases.

(2) **Right to counsel on appeal.** In *Douglas v. California*, 372 U.S. 353 (1963), the United States Supreme Court held that an indigent defendant must be given the assistance of counsel in taking an initial appeal. But *Ross v. Moffit*, 417 U.S. 600 (1974), refused to extend *Douglas* to discretionary appeals.

c) **Civil cases.**

(1) In *Boddie v. Connecticut*, 401 U.S. 371 (1971), the Court used the Due Process Clause to hold that states may not require the payment of court fees, as a condition for judicial dissolution of marriage, from indigents who in good faith seek a divorce. The Court limited the scope

of the decision by noting (i) the basic position of the "marriage relationship" in society, and (ii) the "state monopolization of the means for legally dissolving this relationship." It reasoned that due process requires that "absent a countervailing state interest of overriding significance, persons forced to settle their claims . . . through the judicial process must be given a meaningful opportunity to be heard."

(2) When the issue of the applicability of *Boddie* in other civil contexts reached the Court, the Court read *Boddie* narrowly. In *United States v. Kras*, 409 U.S. 434 (1973), the Court held that the Bankruptcy Act filing fee requirement as a condition for discharge is "rational" and does not violate equal protection as applied to indigent persons who seek voluntary bankruptcy. The right to bankruptcy is not a "fundamental" interest but is in the "area of economics and social welfare."

(3) The same rationale was used for *Ortwein v. Schwab*, 410 U.S. 656 (1973) (filing fee for judicial review of administrative ruling on welfare decision).

d) **Conclusion.** The equal protection and due process arguments do not mean that the poor person gets whatever the rich person does. The United States Supreme Court is aware of the fact that the present resources of the economic and judicial systems could not support such a result. Therefore, the equal protection and/or due process principles are probably violated when discriminations based on wealth work an inequality so significant as to amount to "fundamental unfairness." Thus, a state must provide blood grouping tests to an indigent defendant in a civil paternity suit where the state was a party and the defendant's testimony, by itself, could not prevail over the mother's testimony. [Little v. Streater, 452 U.S. 1 (1981)] However, the Court also held that counsel need not be appointed when the state seeks to terminate an indigent's parental rights, except in particular circumstances. [Lassiter v. Department of Social Services, 452 U.S. 18 (1981)]

2) **Welfare.**

a) **Introduction.** There is no constitutional right to receive public welfare benefits. Classifications made by state agencies in administering or distributing welfare benefits are therefore subject only to the traditional equal protection test (unless a "fundamental" right is affected thereby).

b) **Amount of assistance and family size--**

Dandridge v. Williams,

Facts. Maryland imposed an upper limit of $250 per month per family for federal aid to families with dependent children. Williams (P) challenged the statute as denying equal protection since large families received less aid per child than small families. The lower court held the statute invalid, and Dandridge (D) appeals.

Issue. Does imposition of a ceiling on welfare benefits deny equal protection to large families, who receive less assistance per family member than do smaller families?

Held. No. Judgment reversed.

- No fundamental right is at stake here. In areas of economics and social welfare, a state does not deny equal protection merely because the classifications made by its laws are imperfect.
- The Fourteenth Amendment does not grant federal courts power to set economic or social policy on the states. It is enough that the state's action be rationally based and free from invidious discrimination. This statute, intended to encourage gainful employment, meets that test.

Dissent (Marshall, Brennan, JJ.). A state may not, in the provision of important services or the distribution of governmental payments, supply benefits to some individuals while denying them to others who are similarly situated. This case illustrates the impropriety of the abstract dichotomy between the "traditional test" and the "strict scrutiny test." The Court equates the interest of these needy children with the interests of utilities and other corporations by classifying their interests as "economic."

c) **Abortion funding--**

Harris v. McRae,

Facts. The Medicaid Act, which mandates compliance with all its requirements by all states that elect to participate in its reimbursement program, was amended annually by various Hyde amendments, which denied public funding for certain medically necessary abortions. McRae (P), a Medicaid recipient in the first trimester of pregnancy and seeking an abortion, sought to enjoin enforcement of the funding restriction. The district court found all versions of the Hyde amendment unconstitutional. Harris (D), Secretary of Health, Education and Welfare, appeals.

Issue. May Congress, consistent with due process and the Establishment of Religion Clause, deny public funding for certain medically necessary abortions while funding substantially all other medical costs, including costs of carrying a pregnancy to term?

Held. Yes. Judgment reversed.

- A law is presumptively unconstitutional if it impinges on a recognized constitutional right. P asserts that *Roe v. Wade, supra*, recognized a constitutional right to the liberty to choose whether to terminate a pregnancy. However, a legitimate state interest in protecting potential human life was also recognized. That case placed limits on the state's ability to interfere with that choice; here, P contests a completely different form of activity—state encouragement of an alternative activity consonant with legislative policy. *Wade* recognized no constitutional entitlement to the financial resources needed to pursue the protected choice, and no such entitlement exists.

- P contends that the Hyde amendments tend to establish certain religious doctrines, in violation of the First Amendment Establishment Clause. However, the fact that a statute coincides with a religious tenet does not, by itself, show the establishment of any religion; there must be a more substantial showing under the traditional Establishment Clause tests.

- A classification is unconstitutional if based on "suspect" criteria, or if not rationally related to a legitimate government objective. Earlier cases, such as *Maher v. Roe*, 432 U.S. 464 (1977), have held that poverty, standing alone, is not a suspect classification. The amendments do clearly bear a rational relationship to the legitimate interest in protecting the potential life of the fetus. Therefore, there is no denial of equal protection.

Dissent (Brennan, Marshall, Blackmun, JJ.). The amendments intrude on the constitutionally protected decision of abortion by coercing indigent pregnant women to bear children they would otherwise choose not to have.

Dissent (Marshall, J.). The amendments deny the constitutional right of choice to poor women at the cost of serious and long-lasting health damage.

Dissent (Blackmun, J.). Ignoring the economic realities is unjustifiable.

Dissent (Stevens, J.). The government rules with partiality when it denies otherwise available medical benefits to a woman solely to further an interest in potential life, at the risk of that woman's health.

e. **The right to education.** Because there is no constitutional right to education, regulation of education is judged only by the traditional (rational basis) test.

1) **State spending schemes--**

San Antonio Independent School District v. Rodriguez,

Facts. Rodriguez (P), a Mexican-American, challenged the Texas state system of financing public education. The system involved a combination of state, local, and federal funding, and was operated so that state and local expenditures per pupil varied according to the market value of taxable property per pupil within the various districts. P claimed that the system denied equal protection by invidiously discriminating against the poor. The district court found the system unconstitutional. The San Antonio Independent School District (D) appeals.

Issue. Must a state system of financing public education that closely correlates spending per pupil and the value of local taxable property pass strict judicial scrutiny in order to be valid?

Held. No. Judgment reversed.

- ♦ D's system might be regarded as discriminating against functionally indigent persons, against persons who are relatively poorer than others, or against all who, regardless of their personal incomes, happen to reside in relatively poorer school districts. However, there is no evidence to support a finding that any persons in the first two groups are discriminated against, and the third group clearly cannot fit the traditional definition of a suspect class.

- ♦ Although the system does not operate to the peculiar disadvantage of any suspect class, strict review is still required where the state's action impermissibly interferes with the exercise of a "fundamental" right, which P claims includes education. Although education is an important state service, that importance is not determinative of equal protection examination. Only those rights explicitly or implicitly guaranteed by the United States Constitution are "fundamental" for purposes of equal protection. Education is neither explicitly nor implicitly guaranteed. Additionally, D's system was implemented to extend public education, not to interfere with any rights. Finally, courts ought not interfere with state fiscal policies if not necessary. Therefore, D's system is not subject to strict judicial scrutiny.

- ♦ D concedes that its system is not perfect, yet claims that it bears the necessary rational relationship to a legitimate state purpose. It is based on the state's experience and extensive consideration. Because the statute rationally furthers a legitimate state purpose, it is justifiable under the Equal Protection Clause.

Concurrence (Stewart, J.). The Equal Protection Clause confers no substantive rights but merely measures the validity of classifications created by state laws.

Dissent (Brennan, J.). Education is so closely linked to First Amendment rights that any classification affecting it must be subjected to strict judicial scrutiny. D concedes that this system cannot pass such scrutiny, and it should be held unconstitutional.

Dissent (White, Douglas, Brennan, JJ.). The Court merely requires D to establish that unequal treatment is in furtherance of a permissible goal, but it should also require D to show that the means chosen to effectuate that goal are rationally related to its achievement.

Dissent (Marshall, Douglas, JJ.). The Court appears to find only two standards of equal protection review—strict scrutiny or mere rationality. In reality, there is a wide spectrum of review depending on the constitutional and societal importance of the interest adversely affected and the recognized invidiousness of the classification. The amount of review accorded to nonconstitutional rights or interests varies according to the nexus between those rights and specific constitutional guarantees. Discrimination on the basis of group wealth in this case calls for careful judicial scrutiny.

---

2) Education of children of illegal aliens--

Plyler v. Doe,

Facts. Texas enacted a statute that withheld state funds for the education of illegal alien children and that allowed local school districts to deny enrollment to such children. Doe (P) challenged the constitutionality of the statute. The lower courts found the law unconstitutional, and Plyler (D) appeals.

Issue. May a state deny free public education to undocumented school-age children that it provides to citizens and legally admitted aliens?

Held. No. Judgment affirmed.

- The Fourteenth Amendment guarantees equal protection and due process to "any person within (a state's) jurisdiction." Even illegal aliens are entitled to this protection.
- Equal protection analysis does not require that illegal aliens be treated as a suspect class just because their illegal presence is not a constitutional irrelevancy. Education is not a fundamental right, although it is more than a mere government benefit. However, this case presents another consideration. The

statute imposes a lifetime stigma on children who are not accountable for their disabling status. Therefore, the discrimination cannot be allowed unless it fulfills a substantial state purpose.

♦ Although national policy does not support unrestricted immigration, no policy exists that would deny these children an elementary education. The state policies—protection against excessive illegal immigration, avoidance of the special burden of educating such children, and the likelihood that the children will not remain in the state—are not furthered by the means chosen, even assuming the policies are legitimate. Because no showing of furthering a state interest was made, the statutory discrimination is unconstitutional.

Concurrence (Marshall, J.). An individual's interest in education is fundamental. This case is further proof that a rigid approach to equal protection is impractical.

Concurrence (Blackmun, J.). Because of the political disadvantage incurred by uneducated persons, denial of an education is the analogue of denial of the right to vote. To uphold a discriminatory denial of education, the state must give more than a rational basis for the classification.

Concurrence (Powell, J.). The children discriminated against here are innocent with respect to their status. The legislative classification threatens the creation of an underclass of future residents. Therefore, the state must show a fair and substantial relation to substantial interests. This D has failed to do.

Dissent (Burger, C.J., White, Rehnquist, O'Connor, JJ.). Although it is foolish and wrong to create an illiterate segment of society in the manner at issue here, the courts were never intended to set policy. The only issue here is whether Texas has a legitimate reason to distinguish between legal and illegal residents. The state purpose of preserving its limited resources for school financing is rationally related to the legislative classification. The majority admits that traditional equal protection analysis does not require a different result. Instead, the majority decided what the best result should be and then created an analysis to reach that result.

Comment. A state may refuse to provide free tuition to public schools for children who live apart from parents and guardians so as to attend the free public school. [*See* Martinez v. Bynum, 461 U.S. 321 (1983)]

D. DEFINING THE SCOPE OF "LIBERTY" AND "PROPERTY" PROTECTED BY THE DUE PROCESS CLAUSE—THE PROCEDURAL DUE PROCESS CASES

Both the Fifth and Fourteenth Amendments protect against the deprivation of "life, liberty, or property without due process of law." The Due Process Clause is most often utilized to provide persons accused of a crime with the various procedural safeguards in the Bill of Rights (*e.g.,* Sixth Amendment right to a "public trial"). But due process also protects a range of "liberty" and "property" interests outside the criminal context.

1. **Deprivations of Liberty or Property that Require a Hearing.**

   a. **Definitions of liberty and property.** The liberty and property interests of which persons cannot be deprived without due process do not turn upon whether the interest involved is a "right" rather than a "privilege." Such formalistic procedures have been rejected by the Court. However, exactly what constitutes "liberty" or "property" subject to due process has not been precisely defined.

      1) **Liberty.** It is clear that "liberty" connotes more than freedom from the bodily restraints imposed by the criminal process: it includes at least the right to contract, to engage in gainful employment, and "generally to enjoy those privileges long recognized at common law as essential to the orderly pursuit of happiness by free men." [Meyer v. Nebraska, 262 U.S. 390 (1923)—also including the right to marry, raise children, and acquire useful knowledge]

      2) **Property.** Similarly, "property" denotes more than just actual ownership of realty, chattels or money—it includes "interests already acquired in specific benefits." However, there must be more than a mere abstract need or desire for (or unilateral expectation of) the benefit, since the Constitution does not create property interests. There must be a legitimate claim to an existing interest already derived from state (or federal) law.

   b. **Hiring of government employees--**

Board of Regents of State Colleges v. Roth,

Facts. Roth (P) was hired as a teacher in a public university for a fixed term of one academic year. He was not rehired, but was given no reason for the decision. State law allows tenure only after four years' employment, and leaves hiring decisions for nontenured teachers to the discretion of university officials. P sued the Board of Regents of State Colleges (D), claiming he was deprived of liberty and property without a constitutionally required hearing. The lower court held for P, and D appeals.

Issue. Does a government employee have a constitutional right to a statement of reasons and a hearing on his employer's decision not to rehire him?

Held. No. Judgment reversed.

♦ Liberty and property interests protected by the Fourteenth Amendment are broadly construed, but not infinite. Certain boundaries must be respected to give the word meaning. P simply was not rehired, and D did nothing to interfere with or restrict his freedom to seek another job. The concept of "liberty" does not extend to an otherwise nonexistent right to be employed by a certain employer.

- Property interests are not created by the United States Constitution but by independent sources, such as a state law, which also define their dimensions. P here was given no specific contractual interest in being rehired, nor did state law recognize any such property interest. P has only an abstract concern in being rehired, which cannot be considered a property interest to be protected by the Fourteenth Amendment. Therefore, the United States Constitution does not require that P be given a hearing before not being rehired.

Dissent (Marshall, J.). Every citizen is entitled to every government job for which he applies unless the government can establish a reason for denying employment. This is a property right protected by the Fourteenth Amendment. It is also liberty to work, which is likewise protected.

Comment. A plaintiff can establish a prima facie case by showing that the government had an improper purpose that was a motivating factor in its decision not to rehire, which the government can rebut only by showing it would have made the same decision even were the improper purpose not present.

---

c. **Parental rights of adulterous natural father--**

Michael H. v. Gerald D. *See* *supra*

d. **Creation of liberty interests by limiting government discretion--**

Sandin v. Conner,

Facts. Conner (P) was serving a sentence of 30 years to life in a Hawaii prison. During a strip-search, he reacted angrily and was charged with both "high misconduct" and "low moderate misconduct." P was allowed to appear at a hearing on the charges before an adjustment committee, but was not allowed to present witnesses. He was found guilty and required to serve 30 days in disciplinary segregation. P appealed, and several months after P served the segregation, the deputy administrator of the prison found the high misconduct charge unsupported. The charge was expunged from P's record. P sued Sandin (D) and other prison officials in federal court, claiming a deprivation of procedural due process because he had not been allowed to present witnesses. The district court granted summary judgment for D. The court of appeals reversed on the ground that P had a liberty interest in remaining free from disciplinary segregation because the prison regulations allowed such punishment only based on findings from the committee. The Supreme Court granted certiorari.

Issue. Does a prison regulation that requires an administrative hearing before an inmate may be placed in disciplinary segregation create a protected liberty interest entitling the inmate to procedural due process?

Held. No. Judgment reversed.

- ♦ In *Wolff v. McDonnell*, 418 U.S. 539 (1974), the Court held that a state statute, by providing for good time credits, created a liberty interest in a shortened prison sentence under the Due Process Clause such that credits could not be revoked without adequate procedures. Subsequent cases focused on whether state action was mandatory or discretionary to determine whether liberty interests were created.

- ♦ As a result of this line of cases, inmates no longer had to show that they had suffered a "grievous loss" of liberty retained even after being sentenced to prison. Judicial inquiry focused on the language of a particular regulation instead of the nature of the deprivation. Under this approach, states can avoid creation of liberty interests by eliminating regulations or by conferring standardless discretion on correctional personnel, which is undesirable. This approach also has the undesirable effect of involving federal courts in day-to-day management of prisons.

- ♦ For prison inmates, the type of liberty protected by the Due Process Clause is freedom from restraint that either (i) exceeds the sentence in an unexpected manner, such as a transfer to a mental hospital or an involuntary administration of psychotropic drugs, or (ii) imposes atypical and significant hardship on the inmate in relation to the ordinary incidents of prison life. Imprisonment necessarily includes the withdrawal or limitation of many privileges and rights. Discipline by prison officials in response to inmate misconduct is within the expected parameters of a sentence.

- ♦ The disciplinary segregation imposed on P in this case was not a dramatic departure from the basic conditions of his sentence, and was not the type of significant deprivation in which a state might create a liberty interest. Neither D's regulation nor the Due Process Clause itself gave P a protected liberty interest that entitled him to the procedural protections set forth in *Wolff.*

Dissent (Ginsburg, Stevens, JJ.). The Court's prior approach is flawed because basing fundamental rights on the language of prison regulations makes those rights depend on the jurisdiction where the prisoner is incarcerated. It also gives states an incentive for ruleless prison management. However, P had a liberty interest under the Due Process Clause itself to be free from disciplinary confinement without appropriate procedural safeguards.

Dissent (Breyer, Souter, JJ.). The Court has previously held that certain changes in prison conditions may be so severe or so different from ordinary confinement conditions that the state may not impose them without minimum due process procedures, regardless of whether the state law gives state authorities broad discretionary power to impose them. In addition, deprivations that are less severe may implicate procedural due process if the state law narrowly cabins the legal power of authorities to impose the deprivation. The majority's approach in this case leaves a broad middle category of restraints and deprivations that are not obviously within or outside the protection of the Due Process Clause, with no clear line for analysis. Using state law as a factor helps to draw the line. In this case, P suffered a significant deprivation under rules that cabin official discretion sufficiently that P was deprived of liberty under the Due Process Clause.

---

e. **Due process not implicated by ordinary negligence--**

Daniels v. Williams,

Facts. Daniels (P), an inmate at a city jail, slipped on a pillow that Williams (D), a corrections officer, negligently left on the stairs. P suffered back and ankle injuries from the fall. P sued under 42 U.S.C. section 1983, claiming that D deprived P of his liberty interest in freedom from bodily injury. P claims that he was deprived of an adequate state remedy because D is protected under sovereign immunity, so that P was deprived of liberty without due process of law. The district court granted summary judgment for D, and the court of appeals affirmed. The Supreme Court granted certiorari.

Issue. May the negligent conduct of a government official constitute a deprivation of liberty under the Due Process Clause?

Held. No. Judgment affirmed.

- In *Parratt v. Taylor*, 451 U.S. 527 (1981), a prisoner's property was misplaced. The state provided a tort remedy for the deprivation. The Court held that the prisoner had been deprived of property under the Due Process Clause but that the state remedy provided the process that was due. To the extent that *Parratt* holds that lack of due care by a state official may constitute deprivation under the Fourteenth Amendment, that case is overruled.

- The Due Process Clause has always been applied to deliberate decisions by government officials to deprive a person of life, liberty, or property. The clause was intended to protect the individual from arbitrary exercise of governmental power by permitting deprivations only through appropriate procedures.

- ♦ The negligence of a government official such as D is not an abuse of power but just a failure to act as a reasonable person. It does not implicate the Due Process Clause. No compensation procedure is constitutionally required when a government official negligently causes injury to life, liberty, or property. If P has a remedy, it is under tort law or state law, not the Fourteenth Amendment.

---

2. **Irrebuttable Presumptions.** The use of irrebuttable presumptions as to membership in a class may deny equal protection to individuals who meet the class qualifications but whose particular situations are divergent from the legislative purpose for the classification. Such persons have a right to a hearing to rebut the presumption of class membership.

   a. **State residency--**

Vlandis v. Kline,

Facts. Connecticut had a differential tuition plan based on residence within the state. Students like Kline (P), who were nonresidents when applying for admission, were automatically required to pay nonresident tuition for the duration of their attendance at state schools. P had become a bona fide resident while at school but was prevented from proving this status in order to obtain the lower resident tuition. P challenged the state's conclusive presumption of nonresidence. The district court ruled for P. Vlandis (D), representing the state, appeals.

Issue. May a state create a permanent irrebuttable presumption of nonresidence for students who are nonresidents when applying to state schools?

Held. No. Judgment affirmed.

- ♦ Statutes that create permanent irrebuttable presumptions are not favored under the Due Process Clause of the Fifth and Fourteenth Amendments. D is properly concerned with residency in assessing tuition, but its denial to certain students of an opportunity to prove residency violates the standards required for due process.

- ♦ Therefore, the irrebuttable presumption created by the state statute is unconstitutional. States are, however, permitted to establish reasonable criteria for in-state status to ensure that students who claim residency are, in fact, bona fide residents.

Concurrence (Marshall, Brennan, JJ.). The Court is correct except where it seems to endorse the state's one-year residency requirement, which was not at issue here.

Dissent (Rehnquist, J., Burger, C.J., Douglas, J.). The Court improperly relies on notions of substantive due process and invalidates a proper solution to the acute problems facing state universities.

b. Incapacity resulting from pregnancy--

Cleveland Board of Education v. LaFleur,

Facts. LaFleur (P), a teacher, was required to give two weeks' advance notice before taking mandatory maternity leave without pay five months before the expected birth of her child, despite her desire to finish the school term. P challenged the rule created and enforced by the Cleveland Board of Education (D). The district court upheld the rule, but the court of appeals reversed. D appeals.

Issue. May a school board require that pregnant teachers take a maternity leave after four or five months of pregnancy?

Held. No. Judgment affirmed.

- ♦ Freedom of personal choice in matters of marriage and family life is one of the liberties protected by the Due Process Clause of the Fourteenth Amendment. D's rule burdens P's exercise of this freedom and violates due process unless it is not needless, arbitrary, or capricious.
- ♦ The advance notice rule, by itself, is valid since it is rational and perhaps necessary to ensure continuity of instruction.
- ♦ Mandatory maternity leave at early stages of pregnancy is not closely tied to D's interest in continuity of instruction nor to assurance of physically capable teachers. It creates an irrebuttable presumption of incapacity that violates due process. Nor may it be justified by administrative convenience.

Concurrence (Powell, J.). The result is correct, but it should have been reached through equal protection analysis.

Dissent (Rehnquist, J., Burger, C.J.). The Court recognizes that if D's rule had required maternity leave at a later stage of pregnancy, it might be valid. If legislatures are permitted to draw a general line anywhere short of the delivery room, no judicial standard could invalidate those actually chosen.

c. Social Security benefits--

Weinberger v. Salfi,

Facts. Salfi (P) married a wage earner who died less than six months after the marriage. P was denied Social Security benefits solely on the basis of the duration-of-relationship requirements. P sued Weinberger (D), Secretary of Heath, Education, and Welfare, to have the requirements invalidated. The district court granted P relief, and D appeals.

Issue. May Congress establish generalized rules for distribution of public benefits that, in particular cases, deny benefits to persons not involved in the abuses that the generalized rules were designed to prevent?

Held. Yes. Judgment reversed.

- ♦ A noncontractual claim to receive funds from the public treasury enjoys no constitutionally protected status. P's only constitutional claim, once having failed to meet the specified requirements, is that the test is not sufficiently rational to justify deprivation of benefits to P that are available to those meeting the requirements. However, Congress may rationally conclude not only that generalized rules are appropriate to its purpose and concerns (here, preventing sham relationships created solely to collect Social Security benefits), but also that the difficulties of individual determinations outweigh the marginal increments in the precise effectuation of congressional concern that they might be expected to produce.
- ♦ The district court based its decision on a theory that the statute created an improper conclusive presumption under *Vlandis* and *LaFleur, supra.* Extending those holdings to these eligibility requirements would turn that doctrine into a virtual engine of destruction of countless legislative judgments previously permitted, and would involve extensive and improper judicial involvement in the legislative function.

Dissent (Douglas, J.). The law intended to prevent sham marriages. P should be allowed to show that her marriage was not a sham.

Dissent (Brennan, Marshall, JJ.). The Court's holding is flatly contrary to *Vlandis* and other relevant cases.

E. APPLICATION OF THE POST-CIVIL WAR AMENDMENTS TO PRIVATE CONDUCT: CONGRESSIONAL POWER TO ENFORCE THE AMENDMENTS

1. **Early Interpretation.** Both the Fourteenth and Fifteenth Amendments indicate that only "state action" (as opposed to private, nongovernmental action) that violates the amendments is prohibited. The early cases held that these amendments therefore did not apply to private acts of discrimination; *i.e.,* that individuals were free to discriminate if they chose to do so.

   a. **Nineteenth century approach--**

The Civil Rights Cases,

Facts. The Civil Rights Act of 1875 made it unlawful for anyone to deny a person the enjoyment of accommodations at inns, on public transportation, etc., on the basis of race. Certain blacks were excluded from inns, theaters, and a railroad in five separate states. The cases were consolidated before the Supreme Court.

Issue. May Congress prohibit private discriminatory actions by facilities generally open to the public?

Held. No. The Civil Rights Act is unconstitutional.

- The Fourteenth Amendment permits Congress to take corrective action only against state laws or acts done under state authority. The Civil Rights Act is directed toward acts by individuals and cannot be upheld under the Fourteenth Amendment.

- The Thirteenth Amendment permits direct as opposed to merely corrective legislation, but it covers only slavery or involuntary servitude, or the lingering badges of such. Refusing accommodation to a black person does not impose any badge of slavery or servitude. Mere racial discrimination is not a badge of slavery.

- Congress has no power to pass the Civil Rights Act, and Ps must seek a remedy in state law for any cause of action against private individuals or corporations that are discriminating.

Dissent (Harlan, J.). The Court has ignored the substance and spirit of these amendments. Freedom includes immunity from and protection against racial discrimination, especially in the use of public, albeit privately owned, accommodations and facilities licensed by the state.

Comment. The common law of all states at the time of the Civil Rights Act of 1875 held that it was unlawful to deny the facilities of inns and carriers to any person. Therefore, Ps did have a remedy in state law. However, this case illustrates the approach to state action that permitted individuals to discriminate freely if they wanted to.

b. **Defining state action.** The Fourteenth Amendment clearly prohibits state action. Thus, the determinative question is whether particular conduct is state action. The response to that question has changed over the years.

2. Application of the Constitution to Private Conduct.

a. Private performance of "government" functions.

1) **Company towns.** In *Marsh v. Alabama*, 326 U.S. 501 (1946), a private corporation owned a town and posted signs prohibiting peddlers. A Jehovah's Witness distributed religious literature on the streets of the company town and was convicted of violating a state trespass law that made it a crime "to enter or remain on the premises of another" after being warned not to do so. The conviction was reversed because the town's streets, although privately owned, were in effect a ***public place***. The Court held that neither the state nor any private owner can totally ban freedom of expression in public places; nor can state trespass laws be applied to enforce such a ban. However, the Court has since held that the "company town" rationale does ***not*** extend to the passageways in a privately owned shopping center. [Hudgens v. NLRB, 424 U.S. 507 (1976)—*overruling* Amalgamated Foods Employees Union v. Logan Valley Plaza, 391 U.S. 308 (1968)]

2) **City parks.** *Evans v. Newton*, 382 U.S. 296 (1966), involved a city park. United States Senator Bacon had willed a tract of land to the City of Macon, Georgia, for use as a park for white people only. Eventually, the city permitted black people to use it, and Newton and other park managers sued to have the city removed as trustee. Evans and other black citizens intervened. The city resigned as trustee and the state courts approved the appointment of new trustees who pursued the segregation policy. The Court held that the reach of the Fourteenth Amendment can be determined only by sifting facts and weighing circumstances. This park originated as a private grant of private property, but it gradually acquired character as a public facility since it was maintained by the city. Once the tradition of municipal control had become firmly established, mere substitution of trustees could not instantly transfer the park from the public to the private sector. This is especially true where, as here, the property provided a service that was essentially municipal. Therefore, those in charge of the park had to comply with Fourteenth Amendment mandates regardless of who had title under state law.

3) **Commercial rights and remedies--**

Flagg Brothers, Inc. v. Brooks,

Facts. Brooks (P) was evicted and her possessions stored by Flagg Brothers, Inc. (D). When P failed to pay storage charges, D threatened to sell P's possessions, pursuant to procedures established by the New York Uniform Commercial Code ("U.C.C."). P brought an action seeking damages, an injunction, and declaratory relief that the U.C.C. provision was unconstitutional. The district court dismissed the complaint, but the court of appeals reversed, finding state involvement in D's action sufficient to invoke constitutional protections. D appeals.

Issue. Does a warehouseman's sale of goods entrusted to him for storage constitute state action because it is permitted by state law?

Held. No. Judgment reversed.

- ♦ P claims that the state delegated to D a power traditionally exclusively reserved to the states. While many functions have been traditionally performed by governments, very few have been ***exclusively*** reserved to the state. The settlement of disputes between debtors and creditors is not traditionally an exclusive public function, so D's action is not state action under this test.

- ♦ P also claims D's action is state action because the state has authorized and encouraged it by enacting the U.C.C. While private action compelled by a state is properly attributable to the state, mere acquiescence by the state is insufficient. The state has merely refused to provide P a remedy for D's private deprivation of property. Therefore, D's action is not a state action.

Dissent (Stevens, White, Marshall, JJ.). The question is whether a state statute that authorizes a private party to deprive a person of her property without her consent must satisfy due process requirements. Clearly, it should. The court's holding that only state delegation of ***exclusively*** sovereign functions brings private action within constitutional bounds is inconsistent with prior decisions. P should be permitted to challenge the state procedure permitted by state law.

---

b. **Governmental enforcement of "private" decisions.** The denial of judicial relief is not considered sufficient encouragement to constitute state action, but if the state's courts are used to enforce or perpetuate such discrimination, there is sufficient state action, even though such discrimination by private individuals directly might not be condemned.

   1) **Judicial enforcement of discriminatory private agreement prohibited--**

Shelley v. Kraemer,

Facts. Shelley (D), a black person, purchased residential property that, unknown to D, was encumbered by a restrictive agreement that prevented ownership or occupancy of the property by non-Caucasians. Kraemer (P), a neighbor and owner of the other property subject to the restriction, brought suit to restrain D from possessing the property and to divest title out of D. The trial court denied relief, but the Supreme Court of Missouri reversed. D appeals.

Issue. Does the Fourteenth Amendment Equal Protection Clause prohibit judicial enforcement by state courts of restrictive covenants based on race or color?

Held. Yes. Judgment reversed.

- Property rights clearly are among those civil rights protected from discriminatory state action by the Fourteenth Amendment. Early decisions invalidated any government restrictions on residency based on race. Here the restrictions are purely private and, standing alone, are not precluded by the Fourteenth Amendment.

- Actions of state courts are state actions within the meaning of the Fourteenth Amendment. Judicial enforcement of these private racial restrictions constitutes state discrimination contrary to the Fourteenth Amendment and denies D equal protection.

Comment. In *Barrows v. Jackson*, 346 U.S. 249 (1953), the Court affirmed a decision by the California courts to sustain a demurrer to an action for damages for violation of a discriminatory deed restriction.

2) **State as trustee--**

Pennsylvania v. Board of City Trusts,

Facts. The Board of City Trusts (D) was authorized by the Pennsylvania legislature to carry out the provisions of a private will that created and funded a college for poor white male orphans. Two blacks were denied admission solely because of their race. Pennsylvania (P) and others brought suit to force D to admit nonwhites to the college. The state courts upheld D's refusal. P appeals.

Issue. May a state agency, acting as a trustee for a private will, refuse equal treatment to nonwhites?

Held. No. Judgment reversed.

- Even though D acted only as a trustee, it was a state agency and its action constituted discrimination by a state in violation of the Fourteenth Amendment.

Comment. On remand, the Pennsylvania courts determined that the intent to limit the college to white orphan boys dominated the intent to have the city act as trustee. Private trustees were substituted, and exclusion of blacks sustained. The United States Supreme Court denied certiorari, citing lack of jurisdiction.

---

3) State entwinement through participation in school association--

Brentwood Academy v. Tennessee Secondary School Athletic Association,

Facts. The Tennessee Secondary School Athletic Association (D) was a not-for-profit association that was the only entity regulating interscholastic sport among public and private high schools in Tennessee. D's voting membership consisted of high school principals and other school officials. Eighty-four percent of D's member schools were public. D's staff members were not paid by the state, but they were eligible to join the state's public employee retirement system. D determined that Brentwood Academy (P), a private parochial high school that was a member of D, had violated a recruitment policy. D put P on probation and prohibited its football and basketball teams from competing in playoffs for two years. D's board consisted exclusively of public school administrators when D took this action. P sued, claiming that D's action was state action that violated the First and Fourteenth Amendments. The district court granted P summary judgment and enjoined enforcement of D's rule. The Sixth Circuit found no state action and reversed. The Supreme Court granted certiorari.

Issue. Does an enforcement action taken by a statewide association that regulates sport competition among public and private high schools constitute state action?

Held. Yes. Judgment reversed and case remanded.

- The distinction between state action and private conduct is not merely whether the state or people outside governmental organizations acted; conduct by an ostensibly private organization may be treated as state action if a state caused it to be performed. A finding of state action may be based on a variety of factors.

- The key element of state action is whether there is public entwinement in the management and control of ostensibly separate entities. In this case, there is pervasive entwinement of public institutions and public officials in D's composition and operations. Public schools make up 84% of the membership. D conducted its business during school hours, and most of D's revenue comes from gate receipts generated by sporting activities at public schools.

- D depends for its existence and its operations on public school officials who control D and perform all of its functions, save the purely ministerial acts. Even the ministerial employees are treated as state employees for retirement benefits. There are no values that would outweigh a finding of public accountability in this case. Therefore, D's actions are state actions.

Dissent (Thomas, J. Rehnquist, C.J., Scalia, Kennedy, JJ.). The Court has never before found state action based only upon "entwinement." The entwinement test could be extended to a wide variety of private activity, as long as the members of the organization are state employees. Instead, a private organization's acts should only constitute state action when the organization: performs a public function; was created, coerced, or encouraged by the state; or acted in a symbiotic relationship with the state. Tennessee did not create D, did not fund D, and does not pay D's employees. The state's only involvement is to allow public schools to be members of D. Tennessee has never been involved in regulating recruiting, and D's enforcement action should not be attributable to Tennessee.

---

c. **Government financing, regulation, and authorization of private conduct.**

1) **Private use of government property--**

Burton v. Wilmington Parking Authority,

Facts. Burton (P), a black person, was denied service at a private restaurant (the Eagle) located within a building owned and operated by the Wilmington Parking Authority (D), a state agency. D had leased out some of its space to assist in its financing, including the lease to the Eagle. P sued, claiming that although the Eagle was private, it had a sufficient nexus to D to make its discrimination a state action. The trial court granted summary judgment for P; the Delaware Supreme Court reversed on the basis of a state law granting restaurants the right to refuse service to any person whose reception would injure the business. P appeals.

Issue. Are lessees of state property whose leases further state interests and form an integral part of a state operation required to comply with the Fourteenth Amendment?

Held. Yes. Judgment reversed.

- Although private conduct abridging individual rights does not violate the Equal Protection Clause, if any significant state action is involved, the discrimination is unconstitutional. D is so closely involved with the Eagle that it is a joint participant, and the Eagle is not so purely private as to fall beyond the scope of the Fourteenth Amendment.

- D clearly could have required the Eagle to agree to a binding covenant not to discriminate, but its failure to do so does not permit D to abdicate its responsibilities to prevent discrimination. D has, by its inaction, become a party to the discrimination. Lessee Eagle must therefore comply with the Fourteenth Amendment proscriptions.

---

2) **Financial assistance.** The government cannot provide other than generalized assistance to private activities that discriminate, such as private schools with racially discriminatory admission policies. In *Norwood v. Harrison*, 413 U.S. 455 (1973), the Court held that the state could not loan textbooks to such schools, because this was specific financial assistance, as contrasted with water, electricity, and police and fire protection, which may be provided as necessities of life.

3) **Government licensing--**

Moose Lodge No. 107 v. Irvis,

Facts. Irvis (P), a black person, was refused service by the Moose Lodge (D). P claimed D's action was a state action because D was licensed by the state liquor board to sell alcoholic beverages. A three-judge district court held for P on the merits, and D appeals.

Issue. Does state alcoholic licensing of a private club constitute sufficient state action to require that the club observe Fourteenth Amendment prohibitions against discrimination?

Held. No. Judgment reversed.

- A private entity is not covered by the Fourteenth Amendment when it merely receives any sort of benefit or service at all from the state, or if subject to any state regulation. Otherwise, the distinction between private and public would be meaningless. If the impetus for the discrimination is private, state involvement must be significant to implicate constitutional standards.

- Here, the state's liquor regulation in no way fostered or encouraged racial discrimination. However, those regulations did require that licensed clubs must adhere to their own constitutions and bylaws. States may not use sanctions to enforce segregative rules, and P is entitled to an injunction against the enforcement of the state regulation that would require D to enforce its own discriminatory rules.

Dissent (Douglas, Marshall, JJ.). The state's licensing scheme includes a complex quota system. The quota in D's areas has been full for many years; no more club licenses may be issued in the city. Since private clubs are the only places that serve liquor for significant portions of each week, the state has restricted access by blacks to liquor by granting D a license instead of a nondiscriminatory club.

Dissent (Brennan, Marshall, JJ.). The state has become an active participant in the operation of D's bar through its detailed regulatory scheme, and D should be required to observe Fourteenth Amendment standards.

---

4) Business regulation--

Jackson v. Metropolitan Edison Co.,

Facts. Metropolitan Edison Company (D), a private utility regulated by the state, terminated Jackson's (P's) electric service for nonpayment before affording P notice, a hearing, and an opportunity to pay. P sued, contending that D's action constituted state action depriving her of property without due process of law. The lower courts dismissed P's complaint, and P appeals.

Issue. Does termination of service by a heavily regulated private utility, using procedures permitted by state law, constitute state action?

Held. No. Judgment affirmed.

- State regulation of a private business, even if extensive and detailed, does not by itself convert private action to state action for Fourteenth Amendment purposes. There must be a close nexus between the state and the actual activity of the regulated entity. D's monopoly status, by itself, fails to show such a nexus. Nor is D's service a public function, since the state has no obligation to furnish such service. The limited notion that businesses "affected with a public interest" are state actors cannot be expanded to include private utilities.

- The state concededly approved D's termination procedures, but not on specific consideration. The state's approval amounts merely to a finding that the procedures are permissible under state law. For these reasons, D's actions cannot be considered to be state actions.

Dissent (Marshall, J.). The essential nature of D's service requires that D be subject to the same standards as other governmental entities. The interests of diversity and flexibility that favor protection of private entities from constitutional standards are irrelevant in monopoly situations like D's. Finally, the majority's opinion would appear to apply to a broad range of claimed constitutional violations by the company, including racial discrimination.

---

5) **Authorization of discrimination--**

Reitman v. Mulkey,

Facts. Reitman (D) refused to rent to Mulkey (P), who was black, solely because of P's race. P sued for an injunction and damages under the California Civil Code. D claimed that those provisions were null and void as a result of adoption of a state constitutional provision that assured persons of the right to decline to rent residential property to any person, based on personal discretion. The trial court granted D summary judgment, but the state supreme court reversed, finding the state constitutional provision violative of the Fourteenth Amendment. D appeals.

Issue. Does a state constitutional provision that mandates state neutrality in private residential discrimination matters deny due process?

Held. Yes. Judgment affirmed.

- The California Supreme Court determined that the immediate design and intent of the state constitutional provision was to repeal state laws preventing private discrimination and that the provision invalidly involved the state in racial discrimination in the housing market by effectively encouraging discrimination.

- The right to discriminate, by being included in the state constitution, would be a basic state policy. The California Supreme Court's decision is justifiable and affirmed.

Concurrence (Douglas, J.). Real estate brokerage is state licensed and regulated, and must be dedicated to nondiscriminatory service.

Dissent (Harlan, Black, Clark, Stewart, JJ.). The provision merely ensures state neutrality on the issue and no more violates the Fourteenth Amendment than failure to pass antidiscrimination statutes in the first place would have. The California court made conclusions of law, not findings of fact, and its decision does not merit the high deference accorded by the majority. The decision will hamper efforts in other states to enact what must now appear to be unrepealable antidiscrimination statutes.

---

3. **Federal Civil Rights Legislation.** Following the Civil War, Congress enacted numerous statutes to protect the liberated slaves from interference by state officials and private citizens. After a long lull in such legislation, a civil rights act was enacted in 1957 to give greater protection to the right to vote. Other significant recent legislation includes the Civil Rights Act of 1964, which dealt with voting and equal employment opportunities, the Voting Rights Act of 1975, and the Civil Rights Act of 1968, with its fair housing provisions.

4. **Federal Power to Regulate Private Conduct Under the Thirteenth Amendment.**

   a. **Generally.** Only the Thirteenth Amendment applies directly to private, as well as governmental, action. "Neither slavery nor involuntary servitude, except as a punishment for crime whereof the party shall have been duly convicted, shall exist within the United States, or any place subject to their jurisdiction." Congress's power under this amendment is broadly construed, and extends to any "badge or incident of slavery."

   b. **Private discrimination--**

Jones v. Alfred H. Mayer Co.,

Facts. The Alfred H. Mayer Co. (D) refused to sell a home to Jones (P) solely because P was black. P sued for injunctive and other relief under 42 U.S.C. section 1982. The lower court dismissed P's complaint, concluding that section 1982 applies only to state action and does not reach private refusals to sell. P appeals.

Issue. Does the authority of Congress to enforce the Thirteenth Amendment "by appropriate legislation" include the power to eliminate all racial barriers (including private action) to the acquisition of real and personal property?

Held. Yes. Judgment reversed.

- The plain language of section 1982 appears to prohibit ***all*** discrimination, private and public, against blacks in the sale or rental of property.

- The Thirteenth Amendment authorizes Congress to enact appropriate legislation to abolish all badges and incidents of slavery, and such laws may operate on the unofficial acts of private individuals. Congress has determined that free exercise of property rights is essential to abolition of all badges and incidents of slavery; therefore, section 1982 may properly act on actions of private individuals such as D.

- ♦ Were Congress denied the power to enforce the Thirteenth Amendment to this extent, that amendment would constitute a promise that the nation could not keep.

Dissent (Harlan, White, JJ.). This case is unimportant in light of the recently passed Fair Housing Act, and the Court should have dismissed P's writ as improvidently granted.

---

5. **Federal Power to Regulate Private Conduct Under the Fourteenth Amendment.**

   a. **Generally.** The fact that the Fourteenth Amendment does not expressly protect the constitutional rights of individuals from encroachment by other individuals does not mean that the federal government is entirely powerless to prevent private acts of discrimination.

   b. **Effect of Enabling Clauses.** The Fourteenth Amendment contains provisions giving Congress the power to enforce the amendment by "appropriate legislation." However, since it forbids only state action, the question arises whether Congress is limited to laws preventing ***state*** discrimination, or whether the Enabling Clause also confers power on Congress to outlaw even ***private*** acts of discrimination.

      1) **Discriminatory acts by state officials.** In several decisions, the Court has relied on the Enabling Clause to sustain federal statutes authorizing civil damage judgments and/or criminal convictions against ***state or local officials*** who misuse their authority so as to violate the rights protected by such amendments.

         a) Federal legislation punishing persons who, under color of state law, deprive another of any right, privilege, or immunity secured or protected by the United States Constitution has been upheld as applied to ***law enforcement officers*** who knowingly deprived a prisoner of his life without due process of law. [*See* Screws v. United States, 325 U.S. 91 (1945)—police beat a prisoner to death in an effort to obtain a confession]

         b) A federal statute, authorizing a civil damage suit against any person who, under color of state law, subjects another to the deprivation of any right, privilege, or immunity secured by the United States Constitution or Act of Congress, has been upheld as applied to state police officers. [Monroe v. Pape, 365 U.S. 167 (1961)]

      2) **Discrimination by private individuals collaborating with state officials.** When private individuals willfully engage in a "joint activity" with state officials to infringe on the civil rights of oth-

ers, the private individuals as well as the state officers are subject to sanctions under federal law. [United States v. Price, 383 U.S. 787 (1966)—private citizens killed civil rights workers pursuant to plan joined in by local police]

3) **Discrimination by private individuals alone.** And the Court has at least expressed the view that the Enabling Clauses empower Congress to enact legislation regulating the acts of any individual (with or without any state action) in order to protect the rights secured by these amendments—*i.e.,* that the Enabling Clauses give Congress the power to regulate and punish even purely private acts of discrimination. [*See* United States v. Guest, 383 U.S. 745 (1966)]

6. **The Scope of Congressional Power to Redefine the Amendments.** The Enabling Clauses may give Congress the power to legislate against policies and practices that in themselves are not necessarily unconstitutional. This power may be characterized as "remedial" or "interpretive." Exercise of the power will be upheld if there is a basis for the enactment and if the remedies imposed are not themselves unconstitutional.

   a. **Remedial power--**

City of Rome v. United States,

Facts. The Voting Rights Act of 1965, in an attempt to remedy the effects of past discriminatory practices, required preclearance by the Attorney General or the D.C. District Court of any voting plan changes made in covered jurisdictions. Georgia and all its municipalities were covered jurisdictions. Rome, Georgia (P), sought to alter its electoral scheme, and sought preclearance. The Attorney General declined to preclear, and P sought relief from enforcement of the Act. A three-judge district court granted summary judgment to the United States (D) in P's suit, and P appeals.

Issue. May Congress deny an alteration of a concededly nondiscriminatory plan when there is no discriminatory purpose behind the alteration, but the new plan might have discriminatory effects?

Held. Yes. Judgment affirmed.

- The exemption provisions of the Act are available only to states; P by itself may not be exempted. Therefore, it must meet the preclearance requirements.

- The Act permits preclearance only where the new voting plan has neither the purpose nor the effect of discriminating. P claims this exceeds congressional authority under the Fifteenth Amendment, which expressly prohibits only purposeful discrimination. Earlier cases, however, have broadly interpreted the enforcement provisions, so that Congress can do whatever it deems necessary, if not expressly prohibited by the United States Constitution, to enforce the Fifteenth Amendment. Thus, Congress can, as a remedial action, prohibit practices that do not themselves violate the Fifteenth Amendment, as long as the prohibition is appropriate.

- ♦ This holding does not expand federalism beyond the design of the framers of the Civil War amendments.

Concurrence (Stevens, J.). Since Congress can regulate voting practices in Georgia, it can regulate P's voting practices.

Dissent (Powell, J.). Congress may remedy only violations of voting rights, but P has never violated those rights, so P should not be covered by the Act.

Dissent (Rehnquist, Stewart, JJ.). The Court here permits Congress to amend the United States Constitution and impermissibly intrudes on local government by denying P the power to adopt a plan specifically approved in *Mobile v. Bolden, supra.*

Comment. In *Mobile*, the Court required the presence of discriminatory effect and purpose. In *Rome,* the Court says that if Congress finds the effect, no purpose need be shown. By so holding, the Court may mean that Congress can expand the reach of the United States Constitution, or it may merely mean that Congress's fact findings were adequate to infer purpose.

---

b. **Interpretive power.** The Fourteenth Amendment maintains the traditional separation of powers between Congress and the judiciary by conferring substantive rights against the states that are self-executing, while leaving with the judiciary the power to interpret the Constitution in a case or controversy. Congress can act in a preventive or remedial way to protect the actual guarantees of section 1 of the Fourteenth Amendment, but in determining how to do so, Congress cannot define its own powers by altering the meaning of the Fourteenth Amendment. The line between permissible remedial legislation and substantive redefinition is not easy to discern.

1) **Limits on congressional enforcement of Reconstruction amendments--**

City of Boerne v. Flores,

Facts. In *Employment Division, Department of Human Resources v. Smith* (*infra*), the Court held that, except in special circumstances, the Free Exercise Clause was not violated by a facially neutral and secular law, drafted without legislative animus, that had the effect of interfering with a given religious practice. In that case, Smith had been denied unemployment benefits because he had used peyote in a sacramental ceremony. The Court rejected application of the *Sherbert v. Verner* (*infra*), balancing test. In response, Congress passed the Religious Freedom Restoration Act of 1993 ("RFRA"), which required courts to apply the balancing test. Under RFRA, courts would have to determine whether a statute substantially burdened a religious practice, and if it did, whether the burden was justified by a compelling government interest. The city of Boerne (D) denied a building permit to enlarge a church, based on an ordinance governing historic preservation in the area. Flores (P), the Archbishop of San Antonio, challenged the denial under RFRA. The district court held that in enacting RFRA, Congress exceeded the scope of its Section 5 enforcement power under the Fourteenth Amendment. The fifth circuit reversed. The Supreme Court granted certiorari.

Issue. May Congress impose a rule of constitutional interpretation on the Supreme Court through its enforcement of the Fourteenth Amendment?

Held. No. Judgment reversed.

- Congress relied on the Fourteenth Amendment to impose the RFRA requirements on the states. The Fourteenth Amendment gives Congress power to enforce the constitutional guarantee that no state shall deprive any person of "life, liberty, or property, without due process of law," nor deny any person "equal protection of the laws." In enacting RFRA, Congress sought to protect the free exercise of religion.

- While congressional authority under the Fourteenth Amendment is broad, it is not unlimited. Congress does have power to enforce the constitutional right to the free exercise of religion, since the First Amendment liberties are included within the Due Process Clause of the Fourteenth Amendment. This power extends only to enforcement, however. It does not extend to changing or defining what the right of free exercise is. There is a distinction between enforcement and changing governing law.

- The power to interpret the Constitution in a case or controversy is in the Judiciary, not in Congress. Congress does not have a substantive, nonremedial power under the Fourteenth Amendment. If Congress could define its own powers by altering the meaning of the Fourteenth Amendment, the Constitution would no longer be a superior paramount law that cannot be changed by ordinary means.

- Preventive rules may sometimes be appropriate remedial measures, but the means must be appropriate to the ends to be achieved. In this case, there was no record of generally applicable laws that were passed because of religious bigotry. The provisions of RFRA are so out of proportion to a supposed remedial objective that it cannot be treated as responsive to unconstitutional behavior. RFRA is applicable to all state and federal law, whenever enacted. The substantial costs RFRA imposes on government far exceed any pattern or practice of unconstitutional conduct under the Free Exercise Clause as interpreted by *Smith*.

- Each branch of the government must respect both the Constitution and the proper determination of the other branches. RFRA was designed to control cases and controversies, but it is the interpretation of the Constitution that must govern cases and controversies, not RFRA.

Concurrence (Stevens, J.). RFRA is actually a law respecting an establishment of religion in violation of the First Amendment. It gives churches a preference that other organizations do not enjoy.

Concurrence (Scalia, Stevens, JJ.). Historical materials support a result contrary to the *Smith* holding.

Dissent (O'Connor, Breyer, JJ.). The Court should reexamine the *Smith* holding, which was incorrect. That holding allows the government to prohibit, without justification, conduct mandated by an individual's religious beliefs, so long as the prohibition is generally applicable. In so doing, *Smith* harmed religious liberty. If the Court corrected the misinterpretation of the Free Exercise Clause in *Smith*, we could then review RFRA in light of a proper interpretation. But the Court does correctly hold that Congress cannot independently define or expand the scope of constitutional rights by statute.

Dissent (Souter, J.). The Court cannot soundly decide this case without reexamining the free-exercise standard of *Smith*.

Dissent (Breyer, J.). It is not necessary to consider the question whether the Fourteenth Amendment would allow Congress to enact RFRA.

Comments.

- It could be argued that since Congress is specifically mentioned in the Fourteenth Amendment, it does have special authority to determine what rights to enforce. It has such authority under the Thirteenth Amendment.

- In *Kimel v. Florida Board of Regents*, 528 U.S. 62 (2000), the Court held that the Age Discrimination in Employment Act ("ADEA"), which prohibited employment discrimination because of age, was not "appropriate legislation" under Section 5 of the Fourteenth Amendment. States may discriminate on the basis of age, so long as the age classification involved is rationally related to a legitimate state interest. The ADEA prohibited more state employment decisions and practices than would have been held unconstitutional.

---

2) **Congressional power and state immunity.** The Eleventh Amendment grants federal immunity to states from lawsuits filed by private parties. Section 1 of the Fourteenth Amendment prohibits the states from making or enforcing any law that abridges the privileges or immu-

nities of United States citizens, or that denies due process or equal protection. Section 5 of the Fourteenth Amendment gives Congress the right of enforcement by appropriate legislation. The Supreme Court has had to determine how Congress can enforce the Fourteenth Amendment without violating the Eleventh Amendment.

a) **Abrogation of immunity**. The Supreme Court has held that Congress may abrogate the states' Eleventh Amendment immunity (by subjecting nonconsenting states to suit in federal court) only when Congress both unequivocally intends to do so and acts pursuant to a valid grant of constitutional authority. Article I of the Constitution does not grant Congress this authority. Instead, Congress must rely on section 5 of the Fourteenth Amendment.

b) **Limitation of authority.** Because only the Supreme Court can define the substance of constitutional guarantees, Congress cannot unilaterally declare its authority under the Fourteenth Amendment. In *Boerne*, *supra*, the Court determined that, if Congress enacts legislation under section 5 that is beyond the scope of section 1's actual guarantees, such legislation is valid only if it exhibits "congruence and proportionality between the injury to be prevented or remedied and the means adopted to that end."

c) **State employees cannot recover for ADA Title I violations--**

Board of Trustees of the University of Alabama v. Garrett

Facts. Garrett (P) was a nurse employed as a Director of Nursing by the Board of Trustees of the University of Alabama (D). P was diagnosed with cancer and had to take substantial leave from work for her treatments. When she returned to work, she had lost her director position and was transferred to a lower-paying position. In a separate lawsuit, Ash, a security officer for the Alabama Department of Youth Services, requested a modification of his duties and reassignment to the day shift because of his chronic asthma and sleep apnea. Ash's requests were denied. Ps sued D under the Americans with Disabilities Act ("ADA"), claiming that D did not accommodate their physical disabilities. Title I of the ADA protects against discrimination in employment. In each case, the district court granted D summary judgment on the ground that the ADA cannot override the state's immunity under the Eleventh Amendment. Ps appealed, the cases were consolidated, and the Eleventh Circuit reversed. The Supreme Court granted certiorari.

Issue. May state employees recover damages for the state's failure to comply with Title I of the ADA?

Held. No. Judgment reversed.

- To apply the basic principles of Fourteenth Amendment analysis, the first step is identifying the scope of the constitutional right at issue. This case involves the limitations that section 1 of the Fourteenth Amendment places on state treatment of the disabled.

- Under *Cleburne v. Cleburne Living Center, supra*, the Fourteenth Amendment does not require a state to make special accommodations for the disabled as long as the state's action toward such individuals is rational. Such action need only satisfy rational-basis scrutiny.

- Congress has authority under section 5 only to respond to state transgressions; it must identify a history and pattern of unconstitutional employment discrimination by the states against the disabled to legitimately make the ADA apply to the states. Despite the 4.5 million people employed by the states, Congress assembled only a few incidents of unconstitutional state discrimination in employment against the disabled. This does not rise to a pattern of unconstitutional state behavior. However, even if it did, the ADA creates rights and remedies that fail the *Boerne* test, *supra*, of congruence and proportionality.

Concurrence (Kennedy, O'Connor, JJ.). Congress has failed to establish patterns of constitutional violations committed by the states in their official capacity, which is a requirement for a federal statute that allows private persons to sue the states for money damages.

Dissent (Breyer, Stevens, Souter, Ginsberg, JJ.). The Constitution requires only that Congress determine that the remedy is an appropriate way to enforce basic equal protection. Congress assembled a vast record of massive, society-wide discrimination against persons with disabilities which satisfies the Constitutional requirements. The Court should not unduly restrict the power of Congress to remedy discrimination under section 5.

---

d) State employees can recover under FMLA--

Nevada Department of Human Resources v. Hibbs

Facts. Hibbs (P) worked for the Nevada Department of Human Resources (D). P sought leave to care for his sick wife under the Family and Medical Leave Act ("FMLA"), which allows eligible employees to take up to 12 work weeks of unpaid leave to care for family members. FMLA creates a private right of action against any employer, including a public agency, that interferes with FMLA rights. D allowed P to take the 12 weeks of leave, but once he exhausted that leave, D told P he had to return to work by a certain date. P failed to do so, and D terminated P's employment. P sued D in federal court. The district court granted summary judgment for D, holding that the FMLA claim was barred by the Eleventh Amendment. The Ninth Circuit reversed. The Supreme Court granted certiorari.

Issue. May state employees recover damages for the state's failure to comply with the FMLA?

Held. Yes. Judgment affirmed.

- Congress enacted the FMLA in reliance on its power under section 5 of the Fourteenth Amendment, which authorizes Congress to abrogate the states' Eleventh Amendment sovereign immunity. Congress's section 5 power includes prohibiting unconstitutional conduct, but it also includes deterring future violation of guaranteed rights by prohibiting conduct that is not itself forbidden by the Fourteenth Amendment.

- Unlike the rational-basis test for disability-based distinctions used in *Garrett*, *supra*, the standard for demonstrating the constitutionality of a gender-based classification is a heightened level of scrutiny.

- Under *Boerne*, *supra*, to be valid, section 5 legislation must show congruence and proportionality between the injury to be prevented or remedied and the means adopted to that end. FMLA protects the right to be free from gender-based discrimination in the workplace. Congress has created a legislative record that demonstrates widespread gender-based unconstitutional discrimination by the states. This record of discrimination is sufficient to justify FMLA as prophylactic section 5 legislation.

Concurrence (Souter, Ginsburg, Breyer, JJ.). The Court's opinion is correct here, but the dissenting views from *Seminole Tribe of Florida v. Florida*, *supra*, remain valid.

Concurrence (Stevens, J.). The FMLA is a valid exercise of Congress's commerce clause power.

Dissent (Scalia, J.). Congress must find a violation by the state against which the enforcement action is taken to justify a prophylactic congressional action to enforce the Fourteenth Amendment. D should be able to show that the mere fact Nevada is a state and that some states have been bad actors is insufficient to overcome Nevada's Eleventh Amendment immunity, absent a showing that Nevada has violated the Fourteenth Amendment.

Dissent (Kennedy, Scalia, Thomas, JJ.). There is insufficient evidence here of a pattern of unlawful conduct that would warrant the remedy of opening state treasuries to private suits. The FMLA is not a remedy but a benefit program.

---

e) State employees can recover for ADA Title II violations--

Tennessee v. Lane

Facts. Title II of the ADA prohibits a public entity from denying the benefits of its services, programs, or activities to disabled persons. Under the statute, a "public entity" includes state and local governments. Lane and Jones (Ps) were paraplegics who used wheelchairs. Lane was required to answer a set of criminal charges, but the courtroom was on the second floor and the courthouse had no elevator. Lane had to crawl up two flights of stairs to get to the courtroom. He refused to do so again for a subsequent appearance and he was jailed for failure to appear. Jones was a court reporter who lost work and the opportunity to participate in the judicial process because she was unable to gain access to a number of county courthouses. Ps sued Tennessee (D) under Title II of the ADA. The district court denied D's motion to dismiss. The Sixth Circuit affirmed, concluding that *Garrett*, *supra*, barred private ADA suits against states based on equal protection principles but not suits based on due process principles. The Supreme Court granted certiorari.

Issue. May Congress abrogate state immunity from suits brought under Title II of the ADA for denial of public services to disabled individuals?

Held. Yes. Judgment affirmed.

- ♦ The legislative history of the ADA includes congressional findings that individuals with disabilities are a discrete and insular minority who have been subjected to a history of purposeful unequal treatment based on characteristics beyond their control. Title II prohibits any public entity from discriminating against disabled persons in the provision of public services. The term "public entity" includes state and local governments.

- ♦ D claims that Congress did not have power under Section 5 to abrogate state immunity under the Eleventh Amendment. In *Garrett*, the Court applied the *Boerne* test, *supra*, to reject Title I of the ADA as a valid exercise of Congress's power because Title I was not supported by a relevant history and pattern of constitutional violations, and because Title I's remedial scheme was not sufficiently targeted to prevent unconstitutional discrimination in public employment.

- ♦ Unlike Title I, Title II involves rights of access to the courts that are protected by the Due Process Clause as well as the Confrontation Clause of the Sixth Amendment. The legislative history of Title II demonstrates a systematic deprivation by the states of the fundamental rights of disabled people. Title II is aimed at enforcing basic rights.

- ♦ Title II is an appropriate response to the history and pattern of unequal treatment because its requirement of program accessibility is congruent and proportional to its object of enforcing the right of access to the courts. This is an appropriately limited remedy.

Concurrence (Souter, Ginsburg, JJ.). It is appropriate for Congress to address the situation of disabled access to the courts since the courts themselves have, in the past, contributed to the imposition of legal impediments for disabled persons.

Concurrence (Ginsburg, Souter, Breyer, JJ.). Congress should not be required to indict each state for disregarding the equal-citizenship stature of disabled persons before exercising its authority under section 5 to require government actors to respect the dignity of disabled persons.

Dissent (Rehnquist, C.J., Kennedy, Thomas, JJ.). The majority's decision is irreconcilable with *Garrett*. The majority identifies few, if any, constitutional violations perpetrated by the states against disabled persons, and certainly no patterns of such violations. As noted in *Garrett*, a law requiring special accommodations for the disabled would have to come from positive law and not through the Equal Protection Clause. The majority claims Title II vindicates fundamental rights protected by the Due Process Clause, but it is not tailored to provide protection of these rights. Finally, the majority cures Title II's overbreadth by considering it as applied, but this assumes a hypothetical statute; the real Title II applies to all services and activities of the states.

Dissent (Scalia, J.). The *Boerne* test, resting on such malleable standards as "proportionality," leaves the decision of these cases up to the individual judges' policy preferences. The Court should avoid constitutional rules that result in constant conflicts with Congress, especially when the rule has no demonstrable basis in the text of the Constitution and cannot objectively be shown to have been met or to have failed. Nothing in section 5 allows Congress to go beyond the provision of the Fourteenth Amendment to remedy conduct that does not in itself violate the Fourteenth Amendment. Congress only has power to impose prophylactic section 5 legislation on those states in which there has been an identified history of relevant constitutional violations. Requiring access for disabled persons to all public buildings cannot remotely be considered a means of "enforcing" the Fourteenth Amendment.

Dissent (Thomas, J.). *Hibbs*, *supra*, was wrongly decided, as is this case.

3) Limit on congressional interpretation of the Constitution--

Dickerson v. United States,

Facts. After the decision in *Miranda v. Arizona*, 384 U.S. 436 (1966), Congress adopted 18 U.S.C. section 3501, which provided that the admissibility of statements made during custodial interrogation should turn only on whether they were voluntary. Dickerson (D) was indicted for bank robbery and other related offenses. Prior to trial, D moved to suppress a statement he had made at an FBI office, claiming he had not received his *Miranda* warnings before being questioned. The district court granted his motion, but the court of appeals reversed. Although agreeing that D had not received the *Miranda* warnings, the court held that, under section 3501, admissibility depends solely on whether D made the statements voluntarily, because *Miranda* was not a constitutional holding, and thus Congress could have the final say on the question of admissibility. The Supreme Court granted certiorari.

Issue. May Congress overrule the principle set forth in *Miranda v. Arizona*?

Held. No. Judgment reversed.

- Prior to *Miranda*, the courts applied a voluntariness test to determine the admissibility of a suspect's confession. Originally, this test was based on the common law, but eventually the Court recognized two constitutional bases for a voluntariness test: the Fifth Amendment right against self-incrimination and the Due Process Clause of the Fourteenth Amendment, which makes the Fifth Amendment applicable to the states.

- *Miranda* was a response to modern custodial police interrogation that pressures the individual and presents a heightened risk of a violation of the Fifth Amendment. The *Miranda* warning was established as a concrete constitutional guideline for law enforcement agencies and courts to follow.

- Congress intended to overrule *Miranda* by adopting section 3501. Congress does have the ultimate authority to modify or set aside any judicially created rules of evidence and procedure, except those required by the Constitution. In *Miranda*, the Court specifically stated that it was establishing a constitutional guideline. The Court has applied *Miranda* to the states, which it can only do if it involves a constitutional requirement since the Court has no supervisory authority over state courts.

- In *Miranda*, the Court recognized that Congress or the states could create alternative methods for protecting the privilege against self-incrimination, but any such alternatives would have to be at least as effective as the *Miranda* warnings. Section 3501 falls short as an adequate substitute for the *Miranda* warnings.

- Whether the Court would now agree with *Miranda*, the principles of stare decisis weigh heavily against overruling it now. *Miranda* has become a routine police practice and is part of our national culture. The totality of the circumstances approach of section 3501 is more difficult for police to comply with and for courts to apply consistently. *Miranda* remains the best approach to protecting the right against self-incrimination.

Dissent (Scalia, Thomas, JJ.). The majority does not merely reaffirm *Miranda*, but provides a radical revision of its rationale. *Marbury v. Madison*, 1 Cranch 137 (1803), provided that the courts will not enforce an act of Congress that violates the Constitution. Yet the majority cannot identify how section 3501 prescribes anything that violates the Constitution. Now, the majority holds that a statute of Congress can be disregarded as well when what it prescribes contradicts a decision of this Court that announced a constitutional rule. In other words, the majority holds that this Court has the power to expand the Constitution, not merely to apply it.

Comment. Recall that in *Saenz v. Roe, supra*, the Court held that the constitutional right to travel superseded state regulations adopted under authority of Congress.

IV. CONSTITUTIONAL PROTECTION OF EXPRESSION AND CONSCIENCE

A. GOVERNMENTAL CONTROL OF THE CONTENT OF EXPRESSION

1. Introduction to Problems of Content Control of Speech.

a. General introduction.

1) **The constitutional provision—The First Amendment.** "Congress shall make no law . . . abridging the freedom of speech, or of the press; or the right of the people peaceably to assemble, and to petition the Government for a redress of grievances."

2) **Balancing interests.** The right to freedom of expression is not an absolute right to say or do anything that one desires; rather, the interests of the government in regulating such expression must be balanced against the very strong interests on which this right is based.

   a) **The rationale.** The rationale behind freedom of speech is (i) that such freedom will lead to the discovery of truth and better ideas through the competition of differing viewpoints, and (ii) that such speech and action are necessary for a free society that is to be governed by democratic principles (*i.e.*, change can be brought about by the will of the people, expressed in nonviolent ways).

   b) **Presumption of validity.** Legislation, even legislation that imposes limitations on freedom of expression, is presumed valid until the person attacking such legislation can show otherwise (*i.e.*, that the interests of the government are outweighed by those interests imposed on by the regulation).

   c) **Invalid on its face.** Note that sometimes the United States Supreme Court will hold that a statute is invalid on its face (*i.e.*, that the statute in all of its possible applications is unconstitutional); in other cases, and far more frequently, the United States Supreme Court will hold that the statute is unconstitutional only as applied to a particular fact situation (the one before the Court at that time).

d) **Content.** Restrictions on content are especially inimical to the values of a free society, and are therefore very closely scrutinized.

b. **World War I and post-war cases.**

1) **Incitement.** *Masses Publishing Co. v. Patten*, 244 F. 535 (S.D.N.Y. 1917), dealt with the case of a New York postmaster who refused to accept for mailing a magazine published by Masses Publishing Co. that contained political arguments. The postmaster claimed that the publication violated the Espionage Act. Judge Learned Hand granted an injunction to the publishing company, finding that the government may not refuse use of the mails to a private magazine that criticizes public policy unless the magazine contains direct advocacy of resistance, or actual incitement. The circuit court did not agree with Judge Learned Hand's incitement test and reversed the decision on appeal.

2) **The clear and present danger test.** In *Schenck v. United States*, 249 U.S. 47 (1919), the Court held that Congress may outlaw speech that presents a clear and present danger to an important government interest. The case involved the Espionage Act of 1917, which made it a crime to cause or attempt to cause insubordination in the military forces or to obstruct recruitment. Schenck and others were charged with such an attempt as a result of publishing a pamphlet that attacked the Conscription Act and encouraged disobedience to it. The defendants' conviction was upheld, with the Court finding that the right of free expression is not absolute but varies with the circumstances; for example, a person is not free to falsely yell "fire" in a crowded theater.

3) **Intent.** In *Abrams v. United States*, 250 U.S. 616 (1919), the Court upheld the conviction of Abrams under amendments to the Espionage Act that broadened its coverage. However, Justice Holmes dissented. He felt that Congress could limit expression only where there was the present danger of immediate evil or an intent to bring it about. Both were lacking in this case. He also felt that the First Amendment did ***not*** leave the common law as to seditious libel in force, and implied that the majority did.

4) **Legislative facts--**

Gitlow v. New York, 268 U.S. 652 (1925).

Facts. Gitlow (D) was convicted and imprisoned for violating a New York law that prohibited language advocating, advising, or teaching the overthrow of organized government by unlawful means. D appeals. There was no evidence of any effect resulting from D's actions.

Issue. May states prohibit advocacy of criminal anarchy when there is no concrete result, or likelihood of such a result, flowing from such advocacy?

Held. Yes. Judgment affirmed.

- ♦ The state has penalized, not doctrinal exposition or academic discussion, but language urging criminal action to overthrow the government. D's expressions clearly fit the statutory prohibition; his words were the language of direct incitement. The state has determined that such activity is so inimical to the general welfare that it may be penalized in the exercise of its police power. The state has sought to suppress the threatened danger in its incipiency. Because the statute is not arbitrary or unreasonable, it must be upheld.

- ♦ If the statute itself is constitutional and the use of language falls within its reach, absence of actual results is irrelevant. The state has determined that these utterances involve sufficient likelihood of causing harm that they must be discouraged, and that determination cannot be shown to be clearly erroneous.

Dissent (Holmes, Brandeis, JJ.). D's words did not constitute a present danger of an actual attempt to overthrow the government; they were too indefinite and ineffective. To say that D's words were an incitement proves nothing, for every idea is an incitement and moves to action depending on outside circumstances.

---

5) **The rationale for free speech.** In *Whitney v. California*, 274 U.S. 357 (1927), the Court ruled that a state may outlaw mere membership in a criminal organization even if the individual member intends no criminal acts. Whitney helped organize and became a member of the Communist Labor Party of California, an organization that advocated, taught, and aided criminal syndicalism as defined by the Criminal Syndication Act of California. She appealed her conviction, claiming that although she remained a member, she did not intend that the party be an instrument of terrorism or violence. The Court affirmed her conviction, holding that the Act was not void for vagueness and that its purpose was clearly proper. A state may exercise its police power to outlaw organizations menacing the peace and welfare of the state. A person who abuses the right of association by joining such an organization is not protected by the Due Process Clause from punishment. Justice Brandeis wrote a concurrence in *Whitney* outlining the rationale behind freedom of expression: (i) freedom of expression is an end in itself; (ii) it is a safety valve for frustration; and (iii) it is a means

for finding the truth through the competition of ideas. According to Brandeis, suppression of free speech can be justified only if: (i) reasonable grounds exist to fear that a serious evil will otherwise result; and (ii) reasonable grounds exist for believing that there is imminent danger that the serious evil will occur. In another case, the Court reversed a conviction under a state criminal syndicalism act where the sole offense charged was that the defendant had assisted in the conduct of an otherwise lawful public meeting held under the auspices of the Communist Party. [*See* De Jonge v. Oregon, 299 U.S. 353 (1937)]

c. **Post-World War II and the Smith Act.**

1) **Introduction.** The Smith Act [18 U.S.C. §2385] makes it unlawful for any person: (i) to knowingly or willfully advocate, abet, advise, or teach the duty, necessity, desirability, or propriety of overthrowing any government in the United States by force or violence; (ii) to attempt to commit or to conspire to commit any of such acts; or (iii) to become a member of any organization advocating such acts, knowing its purposes. [18 U.S.C. §2385] The Court upheld the Smith Act in *Dennis v. United States*, 341 U.S. 494 (1951). In *Dennis*, the defendants had been holding classes, giving speeches, and writing articles that advocated overthrow of the government. This was the illegal advocacy involved. Although in *Dennis* the defendants were ringleaders, it was thereafter thought that all that need be shown for a conviction of any person was that he was linked with the organization (which advocated overthrow as fast as possible). In all cases, of course, there had to be shown some connection between the advocacy and the proscribed evil (this was the clear and present danger aspect of the case). However, this connection could be supplied by judicial notice. After the Court in *Dennis* held the Smith Act constitutional, the government brought many actions against alleged Communists.

2) **Mere advocacy.** The Smith Act does ***not*** prohibit "mere advocacy" or teaching of forcible overthrow as an abstract principle, apart from an effort to instigate action to that end. This is true even though such advocacy is engaged in with evil intent and uttered with the hope that it may ultimately lead to violent revolution. The urging of ***action*** for forcible overthrow is a necessary element of the proscribed advocacy.

a) **Advocacy of abstract doctrine--**

Yates v. United States, 354 U.S. 298 (1957).

Facts. Yates (D) and others were convicted under the Smith Act of conspiring to advocate and teach the criminal overthrow of the United States government and to organize a group of persons to so advocate and teach. D appeals the conviction on grounds that the jury instructions failed to distinguish between advocacy of abstract doctrine and advocacy of unlawful action.

Issue. Does the Smith Act reach persons conspiring to advocate mere belief in the desirability of overthrowing the government?

Held. No. Judgment reversed and case remanded (five of the 14 petitioners were acquitted).

- The Court has consistently recognized a distinction between advocacy of abstract doctrine and advocacy directed at promoting unlawful action. The trial court misunderstood *Dennis, supra,* to obliterate the distinction. The distinction is not between advocacy as such and mere discussion or exposition of violent overthrow as an abstract theory, but between advocacy of action and advocacy of belief.

Concurrence and dissent (Black, Douglas, JJ.). All the petitioners should be acquitted because the underlying statutory provisions abridge freedom of speech, press, and assembly.

Dissent (Clark, J.). These convictions should be upheld since all the petitioners were closely involved with the defendants in *Dennis*, whose convictions were upheld.

---

3) Adequacy of proof--

Scales v. United States, 367 U.S. 203 (1961).

Facts. Scales (D) was convicted of violating the membership clause of the Smith Act and appeals, challenging the clause both on its face and as applied.

Issue. May Congress punish active members of an organization that engages in criminal activity based solely on that membership?

Held. Yes. Judgment affirmed.

- Familiar concepts of the law of conspiracy and complicity bring individual associational relationships within the reach of criminal law, even in the absence of specific criminal acts. The Smith Act reaches only "active" members whose membership constitutes a purposeful form of complicity in a group engaging in forbidden advocacy.

- ♦ Because the Smith Act offenses involve subtle elements, strict assessment of the adequacy of proof is necessary. There must be proof of reasonably consistent illegal advocacy, and of ties between the advocacy and the organization itself. The Court had sufficient evidence to justify its findings.

Dissent (Black, J.). The Court improperly uses a balancing test to justify its refusal to fully protect First Amendment freedoms.

Dissent (Douglas, J.). D is punished solely for his mere belief.

Dissent (Brennan, J., Warren, C.J., Douglas, J.). Section 4(f) of the Internal Security Act immunizes D from prosecution under the membership clause.

---

d. Current status of the clear and present danger test--

Brandenburg v. Ohio, 395 U.S. 444 (1969).

Facts. Brandenburg (D), a Ku Klux Klan leader, was convicted under an Ohio statute for advocating criminal terrorism and criminal syndicalism. His activities consisted of inviting television reporters to a secluded gathering where weapons were present and a speech was made. There was no threat of imminent lawless action. The state courts upheld the conviction, and D appeals.

Issue. May a state law prohibit advocacy of civil disruption without distinguishing between mere advocacy and incitement to imminent lawless action?

Held. No. Judgment reversed.

- ♦ The constitutional guarantees of free speech and free press do not permit a state to forbid or proscribe advocacy of the use of force or of law violation except where such advocacy is directed to inciting or producing imminent lawless action and is likely to incite or produce such action. Ohio's law fails to make the required distinction and cannot be upheld. *Whitney*, *supra*, is overruled.

Concurrence (Black, J.). The Court cites *Dennis, supra,* but properly does not agree with the *Dennis* "clear and present danger" doctrine.

Concurrence (Douglas, J.). The line between permissible and impermissible acts is the line between ideas and overt acts. The "clear and present danger" test has no place in the Constitution. Where speech is inseparable from action, a prosecution can be launched for the overt act actually caused. Otherwise, speech is immune from prosecution.

---

2. Vague or Overbroad Regulations and Prior Restraint.

a. **Vagueness and overbreadth.** Although all statutes must be definite and certain in order to be enforceable, this is a fundamental requirement regarding criminal statutes. The statute must give "fair warning" of the conduct that it makes a crime; *i.e.*, it must be sufficiently explicit to inform those who are subject to it exactly what conduct on their part will render them liable to its penalties. Moreover, the requirement of certainty prevents arbitrary and discriminatory enforcement of criminal statutes (*i.e.*, it ensures explicit standards to guide the police as well as the public). In the free speech area, the Court has permitted regulatory statutes to be challenged if they are overbroad on their face (reaching both protected and unprotected expressions) or if they are underinclusive.

1) **Standard of guilt required.** In *Herndon v. Lowry*, 301 U.S. 242 (1937), Herndon was arrested while possessing Communist literature advocating strikes, etc. He was convicted for "attempting to incite insurrection." The Court reversed for failure of proof and because the statute did not provide a sufficiently ascertainable standard of guilt.

2) **Vague definition of "annoy"--**

Coates v. Cincinnati, 402 U.S. 611 (1971).

Facts. Cincinnati (P) made it a criminal offense for "three or more persons to assemble . . . on any of the sidewalks . . . and there conduct themselves in a manner annoying to persons passing by. . . ." Coates (D) was convicted of violating the ordinance, although no facts were given in the record. D appeals, claiming that the ordinance is unconstitutional on its face.

Issue. May a city outlaw all sidewalk assemblies that annoy passersby?

Held. No. Judgment reversed.

- The ordinance is unconstitutionally vague because the meaning of "annoy" is unclear. Possible violators therefore lack adequate notice of the conduct prohibited, in violation of due process.

- The ordinance also permits unconstitutional infringement of the right of free assembly and association. Mere public intolerance or animosity cannot justify restriction of these rights, but the ordinance would make criminal any assembly that "annoys" passersby.

Dissent (White, J., Burger, C.J., Blackmun, J.). The ordinance prohibits conduct clearly within the reach of the law. Although it might apply to some conduct beyond the law's reach, such a determination could only be made where actual facts are presented. Although statutes regulating speech may be invalid on their face if overbroad, this statute deals with conduct, not speech.

Dissent (Black, J.). These issues cannot be adjudicated without a record showing the relevant facts. The case should be remanded.

---

3) **Restriction on partisan political activities upheld.** In *Broadrick v. Oklahoma*, 413 U.S. 601 (1973), the Court sustained state law restrictions on partisan political activities by public employees, despite charges of vagueness and overbreadth. "Although such laws, if too broadly worded, may deter protected speech to some unknown extent, there comes a point where that effect—at best a prediction—cannot, with confidence, justify invalidating a statute on its face and so prohibiting a State from enforcing the statute against conduct that is admittedly within its power to proscribe. . . . [P]articularly where conduct and not merely speech is involved, we believe that the overbreadth of a statute must not only be real, but substantial as well, judged in relation to the statute's plainly legitimate sweep."

b. **Prior restraints.** Government normally cannot regulate in advance what expressions may or may not be uttered or published, even to guard against speech or ideas that, once published, would be constitutionally unprotected and hence subject to state punishment.

1) **Defamatory publications--**

Near v. Minnesota, 283 U.S. 697 (1931).

Facts. Minnesota (P) enacted a statute that provided for the abatement, as a public nuisance, of any "malicious, scandalous, and defamatory" publication. Near (D) published a periodical that criticized law enforcement officers. P brought an action seeking to suppress D's publication. The state courts granted P's request, and D appeals.

Issue. May a state provide for prior restraint of defamatory publications?

Held. No. Judgment reversed.

- Permitting public authorities to suppress publication of scandalous matter relating to charges of official dereliction, restrained only by the publisher's ability to satisfy the judge that the charges are true, is of the essence of censorship.

Liberty of the press under the Constitution has meant, principally, although not exclusively, immunity from previous restraints or censorship. The only permissible restraint is the deterrent effect of actions against defamatory publications arising after publication.

- The burden of instituting the proceedings or proving that the material is protected speech cannot be placed on the censored party.

Dissent (Butler, Van Devanter, McReynolds, Sutherland, JJ.). The previous restraints precluded by the First Amendment refer to subjection of the press to the arbitrary will of an administrative officer. There is no similarity between such impermissible previous restraint and the decree authorized by this statute to prevent further publication of defamatory articles, and the statute should be upheld.

---

2) **Judicial review of censorship.** In *Freedman v. Maryland*, 380 U.S. 51 (1965), the Court articulated certain steps that must be taken to guard against the dangers inherent in a censorship system.

   a) The burden of instituting judicial proceedings, and of proving that the material is "obscene" or otherwise unprotected, must rest on the censor.

   b) Any restraint on the speech or publication pending judicial review can be imposed only for a specified brief period, and only for the purpose of preserving the status quo.

   c) A prompt and final determination must be ensured.

3) **Permit requirement--**

Watchtower Bible and Tract Society of New York v. Village of Stratton, 536 U.S. 150 (2002).

Facts. The Village of Stratton (D) adopted an ordinance that regulated uninvited peddling and solicitation on private property by requiring a permit from the Mayor to engage in door-to-door advocacy, including the promoting of any "cause." A holder of such a permit must display the permit, with his name on it, to any police officer or resident who requests to see it. The ordinance also prohibits uninvited canvassers from entering any property where a "No Solicitation" sign is posted. Watchtower Bible and Tract Society of New York (P) coordinated preaching activities of Jehovah's Witnesses throughout the United States, including in D. P's preachers did not solicit contributions, but offered free literature and accepted donations. P sued D to get an injunction against enforcement of the ordinance, claiming it violated the First Amendment. The district court upheld the ordinance. The Sixth Circuit affirmed. The Supreme Court granted certiorari.

Issue. May a city require people to get a permit before engaging in the door-to-door advocacy of a political or religious cause?

Held. No. Judgment reversed and case remanded.

- The Court has invalidated restrictions on door-to-door canvassing and pamphleteering for many years, mostly in cases involving Jehovah's Witnesses, for whom canvassing is part of their religion. These cases implicate First Amendment interests in the free exercise of religion, freedom of speech, and freedom of the press.

- Door-to-door canvassing and pamphleteering have historically been important vehicles for the dissemination of ideas. However, local governments such as D have an interest in some form of regulation to prevent fraud, such as where solicitation for money is involved, and to prevent crimes such as burglary. Therefore, any regulation must balance these interests with First Amendment rights.

- D asserts that its ordinance serves the proper governmental interests of preventing fraud, preventing crime, and protecting residents' privacy. However, the ordinance applies to promoters of any "cause," not merely to commercial activities and the solicitation of funds. As such, it applies to religious causes and political activity.

- The government may not require citizens to first inform the government of their desire to speak to neighbors and then obtain a permit to do so. D's ordinance is overbroad and is not tailored to D's stated interests. A canvasser who ignores a "No Solicitation" sign is no less annoying because he or she has a permit. The lack of a permit would not preclude criminals from knocking on doors and engaging in conversations not covered by the ordinance, such as asking for directions or posing as census takers.

Concurrence (Breyer, Souter, Ginsburg, JJ.). D did not specifically state that preventing burglaries and violent crimes was an important justification for the ordinance.

Concurrence (Scalia, Thomas, JJ.). While the majority's rationale is largely acceptable, the fact that some people may have a religious objection to applying for a permit should not be a ground for finding D's ordinance invalid.

Dissent (Rehnquist, C.J.). The problem of crime has been associated with door-to-door canvassing for many years. The Court has long held that a town may require a permit for door-to-door canvassers, as long as no discretion is given to the issuing authority. The effect of the Court's decision is likely to cut off door-to-door communication because citizens, left unprotected by the permit requirement, will be forced to resort to posting "No Solicitation" signs. D's ordinance should be upheld.

3. **Speech Conflicting with Other Community Values: Government Control of the Content of Speech.**

a. **Protection of individual reputation and privacy.**

1) **In general.** Speech or writing that is defamatory is not constitutionally protected, and may be punished through criminal libel laws or civil laws awarding damages based on such publications. [*See* Beauharnais v. Illinois, 343 U.S. 250 (1952)—convictions for circulating anti-black literature were upheld under a state "group criminal libel" statute; publications aimed at a group of individuals]

2) **Constitutional privilege—matters of public interest.** The conflict between the need for full disclosure and debate on matters of public interest and the need to protect personal reputations against injurious falsehoods has been resolved by creating a constitutional privilege for certain kinds of defamations. For example, no award of damages for defamation is constitutionally permissible where the publication deals with the official conduct of public officials, unless the publication was made with "actual malice" (knowledge of falsity or reckless disregard as to truth or falsity).

3) **Leading case--**

New York Times Co. v. Sullivan, 376 U.S. 254 (1964).

Facts. Sullivan (P) was a commissioner of the city of Montgomery, Alabama, and supervised the police department. *The New York Times* (D) carried a full-page advertisement that included several false statements regarding repressive police conduct in Montgomery. P sued for damages on grounds that D libeled him; although P's name was not mentioned, the accusations of the ad could be read as referring to him. The trial court awarded damages of $500,000, which was upheld in the state courts. The controlling state rule of law dealt with libel per se, established here merely by showing that D's statements reflected on the agency that P supervised. Once libel per se is demonstrated, the only defense is the truth. D appeals.

Issue. Do the First and Fourteenth Amendments prevent state rules that would allow a public official to recover damages for a defamatory falsehood relating to his official conduct without proof of actual malice?

Held. Yes. Judgment reversed.

- ♦ The Constitution expresses a profound commitment to uninhibited debate on public issues. This protection does not turn on the truth of the ideas or beliefs expressed, nor does concern for official reputation remove defamatory statements from the constitutional shield.

- ♦ The deterrent effect of damage awards—without the need for any proof of actual pecuniary loss—is so great as to severely chill public criticism that should be openly permitted under the First Amendment.

- ♦ Despite First Amendment considerations, a public official may recover damages for a defamatory falsehood to his official conduct if he proves the statement was made with "actual malice," *i.e.*, knowledge of its falsity or reckless disregard as to its truth or falsity. P's proof falls short.

Concurrence (Black, Douglas, JJ.). Malice is too hard to prove or disprove. I reverse on the grounds that D had an absolute, unconditional constitutional right to publish the critical advertisement.

Concurrence (Goldberg, Douglas, JJ.). Citizens have an absolute, unconditional privilege to criticize official conduct despite the harm that may flow from excesses and abuses.

---

4) **Public figures.** The *New York Times* rule, *supra*, relating to defamation of public officials also has been extended to "public figures," on the theory that such persons have the power to counteract false statements.

   a) **Definition and scope.** A person may be deemed a "public figure" (i) for all purposes and in all contexts, if he achieves general fame or notoriety in the community and pervasive involvement in the affairs of society; or (ii) for a limited range of public controversies into which he has voluntarily assumed a central role or into which he has been drawn.

   b) **Persons involved in public issues--**

Gertz v. Robert Welch, Inc., 418 U.S. 323 (1974).

Facts. Gertz (P), an attorney, represented the family of a victim murdered by a police officer in the family's civil suit against the officer. Robert Welch, Inc. (D), publisher of *American Opinion*, published an article concededly untrue that discredited P's reputation and motives. P sued D for libel. After a jury awarded damages to P, the trial court reconsidered and decided that D was protected by application of the *New York Times* rule, *supra* (holding that discussion of any public issue is protected, regardless of the status of the person defamed). Because P was unable to prove that D acted with "actual malice," the court entered a judgment n.o.v. for D. The court of appeals affirmed, and P appeals.

Issue. May a member of the press who published defamatory falsehoods about a person who is neither a public official nor a public figure, but who is involved in a public issue, claim a constitutional privilege against liability for injuries?

Held. No. Judgment reversed.

- The need to avoid self-censorship by the news media must be balanced against the legitimate interest in permitting compensation for harm resulting from defamatory falsehoods. Defamation plaintiffs are not all in the same class, however. Public officials and public figures have more access to the media to counteract falsehoods than do private individuals such as P. Private individuals are also more deserving of recovery because their public exposure is not voluntary. Therefore, the rationale behind the *New York Times* rule does not extend to private individuals.

- Involvement in a public issue, by itself, does not bring a private individual within the class covered by the *New York Times* rule. D was not a public official or public figure. To protect defamations whenever a "public issue" was involved would introduce new uncertainties and broadly expand the scope of the *New York Times* rule.

- States may define their own standards of liability for defamation by a publisher or broadcaster, but may not impose liability without fault. However, states may not permit recovery of presumed or punitive damages in the absence of proof of "actual malice" (knowledge of falsity or reckless disregard for the truth). The only permissible recovery for a private defamation plaintiff who establishes liability under any standard less demanding than the *New York Times* test is compensation for actual injury.

Dissent (Douglas, J.). The Constitution prohibits defamation actions against publishers for the discussion of public affairs.

Dissent (Brennan, J.). The *New York Times* rule should apply to discussions of public issues.

Dissent (White, J.). The states should be free to impose strict liability in cases like this.

Comment. A person is not a "public figure" simply because she is extremely wealthy and engaged in divorce proceedings of interest to the reading public. The fact that she files for divorce (and even holds press conferences during the proceedings) does not mean that she voluntarily chooses to publicize her married life, since going to court is the only way she can legally dissolve her marriage. [*See* Time, Inc. v. Firestone, 424 U.S. 448 (1976)]

---

5) **Private individuals.**

a) **Fault and damages rules.** If the defamed person is neither a public figure nor a public official (or candidate for public office), "free speech" considerations are not as strong. Private individuals are more susceptible to injury because they do not usually have media access to counteract false statements published about them. Consequently, the states may impose whatever standard of defamation liability they choose, except that on matters of public concern:

(1) The factual misstatement must be such as would warn a reasonably prudent publisher or broadcaster of its defamatory potential;

(2) There must be a finding (by the trier of fact or the appellate court) that the publisher or broadcaster was at least negligent in publishing the misstatement (*i.e.*, liability without fault cannot be imposed); and

(3) Damages must be limited to "actual injury" (which includes any out-of-pocket loss plus impairment of reputation, personal humiliation, and mental anguish). An award of "presumed" or punitive damages is permissible only if the publication was made with knowledge of its falsity or in reckless disregard for the truth.

b) **Elimination of media-nonmedia distinction--**

Dun & Bradstreet, Inc. v. Greenmoss Builders, Inc., 472 U.S. 749 (1985).

Facts. Dun & Bradstreet, Inc. (D) was a credit reporting agency. D reported that Greenmoss Builders, Inc. (P) had filed for bankruptcy. The report was false and negligently prepared. P sued for defamation and recovered compensatory and punitive damages. The lower courts upheld the award, and the Supreme Court granted certiorari.

Issue. May a defamed person recover presumed and punitive damages, even without proving actual malice, if the defamation is not speech on a public matter?

Held. Yes. Judgment affirmed.

- When defamatory statements involve no issue of public concern, the court must balance the state's interest in compensating injured parties against the First Amendment interest in protecting the expression. Speech on private matters does not merit the highest First Amendment protection; thus, there are fewer constitutional limits on state libel law in this area.

- Examination of D's credit report indicates that it did not constitute speech on a public issue. It was intended only for the benefit of D and its business audience of five subscribers. The speech was wholly false and clearly damaging to P. Thus, the speech merits little protection.

- There is little danger of chilling due to libel suits, because the market itself provides the incentive to be truthful.

Concurrence (Burger, C.J.). *Gertz, supra*, does not apply here because it is limited to cases involving matters of general public importance.

Concurrence (White, J.). *Gertz* should be overruled, but at any rate this case does not involve a matter of public importance.

Dissent (Brennan, Marshall, Blackmun, Stevens, JJ.). The First Amendment applies equally to citizens and the institutional press. The Court gives no guidance as to what is a protected matter of public concern. Surely a company's filing for bankruptcy is a matter of public concern to the community where the company is located. Bankruptcy is a matter of public record. The speech here was not advertising; even if the credit report is commercial speech, the appropriate remedy should be actual damages, or, on a showing of actual malice, presumed or punitive damages.

Comment. A majority of the Justices indicated that the *Gertz* rules would apply equally to media and nonmedia defendants.

---

6) Disclosure of private facts--

Florida Star v. B.J.F., 491 U.S. 524 (1989).

Facts. A Florida statute made it illegal to print, publish, or broadcast, in any instrument of mass communication, the name of the victim of a sexual offense. The Florida Star (D) obtained the name of B.J.F. (P), a rape victim, from a publicly released police report, and published P's name. P sued D and recovered $100,000 in damages. D appeals, claiming its publication was protected by the First Amendment.

Issue. May a state prohibit the press from publishing the name of a victim of a sexual offense if the name is released in a public police report?

Held. No. Judgment reversed.

- As a general rule, a newspaper that lawfully obtains truthful information about a matter of public significance may not be punished by state officials for publishing the information, absent a need to further a state interest of the highest order.

- In this case, the information published by D was truthful. D lawfully obtained P's name when the police released her name, even though the police were not required to disclose the information. The information about the violent crime is clearly a matter of public import.

- P claims that the statute furthers three important state interests: (i) the privacy of the victims; (ii) the physical safety of such victims; and (iii) the goal of encouraging victims to come forward. While these are highly significant interests, they are insufficient in this case because, where the state itself disclosed the information, punishing the press is not a narrowly tailored means of safeguarding anonymity. In addition, the statute imposes a negligence per se standard so that liability follows automatically from publication; this means D would be liable even if P's name were otherwise known. Finally, the statute is underinclusive because it does not apply to dissemination of the victim's name through means other than an instrument of mass communication.

Concurrence (Scalia, J.). The third ground of underinclusiveness is sufficient to decide the case. The statute appears to prohibit the press from doing something that society in general is not prohibited from doing. Hence, the statute cannot be said to protect an interest "of the highest order."

Dissent (White, J., Rehnquist, C.J., O'Connor, J.). The reasons given by the Court do not support its result. D obtained the report that inadvertently included P's name in a room that contained signs that made it clear that the names of rape victims were not matters of public record and were not to be published. The government did not thus consider dissemination lawful. It is not too much to ask the press not to publish a victim's name. The negligence per se standard is inapposite here because the jury found that D acted with reckless indifference toward P, but, on its face, the legislature could properly determine that disclosure of the fact that a person was raped is categorically a revelation that reasonable people find offensive. Finally, the law applies to all instruments of mass communication because the widespread distribution of rape victims' names is the objective aimed at.

Comment. The Court expressly declined to adopt a broad rule that truthful publication may never be punished, thereby preserving the need to assess the interaction between First Amendment and privacy rights on a case-by-case basis.

---

7) Disclosure of intercepted cell phone call--

Bartnicki v. Vopper, 532 U.S. 514 (2001).

Facts. During contentious union negotiations between a teachers' union and the school board, Bartnicki (P1), the union's chief negotiator, used a cell phone to talk with Kane (P2), the union's president. Ps discussed the status of the negotiations, which were contentious and were covered in the media. An unknown person intercepted and recorded Ps' conversation. During the call, Kane said, "If they're not gonna move for three percent, we're gonna have to go to their, their homes. . . . To blow off their front porches, we'll have to do some work on some of those guys." Vopper (D1), a radio commentator, had previously criticized the union. When the union and school board reached a settlement, Vopper played a tape of the intercepted conversation on his radio show. The media then further publicized it. Vopper had received the tape from Yocum (D2), the leader of a taxpayers' organization that opposed the union's demands, who had discovered the tape in his mailbox. Yocum had played it for members of the school board before delivering it to Vopper. Ps sued for damages. Both parties sought summary judgment. The district court granted a motion for an interlocutory appeal, and the court of appeals remanded the case with instructions to enter summary judgment for Ds. The Supreme Court granted certiorari.

Issue. Does the First Amendment protect the disclosure of a communication concerning matters of public concern if the communication had been illegally intercepted by someone other than the person disclosing it?

Held. Yes. Judgment affirmed.

- Title III of the Omnibus Crime Control and Safe Streets Act of 1968, which covers wiretapping and electronic surveillance, was enacted to effectively protect the privacy of wire and oral communications. Title III prohibits private persons from willfully disclosing the contents of electronic, wire, or oral communications that were illegally intercepted. Under a 1994 amendment, this includes the interception of conversations over both cellular and cordless phones.

- Ps' complaint alleges that Ds intentionally disclosed the contents of the conversations illegally recorded on the tapes and that Ds knew, or had reason to know, that the recording was illegal. For purposes of summary judgment determination, these allegations must be accepted as true.

- Although Ds did not participate in the illegal interception, and although they obtained the tape lawfully, Ds' disclosures fall within the scope of Title III. Thus, if Title III is valid, Ps would be entitled to recover damages.

- The tape involves a matter of public concern. Title III is not content based. To fulfill its purpose of protecting privacy, the statute applies to any illegally intercepted conversation. However, Title III does not regulate conduct; it is a regulation of pure speech. Generally, state action to punish the publication of truthful information is unconstitutional.

- The government has a legitimate interest in protecting privacy, which it protects by prohibiting an interceptor from using information acquired illegally. If the sanctions are inadequate to deter illegal actions, perhaps they should be made more severe, but the government cannot suppress speech by a law-abiding possessor of information in order to deter the conduct of a non-law-abiding third party.

- The government claims that it is necessary to protect the privacy of confidential communications to encourage the uninhibited exchange of ideas and information; the fear of public disclosure of private conversations might have a chilling effect on private speech. Nevertheless, in balancing the competing interests, privacy concerns must yield to the interest in publishing matters of public importance.

Concurrence (Breyer, O'Connor, JJ.). The majority's holding is correct based on the special circumstances of this case, where Ds acted lawfully prior to their disclosures, and the material published involved a matter of unusual public concern. The holding should not be read to extend beyond these circumstances.

Dissent (Rehnquist, C.J., Scalia, Thomas, JJ.). This decision diminishes, instead of enhances, the purposes of the First Amendment by chilling the speech of millions of Americans. Congress and the 40 states that have statutes similar to Title III should be allowed to prohibit knowing disclosure of illegally intercepted communications.

---

b. **Control of obscenity.**

1) **The rationale for prohibiting obscenity--**

Paris Adult Theatre I v. Slaton, 413 U.S. 49 (1973).

Facts. Slaton (P), a local state district attorney, filed civil complaints against the Paris Adult Theatre I (D), seeking to enjoin exhibition of films claimed to be obscene. The films were available only to "consenting adults." The trial judge dismissed the complaint but the Georgia Supreme Court reversed, holding that the films were without First Amendment protection. D appeals.

Issue. May a state prohibit commercial exhibition of "obscene" films to consenting adults?

Held. Yes. Judgment vacated and case remanded.

- The state afforded D the best possible notice, as no restraint on exhibition was imposed until after a full judicial proceeding determined that the films were obscene and therefore subject to regulation.

- Obscene, pornographic films do not acquire constitutional immunity from state regulation merely because they are shown to consenting adults only. The states have power to make a morally neutral judgment that public exhibition of obscene material, or commerce in such material, has a tendency to injure the community as a whole, even if actual exposure is limited to a few consenting adults.

- While the right of privacy may preclude regulation of use of obscene materials within the home, commercial ventures such as D's are not "private" for the purpose of civil rights litigation. Commerce in obscene material is unprotected by any constitutional doctrine of privacy.

- Incidental effects on human "utterances" or "thoughts" do not prevent state action to protect legitimate state interests where the communication is not protected by the First Amendment and where the right of privacy is not infringed on. Such state action is permitted as long as it conforms to the standards of *Miller, infra.*

Dissent (Brennan, Stewart, Marshall, JJ.). The Court's attempts to define obscenity have clearly failed. Government cannot constitutionally bar the distribution of even unprotected material to consenting adults.

Dissent (Douglas, J.). The First Amendment protects all expression, even "obscenity."

---

2) **The problem of definition.** Pornography and obscenity are not synonymous. The definition of obscenity posed a difficult problem for the Court. Even with the *Miller* definition, application can be difficult.

a) **The standard definition--**

Miller v. California, 413 U.S. 15 (1973).

Facts. Miller (D) was convicted under a California statute of knowingly distributing obscene matter to unwilling recipients. The statute incorporated the *Memoirs v. Massachusetts*, 383 U.S. 413 (1966), test of obscenity, namely, that to be unprotected by the First Amendment, the material must meet three criteria: (i) the dominant theme of the material taken as a whole appeals to a prurient interest in sex; (ii) the material is patently offensive because it affronts contemporary community standards relating to the description or representation of sexual matters; and (iii) the matcrial is utterly without redeeming social value. D appeals the conviction.

Issue. Is the *Memoirs* test the appropriate measure of obscene expressions?

Held. No. Judgment vacated and case remanded.

- Obscenity is not within the area of constitutionally protected speech or press. In *Roth v. United States*, 354 U.S. 476 (1957), obscenity was presumed to be "utterly without redeeming social value," but the *Memoirs* case transformed that presumption into a necessary element of proof. *Memoirs* thus requires the prosecution to prove a negative, and that test cannot be upheld.

- Regulation of obscene material is restricted to works that depict or describe sexual conduct, and must specifically define that conduct. The basic guidelines for the trier of fact must be: (i) whether the average person applying contemporary community standards would find that the work, taken as a whole, appeals to the prurient interest; (ii) whether the work depicts or describes, in a patently offensive way, sexual conduct specifically defined by the applicable state law; and (iii) whether the work, taken as a whole, lacks serious literary, artistic, political, or scientific value. Thus, material can be regulated without a showing that it is "***utterly*** without redeeming social value."

Dissent (Douglas, J.). The people through constitutional amendment, and not the courts, should decide what is and is not obscene.

Dissent (Brennan, Stewart, Marshall, JJ.). The challenged statute is unconstitutionally overbroad, hence invalid on its face.

---

b) Application of the *Miller* definition--

Jenkins v. Georgia, 418 U.S. 153 (1974).

Facts. Jenkins (D) was convicted of distributing obscene material for showing the film *Carnal Knowledge*. D appeals, claiming that, although the jury found the film obscene, it was not obscene by constitutional standards.

Issue. Does a jury's verdict as to obscenity preclude all further appellate review of a defendant's First Amendment protection claim?

Held. No. Judgment reversed.

- Although questions of appeal to the "prurient interest" or of patent offensiveness are questions of fact, juries do not have unrestrained discretion in their determinations. Although contemporary community standards are to be applied, no prosecutions are permissible unless the materials depict or describe patently offensive "hard core" sexual conduct.

- Appellate courts therefore have a duty to ensure that a jury's determination falls within these standards. This film, although dealing with sex and containing occasional scenes of nudity, lacked the patently offensive portrayal of sexual conduct that must be present to withdraw the material from constitutional protection.

Concurrence (Brennan, Stewart, Marshall, JJ.). The case illustrates the difficulties of the Court's attempt to define obscenity. As a result, case-by-case determinations of obscenity will be necessary.

Concurrence (Douglas, J.). Any ban on obscenity is unconstitutional.

Comment. A state may prohibit distribution of all child pornography, even without requiring that it be legally obscene. [New York v. Ferber, 458 U.S. 747 (1982)]

---

3) "Virtual" child pornography--

Ashcroft v. The Free Speech Coalition, 535 U.S. 234 (2002).

Facts. The Child Pornography Prevention Act of 1996 ("CPPA") expanded the federal prohibition of child pornography to include "virtual child pornography," which is sexually explicit images that appear to depict minors but are produced without using any real children, whether by using computer imaging or by using adults made to look like children. The CPPA did not require such pornography to be obscene under *Miller v. California, supra*, but prohibited all child pornography, real or virtual. The Free Speech Coalition (P), a trade association for the pornography or adult-entertainment industry, challenged the constitutionality of the CPPA. The district court granted summary judgment for Ashcroft (D), the U.S. Attorney General. The Ninth Circuit reversed, holding that pornography can be banned only if obscene under *Miller* or if it depicts actual children under *New York v. Ferber, supra*. The Supreme Court granted certiorari.

Issue. May Congress prohibit "virtual" child pornography?

Held. No. Judgment affirmed.

- Congress determined that children can be threatened by virtual pornography, even when they are not harmed in the production process, because pedophiles might use the materials to encourage children to participate in sexual activity. Virtual child pornography might also prompt the sexual appetites of pedophiles. The harm Congress identified flows from the content of the images, not from the means of production.

- Modern imaging technology also makes it harder to prosecute pornographers who use real minors. Innocent pictures of real children can be modified to make it appear that the children are engaged in sexual activity.

- The CPPA would be unconstitutional on its face if it prohibited a substantial amount of protected expression. The CPPA prohibits any depiction of sexually explicit activity, even if in a psychology manual or in a movie about the horrors of sexual abuse. It applies to depictions of persons under 18 years of age, which is higher than the legal age for marriage in many states, and higher than the age of consent. However, teenage sexual activity has been the topic of countless literary works, from Shakespeare to acclaimed modern movies.

- Congress cannot prohibit speech that adults have a right to hear in an attempt to shield children from that speech. It also cannot prohibit otherwise protected speech because pedophiles might use it for illegal purposes. The tendency of speech to encourage unlawful acts is not a sufficient reason for banning it.

- Under *Ferber*, the creation of the child pornography was itself the crime. In the case of virtual child pornography, there is no underlying crime. Virtual images would drive actual images from the market because producers of actual images would face severe prosecution, while producers of virtual images would not.

- D's argument that virtual pornography makes it difficult to prosecute actual child pornography is an argument that protected speech may be banned as a means to ban unprotected speech. However, D may not suppress lawful speech as the means to suppress unlawful speech. Protected speech does not become unprotected merely because it resembles unprotected speech.

- D suggested a rule that the CPPA would shift the burden to P to prove an affirmative defense. Creating such an affirmative defense would be ineffective because, under the CPPA, it wouldn't matter if the depicted sexual activity was "virtual" or real. Mere possession would be illegal, so it wouldn't matter whether the defendant could show that no children were harmed in producing the images.

Concurrence (Thomas, J.). If imaging technology develops to the point that the government cannot prove that child pornography depicts real children, it may be necessary to regulate virtual child pornography as long as there is an appropriate affirmative defense.

Concurrence and dissent (O'Connor, J., Rehnquist, C.J., Scalia, J.). The part of the CPPA that prohibits material that "conveys the impression" that it contains pornographic images of minors is properly held unconstitutional. However, the prohibition of pornographic images that "appear to be" of a minor should be struck down only where it is applied to the class of youthful-adult pornography. D's concern about the advances in computer-graphics technology is reasonable. The CPPA is narrowly tailored if the "appears to be" language is interpreted to mean "virtually indistinguishable from."

Dissent (Rehnquist, C.J., Scalia, J.). Congress has a compelling interest in making it possible to enforce prohibitions of actual child pornography. The CPPA need not be interpreted so as to reach films or other literature that has literary or artistic value.

---

4) **Limits on cable broadcasting--**

United States v. Playboy Entertainment Group, Inc., 529 U.S. 803 (2000).

Facts. The Telecommunications Act of 1996 contained regulations regarding cable operators who provide sexually oriented programming. Section 504 allows parents to tell cable operators to keep any channel out of their home. Section 505 requires cable operators to either fully scramble sexually oriented channels or to limit their transmission to between 10 p.m. and 6 a.m. When signals are not fully scrambled, the signal can occasionally bleed through to the viewer, but the technology to fully scramble signals was expensive, so most cable owners chose the limited transmission option. Playboy Entertainment Group, Inc. (P) challenged the regulations. The district court found that section 505's content-based restriction on speech violated the First Amendment because the government might further its interests in less restrictive ways. The United States (D) appeals.

Issue. May Congress require cable operators to limit the transmission of sexually oriented programming to nighttime hours?

Held. No. Judgment affirmed.

- The only reasonable way for many cable operators to comply with section 505 is to limit their broadcast to the eight specified nighttime hours, regardless of the wishes of the viewers. The record shows that as much as half of all adult programming is viewed by households prior to 10 p.m., so this regulation is a significant restriction of communication.

- Whether a regulation is a ban or a burden on speech, a content-based regulation must satisfy the same rigorous scrutiny. Because the statute is content-based, it must be narrowly tailored to promote a compelling government interest.

- The key difference between cable television and broadcasting media is that cable systems can block unwanted channels on a household-by-household basis. Targeted blocking is less restrictive than banning, so the government should not be allowed to ban speech if targeting blocking is reasonably available.

- Under section 504, parents can request blocking of sexually oriented programming to their homes. This approach is narrowly tailored to the government's goal of supporting parents who oppose this type of material. The government cannot impose a more burdensome restriction such as section 505 without showing that the less restrictive alternative is ineffective to meet its goals.

Concurrence (Stevens, J.). Justice Scalia, relying on *Ginzburg v. United States*, 383 U.S. 463 (1996), would treat programs whose content is protected by the First Amendment as though they were obscene because of the way they are advertised. The very fact that P's programs are offensive to many viewers justifies truthful statements about their content.

Concurrence (Thomas, J.). D has ample authority to completely prohibit the broadcasting of programming affected by section 505. But in the absence of factual findings, I am unwilling to rely on the view that some of the relevant programming is obscene.

Dissent (Scalia, J.). Section 505 can be upheld by simply finding that it regulates the business of obscenity. Even assuming the broadcasts are protected by the First Amendment, under *Ginzburg*, commercial entities that engage in pandering by deliberately emphasizing the sexually provocative aspects of their nonobscene products are not protected by the Constitution. Justice Breyer's analysis focuses on protection of children, but adults may also be offended by P's programming. The government could completely block these transmissions, so it should also be allowed to take the less drastic step of dictating how, and during what times, they may occur.

Dissent (Breyer, J., Rehnquist, C.J., O'Connor, J., Scalia, J.). Section 504's opt-out alternative may be less restrictive, but it is not similarly practical and effective as a way to protect children. Section 505 protects children against sexually oriented programming where parents are unaware of what the children are watching, cannot supervise television viewing habits, or are simply unavailable at critical times. It serves the same purpose as laws denying access to children to adult movies.

Comment. The majority addressed the dissent by stating that, even if the government has an interest in substituting itself for informed and empowered parents, its interest is not sufficiently compelling to justify a widespread restriction on speech.

---

5) Community standards on harmfulness to minors--

Ashcroft v. American Civil Liberties Union, 535 U.S. 564 (2002).

Facts. In response to the easy access of web-based pornography, Congress enacted the Communications Decency Act of 1996 ("CDA"), which prohibited the knowing transmission over the Internet of obscene or indecent messages to any recipient younger than 18 years of age. In *Reno v. American Civil Liberties Union*, 521 U.S. 844 (1997), the Court held that the CDA violated the First Amendment, partly because there was no technology that allowed communication to adults while denying it to minors, and partly because it was overbroad and lacked narrow tailoring. Subsequently, Congress enacted the Child Online Protection Act ("COPA"), which prohibits any person from knowingly making any communication for commercial purposes that is available to any minor and includes any material that is harmful to minors. The scope of COPA was limited to material displayed on the Internet and did not cover e-mail. COPA also was limited to commercial material that was harmful to minors. While COPA is more narrowly tailored than CDA, the ACLU (P) challenged the statute. The district court granted P a preliminary injunction. The Third Circuit affirmed. The Supreme Court granted certiorari.

Issue. May Congress use "community standards" to identify and prohibit "material that is harmful to minors" under the Child Online Protection Act?

Held. Yes. Judgment vacated.

- ♦ The *Miller* (*supra*) test of obscenity preserved the use of community standards, thereby making certain that material will be judged by its impact on an average person, rather than a particularly sensitive or insensitive person. COPA relies on this test to define "material that is harmful to minors," which COPA prohibits. The use of the *Miller* definition of obscenity, including the exclusion of material with serious value for minors, sufficiently limits COPA.

- ♦ The court of appeals determined that since access to the World Wide Web cannot be limited on a geographic basis, the "community standards" component of COPA would require all speakers on the Web to conform to the "most puritan" community's standards. However, in *Hamling v. United States*, 418 U.S. 87 (1974), the Court held that the First Amendment is not violated when a speaker disseminating material to a national audience must observe varying community standards. The unique characteristics of the Internet do not justify an approach different from *Hamling*.

Concurrence (O'Connor, J.). While P has not proven substantial overbreadth on this facial challenge, it may be possible for regulation of obscenity under COPA to raise First Amendment "as-applied" challenges in the future.

Concurrence (Breyer, J.). By using the term "community," Congress meant to describe the nation's adult community taken as a whole, instead of the adult community in geographically separate local areas.

Concurrence (Kennedy, Souter, Ginsburg, JJ.). The "community standards" criterion, in the context of the Internet, means that any communication available to a nationwide audience will be judged by the standards of the community most likely to be offended by the message. *Hamling* involved a completely different form of media and does not address the problems of Internet communication.

Dissent (Stevens, J.). The inability to limit geographic access to the Internet means that the community standards rules become a sword instead of a shield. The free speech rights of adults cannot be limited to what is acceptable for children.

6) Restricting Internet speech to protect minors--

Ashcroft v. American Civil Liberties Union, 542 U.S. 656 (2004).

Facts. This case is based on the same facts as *Ashcroft v. ACLU*, 535 U.S. 564 (2002), *supra*. On remand, the Third Circuit affirmed the original issuance of a preliminary junction, this time on the ground that COPA was not the least restrictive means available for D to serve the interest of preventing minors from using the Internet to gain access to harmful materials. The Supreme Court granted certiorari.

Issue. May the government restrict Internet speech to protect minors if there is a less restrictive means available to accomplish the government's legitimate objectives?

Held. No. Judgment affirmed.

- COPA imposes criminal penalties of a $50,000 fine and six months in prison for knowingly posting on the World Wide Web, for commercial purposes, content that is "harmful to minors" as defined in the statute. COPA provides an affirmative defense to those who use specified means to prevent minors from accessing the prohibited material, such as by requiring the use of a credit card, adult access code, or by any other reasonable measures that are feasible under available technology.

- In a challenge to a content-based speech restriction, D has the burden to prove that the proposed alternatives will not be as effective as the challenged statute. P has offered alternative, less restrictive means, such as blocking and filtering software, but D failed to show that it would be likely to disprove the effectiveness of P's alternative at trial. Filters are less restrictive because they impose selective restriction on speech at the receiving end. They may also be more effective than COPA because they may prevent minors from seeing pornography posted on the Web from countries outside the U.S.

- Review of a preliminary injunction is based on the abuse of discretion standard. D has not shown that the district court abused its discretion in issuing this injunction. There are several factual disputes in the case, and leaving the injunction in place will require D to meet its burden of proof. In addition, the record in this case does not reflect current technological reality, which changes rapidly, since the fact-findings were entered over five years ago.

Concurrence (Stevens, Ginsburg, JJ.). The Third Circuit originally held that the use of "contemporary community standards" to identify materials that are harmful to minors was a likely fatal defect, and that position was correct. But COPA also violates the First Amendment because it uses criminal prosecution to regulate speech, which could possibly punish a mistaken judgment about the scope of the category of "harmful to minors."

Dissent (Scalia, J.). COPA is constitutional, and it should not be subjected to strict scrutiny. The First Amendment does not entitle commercial pornography to that exacting standard of review.

Dissent (Breyer, J., Rehnquist, C.J., O'Connor, J.). COPA's burden on protected speech is no more than modest. It applies only to material that is not protected by the First Amendment, *i.e.*, legally obscene material. It does not censor even that material. It merely requires providers to restrict minors' access to material defined to be "harmful to minors." COPA advances the compelling interest of protecting minors from exposure to commercial pornography. The filtering software option cited by the majority is not an alternative legislative approach to the problem; it is part of the status quo. The problem COPA addresses is that, despite the existence of filtering software, children are still being exposed to harmful material on the Internet.

---

7) Pornography and discrimination against women--

American Booksellers Association, Inc. v. Hudnut, 771 F.2d 323 (7th Cir. 1985), *aff'd mem*

Facts. American Booksellers Association, Inc. (P) sued Hudnut (D), the mayor of Indianapolis, to prevent enforcement of an ordinance that defined "pornography" as a practice that discriminates against women, subjecting it to regulation and remedies used for other forms of discrimination. Rather than applying the "obscene" definition of *Miller*, the ordinance defined pornography as "the graphic sexually explicit subordination of women, whether in pictures or words, that also includes one or more of the following: (i) women are presented as sexual objects who enjoy pain or humiliation; (ii) women are presented as sexual objects who experience sexual pleasure in being raped; (iii) women are presented as sexual objects tied up or cut up or mutilated or bruised or physically hurt, or as dismembered or truncated or fragmented or severed into body parts; (iv) women are presented as being penetrated by objects or animals; (v) women are presented in scenarios of degradation, injury, abasement, torture, shown as filthy or inferior, bleeding, bruised, or hurt in a context that makes these conditions sexual; or (vi) women are presented as sexual objects for domination, conquest, violation, exploitation, possession, or use, or through postures or positions of servility or submission or display." The ordinance precludes trafficking in pornography, coercing others into performing in pornographic works, forcing pornography on a person, or assaulting anyone in a way that is directly caused by specific pornography, for which a right of action arises under the statute against pornography makers or sellers. The district court held that the ordinance was unconstitutional and prevented its enforcement. D appeals.

Issue. May the government restrict pornographic speech that conveys a message of discrimination against women?

Held. No. Judgment affirmed.

- ♦ D's ordinance does not judge the work as a whole, but focuses on particular depictions, so that it is irrelevant whether the work has literary, artistic, political, or scientific value. D notes that the ordinance is not intended to vindicate community standards of offensiveness, but to alter the socialization of men and women.

- ♦ There are many arguments for and against the ordinance, but basically the ordinance discriminates against expression on the ground of the content of the speech. Speech treating women in the approved way, with sexual encounters premised on equality, is lawful regardless of how sexually explicit, while speech treating women in an unapproved way is unlawful, regardless of the literary, artistic, or political qualities of the work taken as a whole.

- ♦ The First Amendment prevents the government from evaluating ideas and regulating based on content. Yet this statute expressly regulates speech based on its viewpoint. D claims that the regulation is justified because the prohibited form of pornography is not an idea, but an injury, because it does not persuade people but it changes and socializes them by establishing what conduct is permissible.

- ♦ D's position demonstrates the power of pornography as speech. Its adverse effects depend on mental intermediation. This is also true of speech advocating racial bigotry, anti-Semitism, violence, and other undesirable social activity. Many types of speech have the effect of social conditioning, including religious ceremonies and school curriculum. If the government could regulate speech based on its effect on people, there would be no free speech.

- ♦ D also claims that women are harmed while making pornographic films and pictures. To the extent that there is actual harm to the actors, these harms may be unlawful. But the image of pain is not necessarily pain. It is common in films to show violent or painful images, but the actors are not actually harmed.

- ♦ D's argument is that pornography is low value speech, similar to obscenity. But the Supreme Court's definition of obscenity is not based on the point of view of the particular work. D's approach focuses on the message of the speech, and is therefore unconstitutional. Any rationale to support D's ordinance could not be limited to sex discrimination. There is no way to construe D's ordinance that would make it constitutional.

---

c. **Restrictions on "offensive words" and publicly offensive speech.** This is a major area of confrontation between freedom of expression and the legitimate interests of government in curbing certain kinds of expression likely to cause disruptions or grave damage to societal interests. Speech or writing that by its very utterance tends to incite an immediate breach of the peace is not constitutionally protected, and may be prevented or punished by the state.

1) Public display of offensive speech permitted--

Cohen v. California,

Facts. Cohen (D) wore a jacket in a Los Angeles courthouse corridor bearing the words "Fuck the Draft." D was convicted of violating a state statute that prohibited disturbing the peace by offensive conduct. D appeals after the state courts upheld his conviction.

Issue. May a state excise as "offensive conduct" public use of an offensive word?

Held. No. Judgment reversed.

- Government has special power to regulate speech that is obscene, that constitutes "fighting words," or that intrudes on substantial privacy interests in an essentially intolerable manner. D's expression falls within none of these categories. D's jacket could not be considered erotic. Nor would D's jacket violently provoke the common citizen in the manner of fighting words. Finally, persons present in the courthouse were not unwilling captives of the offensive expression; they could simply avert their eyes.
- The state's regulatory attempt must fail because it would permit the state to outlaw whatever words officials might deem improper, thus running a substantial risk of suppressing ideas. Such power would permit official censorship as a means of banning the expression of unpopular views.

Dissent (Blackmun, J., Burger, C.J., Black, J.). D's antic was mainly conduct and little speech.

Comment. In *Cantwell v. Connecticut*, 310 U.S. 296 (1940), the Court reversed a conviction for breach of the peace when the only offense was the public playing of a record attacking the religion of two men who threatened the defendant with physical harm unless he went away. The defendant left upon being threatened. In *Chaplinsky v. New Hampshire*, 315 U.S. 568 (1942), the Court upheld the conviction of a defendant who, during an altercation with a city marshall, told the officer he was a "God-damned racketeer" and a "damned Fascist."

2) Precision requirement--

City of Houston v. Hill,

Facts. The city of Houston (D) adopted a municipal ordinance that made it an offense for any person to "oppose, molest, abuse or interrupt any policeman in the execution of his duty." Hill (P) was charged with violating this ordinance when he began shouting at police officers who were approaching one of P's friends, who was stopping traffic on a busy street. P was acquitted after a nonjury trial, but he sued in federal court, claiming that the statute was unconstitutional. The district court found that the ordinance had not been unconstitutionally applied. The court of appeals reversed, and D appeals.

Issue. May a city make it unlawful to interrupt a police officer in the performance of his duties?

Held. No. Judgment affirmed.

- D claims that its ordinance does not prevent the exposition of ideas, but only core criminal conduct, such as P's actions. However, the terms used in the ordinance clearly apply to verbal interruptions of police officers.

- The First Amendment protects a significant amount of verbal criticism and challenge directed at police officers, even if provocative, as long as it is not likely to produce a clear and present danger of a serious substantive evil that rises far above public inconvenience, annoyance, or unrest. In a free nation, individuals must be able verbally to oppose or challenge police action without risking arrest.

- A city may protect police officers from physical obstruction, disorderly conduct, or fighting words, but it must narrowly tailor the ordinance it uses. D's ordinance makes criminal a substantial amount of constitutionally protected speech and also gives police excessive discretion in enforcement.

Concurrence and dissent (Powell, O'Connor, JJ., Rehnquist, C.J., Scalia, J.). The Court should not have reached the merits, but the ordinance does violate the Fourteenth Amendment. The ordinance applies not only to speech but also to conduct. D should be allowed to punish individuals who use speech, even conversation, to disrupt an investigation of possible criminal conduct. The defect in this statute is that it confers on police officers a virtually unrestrained power to arrest. Neither D nor any Texas court has limited this broad discretion. In fact, the ordinance has been used to charge people with failing to remain silent and with talking. Thus, the ordinance is too vague. It should apply only to speech that is intended to interfere with the performance by a police officer of lawful duties.

---

3) Statutory inference of intent from conduct not allowed--

Virginia v. Black

Facts. The State of Virginia prohibited the burning of a cross with "an intent to intimidate a person or group of persons." Black and others (Ds) were tried for violating the statute. At the trial, the jury was instructed that Ds' burning of the cross, by itself, was sufficient evidence from which the jury could infer the required intent to intimidate. Ds were convicted and the court of appeals affirmed. The Virginia Supreme Court held that the cross burning statute was facially unconstitutional under the First Amendment. The Supreme Court granted certiorari.

Issue. May a criminal statute provide that the burning of a cross is prima facie evidence of an intent to intimidate when such an intention is one of the elements of the crime?

Held. No. Judgment affirmed in part, vacated in part, and case remanded.

- In the United States, cross burning has been closely tied to the Ku Klux Klan, which uses cross burnings to communicate threats of violence and intimidation. The Klan also uses cross burnings as symbols of shared group identity and ideology. Thus, although the cross burning does not inevitably convey a message of intimidation, when it is used to intimidate, it is a powerful message.

- The government may regulate categories of expression, including fighting words and incitement, as well as true threats. Intimidation is a type of true threat, where the speaker directs a threat to a person with the intent of making the victim fear bodily harm or death. Some cross burnings fit within this definition of intimidating speech.

- The Supreme Court of Virginia held that the statute was unconstitutional because it discriminates on the basis of content and viewpoint under *R.A.V. v. City of St. Paul,* 505 U.S. 377 (1992). *R.A.V.* does not hold that all forms of content-based discrimination within a proscribable area of speech are unconstitutional. The Virginia statute here, unlike the statute in *R.A.V.*, does not single out only that speech directed at one of the specified disfavored topics. The Virginia statute is aimed at burning a cross with intent to intimidate regardless of the victim's race, gender, religion, or other characteristics.

- Virginia may properly outlaw cross burnings done with the intent to intimidate because such activity is a particularly virulent form of intimidation, given its history as a signal of impending violence.

- However, the statute is unconstitutional because the prima facie evidence provision allows a conviction without proof of the very element that makes it constitutional for Virginia to ban cross burning—the intent to intimidate. Virginia could not ban cross burning alone, without the intimidation intent as an element of the offense, so it cannot simply provide that cross burning constitutes prima facie evidence of the required intent. The statute does not distinguish between cross burning with intent to intimidate and cross burning as a political statement not intended to intimidate.

Concurrence and dissent (Scalia, Thomas, JJ.). The prima facie evidence part of the statute is not unconstitutional, at least on a facial challenge. Only a limited class of persons, those who abstain from presenting a defense to rebut the prima facie evidence, could be wrongly convicted under that statute. Thus, the statute is not overbroad.

Concurrence and dissent (Souter, Kennedy, Ginsburg, JJ.). The statute makes a content-based distinction within the category of punishable intimidating expression, which is unconstitutional. This content-based proscription of cross burning could be an effort to ban not only intimidation, but also the messages communicated by non-threatening cross burning. No content-based statute should survive under *R.A.V.* without a high probability that no official suppression of ideas is afoot. The statute here is not narrowly tailored, since a content-neutral statute banning intimidation would accomplish the same objective without singling out particular content.

Dissent (Thomas, J.). Whatever expressive value cross burning may have, the legislature wrote it out by banning only intimidating conduct undertaken by a particular means. The statute addressed conduct only, not speech, and should not fall within the First Amendment. Even if the statute did implicate the First Amendment, permitting a jury to draw an inference of intent to intimidate from the cross burning itself is permissible. The inference is rebuttable, and the jury still has to find the existence of each element of the offense beyond a reasonable doubt. The Court values physical safety less than the right to be free from unwanted communications.

---

d. **Regulation of commercial advertising.** Commercial speech is entitled to protection, although subject to more stringent regulation than would be permissible with respect to noncommercial speech. The free speech interest in the contents of the speech must be weighed against the public interest served by the governmental regulation.

   1) **Scope of protection--**

Virginia State Board of Pharmacy v. Virginia Citizens Consumer Council, Inc.,

Facts. The Virginia State Board of Pharmacy (D) prohibited advertisement of the retail prices of prescription drugs by pharmacists. The Virginia Citizens Consumer Council, Inc. (P), for itself and on behalf of users of prescription drugs, sought an injunction against the enforcement of D's rule. The three-judge district court granted the injunction, and D appeals.

Issue. Is purely commercial speech wholly outside First Amendment protection?

Held. No. Judgment affirmed.

- First Amendment protection extends to the communication, to its source, and to its recipients. P, as a potential recipient, has standing to bring this action.

- The speech in question—commercial advertising—is not qualified from protection merely because the speaker's interest is purely economic. The particular consumer has a vital interest in the free flow of commercial information, possibly a greater interest than in current political debates, which are clearly protected. Society in general also has a strong interest in the free flow of commercial information. Actually, such a free flow is essential to the proper functioning of our economic system; it is likely that no line can properly be drawn between "important," and hence protected, advertising and the opposite kind.

- D claims an interest in protecting the public from unscrupulous pharmacists who would use advertising to their own advantage and the public's detriment. But the choice between the dangers of suppressing information and the dangers of its misuse, if it is freely available, has been made by the First Amendment. Therefore, D cannot prohibit commercial advertising of the type involved here.

- Although commercial speech is protected, it remains subject to proper restrictions, *e.g.*, time, place, and manner restrictions; false and misleading advertising prohibitions; and prohibitions against advertising illegal transactions.

Concurrence (Burger, C.J.). The Court expresses no opinion as to regulation of advertising by other professionals, such as lawyers.

Concurrence (Stewart, J.). Commercial price and product advertising differs markedly from ideological expression because it is confined to the promotion of specific goods or services. Commercial expression is protected because of the information of potential interest and value conveyed, rather than because of any direct contribution to the interchange of ideas. Therefore, commercial speech is subject to proper regulation assuring its accuracy and reliability.

Dissent (Rehnquist, J.). The Court expands the standing requirements and extends First Amendment protection beyond what is necessary.

---

2) **Four-part analysis--**

Central Hudson Gas & Electric Corp. v. Public Service Commission,

Facts. The Public Service Commission (D), in response to an energy shortage, temporarily banned all advertising by electric utilities that "promote the use of electricity." Over the objections of the Central Hudson Gas & Electric Corp. (P), D extended the ban and distinguished between promotional advertising, which was totally prohibited, and institutional and informational advertising, which D permitted. The state courts upheld D's order, and P appeals.

Issue. Does a public service commission's prohibition of promotional advertising by an electric utility violate the utility's First Amendment rights?

Held. Yes. Judgment reversed.

- Although D's regulation applies only to commercial speech, such speech is protected by the First Amendment because of its informational functions. Thus, a four-part analysis has developed regarding commercial speech.

  (i) Is the expression protected? If it concerns lawful activity and is not misleading, it generally is; P's speech is protected.

  (ii) Is the asserted governmental interest in regulation substantial? D based its regulation on the need for energy conservation, clearly a substantial interest.

  (iii) Does the regulation directly advance the governmental interest? If demand for electricity were unaffected by advertising, P would not have brought this suit. Therefore, D's regulation does advance the governmental interest.

  (iv) Is the regulation more extensive than necessary? Here, D's regulation fails, since it would prohibit information about electric devices or services that would not increase net energy use, although they might increase electric use, *e.g.,* use of electricity as a back-up to solar heating. D's rule is overbroad, and, in the absence of a showing that a more limited rule could not serve D's interests, it cannot be upheld.

Concurrence (Blackmun, Brennan, JJ.). The four-part test is inadequate in that it permits deprivation of information needed by the public to make a choice. D attempts to manipulate choices of private persons by withholding information rather than by persuasion or direct regulation. Such covert attempts are illegal regardless of their "necessity."

Concurrence (Stevens, Brennan, JJ.). The issue is whether D has banned nothing but commercial speech. D's ban covers more than purely commercial speech and is therefore invalid, regardless of the four-point analysis.

Dissent (Rehnquist, J.). D here is placing an essentially economic regulation on a heavily regulated state-created monopoly. Economic regulation traditionally merits virtually complete deference by the Court. D's regulation should also.

---

3) Ban on truthful advertising of legal activity--

44 Liquormart, Inc. v. Rhode Island,

Facts. Rhode Island (D) prohibited advertising of the retail price of alcoholic beverages, except on price tags or signs within licensed premises and not visible from outside. In addition, news media within D could not broadcast any advertisements referring to the price of such beverages, even if they merely referred to sales in other states. 44 Liquormart, Inc. (P) operated a liquor store in D. (Co-petitioner Peoples Super Liquor Stores, Inc. operated stores in Massachusetts that were patronized by D's residents.) P placed an ad in a Rhode Island newspaper that did not advertise the price of its alcohol, but implied low prices by stating low prices for snacks and mixers and placing the word "wow" next to pictures of certain alcoholic beverages. D began enforcement proceedings and eventually fined P $400. P sought a declaratory judgment that the advertising ban was unconstitutional. The district court found for P, but the court of appeals reversed. The Supreme Court granted certiorari.

Issue. May a state prohibit advertising about retail prices for alcoholic beverages?

Held. No. Judgment reversed.

- ♦ In *Central Hudson, supra*, the Court noted that special concerns arise from "regulations that entirely suppress commercial speech in order to pursue a nonspeech-related policy."

- ♦ A state regulation of commercial speech that is intended to protect consumers from misleading or deceptive information is consistent with the reasons such speech is protected by the Constitution and thus receives less than strict review. But when a state prohibits the dissemination of truthful and nonmisleading commercial messages for other public policy reasons, there is less reason to depart from ordinarily rigorous First Amendment review.

- ♦ Complete bans serve to obscure underlying governmental policies that could be implemented in other ways without regulating speech. As such, they typically are based on the assumption that the public will respond to the truth in a manner disfavored by the government. The First Amendment clearly disfavors regulations that seek to keep people in the dark for what the government perceives to be their own good. D's rationale for the ban is that it advances D's substantial interest in promoting temperance. Theoretically, a ban on price advertising mitigates competition, thus keeping prices higher and demand lower. But D has produced no evidence of any connection between the ban and a significant change in alcohol consumption. Besides, there are several actions D could take to accomplish its objective without restricting speech, such as increasing prices through higher taxation or educational campaigns.

- D argues that under *Posadas de Puerto Rico Associates v. Tourism Co. of Puerto Rico*, 478 U.S. 328 (1986), the Court should give particular deference to D's choice because D could, if it chose, ban the sale of alcoholic beverages outright. While *Posadas* did hold that a state could reduce gambling by suppressing in-state casino advertising, the Court in that case erroneously applied the First Amendment analysis. The Court should not have held that the legislature could choose suppression over a less speech-restrictive policy. *Posadas* was also erroneous in applying a "greater-includes-the-lesser" approach that would allow a state that can ban activity outright to ban speech regarding the activity. The power to prohibit an activity is not necessarily greater than the power to suppress speech about it. Under the First Amendment, it should be more difficult for the government to suppress speech than to suppress conduct.

- *Posadas* also held that an advertising ban was permissible if it targets commercial speech relating to a "vice" activity. The scope of any "vice" exception to First Amendment protections would be impossible to define. Labeling an activity a "vice" cannot permit greater speech restrictions, especially where there is no corresponding prohibition against the commercial behavior involved.

- The Twenty-First Amendment grants the states authority over commerce that might otherwise be reserved to the federal government, but it does not limit other constitutional provisions.

Concurrence (Scalia, J.). Both sides in this case accepted the *Central Hudson* approach, which should be reexamined in favor of a test based on state legislative practices prevalent at the time the First and Fourteenth Amendments were adopted.

Concurrence (Thomas, J.). When the government asserts an interest in keeping legal users of a product ignorant in order to manipulate their choices in the market, the interest should be deemed per se illegitimate without applying the *Central Hudson* test. The majority implies that if the ban had been more successful in decreasing alcohol consumption by keeping consumers ignorant, it might have been upheld under *Central Hudson.*

Concurrence (O'Connor, J., Rehnquist, C.J., Souter, Breyer, JJ.). The Court should apply *Central Hudson* to these facts. Even assuming that the first three prongs are satisfied, D's ban does not meet the final prong because the ban is more extensive than is necessary to serve D's interest. There are several readily available alternatives that would not suppress speech. Since *Posadas*, the Court has required a closer look at the final prong.

---

4) Attempted restriction of broadcasting--

Greater New Orleans Broadcasting Association v. United States,

Facts. Pursuant to 18 U.S.C. section 1304, the Federal Communications Commission ("FCC") prohibited radio and television broadcasters from carrying advertising about privately operated commercial casino gambling, regardless of the station's or casino's location. The Greater New Orleans Broadcasting Association (P) sought to run ads for casinos in Louisiana and Mississippi. They sued for a declaration that section 1304 and the FCC's regulations violated the First Amendment. The United States (D) and P each moved for summary judgment. The district court granted D's motion. The court of appeals affirmed. The Supreme Court granted certiorari.

Issue. May the government prohibit radio and television broadcasting of advertising for lawful private casino gambling if the broadcasts may reach states where such gambling is illegal?

Held. No. Judgment reversed.

- Under *Central Hudson,* a court applies a four-part test that asks (i) whether the speech at issue concerns lawful activity and is not misleading; (ii) whether the asserted governmental interest is substantial; (iii) whether the regulation directly advances the governmental interest asserted; and (iv) whether it is not more extensive than is necessary to serve that interest.

- P's advertising is clearly commercial speech that satisfies the first part of the *Central Hudson* test. D also has "substantial" interests, including reducing the social costs associated with gambling and assisting states that restrict or prohibit gambling. However, many states have concluded that the social costs of suppressing gambling are outweighed by other policies, and Congress has left the issue to the states. This uncertainty undermines the importance of D's expressed interests.

- In this case, section 1304 cannot satisfy the third and fourth parts of the *Central Hudson* test. The many exemptions and inconsistencies in section 1304 and its implementing regulations suggest that D's interest in reducing the social costs of gambling is not the real reason for the challenged rules. For example, federal law exempts advertising about state-run casinos and tribal casino gambling even if the broadcaster is located in or broadcasts to a jurisdiction with strict antigambling policies. This suggests that D is actually committed only to prohibiting certain accurate product information, not commercial enticements of all kinds, and then only for certain brands of casino gambling.

- D's second asserted interest of "assisting" states with policies that disfavor private casinos is also unconvincing. Even if the state policies about gambling are more coherent than the federal policies, section 1304 sacrifices more truthful speech about lawful conduct than it should when compared to the diverse policies at stake and the social ills that one could reasonably hope such a ban would eliminate.

Concurrence (Rehnquist, C.J.). If this regulation had been part of a substantive regulation of the gambling industry, it might be permissible, but as a mere regulation of commercial speech, *Central Hudson* requires a more demanding standard of review that is not met here.

Concurrence (Thomas, J.). The *Central Hudson* test should not be applied and can no more justify regulation of "commercial speech" than it can justify regulation of "noncommercial speech."

---

5) Limited ban on tobacco products--

Lorillard Tobacco Co. v. Reilly

Facts. Reilly (D), the Attorney General of Massachusetts, promulgated comprehensive regulations on the advertising and sale of tobacco products. The regulations included a prohibition on outdoor advertising within 1,000 feet of a school or playground and a point-of-sale regulation that prohibited indoor advertising lower than five feet from the floor. Lorillard Tobacco Co. and other tobacco manufacturers and retailers (Ps) challenged the constitutionality of the regulations. The district court found the regulations valid, except for the point-of-sale regulation. The First Circuit reversed the ruling on the indoor advertising issue, but upheld the district court's decision that the regulations were not preempted by the Federal Cigarette Labeling and Advertising Act ("FCLAA"). The Supreme Court granted certiorari.

Issue. Does the First Amendment prohibit a state from placing a comprehensive ban on the advertising of smokeless tobacco and cigars, even if the ban is limited to advertising near schools?

Held. Yes. Judgment reversed in part.

- ♦ D's regulation was intended to "close holes" in the settlement agreement between 40 states and major cigarette manufacturers, in which the manufacturers agreed to pay damages in return for the states settling their claims. However, Congress enacted the FCLAA in part to preempt state cigarette advertising regulations. Consequently, D's regulations regarding outdoor and point-of-sale advertising of cigarettes are preempted.
- ♦ D's sales practices regulations for all tobacco products, and D's advertising regulations for smokeless tobacco and cigars, while not preempted, are still subject to First Amendment requirements. The *Central Hudson* (*supra*) four-part analysis applies to this case. Only the last two steps are at issue.

- The ban on outdoor advertising within a 1,000-foot radius of a school is supported by D's evidence of the problem with underage use of smokeless tobacco and cigars, as well as evidence that limiting youth exposure to advertising will decrease such use. This satisfies the third step of *Central Hudson*, which concerns the relationship between the harm that underlies the state's interest and the means identified by the state to advance that interest.

- The fourth *Central Hudson* step requires narrowly tailored means. The broad sweep of D's regulations does not suggest careful calculation of the costs and benefits associated with the burden on speech imposed. D's ban affects a substantial portion of the metropolitan areas in the state, and would constitute nearly a complete ban in some areas. The ban includes oral communications, such as a retailer's response to inquiries about its tobacco products if the communication takes place outdoors. While D has a compelling interest in preventing underage tobacco use, adult usage of these products is legal. Retailers may have no alternative to outdoor advertising.

- D's regulation of point-of-sale advertising for smokeless tobacco and cigars fails both the third and fourth steps of *Central Hudson*, since the five-foot rule does not seem to advance D's stated goal. However, D has demonstrated a substantial interest in preventing minors' access to tobacco products, and D's regulations regarding the placement of self-service displays is an appropriately narrow means of advancing that interest.

Concurrence (Kennedy, Scalia, JJ.). As the outdoor advertising restrictions fail the fourth part of the *Central Hudson* test, there is no need to consider the third part of the test.

Concurrence (Thomas, J.). All of D's restrictions should be subject to strict scrutiny. Under that approach, they violate the First Amendment. D cannot regulate all advertising on the ground that some of its viewers may not legally act on it, or on the premise that an indirect solicitation of children must be suppressed.

Concurrence and dissent (Stevens, Ginsburg, Breyer, Souter, JJ.). The FCLAA does not preempt D's regulations. The case should be remanded for further fact-findings regarding the tailoring of D's regulations. The point-of-sale advertising restrictions and sales practice restrictions do not implicate First Amendment concerns and should be upheld.

---

6) Prohibition on advertising of compounded drugs--

Thompson v. Western States Medical Center,

Facts. The Food and Drug Administration Modernization Act of 1997 ("FDAMA") exempted "compounded drugs" from the Food and Drug Administration's ("FDA") standard drug approval requirements, provided that the providers of the compounded drugs refrain from advertising the drugs. Compounded drugs are created by a pharmacist by combining, mixing, or altering ingredients to create a medication adapted to the needs of an individual patient, based on a doctor's prescription. Western States Medical Center (P), a group of pharmacies that engaged in compounding drugs, sued Thompson (D), Secretary of Health and Human Services, seeking an injunction against enforcement of the advertising ban. The district court granted summary judgment for P on the ground that the restrictions did not satisfy *Central Hudson*, *supra*. The Ninth Circuit affirmed. The Supreme Court granted certiorari.

Issue. May the government prohibit advertising of compounded drugs?

Held. No. Judgment affirmed.

- D cites several governmental interests, including the need to draw a line between small-scale compounding and large-scale drug manufacturing, and that advertising is a fair proxy for such a line. However, D failed to show that the speech restrictions are not more extensive than is necessary to serve D's interests.

- D could rely on nonspeech-related means to draw its line, including the factors the FDA relied on to distinguish compounding from manufacturing in its own guidelines. D could prohibit Ps from compounding drugs in advance of receiving prescriptions, or it could limit the amount of compound drugs that Ps can make. Nothing in the legislative history shows why forbidding advertising was a necessary, instead of merely convenient, means to achieve D's interests.

- The government does not have a legitimate interest in preventing the dissemination of truthful commercial information to prevent members of the public from making bad decisions with the information. Beyond these problems with the FDAMA, the ban on speech would prevent pharmacists from telling doctors about alternative drugs available for their patients.

Concurrence (Thomas, J.). The Court properly applies *Central Hudson*, but *Central Hudson* shouldn't be applied to this type of case.

Dissent (Breyer, J., Rehnquist, C.J., Stevens, Ginsburg, JJ.). The Court undervalues the importance of D's interest in protecting the health and safety of the public. The FDAMA restricts advertising to directly advance its important safety objective—confining the sale of untested, compounded drugs to where they are medically needed. The FDAMA exempts compounded drugs from testing requirements, but this creates risks by giving untested drugs to consumers. This risk is justifiable only where the consumer has a specific medical need for a specially tailored drug. On the other hand, consumer-oriented advertising will create a strong consumer-driven demand for the drugs, which could lead to doctors issuing prescriptions they would not otherwise issue. Congress could not have achieved its safety objective in significantly less restrictive ways.

B. RESTRICTIONS ON TIME, PLACE, OR MANNER OF EXPRESSION

The issue here concerns the need for public order (quiet, traffic control, etc.) versus the right of free speech. In each instance, the public interest involved must be specifically identified and weighed against the right of free speech. The following questions are determinative: Where is the person attempting to speak? When does it occur? Who is the audience? How is the speaker attempting to speak? What is the content of the speech? Pursuant to the concept of ordered liberty, courts have permitted restrictions on the First Amendment rights of expression that are necessary to ensure order. These restrictions typically involve time, place, or manner of expression. However, even these restrictions must be well justified; that is, they cannot be discriminatory.

1. The Traditional Public Forum: Speech Activities in Streets and Parks.

a. Restrictions on use of streets and parks.

1) **Littering.** An ordinance that bans the unlicensed communication of any views, or the advocacy of any cause, from door to door, and permits canvassing in public only subject to the power of a police officer to determine, as a censor, what literature may be distributed from house to house and who may distribute it, has been held invalid. The claimed interest of the community in the prevention of littering the streets could be achieved by a statute specifically directed at that practice. [*See* Schneider v. New Jersey, Town of Irvington, 308 U.S. 147 (1939)]

2) **Noise.** A city ordinance that prohibited operation on public streets of sound trucks that emitted any message amplified to a "loud and raucous volume" has been upheld, even though the message involved was of public interest. The rationale was that any public policy favoring free speech in such cases was outweighed by the community interest in order and tranquility. Free speech cannot be exercised in a manner that constitutes a public nuisance. [*See* Kovacs v. Cooper, 336 U.S. 77 (1949)]

3) **Permit requirements.** A state cannot condition the right of a person to publicly express his views on obtaining a permit to do so from local authorities if such permits are given on a purely discretionary basis. There must be some reasonable standard established on which to decide who gets a permit, when, and why.

a) **Permit to distribute circulars.** In *Lovell v. City of Griffin*, 303 U.S. 444 (1938), the Court held that a city may not prohibit all distribution of all literature without prior written approval of a government agent. The ordinance was overbroad because it prohibited distribution that did not interfere with proper government functions.

b) **Permit to demonstrate.** A state statute prohibiting a parade or procession on public streets without a special license specifying the day and hour of the procession, applied nondiscriminatorily, was sustained based on the state's police power over traffic and safety. [*See* Cox v. New Hampshire, 312 U.S. 569 (1941)] In *Poulos v. New Hampshire*, 345 U.S. 395 (1953), the Court upheld a prosecution for conducting an unlicensed meeting in a public park. Although a license had been improperly denied, the defendant should have challenged the denial instead of holding the unlicensed meeting, since the statute itself was not invalid.

c) **Mass demonstrations.**

(1) Mass demonstrations are legitimate objects of state regulation to preserve order, free passage of traffic, etc. The rights of those who seek to communicate their ideas by such demonstrations are simply not as broad as those who communicate their ideas by speech alone. [*See* Walker v. Birmingham, 388 U.S. 307 (1967)]

(2) Such regulation must be circumscribed by reasonable standards, and local officials cannot be given completely unfettered discretion in applying the law. That is, an ordinance vesting in local officials the power to grant or deny parade permits based on their judgment as to the effect of the parade on the "welfare" or "morals" of the community was held unconstitutional for lack of adequate standards. [*See* Shuttlesworth v. City of Birmingham, 394 U.S. 147 (1969)]

(3) In certain instances, injunctions may be used to curtail demonstrations. In *Carroll v. President & Commissioners of Princess Anne*, 393 U.S. 175 (1968), the Supreme Court held that an ex parte order that enjoined the petitioners from holding further rallies (on the basis that they endangered peace in the area) was improper unless it could be shown that it was impossible to notify the opposing parties and give them an opportunity to participate in the proceedings leading to the injunction

(particularly in the situation where a political speech is involved, since here the element of timeliness is especially important).

b. **Content-neutral controls--**

Frisby v. Schultz,

Facts. Schultz and others (Ps) engaged in six separate antiabortion picketings outside the residence of a doctor who performed abortions. Ps' picketing was orderly and peaceful, but produced many complaints. In response, the Town Board adopted an ordinance prohibiting all picketing in residential neighborhoods, with the exception of labor picketing. This was later replaced with a complete ban on residential picketing of any type. The purpose was to protect and preserve the home and to eliminate the harassment of residential occupants. Ps ceased their picketing and sought declaratory and injunctive relief against the ordinance. The district court granted a preliminary injunction that would automatically become permanent unless Frisby (D) requested a trial or an appeal. The court of appeals affirmed, and D appeals.

Issue. May a city completely ban picketing "before or about" any residence?

Held. Yes. Judgment reversed.

- ♦ Time, place, and manner restrictions may be applied consistent with the First Amendment. The validity of place restrictions depends on the character of the property at issue, of which there are three basic types: (i) the traditional public forum; (ii) the public forum created by government designation; and (iii) the nonpublic forum.

- ♦ Public streets are traditional public forums. D's suggestion that residential streets should be considered nonpublic has been rejected. Thus, D's ordinance is subject to the stringent review applicable to restrictions on speech in a traditional public forum. Even though D's ordinance is content-neutral, it must: (i) be narrowly tailored, (ii) serve a significant government interest, and (iii) leave open ample alternative channels of communication.

- ♦ Narrowly construed, the ordinance applies to focused picketing taking place solely in front of a particular residence, but not to a more general marching or even walking a route in front of an entire block of houses. Thus, it permits alternative communications, such as general dissemination of a message throughout a neighborhood.

- ♦ The ordinance also serves a significant government interest—protection of residential privacy—in recognition of the unique nature of the home. An important aspect of this is protection of an unwilling listener. Individuals may not be forced to welcome unwanted speech into their own homes.

- The ordinance is narrowly tailored at focused picketing, directed at the household instead of the public and intended to offensively intrude on residential privacy. The target of such picketing is a captive audience who is presumptively unwilling to receive the unwanted speech and cannot avoid it. Thus, the ordinance is not unconstitutional.

Concurrence (White, J.). An ordinance that forbade picketing before a single residence would not be unconstitutional on its face.

Dissent (Brennan, Marshall, JJ.). The Court's construction of the ordinance still covers significantly more speech than is necessary to achieve the government's interest. Regulation intended to neutralize the intrusive aspects of residential picketing—such as restrictions on the number of picketers, the time of such pickets, and the permissible noise level—would address the interests without prohibiting the expression completely.

Dissent (Stevens, J.). The ordinance even as construed still leaves too much discretion to enforcement officials.

Comment. Consider *Capitol Square Review & Advisory Board v. Pinette*, *infra*, at page 354.

---

c. Injunction against protestors--

Madsen v. Women's Health Center, Inc.,

Facts. Women's Health Center, Inc. (P) operated abortion clinics in Florida. Madsen and others (Ds) picketed and demonstrated against one of P's clinics. P obtained an injunction from a Florida state court that prohibited Ds from blocking or interfering with public access to the clinic and from physically abusing persons entering or leaving the clinic. Six months later, the court found that Ds had continued to impede access to the clinic by congregating on the paved street leading to the clinic and by marching in front of the clinic's driveways. Ds, who at times numbered as many as 400 persons, also made noise with loudspeakers, singing, and chanting. The court found that the protests increased the level of anxiety of patients, requiring higher levels of sedation for surgical procedures, and stressing patients who were recuperating. The court then entered a more restrictive injunction that prohibited Ds from: (i) entering P's premises and property; (ii) blocking or interfering with access to any building or parking lot of P's; (iii) congregating on a public right-of-way or private property within 36 feet of P's property line, except actual titled holders of adjacent property could enter their own property so long as they did not act in concert with Ds; (iv) making noise or displaying images observable to, or within earshot of, the patients inside the clinic between 7:30 a.m. and noon; (v) physically approaching P's clients within 300 feet of the clinic; (vi) demonstrating within 300 feet of the residence of any of P's employees; (vii) physically crowding or assaulting persons entering or leaving P's clinic or any of the homes of P's owners, staff, or patients; (viii) harassing any present or former staff member or volunteer of P; and (ix) encouraging other persons to commit any of the prohibited acts. Ds challenged the constitutionality of the second injunction. The Florida Supreme Court upheld it on the ground that it was content-neutral. The Eleventh Circuit, in a separate challenge, held that the injunction was content-based and neither necessary to serve a compelling state interest nor narrowly drawn. The Supreme Court granted certiorari.

Issue. When evaluating a content-neutral injunction, must a court apply a more stringent test than the standard time, place, and manner analysis?

Held. Yes. Judgment reversed in part.

- An injunction, by its very nature, applies only to a particular group. It must regulate the activities, and hence even the speech, of that group, but it applies because of that group's past actions, not because of the content of the speech. Nothing in the injunction was directed at the content of Ds' message, but only against the time, place, and manner of expression. The fact that Ds shared a common message does not make the injunction content- or viewpoint-based, so the heightened scrutiny set forth in *Perry Education Association*, *infra,* does not apply.

- A content-neutral, generally applicable statute is evaluated by determining whether the time, place, and manner restrictions were "narrowly tailored to serve a significant governmental interest." An injunction, however, carries greater risks of censorship and discriminatory application than does a general ordinance. Therefore, a more stringent application of the First Amendment must apply. The courts must inquire whether the challenged provisions of an injunction "burden no more speech than necessary to serve a significant government interest."

- There are several significant government interests protected by the injunction, including protection of a woman's freedom to seek lawful medical or counseling services for her pregnancy, ensuring public safety and order, and protecting residential privacy. These interests are sufficient to justify an appropriately tailored injunction to protect them.

- The 36-foot buffer zone prevented Ds from blocking traffic on the street. Because Ds had disobeyed the prior injunction that protected access to P's clinic, the court could not allow Ds to remain on the clinic's sidewalk and driveway. Under these circumstances, the 36-foot buffer zone burdens no more speech than necessary to accomplish the governmental interest at stake.

- The 36-foot buffer zone on private property on the back and side of the clinic was imposed to protect access, but nothing in the record shows that Ds' activities on this private property obstructed access to the clinic or blocked traffic on the street. This portion of the injunction fails to serve the significant governmental interest and thus burdens more speech than necessary to protect access to the clinic.

- The injunction against noise that can be heard within the clinic burdens no more speech than necessary to ensure the health and well-being of P's patients, but the prohibition against "images observable" does, because the only reason a patient would be bothered by such images is if the patient found the expression contained in such images disagreeable. While the clinic cannot block out sound, it can simply pull its curtains.

- The prohibition on physically approaching any person seeking services of the clinic within 300 feet of the clinic also burdens more speech than necessary to prevent intimidation and to ensure access to the clinic. Ds' conduct would have to be independently proscribable, such as "fighting words," or constitute a threat of physical harm to be so restricted. The ban on picketing within 300 feet of the residences of clinic staff likewise burdens more speech than necessary because a smaller zone could have accomplished the desired result.

Concurrence and dissent (Stevens, J.). Injunctive relief should be judged by a more lenient standard than legislation because it is imposed on those who have engaged in illegal activity.

Concurrence and dissent (Scalia, Kennedy, Thomas, JJ.). The injunction in this case would be a candidate for summary reversal if the context were not abortion, which has distorted the Court's constitutional jurisprudence in other areas as well. The injunction simply prohibits a particular group, which had broken no law, from exercising its rights of speech, assembly, and association within a specified area. This is profoundly at odds with the First Amendment. The majority's new standard for analysis, created for an abortion-related case, falls short of strict scrutiny. However, content-neutral injunctions are at least as deserving of strict scrutiny as a statutory, content-based restriction. But in this case, the injunction was content-based. It was directed at Ds and those who were deemed to be "acting in concert or participation" with Ds. The judge himself noted that this meant those who had taken a certain position adverse to the clinic. The second injunction prohibited acts not covered by the first injunction, so Ds could not have violated the first injunction regarding those acts. The trial court could have simply limited the number of demonstrators permitted on the clinic's sidewalks and forbidden them to walk on the driveways. This case now stands for the propositions that injunctions against speech are subject to the intermediate scrutiny applied to time, place, and manner legislative restrictions; injunctions against speech need not be closely tied to any violation of law but may simply implement sound social policy; and reviewing courts may simply accept trial court conclusions permitting injunctions without inquiring into the findings of fact.

d. Permissible restriction near a health care facility--

Hill v. Colorado,

Facts. Colorado Rev. Stat. section 18-9-122(3) made it unlawful for any person within 100 feet of a health care facility's entrance to "knowingly approach" within eight feet of another person, without that person's consent, in order to pass "a leaflet or handbill to, displa[y] a sign to, or engag[e] in oral protest, education, or counseling with [that] person. . . ." Hill and others (Ps) sought to enjoin enforcement of the statute, claiming it was facially invalid. The trial court dismissed the complaint, holding that the statute imposed content-neutral time, place, and manner restrictions narrowly tailored to serve a significant government interest. The court of appeals affirmed, and the state supreme court denied review. The United States Supreme Court remanded that judgment in light of its holding in *Schenck v. Pro-Choice Network of Western New York*, 519 U.S. 357 (1997), that the state could not create a speech-free floating buffer zone with a 15-foot radius. On remand, the state courts distinguished *Schenck*, concluding that the statute was narrowly drawn to further a significant government interest, rejecting Ps' overbreadth challenge, and concluding that ample alternative channels of communication remained open to Ps. The Supreme Court granted certiorari.

Issue. May a state restrict free speech rights within close proximity to the entrance of a health care facility?

Held. Yes. Judgment affirmed.

- Ps have clear and undisputed First Amendment interests. At the same time, D's police powers allow it to protect its citizens' health and safety, especially to protect access to health care facilities and to avoid potential trauma to patients associated with confrontational protests. The statute protects listeners from unwanted communication; it does not restrict a speaker's right to address a willing audience.

- Section 18-9-122(3) passes the content-neutrality test outlined in *Ward v. Rock Against Racism*, 491 U.S. 781 (1989), for three independent reasons. First, it is a regulation of places where some speech may occur, not a "regulation of speech." Second, it was not adopted to target any particular viewpoint, but is content-neutral. Third, D's interests are unrelated to the content of the demonstrators' speech.

- Ps claim that, because the statute applies to those who "knowingly approach" within eight feet of another to engage in "oral protest, education, or counseling," it is "content-based" under *Carey v. Brown*, 447 U.S. 455 (1980), as it requires examination of the content of a speaker's comments. However, it is not improper to look at a statement's content to determine whether a rule of law applies to a course of conduct. Here, the state does not need to know the exact words spoken to know whether sidewalk counselors are engaging in oral protest, education, or counseling rather than social or random conversation. By contrast, *Carey* involved a statute that prohibited all picketing except for picketing of a place of employment in a labor dispute, thus preferring expression concerning one particular subject.

♦ The statute is also a valid time, place, and manner regulation under *Ward*, for it is "narrowly tailored" to serve the state's significant and legitimate governmental interests and it leaves open ample alternative communication channels. A content-neutral regulation need not be the least restrictive or intrusive means of serving the statutory goal if it does not entirely foreclose any means of communication. The eight-foot zone should not adversely impact a reader's ability to read demonstrators' signs.

♦ Unlike the "floating buffer zone" rejected in *Schenck*, D's zone in this case allows the speaker to communicate at a "normal conversational distance," and to remain in one place while other individuals pass within eight feet. The "knowing" requirement protects speakers who thought they were at the proscribed distance from inadvertently violating the statute. Whether the eight-foot interval is the best possible accommodation of the competing interests, deference must be accorded to the Colorado legislature's judgment. The burden on the distribution of handbills is more serious, but the statute does not prevent a leafletter from simply standing near the path of oncoming pedestrians and proffering the material, which pedestrians can accept or decline.

♦ The statute is not overbroad, because it does not ban any forms of communication, only the places where communication may occur. Nor is it unconstitutionally vague, since it requires scienter and the language of the statute is plain. It provides adequate guidance to law enforcement officials to prevent arbitrary enforcement.

Concurrence (Souter, O'Connor, Ginsburg, Breyer, JJ.). A restriction is content-based only if it is imposed because of the content of the speech and not because of offensive behavior identified with its delivery. If the ostensible reason for regulating is really something about the ideas, the regulation is invalid. In this case, the ostensible reason is the true reason. The regulation prohibits close encounters; it is the behavior of the protestors, not their antiabortion message, that is regulated.

Dissent (Scalia, Thomas, JJ.). The Court has concluded that a regulation requiring speakers on the public thoroughfares bordering medical facilities to speak from a distance of eight feet is "not a 'regulation of speech,'" but "a regulation of the places where some speech may occur," and that a regulation directed to only certain categories of speech (protest, education, and counseling) is not "content-based." It then holds that the regulation survives the less rigorous scrutiny afforded content-neutral time, place, and manner restrictions because it is narrowly tailored to serve the government's interest in protecting citizens' "right to be let alone," even though such an interest is incompatible with the guarantees of the First Amendment. The Court applies this unusual analysis because the regulation in this case is directed against the opponents of abortion. Having deprived abortion opponents of the political right to persuade the electorate that abortion should be restricted by law, the Court now restricts their individual right to persuade women contemplating abortion that what they are doing is wrong. Because, like the rest of our abortion jurisprudence, today's decision is in stark contradiction of the constitutional principles we apply in all other contexts, I dissent.

Dissent (Kennedy, J.). The law here imposes a content-based restriction on speech and is intended to restrict only speakers who protest abortions. It creates a right for citizens to avoid unpopular speech in a public forum. This holding contradicts 50 years of First Amendment cases by approving a law that bars a private citizen from passing a message, in a peaceful manner and on a profound moral issue, to a fellow citizen on a public sidewalk. This holding will lead to the elimination of the proud tradition of free and open discourse in a public forum. There are less burdensome alternatives to address the law's purported concerns. In addition, the Court's decision conflicts with the essence of the joint opinion in *Carey*, *supra*.

---

2. The Nontraditional Forum.

a. Speech activities on public property other than parks and streets.

1) Jails--

Adderley v. Florida,

Facts. Adderley and others (Ds) were convicted for trespassing on the premises of a county jail. Ds had entered the premises to protest the arrest of fellow students and had refused to leave after being notified that they would be arrested for trespass. Ds claim that the conviction violated their constitutional right of assembly, and appeal.

Issue. May a state use a trespass action to prohibit peaceful assembly on special-purpose public property?

Held. Yes. Judgment affirmed.

- The record reveals that the sheriff objected not to Ds' ideas or protests but only to their presence on that part of the jail grounds reserved for jail uses. The area occupied by Ds was not open to the general public but was reserved for those having specific jail duties. The state has power to preserve its property for the use to which it is lawfully dedicated, and the sheriff did not discriminate against these particular defendants.

- Ds presume that people who want to propagandize protests or views have a constitutional right to do so whenever, however, and wherever they please, but this Court has previously rejected such a concept.

Dissent (Douglas, J., Warren, C.J., Brennan, Fortas, JJ.). A prison is a seat of government and an obvious center for protest against unjust confinement. We do violence to the First Amendment by permitting this "petition for redress of grievances" to be turned into a trespass action.

---

2) **Military bases.** Military bases may be closed to political speeches and distribution of leaflets, if done evenhandedly. This is true even if the public is generally permitted to visit the base because of the strong government interest in keeping the military free of partisan political entanglements. [*See* Greer v. Spock, 424 U.S. 828 (1976)]

3) **State fair.** In *Heffron v. International Society for Krishna Consciousness, Inc.*, 452 U.S. 640 (1981), the Court held that a state may restrict the sale of literature and solicitation of funds at a state fair by requiring that it be conducted from a fixed booth. The restriction was not content-based, and it served the significant governmental interest in protecting the safety and convenience of the fairgoers. At the same time, the restriction did not foreclose all means of expression.

4) **Letter boxes.** The First Amendment does not guarantee a civic association the right to deposit literature, without payment of postage, in mail depositories authorized by the United States Postal Service. [United States Postal Service v. Council of Greenburgh Civic Associations, 453 U.S. 114 (1981)] The Postal Service's interest in efficient mail service justified this restriction, and such letter boxes are not a "public forum."

5) **School mailboxes.** A school district may restrict access to its mail system so that an exclusive labor bargaining representative may use them but not a challenger. [Perry Education Association v. Perry Local Educators' Association, 460 U.S. 37 (1983)] The public school mail system fell within the category of public property that is not by tradition or designation a public forum. Access to such property may be limited so long as the restriction on speech is reasonable, and not an arbitrary suppression of ideas.

6) **Access to government charity drive.** The President may exclude political activist organizations from eligibility for participation in a federal charitable campaign. [Cornelius v. NAACP Legal Defense and Education Fund, Inc., 473 U.S. 788 (1985)] Participation in the Combined Federal Campaign ("CFC") is a form of charitable solicitation of funds, which is protected speech. The

Court held that the CFC was a nonpublic forum limited to charitable organizations.

7) **Utility poles.** Los Angeles prohibited the posting of signs on public property. In *Los Angeles v. Taxpayers for Vincent*, 466 U.S. 789 (1984), the Court held that the city had a constitutional power to enhance its appearance that justified the ordinance. The interest was unrelated to the suppression of ideas.

8) **Airports--**

International Society for Krishna Consciousness, Inc. v. Lee,

Facts. Members of the International Society for Krishna Consciousness, Inc. (P) performed a religious ritual known as sankirtan, which consisted of going into public places, disseminating religious literature, and soliciting funds to support the religion. P desired to perform sankirtan at the airports in the New York City area. Lee (D) was the police superintendent of the airports and was responsible for enforcing a regulation that prohibited the repetitive sale of merchandise, the solicitation of money, or the distribution of literature within the interior areas of buildings at the airport. Such activities were permitted on the sidewalks outside the terminal buildings. P challenged the regulation. The district court granted P summary judgment. The court of appeals affirmed with regard to the ban on distributing, but reversed with regard to the ban on solicitation. The Supreme Court granted certiorari.

Issue. May an airport terminal operated by a public authority prohibit solicitation in the interior of its buildings?

Held. Yes. Judgment affirmed.

♦ Solicitation is clearly a form of protected speech, but the government need not permit all forms of speech on property it owns and controls. Prior cases reflect a "forum-based" approach to assess government restrictions on the use of its property. There are three categories of government property:

  (i) ***Traditional public forums***—property that has traditionally been available for public expression. Regulation of speech on this type survives only if it is narrowly drawn to achieve a compelling state interest.

  (ii) ***Designated public forums***—property that the government has opened for expressive activity by part or all of the public. Regulation of speech on this type also survives only if it is narrowly drawn to achieve a compelling state interest.

(iii) ***All remaining public property***. Regulation of speech on this type survives if it is reasonable, so long as the regulation is not an effort to suppress the speaker's activity due to disagreement with the speaker's views.

♦ A traditional public forum exists where the property has been immemorially held in trust for the use of the public and has been used for purposes of assembly, communicating thoughts between citizens, and discussing public questions. Examples include streets and parks. Designated public forums are areas that are intentionally dedicated for use in public discourse.

♦ Airports do not meet these requirements. For one thing, they have not been in existence for many years. For another, they have not historically been made available for speech activity, except when ordered to by the courts. Airports are not just "transportation nodes" like bus and rail terminals, but have special characteristics. The purpose of an airport is to facilitate travel and to make a regulated profit, not to promote expression.

♦ Because an airport is not a public forum, D's regulations are permissible so long as they are reasonable. P's proposed solicitation had a disruptive effect on airport travelers who are typically in a hurry and for whom a delay can mean a lost flight and severe inconvenience. Face-to-face solicitation presents a risk of duress and fraud that D can properly attempt to avoid. Therefore, D's ban on solicitation is sustained.

Concurrence (O'Connor, J.). An airport is clearly not a public forum. It could be closed to everyone except those who have legitimate business there, unlike public streets and parks, but government officials make airports open to the public as a convenience. The airport does contain restaurants, shops, newsstands, and other facilities not directly related to travel, but D's regulations are reasonably related to maintaining the multipurpose environment created by D. At the same time, the ban on leafleting cannot be upheld as reasonable, since distributing literature does not present the same problems as soliciting funds.

Concurrence (Kennedy, Blackmun, Stevens, Souter, JJ.). The areas of an airport that are outside the passenger security zones are public forums. The Court's categorical approach to classifying government property leaves no room for the development of new public forums without government approval. The traditional three-part analysis provides a better, more objective approach, based on the actual, physical characteristics and uses of the property. An airport, for example, is not much different from a street and sidewalk, since both have a principal purpose of facilitating transportation, not public discourse. So long as expressive activity would be appropriate and compatible with the actual uses of public property, the property should be considered a public forum. Under this analysis, passenger convenience would not be a sufficiently strong rationale for banning solicitation. The ban on solicitation and receipt of funds is nevertheless a proper time, place, and manner restriction. The ban does not prevent solicitation that does not involve the immediate receipt of money.

Concurrence and dissent (Souter, Blackmun, Stevens, JJ.). The traditional public forums are only "archetypes" of property from which the government may not exclude speech, and the airports involved in this case fit the archetype. The ban on solicitation is not sufficiently narrowly tailored to further a significant state interest and should not be sustained.

Comment. In the companion case, *Lee v. International Society for Krishna Consciousness, Inc.*, 505 U.S. 830 (1992), the Court held that the ban on the distribution of literature was invalid, citing the concurrences above.

---

9) **Access to televised debate--**

Arkansas Educational Television Commission v. Forbes,

Facts. The Arkansas Educational Television Commission (D), a state-owned public television broadcaster, sponsored a debate between the major party candidates for a congressional seat. Forbes (P), an independent, sought to participate, but D denied his request. P sued. The district court found for D. The court of appeals held that the debate was a public forum for which P had a presumptive right of access, and that D's rejection of P for lack of political viability was neither a compelling nor a narrowly tailored reason for excluding him. The Supreme Court granted certiorari.

Issue. Is a political candidate debate on public television a public forum such that restrictions on candidate access are subject to strict scrutiny?

Held. No. Judgment reversed.

♦ Candidate debates on public television are subject to scrutiny by the courts under the public forum doctrine. However, the doctrine applies differently to broadcasts of candidate debates than it does to the traditional public streets and parks.

♦ A broad right of access to broadcasts, even of political candidate debates, would undermine the editorial discretion that broadcasters must exercise to fulfill their statutory obligations and journalistic purpose. But candidate debates require scrutiny because they are designed for expression of the candidates' views, not D's, and because candidate debates are exceptionally important to the electoral process. These factors make D's debate a public forum.

♦ There are three types of speech forums: (i) the traditional public forum; (ii) the public forum created by government designation; and (iii) the nonpublic forum. The government can exclude a speaker from a traditional public forum only when the exclusion is necessary to serve a compelling state interest and is narrowly drawn to achieve that interest. The government must also satisfy strict scrutiny to exclude from a designated public forum a speaker who falls within the class to which such a forum is made generally available. However, access to a nonpublic forum can be restricted with merely reasonable restrictions, so long as the government is not trying to suppress views public officials oppose.

♦ D's debate was a nonpublic forum. A designated forum is not created merely by the government reserving eligibility for access to a particular class of speakers. D did not open its debate to all candidates for the office; it reserved eligibility to those candidates that it selected. P was excluded solely because he had not generated appreciable public interest, which was a reasonable restriction not based on P's viewpoint.

Dissent (Stevens, Souter, Ginsburg, JJ.). The Court gives D too much flexibility in applying its standard for selection of participants, so that D had nearly limitless discretion based on ad hoc justifications.

Comment. The Court noted that, generally, the public forum doctrine does not apply to state-owned television stations. Such stations have a responsibility to make programming decisions that make it impractical for them to be considered a forum at all.

---

3. **Speech on Private Premises.**

   a. **Introduction.** As indicated *supra*, the location of the speech has a significant impact on the protection afforded to the speech. Speech in nonpublic forums—private premises—receives the lowest level of protection from time, place, and manner restrictions.

   b. **Residential signs--**

City of Ladue v. Gilleo,

Facts. The city of Ladue (D) adopted an ordinance prohibiting homeowners from displaying any signs on their property other than "residence identification" signs, "for sale" signs, and signs that warn about safety hazards. Gilleo (P) owned a house in D. She placed a sign on her front lawn that expressed disapproval of the war in the Persian Gulf. Someone removed this sign, and a replacement sign P put up was knocked down. P reported the incidents to the police, who informed her that D prohibited such signs. P sought a variance, which D denied. P sued, and the district court enjoined enforcement of the ordinance. D then adopted a new ordinance that contained 10 exceptions to the sign ban. However, signs such as P's were still prohibited. The lower courts found the new ordinance unconstitutional, and the Supreme Court granted certiorari.

Issue. May the government prohibit all signs on residential property except identification signs, "for sale" signs, and safety warning signs?

Held. No. Judgment affirmed.

- Signs are subject to police powers because, although they are protected speech, they take up space and may obstruct views, distract motorists, and create other problems. In *Linmark Associates, Inc. v. Willingboro*, 431 U.S. 85 (1977), the Court held that a government may not prohibit "for sale" signs on residential property without also banning all other types of signs. The *Linmark* ban was concerned with the content of the speech. In this case, D has allowed such signs and relied on the content-neutral justification of promoting aesthetic values to ban all signs not specifically covered by the exceptions.

- D claims that its purposes are content-neutral. Yet the exemptions in the ordinance reflect a finding that certain messages are so important that they outweigh D's aesthetic interests.

- D's interest in minimizing visual clutter is valid, as it was in *Linmark*, but the burden imposed by D is greater than the burden in *Linmark*. D has eliminated a unique and important means of political expression. There is no alternative channel for communication that substitutes for residential lawn signs. Such signs are "an unusually cheap and convenient form of communication." A respect for individual liberty in one's home makes a ban on speech at the home particularly sensitive.

- D's ban is simply not sufficiently justified in light of its serious impact on freedom of speech.

Concurrence (O'Connor, J.). Content discrimination in regulating the speech of private citizens on private property is presumed to be impermissible. Normally, the courts determine whether a regulation is content-based or content-neutral, and then apply the appropriate level of scrutiny. This approach should have been used in this case.

---

c. **Regulation of speech based on secondary effects--**

City of Los Angeles v. Alameda Books, Inc.,

Facts. The city of Los Angeles (D) determined that concentrations of adult businesses were associated with higher rates of crime, including prostitution, robbery, assaults, and thefts. D adopted an ordinance that prohibited the establishment of an adult entertainment facility within 1,000 feet of another such enterprise or within 500 feet of any religious institution, school, or public park. To avoid the creation of an adult-oriented department store to replace a strip of such stores, D adopted an ordinance that prohibited having more than one adult entertainment business in the same building. Ps are two adult establishments that each operated an adult bookstore and an adult video arcade in the same building. Ps challenged D's ordinance under the First Amendment. The district court granted summary judgment for Ps. The Ninth Circuit affirmed. The Supreme Court granted certiorari.

Issue. May a city prohibit the operation of more than one adult entertainment business in any one building even if it does not specifically study the negative effects of this type of concentration of adult businesses?

Held. Yes. Judgment reversed and case remanded.

- In *Renton v. Playtime Theatres, Inc.*, 475 U.S. 41 (1986), the Court held that a city can prohibit the operation of adult movie theaters within 1,000 feet of residences, churches, parks, and schools. Such an ordinance is not a ban, but merely a time, place and manner regulation. The ordinance was aimed not at the content of the films, but at the secondary effects of such theaters on the surrounding community. Because the ordinance served a substantial government interest and no reasonable alternatives were available, it was permissible.

- The Ninth Circuit applied *Renton* to D's ordinance in this case, but determined that D failed to satisfy the third step of *Renton* because D's prohibition on multiple-use adult establishments was not designed to serve D's substantial interest in reducing crime. The study D relied on focused on a concentration of establishments, not a concentration of operations within a single building.

- The Ninth Circuit misunderstood the implications of D's study and erred in requiring D to prove that its theory about a concentration of adult operations attracting crowds of customers was a necessary consequence of the study. The court simply replaced D's theory with its own, but D is not required to prove that its own theory is the only conclusion that can be drawn from the study. Instead, D may rely on any evidence that is reasonably believed to be relevant.

- On remand, Ps may introduce evidence to cast doubt on D's rationale, which would require D to provide more evidence to support its theory. Under *Renton*, municipal ordinances receive only intermediate scrutiny if they are content neutral.

Concurrence (Scalia, J.). It is not necessary for a city to rely on "secondary effects" in this type of case because the Constitution does not prevent communities from regulating, or even entirely suppressing, the business of pandering sex.

Concurrence (Kennedy, J.). Speech can produce tangible consequences, from the pollution of a newspaper factory to impaired property values caused by high concentrations of adult businesses. A city can use its zoning authority to address these secondary consequences as long as it results in only a trivial decrease in the quantity of speech. As long as a city has some basis to show that its regulation has the purpose and effect of suppressing secondary effects, while leaving the quantity and accessibility of speech substantially intact, it should be allowed to adopt the regulation.

Dissent (Souter, Stevens, Ginsburg, Breyer, JJ.). D's latest ordinance moves from a policy of dispersing adult establishments to a policy of dividing them in two. The study D relies on, which it used for its original ordinance, does not support the breakup policy. This type of secondary-effects zoning regulation is not the same as a time, place, or manner regulation because it is based on the content of the material in Ps' establishments. D failed to show any causal relationship between its breakup policy and elimination of secondary effects.

---

d. Public utility billing inserts--

Consolidated Edison Co. v. Public Service Commission,

Facts. Consolidated Edison Company (P) included written material advocating nuclear power in its billing envelopes. Upon application by an environmental group for equal access, the Public Service Commission (D) decided to prohibit all such use of billing envelopes for the discussion of political matters, but permitted P to send bill inserts that did not cover controversial issues of public policy. P sought review, and the state courts held D's regulation to be a valid time, place, and manner regulation. P appeals.

Issue. Does a public service commission deny a utility's First Amendment rights by prohibiting monthly billing inserts discussing controversial matters of public policy but not prohibiting noncontroversial topics?

Held. Yes. Judgment reversed.

- The utility, like other corporations, clearly is entitled to freedom of speech. Time, place, or manner regulations may limit that freedom, but they cannot be based on subject matter. D's rule is therefore invalid.

- D claims that since it bans all discussion of nuclear power, pro and con, its rule is permissible. However, the First Amendment protects complete public discussion as well as particular viewpoints. D also argues that its rule protects a captive audience, but P's customers do not fit within that class, since they can avoid P's possibly objectionable speech merely by not reading it. D's claim that its rule prevents ratepayers from being forced to subsidize P's communication is not supported by the facts; D could require allocation of costs to P's shareholders rather than to P's ratepayers.

Concurrence (Stevens, J.). Time, place, and manner restrictions may relate to content, as does the Court's own regulation of oral argument. The fallacy of D's rule is that it denies P the right to address a selected audience on a controversial issue of public policy.

Dissent (Blackmun, Rehnquist, JJ.). P's monopoly status and rate structure results in ratepayer subsidy of its speech; the First Amendment does not require this.

---

4. **Speech in Public Schools.**

   a. **Introduction.** Public schools are special forums in the sense that although they are public, and are devoted to education and the exchange of ideas, they also are intended to promote responsible citizenship and social values. Accordingly, when confronted with a challenge to regulation of speech in public schools, the courts must balance these interests, taking into consideration the context of the speech and the age and maturity of the intended or actual audience, as well as the effect of the speech on the mission of the schools.

   b. **Wearing of armbands in public schools--**

Tinker v. Des Moines School District,

Facts. Tinker and other students (Ps) wore black armbands to school to protest the Vietnam War, despite a school policy against such action. Ps were suspended and sought an injunction against the Des Moines School District (D) to prevent D from disciplining them. The lower courts upheld D's action as reasonable to maintain school discipline, and Ps appeal.

Issue. May school officials ban a silent, peaceful expression of opinion, such as wearing an armband, and punish offenders?

Held. No. Judgment reversed.

- Wearing an armband is a symbolic act worthy of First Amendment protection. Constitutional rights are not abandoned at the schoolhouse gate. Yet, school authorities may properly prescribe and control conduct in the schools.

- Ps' expression was silent and passive, unaccompanied by disorder or interference with the school's work. Prohibition of a particular expression of opinion is justified only by a showing that the expression would materially interfere with the school's discipline, which D has failed to show. Avoidance of the controversy attending unpopular opinion is an inadequate reason to ban expression of such opinions.

Concurrence (Stewart, J.). The Court goes too far in assuming that the First Amendment rights of children are coextensive with those of adults.

Dissent (Black, J.). Ps' actions did in actuality divert at least some students' minds from their classwork. There is no constitutional right to say whatever a person pleases, where and when he pleases. The school rules were proper and ought to be upheld.

Comment. The Court has upheld an ordinance prohibiting demonstrations near schools, during school hours, that materially disrupt classwork. Although school property (or adjacent property) cannot be declared "off limits" for expressive activity, such activity cannot be permitted to invade the rights of students to an education. [*See* Grayned v. City of Rockford, 408 U.S. 104 (1972)]

---

c. Student's lewd speech at school assembly--

Bethel School District No. 403 v. Fraser,

Facts. Fraser (P) delivered a nominating speech at a high school-sponsored assembly for election of student officers. P's speech was constructed around an explicit sexual metaphor that provoked numerous crowd reactions. Several teachers wrote reports of P's speech that the school principal used to suspend P for three days pursuant to a rule against the use of obscene language in school. P's suspension was upheld through the grievance procedures followed by the Bethel School District No. 403 (D). P then brought a federal suit, claiming damages for violation of his First Amendment rights. The district court found for P, and the court of appeals affirmed. The Supreme Court granted certiorari.

Issue. May a high school discipline one of its students for giving a lewd speech at a school assembly?

Held. Yes. Judgment reversed.

- P's speech is significantly different from the political message of the armband that was protected in *Tinker, supra*. The *Tinker* speech did not intrude upon the work of the schools or the rights of other students. By contrast, P's speech was plainly offensive to teachers and students; one teacher had to spend class time the next day to discuss the speech.

- A basic purpose for public education is to promote and develop habits and manners of civility. While there is a First Amendment interest in advocacy of unpopular and controversial views, even in schools, this interest must be balanced against the interest in teaching students the boundaries of socially appropriate behavior. Public schools must be allowed to prohibit the use of vulgar and offensive terms in public discourse.

Concurrence (Brennan, J.). P's speech is hardly as obscene as the Court makes it out to be, but D should have authority to discipline high school students for giving speeches at a school-sponsored assembly that disrupt the school's educational mission.

Dissent (Marshall, J.). D failed to prove that P's speech was actually disruptive.

Dissent (Stevens, J.). P did not have fair notice of the scope of the prohibition against offensive speech.

---

d. Removal of books from public secondary school libraries--

Board of Education v. Pico,

Facts. The Board of Education (D) obtained a list of "objectionable" books and removed them from the high school library for review by Board members. D appointed a committee to recommend whether the books should be retained in the library, then rejected the recommendations and returned only one of the removed books. D based its decision on the claim that the books were anti-American and that they presented moral danger to the students. Pico and others (Ps) challenged the decision in federal court. The district court granted summary judgment for D, but the court of appeals reversed and remanded the case for trial. D appeals.

Issue. Does the First Amendment impose limitations on a local school board's discretionary removal of books from a high school library?

Held. Yes. Judgment affirmed.

- ♦ This case does not involve the use of books in the classroom, but merely optional library books, nor does it involve acquisition of books. Because of the procedural posture, the judgment must be affirmed if there is any question of fact.

- ♦ Local school boards have discretion in managing school affairs. However, this discretion is subject to the First Amendment rights of the students. These rights may be impinged on by the removal of books from a school library. D's discretion may not be exercised so as to deny students access to ideas with which the board members disagree, although they could remove books that were pervasively vulgar or educationally unsuitable.

- ♦ The evidence as to D's motive in removing the books is unclear. There is evidence that D acted out of disagreement with the ideas contained in the books. By disregarding the committee's recommendations, the board acted in an ad hoc manner. The case must be remanded for necessary fact findings.

Concurrence (Blackmun, J.). The state may not suppress exposure to ideas without a sufficiently compelling reason. And it may not deny access to an idea simply because state officials disapprove of or disagree with the idea. However, there is no right to receive ideas on the part of students. The determinative question is the motive of the school officials.

Concurrence (White, J.). There is no need to decide the question in the absence of a complete factual record.

Dissent (Burger, C.J., Powell, Rehnquist, O'Connor, JJ.). School boards, not judges and students, are charged with administering schools. Such boards are responsive to the voters and therefore reflect the views of the community. The values of morality, good taste, and relevance to education may properly be considered by the elected officials in performing their duty.

Dissent (Rehnquist, J., Burger, C.J., Powell, J.). D did not deprive the public generally of the ideas in the books. Education, especially short of the university level, is necessarily selective, and those charged with providing the education must be free to determine what is necessary and what is not. The First Amendment right to receive information does not apply to an institution that is necessarily selective in the ideas it may impart.

---

e. School's control over contents of student-produced newspaper--

Hazelwood School District v. Kuhlmeier,

Facts. Kuhlmeier and other students (Ps) were staff members of a high school newspaper. The principal of the school would review page proofs before the paper was published. The principal objected to two articles Ps wanted to publish: one dealt with three students' experiences with pregnancy, and the other with the impact of divorce on students. The principal approved publication of the paper without the stories. Ps sued the Hazelwood School District (D) for an injunction and for damages for violation of their rights. The district court denied an injunction, but the court of appeals reversed. The Supreme Court granted certiorari.

Issue. May a high school exercise control over the content of the student-produced high school paper?

Held. Yes. Judgment affirmed.

- The newspaper was not a public forum unless the school had opened it for indiscriminate use by the general public or by some segment of the public. In this case, D supported the newspaper solely as part of the curriculum and for its educational benefits. Thus, D was entitled to regulate the contents of the paper in any reasonable manner.

- ♦ This case involves the question whether the First Amendment requires a school affirmatively to promote particular student speech, a different question from that involved in *Tinker*, *supra*—whether a school must tolerate particular student speech. Because the newspaper is school sponsored, the public might reasonably perceive it to bear the imprimatur of the school, and educators may exercise greater control over this type of student expression to preserve its educational value as well as protect against attribution of the expression to the school. Judicial intervention would be appropriate only if the newspaper had no educational purpose.

- ♦ The principal in this case acted reasonably in deleting the specific articles involved.

Dissent (Brennan, Marshall, Blackmun, JJ.). This is the first case to distinguish between personal and school-sponsored speech. Under *Tinker*, official censorship intended to protect the audience or dissociate the sponsor from the expression is not permitted. Censorship does not further the curricular purposes of a student newspaper.

---

f. Student banner with cryptic message involving drugs--

Morse v. Frederick,

Facts. Morse (D), a high school principal, permitted students to watch the Olympic Torch Relay as it passed in front of the school during school hours. Frederick (P), a student at the school, watched with friends across the street from the school. As the torchbearers and camera crews passed by, P and his friends unfurled a 14-foot banner that read "BONG HITS 4 JESUS." D demanded the banner be taken down. Everyone but P complied. D confiscated the banner and suspended P from school for 10 days on the ground that the banner encouraged illegal drug use in violation of school policy. Administrative appeals upheld D's action. P sued in federal court. The district court found for D, but the court of appeals reversed. The Supreme Court granted certiorari.

Issue. May school officials confiscate a pro-drug banner on school grounds and suspend the students who created and displayed it?

Held. Yes. Judgment reversed.

- ♦ Although P was late for school that day, he was standing with fellow students, during school hours, at a school-sanctioned activity. He cannot claim that he was not at school. Therefore, this is a school speech case.

- D's interpretation of the banner's wording as celebrating or promoting illegal drug use was reasonable. Under *Tinker*, *supra*, student expression may not be suppressed unless it will materially and substantially disrupt the work and discipline of the school. But in *Kuhlmeier*, *supra*, this Court recognized that school officials know the impact of peer pressure in leading kids to use drugs. P's banner in this setting presented a serious and palpable danger. Under these circumstances, D's response was reasonable. The First Amendment does not require school officials to tolerate this type of student expression at school events.

Concurrence (Thomas, J.). I join the Court's opinion because it erodes *Tinker*; I believe that the *Tinker* approach should be rejected. The First Amendment's freedom of speech does not extend to a student's right to speak in public schools.

Concurrence (Alito, Kennedy, JJ.). The Court today merely holds that a public school may restrict speech that a reasonable observer would interpret as advocating illegal drug use. It does not support a restriction of speech that can be interpreted as commenting on any political or social issue. Public schools are not free to censor all student speech that interferes with a school's "educational mission." The *Tinker* "substantial disruption" standard allows school officials to step in before actual violence erupts. Because advocacy of illegal drug use is a serious threat to student safety, it may properly be banned, although this is at the far reaches of what the First Amendment permits.

Concurrence and dissent (Breyer, J.). This case can be resolved by holding that qualified immunity bars P's claim for monetary damages. The Court's opinion goes further than necessary to decide the case and could be used to justify further viewpoint-based restrictions.

Dissent (Stevens, Souter, Ginsburg, JJ.). The Court's opinion invites viewpoint discrimination. D disciplined P because she disagreed with P's message. It is one thing to restrict speech that advocates drug use; it is another thing entirely to prohibit an obscure message with a drug theme that a third party subjectively thinks is the same as expressing advocacy. D must show that P's supposed advocacy stands a meaningful chance of making students try marijuana when they otherwise would not. The Court instead allows the censorship of any student speech that mentions drugs if someone could interpret the speech as containing a latent pro-drug message.

---

5. Government Subsidies to Speech--

Rust v. Sullivan,

Facts. Congress enacted Title X of the Public Health Service Act, which provided federal funding for family-planning services. However, the Act provided that none of the funds could be used in programs where abortion is a method of family planning. Sullivan (D), Secretary of the Department of Health and Human Services, promulgated new regulations that (i) specified that a Title X project cannot provide counseling concerning abortion or referrals for abortion; (ii) prohibited a Title X project from engaging in activities that encourage, promote, or advocate abortion as a method of family planning; and (iii) required that Title X projects be physically and financially separate from prohibited abortion activities. Rust (P) challenged the facial validity of the regulations, claiming they violated the First and Fifth Amendments to the Constitution. The lower courts upheld the regulations, and the Supreme Court granted certiorari.

Issue. May the federal government condition the acceptance of federal funds by a particular project on the project's agreement to refrain from promoting or even discussing abortion?

Held. Yes. Judgment affirmed.

- D's regulations do not exceed D's authority so long as they reflect a plausible construction of the plain language of the statute and do not otherwise conflict with Congress's expressed intent. The language of the statute is ambiguous and broad enough to allow D's interpretation. Courts normally must defer to the expertise of the agency charged with administering the law. The fact that the regulations are a change from the prior regulations is justified by D's experience under the prior policy.

- Ps claim that the regulations are discrimination based on viewpoint because they promote childbirth over abortion. But D has merely chosen to fund one activity to the exclusion of the other. The government has no obligation to subsidize counterpart rights once it decides to subsidize one protected right. D's regulations do not deny anyone a benefit, but merely require that public funds be spent for the purposes for which they were authorized. And they apply to the project, not to the grantee, who is left free to perform abortions and to advocate abortion in other contexts.

- Ps also claim that D's regulations violate a woman's Fifth Amendment right to choose whether to terminate her pregnancy. But Congress's refusal to fund abortion counseling and advocacy leaves a pregnant woman with the same choices as if Congress had chosen not to fund family-planning services at all. D's regulations do not affect a doctor's ability to provide information about abortion outside the context of a Title X project.

Dissent (Blackmun, Marshall, Stevens, O'Connor, JJ.). D's regulations clearly constitute content-based regulation of speech aimed at suppressing "dangerous ideas." They are also viewpoint based, since they prohibit abortion advocacy but do not regulate anti-abortion advocacy.

Comment. The Court noted that government funding is not always sufficient by itself to justify government control over the content of expression. For example, government ownership of real property does not justify restriction of speech in such areas if they have been traditionally open to the public for expressive activity, and government payments to universities do not justify control of speech there. In this case, D's regulations do not significantly impinge upon the doctor-patient relationship because they do not apply to post-conception medical care, and the doctor can make it clear that advice regarding abortion is beyond the scope of the Title X program.

---

6. **Government Support for Religious Viewpoints--**

Rosenberger v. Rector & Visitors of the University of Virginia. *See infra*

7. **Decency Standards for Federal Spending--**

National Endowment for the Arts v. Finley,

Facts. The National Endowment for the Arts (D) was funded by Congress. Applications for funding by D were reviewed by advisory panels of experts who in turn reported to the national council, who then advised D's chairperson, who awarded the grants. After D funded some controversial projects, Congress amended the statute to require the chairperson to consider "general standards of decency and respect for the diverse beliefs and values of the American people" in establishing procedures to judge the artistic merit of grant applications. Finley and other artists (Ps) applied for grants before the amendment was adopted. Ps were denied funding, and they sued, claiming D denied their First Amendment rights by rejecting their applications on political grounds. The district court denied D's motion for judgment on the pleadings. The court granted summary judgment to Ps on their facial challenge to the amendment and enjoined D from enforcing it. The court of appeals affirmed. The Supreme Court granted certiorari.

Issue. May Congress impose decency standards on discretionary spending of federally appropriated funds?

Held. Yes. Judgment reversed.

- The amendment, section 954(d)(1), does not impose a categorical requirement. It consists of advisory language only, and is aimed at reforming procedures rather than precluding speech. There is no realistic danger that the provision will compromise First Amendment values.

- It is also unlikely that the provision will introduce any greater element of selectivity than the determination of "artistic excellence" itself. The nature of arts funding requires content-based considerations. Some constitutionally protected expression will be rejected regardless of the criteria used.

- In *Rosenberger v. Rector & Visitors of the University of Virginia*, *infra*, the Court held that a school could not exclude religious student publications when it encouraged a diversity of views from private speakers. In this case, however, D is not indiscriminately encouraging a diversity of views; it is trying to make aesthetic judgments on the content of submissions.

- The government may allocate competitive funding according to criteria that would be impermissible if it were directly regulating speech. It may selectively fund programs by making choices between and among the alternatives.

- The language of section 954(d)(1) is vague, but when the government acts as patron rather than as sovereign, the consequences of imprecision are not constitutionally severe. Thus, the amendment is not unconstitutionally vague. The provision simply adds some imprecise factors to an already subjective selection process.

Concurrence (Scalia, Thomas, JJ.). Section 954(d)(1) properly establishes content- and viewpoint-based criteria upon which D is to evaluate grant applications. There is a fundamental difference between abridging speech and funding it.

Dissent (Souter, J.). D has failed to show why the statute should be exempted from the fundamental rule of the First Amendment that viewpoint discrimination in the exercise of public authority over expressive activity is unconstitutional. Once the government decides to subsidize expressive conduct at large, it cannot discriminate on the basis of the content.

---

a. Government support of legal services--

Legal Services Corporation v. Velazquez

Facts. Congress created the Legal Services Corporation (D) through the Legal Services Corporation Act. D was a nonprofit corporation with a mission to distribute federal funds to eligible organizations to provide financial support for legal assistance in noncriminal proceedings. Congress provided that D's funds could not be used on legal representation that involved an effort to amend or otherwise challenge existing welfare law. Velazquez and other interested lawyers and clients (Ps) sought to have the restriction declared invalid. The district court declined to issue an injunction, but the Second Circuit approved an injunction. The Supreme Court granted certiorari.

Issue. If Congress grants federal funds for use in providing legal services for indigent persons, may it prohibit the use of those funds to pay for challenges to welfare laws?

Held. No. Judgment affirmed.

- Congress has always restricted D's use of funds, such as prohibiting D's grantees from using funds for political party activities, criminal proceedings, litigation involving nontherapeutic abortions, and other specific types of cases. D allows its grantees to challenge welfare agency determinations of benefit ineligibility, but not to challenge the welfare law itself.

- Under *Rust*, *supra*, Congress may choose to fund one activity to the exclusion of another without discriminating against viewpoints. When it acts in this manner, Congress does not single out a particular idea for suppression. It merely prohibits recipients of federal funds from providing counseling outside the scope of the project.

- *Rust* involved the government's own message, which gave the government greater latitude to restrict speech. In this case, however, D was set up to facilitate private speech, not to promote a governmental message. Lawyers funded by D speak for their clients, not the government.

- Although D's program is a subsidy, it has similarities to limited form cases. Restricting D's attorneys in handling their clients' cases distorts the legal system by altering the traditional role of attorneys. This severe impairment of the judicial function would result in questions about the validity of an attorney's representation of her clients. Where the attorney withdraws to avoid violating D's rules, the client would be unlikely to find alternative counsel, which means there is no alternative channel for the expression Congress seeks to restrict.

- The effect of the restriction is to prohibit advice or argumentation that existing welfare laws are unconstitutional or unlawful. By insulating welfare laws from constitutional scrutiny, Congress has implicated central First Amendment concerns. If Congress decides to fund D's attorneys, it is not required to fund the whole range of representation. However, it cannot define the scope of the litigation it does permit so as to exclude certain vital theories and ideas.

Dissent (Scalia, J., Rehnquist, C.J., O'Connor, Thomas, JJ.). In defining the scope of D's spending authority, Congress has not directly regulated speech, it has not established a public forum, and it has not discriminated on the basis of viewpoint. The restriction applies to defense of existing welfare law as well as challenges to it. The program is a subsidy, not a regulation. Simply denying a subsidy does not coerce belief. The attempt to distinguish *Rust* fails because the private doctors' advice in that case is not government speech. D's program neither prevents anyone from speaking nor coerces anyone to change speech, so it is squarely within the *Rust* rule.

8. Requiring Internet Filters in Government-Supported Libraries--

United States v. American Library Association, Inc.,

Facts. After providing funding to help public libraries provide public Internet access, Congress became concerned that its programs were facilitating access to illegal and harmful pornography by minors. The Children's Internet Protection Act ("CIPA") provided that a public library could not receive federal funds to provide Internet access unless the library installed filtering software to prevent minors from accessing harmful material and to block obscenity and child pornography. Although some libraries had begun installing blocking and filtering software prior to CIPA, a group of libraries, library associations, library patrons, Web site publishers, and the American Library Association, Inc. (Ps) challenged CIPA. The district court held that filtering software was a content-based restriction on access to a public forum that was not narrowly tailored. The United States (D) appeals.

Issue. May Congress require public libraries to limit Internet access to certain content as a condition for receiving public funds?

Held. Yes. Judgment reversed.

- Congress has wide latitude to attach conditions to the receipt of federal assistance in order to further its legitimate policy objectives. However, Congress cannot induce the recipient of funds to do something that is unconstitutional.

- The traditional role of a library is to collect materials that would benefit or be of interest to its community. Libraries have never provided universal coverage; they have to exercise judgment in selecting material for their patrons. They have broad discretion in making their decisions, and they necessarily consider content.

- Internet access in public libraries is neither a traditional nor a designated public forum. Adding blocking and filtering software does not change the nature of a library's role; most libraries already exclude pornography from their collections because they consider it inappropriate.

- Even if filtering software can "overblock," by blocking access to constitutionally protected speech outside the categories intended to be blocked, patrons can have the software disabled for particular sites.

- Even if Ps had a claim that Congress was placing unconstitutional conditions on the receipt of government funds, Congress has authority to define the limits of programs that it funds. The lack of a subsidy is not a penalty, so Congress is not penalizing libraries that choose not to install the filtering software.

Concurrence (Kennedy, J.). The government has a legitimate and compelling interest in protecting minors from inappropriate material. Congress's program does not significantly burden the ability of adult library users to access protected material.

Concurrence (Breyer, J.). Because CIPA directly restricts the public's receipt of information, CIPA should be subject to a form of heightened scrutiny that is not quite "strict," but is greater than a "rational basis" review. Any speech-related harm that CIPA may cause is not disproportionate when considered in relation to its legitimate objectives.

Dissent (Stevens, J.). CIPA is a blunt nationwide restraint on adult access to a large amount of constitutionally protected speech. Libraries should be allowed to exercise their discretion in this matter the same way they do when making other decisions about what to include in their collections.

Dissent (Souter, Ginsburg, JJ.). CIPA mandates action (installing blocking and filtering software) that would violate the First Amendment's guarantee of free speech if the libraries took that action entirely on their own. Internet blocking is not the same as a library's selective process of acquiring library materials. Internet access presents no issues of funding or space because the blocking takes place after the money is spent on the Internet connection. Blocking Internet access in public libraries is like removing books from library shelves because of their content.

C. PROTECTION OF PENUMBRAL FIRST AMENDMENT RIGHTS

1. **Symbolic Speech.** The protection afforded unpopular words extends to symbolic conduct that can be considered expression—*i.e.*, conduct undertaken to communicate an idea.

   a. **Draft card burning--**

United States v. O'Brien,

Facts. O'Brien and others (Ds) publicly burned their draft cards in violation of federal law. Ds claimed that their action was intended to influence others to adopt their anti-war beliefs. Ds were convicted, but the court of appeals held that the statute was an unconstitutional abridgment of freedom of speech. The United States (P) appeals.

Issue. When conduct contains both "speech" and "nonspeech" elements, may an important governmental interest in regulating the nonspeech element justify incidental limitations on First Amendment freedoms?

Held. Yes. Judgment reversed.

- The statute does not abridge free speech on its face, but deals with conduct having no connection with speech, *i.e.,* destruction of draft cards.

- Although freedom of expression includes certain symbolic speech, it does not include any and all conduct intended to express an idea. Even conduct that contains a protected communicative element is not absolutely immune from government regulation. A sufficiently important governmental interest in regulating the nonspeech element of conduct can justify incidental limitations on the speech element.

- A government regulation is justified if it is within constitutional authority, if it furthers an important governmental interest, if the interest is unrelated to the suppression of free expression, and if the incidental restriction on First Amendment freedoms is no greater than is essential to the furtherance of that interest. The draft card laws meet these tests; therefore, D may properly be prosecuted for his illegal activity.

---

b. Flag burning--

Texas v. Johnson,

Facts. As part of a political demonstration, Johnson (D) unfurled an American flag, doused it with kerosene, and set it on fire. While the flag burned, the protesters chanted, "America, the red, white, and blue, we spit on you." Observers later testified they were seriously offended by the flag burning, but no one was physically injured or threatened with injury. D was charged with desecration of a venerated object and convicted. He was sentenced to one year in prison and fined $2,000. D appealed. The first appellate court affirmed, but the second reversed. Texas (P) appeals.

Issue. May the government prosecute a person for burning a United States flag in protest when there is no physical injury to any person or property?

Held. No. Judgment affirmed.

- The First Amendment literally applies only to "speech," but this is not limited to spoken or written words. Conduct may possess sufficient communicative elements to constitute "speech" where there is an intent to convey a particularized message and the likelihood is great that the message would be understood by those who view it. For example, the wearing of black armbands, a sit-in, or picketing may constitute "speech."

- Attaching a peace sign to the flag, saluting the flag, and displaying a red flag have all been held to constitute "speech." The very purpose of a national flag is to serve as a symbol of the country it represents. D's conduct in burning the flag was overtly political; his intent was clear and the message apparent to those who observed. It therefore implicated the First Amendment.

- In general, the government has more latitude to restrict expressive conduct than it has in restricting the written or spoken word, but it may not criminalize conduct merely because it has expressive elements. Under the *O'Brien* test, *supra*, P claims two interests in support of its statute that are unrelated to the suppression of expression. The first is preventing breaches of the peace, but in this case there was no breach of the peace. A potential for a breach of the peace is not enough to suppress expressive conduct. The second interest is in preserving the flag as a symbol of nationhood, which D's conduct undermines, but this is precisely the suppression of free expression that cannot be permitted under the First Amendment.

- P claims an interest in preserving the flag as a symbol of nationhood and national unity that justifies its law. Burning the flag to dispose of it because it is dirty or torn is not a violation; D's treatment of the flag violated Texas law only because of the likely communicative impact of his conduct. Because P's law restricts expression based on its content, it must survive the most exacting scrutiny. But the First Amendment forbids the government from prohibiting the expression of an idea simply because society finds the idea itself offensive or disagreeable. Therefore, the Texas law is unconstitutional.

- This decision strengthens the flag's special role in our community, because it reaffirms the principles of freedom and inclusiveness that the flag best represents.

Dissent (Rehnquist, C.J., White, O'Connor, JJ.). Justice Holmes states that "a page of history is worth a volume of logic." The American flag has occupied a unique position as the symbol of our nation for over 200 years. D was punished not for the ideas he sought to convey, which he freely conveyed in a variety of other methods, but for his use of this particular symbol. If the government may conscript men into the Armed Forces and require them to fight and even die for the flag, it should be able to prohibit the public burning of that same flag.

Dissent (Stevens, J.). Even if flag burning could be considered just another species of symbolic speech under the Court's jurisprudence, the use of the American flag has an intangible dimension that makes those rules inapplicable.

Comment. Subsequent to this decision, Congress passed the Flag Protection Act of 1989, which prohibited the mutilation, burning, and trampling on the flag of the United States, regardless of the message intended or the likely effect on onlookers. The Court held the statute unconstitutional in *United States v. Eichman*, 496 U.S. 310 (1990).

c. **Public nudity--**

City of Erie v. Pap's A.M.,

Facts. The city of Erie, Pennsylvania (D), made it an offense to knowingly or intentionally appear in public in a "state of nudity." Pap's A.M. (P) operated "Kandyland," which featured totally nude erotic dancing by women. Under D's ordinance, P's dancers had to wear "pasties" and a "G-string." P sued D, seeking declaratory relief and a permanent injunction against enforcement of the ordinance. The trial court held the ordinance unconstitutional, and the Pennsylvania Supreme Court ultimately agreed, holding that, because the ordinance was related to the suppression of expression and was not content neutral, it was subject to strict scrutiny. The Supreme Court granted certiorari.

Issue. May a municipality ban appearing in public in a state of nudity?

Held. Yes. Judgment reversed and case remanded.

- Government restrictions on public nudity such as D's ordinance should be evaluated under *United States* v. *O'Brien, supra*, for content-neutral restrictions on symbolic speech. Although being "in a state of nudity" is not an inherently expressive condition, nude dancing of the type at issue here is expressive conduct that falls within the outer ambit of the First Amendment's protection.

- The appropriate level of scrutiny depends on whether the ordinance is related to the suppression of expression. If the governmental purpose in enacting the ordinance is unrelated to such suppression, the ordinance need only satisfy the "less stringent," intermediate *O'Brien* standard. If the governmental interest is related to the expression's content, however, the ordinance falls outside *O'Brien* and must be justified under the more demanding, strict scrutiny standard.

- An almost identical public nudity ban was upheld under the First Amendment in *Barnes v. Glen Theatre, Inc.*, 501 U.S. 560 (1991). The ordinance in this case is a general prohibition on public nudity that regulates conduct alone. It does not target nudity that is accompanied by expressive activity, such as an erotic message. The Pennsylvania Supreme Court construed the ordinance's preamble to mean that one of its purposes was to combat negative secondary effects, such as crime, caused by the presence of adult entertainment establishments like Kandyland and not at suppressing the erotic message conveyed by this type of nude dancing.

- Courts should not strike down otherwise constitutional statutes on the basis of allegedly illicit motive. Even if D's public nudity ban has some minimal effect on the erotic message, P's dancers are free to perform wearing pasties and G-strings. Any effect on the overall expression is therefore de minimis. Thus, D's ordinance is valid if it satisfies the *O'Brien* test.

- D's ordinance satisfies *O'Brien*'s four-factor test. First, the ordinance is within D's police power to protect public health and safety. Second, the ordinance furthers the important government interests of regulating conduct through a public nudity ban and of combating the harmful secondary effects associated with nude dancing, as demonstrated in other cases. Although requiring dancers to wear pasties and G-strings may not greatly reduce these secondary effects, *O'Brien* requires only that the regulation further the interest in combating such effects.

- D's ordinance also satisfies *O'Brien*'s third factor, that the government interest is unrelated to the suppression of free expression. The fourth *O'Brien* factor—that the restriction is no greater than is essential to the furtherance of the government interest—is satisfied because the ordinance regulates conduct, and any incidental impact on the expressive element of nude dancing is de minimis. The pasties and G-string requirement is a minimal restriction in furtherance of the asserted government interests, and the restriction leaves ample capacity to convey the dancer's erotic message.

Concurrence (Scalia, Thomas, JJ.). D modeled its ordinance on the public nudity statute upheld in *Barnes*, which was upheld because, as a general law regulating conduct and not specifically directed at expression, it was not subject to First Amendment scrutiny at all. There is no need to identify "secondary effects" associated with nude dancing that D could properly seek to eliminate. The traditional power of government to foster good morals, and the acceptability of the traditional judgment that nude public dancing itself is immoral, have not been repealed by the First Amendment.

Concurrence and dissent (Souter, J.). The record in this case fails to reveal any evidence on which D may have relied, either for the seriousness of the threatened harm or for the efficacy of its chosen remedy. Under *O'Brien*, the incidental speech restriction must be no greater than essential to achieve the government's legitimate purpose. D might have been able to counter secondary effects by the significantly lesser restriction of zoning.

Dissent (Stevens, Ginsburg, JJ.). The Court today holds that secondary effects may justify the total suppression of protected speech and not merely the regulation of the location of indecent entertainment.

---

2. **Compelled Affirmation of Belief.** The First Amendment protects not only the affirmative right to speak out, but also the right to refrain from speaking at all.

   a. **Flag salute.** In *West Virginia State Board of Education v. Barnette*, 319 U.S. 624 (1943), the Court held that a compulsory flag salute ceremony for all school pupils violated religious liberty. "To sustain the compulsory flag salute rule, we are required to say that a Bill of Rights which guards the individual's right to speak his own mind left it open to public authorities to compel him to utter what is not in his mind."

b. **License plate.** In *Wooley v. Maynard*, 430 U.S. 705 (1977), the Court held that the owner of an automobile cannot be compelled to display a state motto on his license plate.

3. **Freedom of Association.**

a. **The right to associate.**

1) **Political membership--**

NAACP v. Alabama,

Facts. The Attorney General of Alabama (P) sued the NAACP (D) to enjoin D's activities in the state. P sought a large number of D's records, including membership lists. D refused to provide the lists and was fined for contempt. D appeals.

Issue. May a state force production of a private association's membership lists?

Held. No. Judgment reversed.

- P's production order clearly entails the likelihood of substantial restraint on D's members' right to freedom of association. D's immunity from state scrutiny of its membership lists, being closely related to its members' right of association, is protected by the Fourteenth Amendment.
- P has shown no controlling justification for its attempt to curb D's members' rights, and the fine levied against D must fail.

b. **Limits on association activities--**

NAACP v. Claiborne Hardware Co.,

Facts. The NAACP (D) initiated a boycott of several white merchants (Ps), including Claiborne Hardware Co., in order to secure equality and racial justice. Isolated incidents of violence related to the boycott occurred, and some black citizens withheld their patronage from Ps' businesses, fearing reprisals. Ps sued for damages and injunctive relief. The state courts upheld an award based on tort theories, and the Supreme Court granted certiorari.

Issue. Is a boycott organized for political, as opposed to economic, purposes protected under the First Amendment?

Held. Yes. Judgment reversed.

- The boycott consisted of meetings, speeches, and nonviolent picketing. This is protected conduct. The right to associate does not lose constitutional protection just because some members of the group have participated in illegal activity. Boycotts may be subject to reasonable governmental economic regulation, such as restrictions on labor union picketing. The boycott in this case involved peaceful political activity, however, not economic concerns, so the government has no right to prohibit it. Thus, the nonviolent elements of D's activities are protected under the First Amendment.

- Because the First Amendment does not protect violence, the state may impose tort liability for business losses caused by violence and threats of violence. Precision of regulation is demanded when such conduct occurs in the context of constitutionally protected activity. Voluntary participation in the boycott would not therefore be a sufficient basis for imposition of liability, absent a showing of agreement to use unlawful means.

---

c. **Limits on association membership policies.**

1) **Exclusive membership based on sex.** In *Roberts v. United States Jaycees*, 468 U.S. 609 (1984), the Court found no infringement on the freedom of association by a state antidiscrimination law requiring an all-male organization to admit women. Although freedom of association includes the right to associate to engage in First Amendment activities and also the right to establish relationships and share ideals and beliefs, the right is not absolute. Infringements may be justified by compelling state interests, unrelated to suppression of ideas, that cannot be achieved by significantly less restrictive means. The law here is content neutral on its face, and as applied. [*See also* Board of Directors of Rotary International v. Rotary Club, 481 U.S. 537 (1987)—applying *Roberts*]

2) **Exclusive membership based on sexual orientation--**

Boy Scouts of America v. Dale,

Facts. The Boy Scouts of America (D) is a private, not-for-profit organization that instills its system of values in young people, including its assertion that homosexuality is inconsistent with those values. Dale (P) was an adult leader within D. When D learned that P is a homosexual and gay rights activist, D revoked P's adult membership in D. P sued in state court, alleging illegal discrimination. The trial court granted summary judgment for D, but the appellate division reversed in pertinent part and remanded. The state supreme court affirmed, holding that D violated the state's public accommodations law by revoking P's membership based on his avowed homosexuality and that P's reinstatement would not compel the Boy Scouts to express any message. The Supreme Court granted certiorari.

Issue. May the Boy Scouts of America prohibit participation by homosexuals?

Held. Yes. Judgment reversed.

- The application of New Jersey's public accommodations law to require D to admit P violates D's First Amendment right of expressive association. The government may not intrude into a group's internal affairs by forcing it to accept a member it does not desire if such forced membership affects in a significant way the group's ability to advocate public or private viewpoints.

- Under *Roberts*, *supra*, freedom of expressive association is not absolute, and it must yield to regulations adopted to serve compelling state interests, unrelated to the suppression of ideas, that cannot be achieved through means significantly less restrictive of associational freedoms. To determine whether a group is protected, the courts must determine whether the group engages in "expressive association." D clearly does so when its adult leaders inculcate its youth members with its value system.

- The next step is to determine whether forcing D to accept P would significantly affect D's ability to advocate public or private viewpoints. D asserts that homosexual conduct is inconsistent with the values embodied in the Scout Oath and Law, particularly those represented by the terms "morally straight" and "clean," and that D does not want to promote homosexual conduct as a legitimate form of behavior. P's presence as a leader within D's organization would significantly burden D's expression of its viewpoints by interfering with D's choice to not propound a viewpoint that is contrary to its beliefs.

- An association's expression may be protected whenever it engages in expressive activity that could be impaired. Expression need not be its only purpose. Application of the New Jersey public accommodation law to force D to accept P as a leader would violate D's First Amendment rights.

- The intermediate standard of review enunciated in *United States v. O'Brien* is inapplicable here. The appropriate level of analysis is found in *Hurley v. Irish-American Gay, Lesbian and Bisexual Group of Boston, Inc.*, 515 U.S. 557 (1995). The state interests embodied in New Jersey's public accommodations law do not justify the severe intrusion on D's freedom of expressive association that P's participation would present. It is not a question whether D's teachings with respect to homosexual conduct are right or wrong because public or judicial disapproval of an organization's expression does not justify the state's interference with a defendant's expressive message.

Dissent (Stevens, Souter, Ginsburg, Breyer, JJ.). The New Jersey Supreme Court provided an expansive coverage to the state's usage of the term "place of public accommodation." This expansive construction does not violate D's constitutional rights. The law does not impose any serious burdens on D's efforts to achieve its goals, and does not force D to communicate any message it does not want to endorse. D's policy statements are officially silent on homosexuality; D has simply adopted an exclusionary membership policy. P's participation did not send a cognizable message to D or to the world. The right of free speech is not effectively an unlimited right to exclude for every organization. The only rationale for this holding is that homosexuals are so different from the rest of society that their presence alone should be singled out for special First Amendment treatment.

Dissent (Souter, Ginsburg, Breyer, JJ.). D never made sexual orientation the subject of any unequivocal advocacy. Therefore D does not have an expressive association claim.

---

3) Military recruiters' access to law schools--

Rumsfeld v. Forum for Academic and Institutional Rights, Inc.,

---

Facts. Because they disagreed with the military's policy on homosexuals, law schools around the country began restricting the access of military recruiters to their students. In response, Congress adopted the Solomon Amendment, which denies certain federal funds to any institution of higher education that denies military recruiters access equal to that provided other recruiters. FAIR (P), an association of law schools and law faculties, sued Rumsfeld (D), the Secretary of Defense, claiming infringement of P's rights of free speech and association. The district court upheld the statute. The court of appeals reversed. The Supreme Court granted certiorari.

Issue. May Congress deny federal funding to an institution of higher education that denies military recruiters access equal to that provided by other recruiters?

Held. Yes. Judgment reversed and case remanded.

- The statute requires law schools to offer military recruiters the same access to their campuses and students that law schools provide to the nonmilitary recruiter that receives the most favorable access. Some law professors acting as amici argue that the Solomon Amendment's equal access requirement is satisfied when a law school treats military recruiters the same as it treats other recruiters, including employers that violate the school's nondiscrimination policy. Under this interpretation, a military recruiter has the same access to campuses and students as a law firm when the law firm is permitted on campus to interview students and the military is not. But this reading is erroneous. The military recruiter does not receive equal access in this situation, regardless of whether the disparate treatment is attributable to the military's failure to comply with the school's nondiscrimination policy.

- The Solomon Amendment was recently revised to codify Department of Defense policy requiring military recruiters' equal access to students once recruiters were on campus. Under amici's interpretation, this legislative change would mean that military recruiters' access could be denied altogether, as long as a nonmilitary recruiter would also be denied access. That is rather clearly not what Congress had in mind when it codified the Department of Defense policy.

- Thus, we read the Solomon Amendment the way both the government and FAIR interpret it. It is insufficient for a law school to treat the military as it treats all other employers who violate its nondiscrimination policy. Military recruiters must be given the same access as recruiters who comply with the policy.

- Congress has broad authority to legislate on matters of military recruiting, but it chose to secure campus access for military recruiters indirectly, through its Spending Clause power. There is a limit on Congress's ability to place conditions on the receipt of funds. However, this case does not require us to determine whether a condition placed on university funding becomes an unconstitutional condition, because a funding condition cannot be unconstitutional if it could be constitutionally imposed directly.

- The Solomon Amendment regulates conduct, not speech. Law schools are free to say what they want about the military employment policy and still retain eligibility for federal funds, as long as they allow the required access. And the Amendment does not mandate speech, except as incidental to its regulation of conduct.

- The compelled-speech cases found constitutional violations when the complaining speaker's own message was affected by the speech it had to accommodate. In this case, law schools are not speaking when they host military recruiters. Recruiting merely helps students find jobs; it is not an expressive activity similar to a parade, newsletter, or newspaper. Nothing about recruiting suggests that law schools agree with any speech by recruiters, and nothing in the Amendment restricts what law schools can say about the military's policies.

- Conduct that is inherently expressive, such as flag burning, is entitled to First Amendment protection. However, the conduct regulated by the Solomon

Amendment is not inherently expressive. When law schools "expressed" their disagreement with the military by treating military recruiters differently from other recruiters, these actions were expressive only because the law schools accompanied their conduct with speech explaining it. If combining speech and conduct were enough to create expressive conduct, conduct could always be transformed into speech just by talking about it.

- The Amendment does not affect a law school's rights of association. Military recruiters are outsiders who visit the campuses for the limited purpose of trying to hire students. They do not become members of the schools. Their mere presence on campus does not violate the school's right of association.

---

d. Compulsory membership and funding for association speech.

1) Compulsory bar membership--

Keller v. State Bar of California,

Facts. The State Bar of California (D) was organized to regulate the state's legal profession, and by law all attorneys in the state had to belong as a condition of practicing law in the state. In addition to its regulation of the practice of law, D participated in lobbying and legal educational activities, filed amicus curiae briefs, and adopted resolutions at its annual meetings regarding issues of public interest. All of D's activities were financed mainly with membership dues. Keller and others (Ps) sued to prevent D from using Ps' membership dues to finance ideological or political activities to which Ps were opposed. The Supreme Court of California held that Ps could be compelled to be members of D and that D could use the dues for any purpose within its broad statutory authority. The Supreme Court granted certiorari.

Issue. May an integrated bar use mandatory dues to finance political activities with which some of its members disagree?

Held. No. Judgment reversed in part.

- The Court has previously held, in *Lathrop v. Donohue*, 367 U.S. 820 (1961), that a lawyer may be compelled to join and financially support a state bar association that lobbies for legislation. However, that holding was limited to mandatory dues and membership and did not address the free speech issue raised by Ps here.

- The Court has also held that agency-shop dues of nonunion public employees could not be used to support the union's political causes unrelated to collective bargaining activities. [*See* Abood v. Detroit Board of Education, 431 U.S. 209

(1977)] The rationale is that under the First Amendment, a person may not be forced to contribute money to propagate opinions to which he objects.

- *Abood* has been applied to several integrated bar associations, but D claims it is different because, as a regulated state agency, it is exempt from any constitutional constraints on the use of its dues. A typical government agency involves the democratic process, and government officials are free to express their views, which presumably reflect those of the majority of their constituents. The government, by its nature, is required to take substantive positions and make decisions, and can speak despite citizen disagreement with its message.

- But D is much more like a labor union than a normal government agency. It obtains its funds directly from its members; membership is limited to those of a specific occupation; and the state supreme court actually admits and disbars or suspends lawyers. D does not participate in the general government of the state, but provides advice to those who ultimately govern the legal profession.

- The state may establish an integrated bar to promote its interest in regulating the legal profession and improving the quality of legal services. D may constitutionally use mandatory dues to fund activities germane to those goals. But it cannot use mandatory dues to fund ideological activities outside those goals. Distinguishing between the two types of activities might be difficult, but as long as a set of procedures is established to challenge the amount of the fee and its uses, the constitutional requirement will be satisfied.

---

2) **Funding of public-sector unions.** In *Davenport v. Washington Education Association*, 551 U.S. 177 (2007), the Court held that a state may prohibit a public-sector labor union from using fees collected from nonunion member employees for election-related purposes. The union was authorized to collect fees from nonmembers, but it had to obtain affirmative authorization from nonmembers to use their funds to operate political committees or otherwise influence elections. The Court rejected the union's assertion that the distinctions were unconstitutional because they were based on the content of the union's speech. Noting that the union had no constitutional entitlement to the nonmembers' fees, which was a state-bestowed entitlement, the Court found that there was no suppression of ideas and no violation of the First Amendment.

3) **Forced funding of advertising in government program--**

United States v. United Foods, Inc.,

Facts. Congress enacted the Mushroom Promotion, Research, and Consumer Information Act, which created a Mushroom Council to pursue the statute's goals. The Council was authorized to impose mandatory assessments on handlers of fresh mushrooms. The funds generated could be used for mushroom promotion, research, consumer information, and industry information, although most of the funds were used for generic mushroom advertising. United Foods, Inc. (D), a fresh mushroom grower, refused to pay its mandatory assessments. The United States (P) sued to compel D to pay. Before the district court ruled on the case, the Supreme Court decided, in *Glickman v. Wileman Brothers & Elliott, Inc.*, 521 U.S. 457 (1997), that the government may require farmers to contribute to a government program that includes generic advertising for their products, even if the farmers object to the advertising. The district court relied on *Glickman* to grant P's motion for summary judgment. The Sixth Circuit reversed. The Supreme Court granted certiorari.

Issue. May the government underwrite and sponsor speech with a certain viewpoint, using special subsidies exacted from a designated class of persons, some of whom object to the idea being advanced?

Held. No. Judgment affirmed.

- D wants to convey a message that its brand of mushrooms is superior to those grown by other producers, and objects to being forced to pay for a message that mushrooms are good to consume whether or not they are branded. This clearly raises a First Amendment issue.

- P claims that the assessments here fall within *Glickman* because: D is not restricted from communicating its own message, D is not required to express views it disfavors, and the program does not require expression of political or ideological views. However, the *Glickman* assessments were ancillary to a more comprehensive program restricting marketing autonomy, while the assessments in this case are principally for advertising.

- The *Glickman* assessments were part of a marketing order and cooperative that restricted freedom of growers to act independently. The Mushroom Council does not involve a cooperative or marketing orders; it primarily collects funds for generic advertising. Therefore, the expression that D is required to support is not germane to a purpose related to an association independent from the speech itself. The government cannot enforce such assessments under the First Amendment.

Concurrence (Stevens, J.). D has been forced to subsidize speech to which it objects. The government does not have a sufficient interest in making one company finance advertising for the benefit of its competitors.

Concurrence (Thomas, J.). Any regulation that compels the funding of advertising is subject to the most stringent First Amendment scrutiny.

Dissent (Breyer, Ginsburg, O'Connor, JJ.). The characteristics of *Glickman* that made that program permissible apply as well to this case. The presence of price or output regulations in *Glickman*, which are not present in this case, should not matter for First Amendment analysis. P's advertising in this case relates directly to the regulatory programs established by statute. This program is a common example of government intervention in the marketplace that involves economic regulation, not "commercial speech."

Comment. The Court has upheld a university's requirement that its students pay an activity fee that is distributed to various student groups even though some students may find the groups offensive to their personal beliefs. [Board of Regents of University of Wisconsin System v. Southworth, 529 U.S. 217 (2000)]

---

4) Compelled funding of government speech--

Johanns v. Livestock Marketing Association,

Facts. Congress enacted the Beef Promotion and Research Act of 1985 to promote the marketing and consumption of beef. Promotional campaigns were funded by an assessment, or "checkoff," of $1 per head on all sales or importation of cattle. Livestock Marketing Association, another association, and several individuals who raised and sold cattle subject to the checkoff (Ps) sued the Department of Agriculture, the board, and the Secretary of Agriculture, Johanns (Ds), claiming that the advertising violated Ps' First Amendment rights because Ds promoted beef as a generic commodity, whereas Ps sought to promote certain types of beef as superior. While the litigation was pending, the Court held, in *United States v. United Foods, Inc., supra*, that a mandatory checkoff for generic mushroom advertising violated the First Amendment. The district court ruled for Ps. The court of appeals affirmed. The Supreme Court granted certiorari.

Issue. May the government compel producers to pay for government speech that promotes a commodity even when the producers disagree with the content of the speech?

Held. Yes. Judgment vacated and case remanded.

- Two types of compelled expression have been held to violate the First Amendment. In true "compelled speech" cases, such as *West Virginia State Board of Education v. Barnette, supra*, individuals are obligated personally to express a government-imposed message with which they disagree. In "compelled subsidy" cases, such as *Keller v. State Bar of California, supra*, the government requires individuals to subsidize a message they disagree with, expressed by a private entity. In these cases, the speech was presumed to be that of an entity other than the government itself. Compelled funding of government speech does not, by itself, raise First Amendment concerns.

- This case involves a different category: government-compelled subsidy of the government's own speech. The promotional campaigns to which Ps object are designed by the Beef Board's Operating Committee, half of which is appointed by D. Ps claim that this means the government does not control the campaigns. However, the message of the promotional campaigns is effectively controlled by the federal government.

- Ps also claim that the promotional program is not government speech because it is funded by a targeted assessment on beef producers, rather than by general revenues. According to Ps, this gives control over the beef program to a narrow interest group that will not listen to Ps' dissenting views, and it creates the perception that the promotions speak for beef producers such as Ps.

- However, citizens have no First Amendment right to refuse to fund government speech, regardless of whether the funds are raised through targeted assessments or by general taxes. Johanns is a politically accountable official who oversees the program and retains absolute veto power over the content of the promotions.

Concurrence (Thomas, J.). Although any regulation that compels the funding of advertising must be subjected to the most stringent First Amendment scrutiny, this principle must be qualified when the regulation compels the funding of government speech. Taxpayers cannot all have a First Amendment objection to taxpayer-funded government speech, even if the funded speech is not "germane" to a broader regulatory program.

Concurrence (Breyer, J.). The checkoff program at issue in this case is virtually identical to the checkoff program in the *United Foods* case, which the Court held violated the First Amendment. But in that case, the Court did not consider the "government speech" theory. The better approach would be to treat the checkoffs in both cases as a form of economic regulation, as I noted in my dissent in *United Foods*, but the "government speech" theory is an acceptable solution.

Concurrence (Ginsburg, J.). The assessments are permissible economic regulation.

Dissent (Kennedy, J.) The speech in this case is not government speech.

Dissent (Souter, Stevens, Kennedy, JJ.). A compelled subsidy, such as the checkoffs in this case, should not be justifiable by speech unless the government must make itself politically accountable by indicating that the speech is its own. Otherwise there is no check on the government's power to compel special speech subsidies. The Court's opinion sanctions government deception; expression that the government does not espouse is not government speech sufficient to justify enforcement of a targeted subsidy to promote it.

e. Compulsory speech access for third parties--

Pacific Gas & Electric Co. v. Public Utilities Commission,

Facts. Pacific Gas and Electric Company (P) distributed an informational newsletter in its billing envelopes. During a ratemaking proceeding, the Public Utilities Commission of California (D) determined that the space P had used for the newsletter was the property of ratepayers and permitted another organization to use this extra space four times in the next two years. P would not have control over the message. P appealed D's order to the state supreme court, which denied review. P appeals.

Issue. May a utility regulatory agency require a privately owned utility company to include in its billing envelopes messages from a third party with which the utility disagrees?

Held. No. Judgment reversed.

- The First Amendment guarantee of free speech represents more than merely the speaker's interest in expression; it also protects the public's interest in receiving information. Under established principles, D's newsletter merits the full protection of the First Amendment.

- The compelled access D imposed on P penalizes P's expression of a particular point of view and forces P to alter its speech to conform with someone else's agenda. In *Miami Herald Publishing Co. v. Tornillo*, *infra*, the Court held that the state could not require a newspaper to publish a candidate's reply to criticism published by the newspaper. The statute in that case deterred the newspaper from expressing its views and interfered with the editorial control of the newspaper. These same concerns apply to P.

- D claims that its access order was to give the public a greater variety of views and to facilitate fundraising by interested parties. This means that access to P's envelopes is not content-neutral; instead, only those that disagree with P can have access. While P does not have the right to freedom from debate, it does have the right to freedom from forced enhancement of its opponents' message. Corporations, like individuals, have the choice of what not to say.

- D also claims that P's customers own the space involved, although D admits that P owns the envelope, the bill, and the physical newsletter. Thus, D is forcing P to use its own property to disperse a message it disagrees with.

- Even though D's order burdens P's protected speech, it could be permitted if it were narrowly tailored to serve a compelling state interest. D claims that its order would improve ratemaking proceedings by involving ratepayers, but there are less burdensome means for serving that interest, nor can D advance some points of view to the detriment of others, even to promote speech by making available a variety of views.

Concurrence (Burger, C.J.). This case is governed by *Wooley v. Maynard*, *supra*, because D is attempting to force P to associate with views with which it disagrees.

Concurrence (Marshall, J.). This case is distinguishable from *PruneYard Shopping Center v. Robins*, 447 U.S. 74 (1980), in that P has never given up its right to exclude others from its property as the mall owner did in *PruneYard.* In addition, D here gives others a right to speak at the expense of P's own rights.

Dissent (Rehnquist, White, Stevens, JJ.). While the government may not directly suppress a corporation's affirmative speech, nothing prohibits it from indirectly and remotely affecting a speaker's speech. *Tornillo* does not apply here, where the deterrent effect is conjectural, since the right of access is independent of whatever P says in its newsletter. The individual freedom of conscience decisions include the notion of a right to remain isolated from other parties' expressive activity, but this should not be extended to corporations any more than the right to remain silent and the right to privacy.

Dissent (Stevens, J.). D could impose many regulations on P's newsletter, such as a requirement to include legal notices of public ratemaking proceedings, and it could require bills to be in a specified format. The order issued here is not constitutionally different.

---

4. Government Regulation of Elections.

a. **Introduction.** Several constitutional provisions relate to voting and elections. For example, the Fourteenth Amendment Equal Protection Clause has been applied to the right to vote, and the Fifteenth, Nineteenth, Twenty-Fourth, and Twenty-Sixth Amendments all specifically apply to voting. The First Amendment freedom of association has also been applied to voting issues. In *Anderson v. Celebrezze*, 460 U.S. 780 (1983), the Court specifically relied on the First Amendment instead of equal protection to invalidate an early filing deadline that applied to independents but not to the nominees of political parties. The Court articulated a balancing test, comparing the restriction's injury to First Amendment rights with the justifications asserted by the state.

b. **Choosing and electing candidates.**

1) **Closed primary system--**

Tashjian v. Republican Party of Connecticut,

Facts. Connecticut law required voters in any party's primary to be registered members of that party. The Republican Party of Connecticut (P) adopted a party rule permitting independent voters to vote in Republican primaries. P then brought suit against Tashjian (D), claiming the state law was unconstitutional. The lower courts found for P, and D appeals.

Issue. May a state restrict primary voting rights to members of the party involved in the primary?

Held. No. Judgment affirmed.

- In evaluating challenges to state election laws, the court must: (i) consider the nature of the alleged injury; (ii) evaluate the state's interests that the law is intended to address; and (iii) consider the extent to which those interests make it necessary to impose the burden that causes the injury.
- P has a clear interest in freedom of association. P's new rule is an attempt to broaden support through increased participation in its candidate selection process. The state's power to control the time, place, and manner of elections does not justify an abridgment of fundamental rights, as P asserts.
- D claims that its statute is narrowly tailored to advance the state's interest in effectively administering the primary system, preventing raiding, avoiding voter confusion, and protecting the responsibility of party government.
- Administrative convenience cannot justify a restraint on freedom of association. While the state may have an interest in preventing raiding, its statute does not do so, as it permits party registration as late as noon on the business day preceding the primary. Nor would P's rule confuse voters—since a candidate still must win at least 20% of the vote at a party convention to be on the primary ballot, the eventual nominee would presumably represent the party.
- D claims that the closed primary system strengthens the party system, but this Court cannot decide whether the state legislature or P was the wiser. Regulation intended to protect parties from infiltration from outside the party has been sustained in the past, but in this case P has taken internal steps to improve its position. D is essentially claiming to protect the integrity of P against P itself. Especially since the state legislature is controlled by P's opponents, this argument has little merit. Accordingly, the closed primary system cannot be sustained.
- Finally, D relies on the Qualifications Clause (Article I, Section 2, Clause 1) and the Seventeenth Amendment. P's rule permits independents to participate in federal and statewide primaries, but not in state legislature primaries. How-

ever, the Qualifications Clause was intended to ensure that a voter qualified to vote for the more numerous house of the state legislature is also qualified to vote in congressional elections. P's rule is consistent with this approach.

Dissent (Stevens, Scalia, JJ.). The Qualifications Clause clearly prohibits a rule that permits a voter to participate in congressional elections but prevents the same person from voting for candidates to the most numerous branch of the state legislature.

Dissent (Scalia, J., Rehnquist, C.J., O'Connor, J.). The concept of freedom of association does not include the casual contact of a single primary vote by an independent voter who is unwilling to join the party. Even under state law, P's members are free to choose their own candidate.

---

2) Forced open primaries not allowed--

California Democratic Party v. Jones,

Facts. Candidates for public office in California may gain access to the general ballot by winning a qualified political party's primary. Traditionally, these primaries were closed so that only a member of the particular party could vote on its nominees. In 1996, Proposition 198 created a blanket primary, in which each voter's ballot lists every candidate regardless of party affiliation and allows the voter to choose freely among them. The winner of each party becomes the respective party's nominee for the general election. The California Democratic Party and three other political parties (Ps) sued Jones (D), the Secretary of State, claiming that the blanket primary violated their First Amendment rights of association. The district court held that the new primary mechanism imposed a minor burden on Ps' associational rights and was justified by substantial state interests. The court of appeals affirmed. The Supreme Court granted certiorari.

Issue. May a state require that all political primaries be open to every voter, regardless of party affiliation?

Held. No. Judgment reversed.

- Although states have a major role in structuring and monitoring the primary election process, political parties have their own power to choose procedures for selecting their own nominees for office. These are not wholly public activities. States can only regulate the parties' internal processes within Constitutional limits.

- Prior cases have held that, when a state prescribes an election process that gives a special role to political parties, the parties' action becomes state action. This does not mean that party affairs are public affairs, however.

- Political parties are associations of citizens to promote candidates who reflect their political views. The First Amendment freedom of association includes the freedom to identify who constitutes the association and to limit the association to those people. The candidate selection process is the most important aspect of the right to exclude others, since that process determines the party's positions on public issues and identifies the party's key representative to the general public.

- Proposition 198 violates the Constitution because it forces party members to dilute their candidate-selection process. Forcing a party to accept those who do not affiliate with it would likely lead to a change in the party's message.

- D claimed several interests to justify this intrusion into Ps' rights of association, including: (i) producing elected officials who better represent the electorate, (ii) expanding candidate debate beyond the scope of partisan concerns, (iii) ensuring that disenfranchised persons enjoy the right to an effective vote, (iv) promoting fairness, (v) affording voters greater choice, (vi) increasing voter participation, and (vii) protecting privacy. None of these are sufficiently compelling, however.

Concurrence (Kennedy, J.). Because the true purpose of this law is to force a political party to accept a candidate it may not want, it cannot stand. It is also doubtful because the Court has denied a political party's freedom to spend its own funds in cooperation with its preferred candidate, which was the remedy the state had offered to support its law.

Dissent (Stevens, Ginsburg, JJ.). California should be allowed to adopt a blanket primary. A quintessential attribute of sovereignty is a state's power to determine how its officials are to be elected. Federalism principles should require respect of the policy choice made by the state's voters who approved Proposition 198. The state can require political parties to use a primary format to select their nominees, even though this restricts the parties' associational freedoms, because elections are basic forms of state action. The Court should not intrude on this aspect of state sovereignty.

---

3) Semiclosed primaries allowed--

Clingman v. Beaver,

Facts. The primary system in Oklahoma was semiclosed, meaning that a political party could invite only its own registered members and voters registered as Independents to vote in its primary. When the Libertarian Party of Oklahoma ("LPO") sought permission from the secretary of the Oklahoma State Election Board (D) to open its upcoming primary to all registered voters, D agreed only as to members of the LPO and to voters registered as Independents. The LPO and several Republican and Democratic voters (Ps) sued for declaratory and injunctive relief, claiming that the semiclosed primary law violated their First Amendment right to freedom of political association. The district court upheld the law, but the court of appeals reversed. The Supreme Court granted certiorari.

Issue. May a state restrict participation in a political party's primary to voters who have registered as members of that party and to voters registered as Independents?

Held. Yes. Judgment reversed and case remanded.

- The states have broad power to prescribe the time, places, and manner of holding elections for senators and representatives. The First Amendment protects the rights of citizens to associate in promoting among the electorate candidates who espouse their political views. But regulations that burden associational rights may be justified where a state has important regulatory interests, as long as the restrictions are reasonable and nondiscriminatory.

- Although Oklahoma is preventing the LPO from inviting Republican and Democratic voters to vote in its primary, Oklahoma is not compelling the party to associate with unwanted members or voters. Those Ps who are not members of the LPO do not wish to associate with the LPO in a formal sense; they want to remain registered with other political parties, while assisting in selecting the LPO's candidate for general election by voting in the LPO's primary. Such a voter who is unwilling to disaffiliate from another party to vote in the LPO primary forms little "association" with the LPO.

- The ordinary and widespread burden of a semiclosed primary system cannot be deemed severe without subjecting virtually every electoral regulation to strict scrutiny. This would hamper states' ability to run efficient and equitable elections and compel federal courts to rewrite state electoral codes, contrary to the Constitution, which gives states authority over elections.

- Oklahoma has important regulatory interests in enforcing a semiclosed primary system, including the preservation of political parties as viable and identifiable interest groups. The system enhances the parties' electioneering and party-building interests and protects against party raiding. Even if the LPO wants to risk the loss of its identity, Oklahoma's interest is independent and concerns the integrity of the primary system. Oklahoma does not want primary election outcomes to confuse or mislead the general voting population to the extent that it relies on party labels as representative of certain ideologies.

- Oklahoma could allow the LPO to invite registered voters of other parties, but this is a choice to be made through the democratic process, not by the courts.

Concurrence in part (O'Connor, Breyer, JJ.). There is no need to minimize Ps' associational interests to decide this case. Standing alone, Oklahoma's semiclosed primary law imposes only a modest, nondiscriminatory burden on those interests, but there could be other laws that restrict the ability to change party affiliation that should be considered. Significant associational interests are at stake when a party invites a voter to participate in its primary and the voter desires to participate.

Dissent (Stevens, Ginsburg, Souter, JJ.). Today's decision diminishes the value of two important First Amendment rights: a citizen's right to vote for the candidate of his choice and a political party's right to define its own mission. A member of one party has a right to participate in a third party's primary, when invited by the third party, that far outweighs any public interest in punishing registered Republicans or Democrats for acts of disloyalty. Also, the LPO has a right to associate with willing voters. Oklahoma's interests do not override these important values, because states have no valid interest in protecting the major parties from competition.

---

c. Regulation of political fundraising and expenditures.

1) Contribution and expenditure limitations--

Buckley v. Valeo,

Facts. Buckley (P) and others brought suit challenging, inter alia, the contribution and expenditure limitations of the Federal Election Campaign Act of 1971. P appeals adverse lower court decisions.

Issue. May Congress impose contribution limitations or expenditure limitations on federal elections?

Held. Yes on the issue of contribution limitations; no on the issue of expenditure limitations.

- The financial limitations imposed on political campaigns cannot be considered as regulation of conduct alone, since exercise of free speech depends largely on the ability to finance that speech.
- The $1,000 limit on campaign contributions has minimal effect on freedom of association or on the extent of political discussion, but it does deal directly with the sources of political corruption and is therefore justified. The other limits on contributions are also valid.
- The expenditure limitations impose more severe restrictions on freedom of political expression and association. Although designed with the arguably valid interest of curbing exorbitant campaign expenditures and of equalizing the relative ability of individuals and groups to influence elections, it is not within the

government's power to determine that spending to promote one's political views is wasteful, excessive, or unwise.

Dissent (Burger, C.J., Blackmun, J.). Contribution limits should be invalid.

Dissent (Marshall, J.). Limits on expenditures of family funds should be valid.

Dissent (White, J.). Limits on expenditures should be valid.

Comment. The Court also held that Congress could impose extensive reporting and disclosure requirements on political contributions to deter corruption, avoid the appearance of corruption, and allow enforcement of the contribution limitations.

---

2) Restriction on corporate political spending--

Austin v. Michigan Chamber of Commerce,

Facts. Section 54(1) of the Michigan Campaign Finance Act prohibited corporations from using corporate treasury funds for independent expenditures to support or oppose political candidates, but corporations could make such expenditures from segregated funds used solely for political purposes. The Michigan Chamber of Commerce (P) challenged the law. The court of appeals held that, under the First Amendment, the law could not be applied to P. Austin (D) appeals.

Issue. May a state prohibit corporations from making independent political expenditures except from a segregated fund maintained solely for that purpose?

Held. Yes. Judgment reversed.

- P's status as a corporation does not remove its use of funds to support a political candidate, which is "speech," from protection by the First Amendment. In *FEC v. Massachusetts Citizens for Life, Inc.*, 479 U.S. 238 (1986), the Court held that a federal statute requiring corporations to make independent political expenditures only through special segregated funds burdens corporate freedom of expression. Thus, D's restriction on such political corporate expenditures may be sustained only if they are narrowly tailored to serve a compelling state interest.

- D claims that corporations have unique legal and economic characteristics that present a danger of corruption if their political expenditures are not regulated. State-conferred advantages make it possible for a corporation to attract capital for reasons unrelated to popular support for the corporation's political ideas. Corporate wealth can unfairly influence elections when it is deployed in the form of independent expenditures. This compelling interest in preventing corruption supports the restriction of the influence of political war chests funneled through the corporate form.

- ♦ D's law is precisely targeted to eliminate the distortion caused by corporate spending while also allowing corporations to express their political views; thus, it is sufficiently narrowly tailored to achieve its goal.

- ♦ P claims that, even if the law is permissible with regard to for-profit corporations, it cannot be applied to a nonprofit ideological corporation such as P. The *Massachusetts Citizens for Life* case held that the federal law could not be applied to a nonprofit organization that was more like a voluntary political association than a business firm. The organization in that case was formed expressly to promote political ideas and could not engage in business activities. P, by contrast, has a non-political purpose in addition to its political purpose. P's business activities are distinct from its political activities, so members who disagree with P's political agenda could still pay dues to participate in the business activities. Finally, P accepts contributions from business corporations, giving them the opportunity to use P to circumvent the Act's regulation of corporate political spending.

- ♦ P also claims that, because the Act exempts unincorporated associations and media corporations, it denies equal protection. But there are valid reasons for these exemptions.

Concurrence (Stevens, J.). The danger of quid pro quo relationships arising from corporate participation in candidate elections provides adequate justification for the regulation of P's expenditures and contributions.

Concurrence (Brennan, J.). The Act does not prohibit P from participating in politics, but merely requires that corporations make independent expenditures either through segregated funds or political action committees.

Dissent (Scalia, J.). The majority has concluded that too much speech is an evil that the democratic majority can proscribe, but the central truth of the First Amendment is that government cannot be trusted to ensure, through censorship, the "fairness" of political debate. Corporations are not the only ones that receive special advantages from the government. Other organizations and even individuals receive tax breaks, contract awards, public employment, and outright cash subsidies. But a state may not require the forfeiture of First Amendment rights as a condition to receipt of these advantages. The Court has not distinguished *Buckley v. Valeo*, *supra*, which held that independent expenditures by individuals and associations do not raise a sufficient threat of corruption to justify prohibition. The Act does not aim at preventing wrongdoing, but at preventing speech. But in our system, there is no such thing as too much speech, and the people, not the government, must separate the wheat from the chaff.

Dissent (Kennedy, O'Connor, Scalia, JJ.). The majority upholds two forms of censorship: D's content-based law that makes it a crime for a nonprofit corporate speaker to endorse or oppose candidates for public office, and the Court's value-laden, content-based speech suppression that creates a preferred class by permitting some nonprofit corporate groups, but not others, to engage in political speech. D discriminates, not only on the content of the speech, but also on the basis of the speaker's identity. D has no compelling interest to support the law, as there is no support for the assertion that corporate political expenditures present a corrosive and distorting effect on the political process. Requiring nonprofit corporations to speak politically through PACs eliminates accountability. And the media exemption ignores the reality that all corporations communicate with the public to some degree, whether it is their primary business or not, and communication is particularly important for nonprofit corporations. It is difficult to untangle the links between media and nonmedia corporations, especially where the latter owns and controls the former.

---

3) Campaign finance reform--

McConnell v. Federal Election Commission

Facts. The Bipartisan Campaign Reform Act of 2002 ("BCRA") restricted the use of soft money and issue ads. It amended the Federal Election Campaign Act of 1971 ("FECA"), which had imposed limitations only on "hard money" contributions, or money used to influence an election for federal office. "Soft money," or money used for state or local elections and for issue ads, was unregulated under FECA. Title I of BCRA (the new section 323(a) of FECA) prohibited national party committees from soliciting, receiving, directing, or spending any soft money. Section 323(b) prevented state and local party committees from using soft money for activities that affect federal elections. Section 323(d) prohibited political parties from donating funds to tax exempt organizations such as the section 527 groups that are organized for the express purpose of engaging in partisan political activity. Section 323(f) imposed restrictions on candidates' use of soft money. Title II of BCRA imposed restrictions on corporations and labor unions to prevent them from funding "electioneering communications," defined as political broadcasts that refer to a clearly identified federal candidate that are made within 60 days before a general election (or 30 days before a primary election). Title III, section 318, prohibited minors 17 years old or younger from making contributions or donations to political parties. Title V, section 504, required broadcasters to keep publicly available records of politically related broadcasting requests. Senator McConnell and others (Ps) challenged the law by suing the Federal Election Commission (D). The district court upheld part of the law and found some parts unconstitutional. Ps appeal.

Issue. May Congress limit the use of soft money contributions and impose detailed restrictions on how organizations can influence elections?

Held. Yes. Judgment affirmed in part and reversed in part.

- The Court has previously held that a contribution limit may impose significant interference with the right of association as long as it is closely drawn to match a sufficiently important interest. The Court must defer to Congress's ability to weigh competing constitutional interests in an area in which it enjoys particular expertise.

- The FECA limits have a marginal impact on political speech. They limit the sources and individual amounts of donations, but they do not limit the total amount of money that the parties can spend.

- The rationale behind the contribution restrictions in section 323(a) is that contributions to a candidate's party to aid the candidate's campaign threaten to create a sense of obligation. Large soft money donations have a corrupting influence. For example, special interests influence the congressional calendar that determines what legislation gets voted on. The six national party committees have menus of opportunities for access to would-be soft money donors, with more access available in return for higher contributions. The best means to prevent these abuses is to identify and remove the temptation, so section 323(a) is not unconstitutional.

- Section 323(b)'s limits on state committees are designed to prevent wholesale evasion of section 323(a). Congress determined that, without this provision, soft money contributors would simply contribute to the state parties, which would create the same sense of obligation on the part of candidates as would contributions to the national parties. The Court must defer to Congress in this area, and the provisions are closely drawn to match the important governmental interests Congress has identified.

- Section 323(d) is not unconstitutional when narrowly construed to ban only donations not raised in compliance with FECA. Without this restriction, the various party committees would have an incentive to use their fundraising system to benefit like-minded tax-exempt organizations that would benefit their candidates, bringing with it all of the corrupting influences Congress was concerned about. This is basically an anti-circumvention measure.

- Section 323(f) prevents candidates from spending soft money on advertising that refers to a clearly identified federal candidate, whether pro or con. It limits contributions, but not expenditures. This is a narrow focus on the soft money donations that have the greatest potential for corruption and is a permissible means for addressing the problems that Congress has identified.

- Title II's restrictions on funding by corporations and labor unions has been established previously, and these institutions are able to engage in express advocacy by forming separate segregated funds to pay for it. Organizations can still fund electioneering communications with PAC (political action committee) money, so there is no complete ban on expression. The regulation of this speech is constitutional.

- ♦ BCRA section 318, prohibiting contributions from minors, is too broad, does not withstand heightened scrutiny, and violates the First Amendment rights of minors.

- ♦ BCRA section 504, requiring broadcasters to keep records of broadcast requests made by or on behalf of a candidate, imposes a comparatively small administrative burden and serves significant governmental interests.

Concurrence and dissent (Kennedy, J., Rehnquist, C.J., Scalia, Thomas, JJ.). The Court's opinion is wrong with respect to Titles I and II. The citizens have the right to judge for themselves the most effective means for expressing political view and to decide for themselves whom to believe. BCRA is the codification of an assumption that the mainstream media alone can protect freedom of speech, and it is an effort by Congress to make sure that civic discourse takes place only through the modes of its own choosing. The Court has moved beyond the anti-corruption rationale of *Buckley* to allow regulation of any conduct that wins goodwill from or influences a Member of Congress. Access, in itself, is not corruption. The new regulations impose far greater burdens on associational rights than do regulations that merely cap the amount of money a person can contribute to a political candidate or committee.

Concurrence and dissent (Scalia, J.). Today, the Court, which sternly disapproves of restrictions on pornography, approves of a law that cuts to the heart of the First Amendment—the right to criticize the government. There are three fallacious propositions that might be thought to justify the provisions of this legislation: (i) money is not speech; (ii) pooling money is not speech; and (iii) speech by a corporation can be abridged. These propositions fail for the following reasons. A law limiting the funding of speech is a direct restriction on speech, and part of freedom of speech is the freedom to associate with others for the dissemination of ideas by pooling financial resources for expressive purposes. As for corporations, corporate (like noncorporate) allies support officeholders who favor their causes; that is the nature of politics.

Concurrence and dissent (Thomas, Scalia, JJ.). Besides continuing the errors of *Buckley*, the Court now expands the anti-circumvention rationale beyond reason. The established right to anonymous speech has been stripped away based on the flimsiest of justifications. The endpoint of this reasoning will be the regulation of the press.

Comment. The Court's opinion was actually delivered by four separate Justices. Justices Stevens and O'Connor delivered the opinion on BCRA Titles I and II; Chief Justice Rehnquist delivered the opinion regarding Titles III and IV; and Justice Breyer delivered the opinion on Title V.

---

4) Pre-election issue advocacy--

Federal Election Commission v. Wisconsin Right to Life,

Facts. Section 203 of the Bipartisan Campaign Reform Act of 2002 ("BCRA") made it illegal for any corporation to broadcast, shortly before an election, any communication that named a federal candidate for elected office and was targeted to the electorate. In *McConnell, supra*, the Court upheld section 203 against a facial challenge as long as the forbidden speech was express campaign speech or its functional equivalent. Wisconsin Right to Life (P) was a 501(c) nonprofit advocacy organization. P planned to run broadcast ads during the election blackout period (within 30 days of Wisconsin's federal primary election). P intended to encourage voters to call Senator Feingold to protest the filibuster of judicial nominees. P filed suit against the Federal Election Commission (D), seeking declaratory and injunctive relief that would permit the running of these ads. The district court denied the injunction, but on remand from the Supreme Court, granted P summary judgment. D appeals.

Issue. May the BCRA be applied to prohibit issue advocacy that mentions a candidate for federal office but is not an appeal to vote for or against a specific candidate?

Held. No. Judgment affirmed.

- ♦ If P's ads are the functional equivalent of speech expressly advocating the election or defeat of a candidate, they can constitutionally be regulated. But if they are genuine issue ads, under the First Amendment, they cannot be regulated.

- ♦ BCRA section 203 is subject to strict scrutiny because it burdens political speech. Thus, D must prove that applying it to P's ads furthers a compelling interest and is narrowly tailored to achieve that interest. Although BCRA survived a facial challenge in *McConnell*, it is still subject to as-applied challenges.

- ♦ The test for an as-applied challenge does not depend on the speaker's intent. An intent-based test would chill political speech and would offer no security for free discussion. The proper standard must be objective. It must focus on the substance of the communication and must give the benefit of any doubt to protecting rather than stifling speech.

- ♦ An ad is the functional equivalent of express advocacy only if it is susceptible of no reasonable interpretation other than as an appeal to vote for or against a specific candidate. Under this test, P's ads are not the functional equivalent of express advocacy. They focus on a legislative issue (the filibuster), take a position on the issue, exhort the public to adopt that position, and urge the public to contact public officials regarding the issue. They do not mention an election, candidacy, political party, or challenger. They also do not take a position on a candidate's character, qualifications, or fitness for office.

- Because P's ads are not the functional equivalent of express advocacy, section 203 may be applied to P's ads only if it is narrowly tailored to further a compelling interest. *McConnell* assumed the governmental interest in preventing corruption in election campaigns justified regulation of express advocacy, and then extended this interest to ads that were the functional equivalent of express advocacy. But there is no basis for further extending the rationale to apply to issue advocacy ads, which are not equivalent to contributions and to which the corruption interest rationale does not apply. Section 203 is unconstitutional as applied to the ads at issue here.

Concurrence (Alito, J.). Section 203, as applied, cannot ban any advertising that may reasonably be interpreted as anything other than an appeal to vote for or against a candidate. Because section 203 is unconstitutional as applied to P's ads, we need not decide today whether section 203 is unconstitutional on its face. However, if the implementation of the as-applied standard chills political speech, in a future case we may need to reconsider the facial validity of section 203.

Concurrence (Scalia, Kennedy, Thomas, JJ.). Although I agree with the Court's judgment, I would overrule that part of the Court's decision in *McConnell* that upheld section 203(a). *McConnell* is unworkable because any acceptable as-applied test cannot validate the facial constitutionality of section 203 of the BCRA.

Dissent (Souter, Stevens, Ginsburg, Breyer, JJ.).

- Campaign finance reform has focused on the concentrations of money supporting political campaigning and on the threat to the integrity of our electoral process. According to a 2002 poll showing the pervasive public cynicism, 71% of Americans think that members of Congress cast votes based on the views of their big contributors, rather than on the members' own beliefs. Congress determined that corporate and union expenditures for fake issue ads should be regulated, and it used a narrow definition of "electioneering communication" to reach only broadcast ads that were the practical equivalents of express advocacy. In 2003, this Court found that the provision was free from vagueness and was justified.

- P is a nonprofit corporation funded largely by contributions from other corporations. P's ads were run after the Senate recessed and did not resume after the election. It was obvious from the ads that Democratic Senator Feingold supported filibusters against Republican presidential judicial nominees, that P opposed his reelection because of his position on filibusters, and that P was telling voters that the senator's position on the filibusters was grounds to vote against him. The ads are constitutionally subject to regulation under *McConnell*, but the Court has effectively overruled *McConnell*.

5) **The Millionaire's Amendment and unequal financing restrictions--**

Davis v. Federal Election Commission,

Facts. Federal law limited the amount of money a candidate for the House of Representatives could receive from individuals to $2,300 per election cycle, with an overall cap of $42,700 for aggregate contributions. There were also limits on coordinated expenditures with political party committees. Section 319(a) of the Bipartisan Campaign Reform Act of 2002, the "Millionaire's Amendment," provided an exception when a candidate's opponent spent more than $350,000 in personal funds (considered to be "self-financing"). Section 319(a) allowed the non-self-financing candidate to receive three times the normal limits from individual contributions until that candidate also collected $350,000. The self-financing candidate had to provide detailed reports on finances, while the non-self-financing candidate faced less extensive disclosure requirements. Davis (P), a candidate for the House of Representatives, spent far more than $350,000 of his own money in each of two campaigns. He filed suit against the Federal Election Commission (D), requesting that section 319 be declared unconstitutional and that it could not be enforced. The district court granted summary judgment for D. P appeals.

Issue. May Congress impose different campaign contribution limits on candidates competing for the same congressional seat so that a non-self-financing candidate can raise more money from individual contributions than can a self-financing candidate?

Held. No. Judgment reversed.

- P claims that 319(a) unconstitutionally burdens his exercise of his First Amendment right to make unlimited expenditures of his personal funds because doing so enables his opponent to raise more money from others than P can and then use that money to counteract P's own speech.

- If 319(a) raised the contribution level for all candidates, there would be no constitutional violation. The problem with 319(a) is that it raises the limits for only the non-self-financing candidate, and then only when the self-financing candidate's expenditures reach a threshold. The Court has never previously upheld a law that imposes different contribution limits for competing candidates.

- Under *Buckley v. Valeo, supra,* Congress cannot cap a candidate's expenditure of personal funds to finance his own campaign speech. While 319(a) does not cap P's expenditure of his own funds, it does impose a penalty on such expenditures by triggering discriminatory fundraising limitations. The substantial burden on the exercise of the First Amendment right to use personal funds for campaign speech must be justified by a compelling state interest in order to stand.

- There is no compelling state interest sufficient to justify this burden. The offered objective of reducing the natural advantage wealthy individuals possess in campaigning for public office is not a legitimate governmental objective. Candidates have different strengths, including celebrity or a well-known family name, in addition to wealth disparities, and Congress cannot use election laws to level electoral opportunities without making an impermissible judgment about which strengths should be allowed to contribute to the outcome of an election.

- To the extent there is a public perception that wealthy people can buy seats in Congress, Congress could raise or eliminate campaign contribution limits. It just cannot impose different limits on different candidates.

- Because the disparate reporting requirements were designed to implement the asymmetrical contribution limits, they are also unconstitutional.

Concurrence and dissent (Stevens, Souter, Ginsburg, Breyer, JJ.). The "Millionaire's Amendment" is a reasonable response to combat the perception that congressional seats are for sale to the highest bidder. It imposes no burden on a self-financing candidate. Because it merely diminishes the unequal strength of the self-financing candidate, it does not violate the Constitution. *Buckley v. Valeo* was incorrect in rejecting the imposition of reasonable limitations on expenditures permitted during any single campaign. Such a limitation would improve the quality of the exposition of ideas, just as it does in appellate advocacy when both sides have time limitations. Even under *Buckley*, the Millionaire's Amendment is a good-faith attempt to regulate a pernicious feature of contemporary political campaigns. It does not quiet any speech. Even if it did burden P's First Amendment rights, the burden is justified by the governmental interest in reducing both the influence of wealth on elections and the appearance that wealth alone dictates those results.

Concurrence and dissent (Ginsburg, Breyer, JJ.). The district court's opinion correctly concluded that the provisions challenged in this case are entirely consistent with *Buckley*. And although I join part of Justice Stevens's opinion, I do not join the conclusion as to *Buckley's* holding regarding expenditure limits. D has not asked us to overrule *Buckley*, and I would leave reconsideration of *Buckley* for a later day and case.

---

6) Impermissibly low expenditure and contribution limits--

Randall v. Sorrell,

Facts. A Vermont campaign finance statute, Act 64, imposed both expenditure limitations on candidates for state office and contribution limitations on their supporters. Incumbents seeking reelection to statewide office could spend no more than 85% of the expenditure limits for a candidate for that office. Contributions from a single individual were limited to $400 per person for state offices during a two-year general election cycle and even lesser amounts for state legislators. Individuals who had run for state office in Vermont, citizens who voted in Vermont elections and contributed to Vermont campaigns, and political parties and committees that participated in Vermont politics (Ps) filed a lawsuit against state officials charged with enforcement of Act 64 soon after it became law (Ds). The district court held that the expenditure limits violated the First Amendment. The court also held that the Act's limits on the contributions of political parties to candidates were unconstitutional, but upheld the other limits on contributions. The court of appeals upheld all of the contribution limits and remanded the issue of expenditure limits for further consideration in light of compelling state interests in preventing corruption or the appearance of corruption and in limiting the amount of time state officials must spend raising campaign funds. The court of appeals then remanded the case to the district court with instructions to determine whether the Act's expenditure limits were narrowly tailored to those interests. The Supreme Court granted certiorari.

Issues.

(i) Do Act 64's expenditure limits violate the First Amendment?

(ii) Do Act 64's contribution limits violate the First Amendment?

Held. (i) Yes. (ii) Yes. Judgment reversed and case remanded.

- Ds ask us to overrule *Buckley* or to distinguish it from the present case on a ground not considered in *Buckley*—that expenditure limits help protect candidates from spending too much time raising campaign funds. However, there is no special justification for overruling *Buckley*. Subsequent case law has not undermined its basic legal principles, and Ds have not shown any dramatic increase in corruption or the appearance of corruption in Vermont or that expenditure limits are the only way to attack that problem. Overruling *Buckley* now would dramatically undermine reliance on our settled precedent.

- Also, we find no significant basis to distinguish this case from *Buckley*. Act 64's expenditure limits are not substantially different from those at issue in *Buckley*, and Vermont's primary justification for imposing its expenditure limits are not significantly different from the rationale for the *Buckley* limits—preventing corruption and its appearance. *Buckley* continues to be controlling precedent; thus, Act 64's expenditure limits violate the First Amendment.

- As to the constitutionality of Act 64's contribution limits, under *Buckley*, limitations on campaign contributions are permissible as long as they are closely drawn to match a sufficiently important interest. The interest advanced in *Buckley*, preventing corruption and the appearance of corruption, was sufficiently important to justify the contribution limits. But contribution limits might sometimes impose burdens on First Amendment interests that, when viewed in light of a statute's legitimate objectives, are disproportionately severe.

- In this case, the contribution limits are the lowest in the nation and are well below the limits this Court upheld in *Buckley*. This raises suspicion that the limits are not closely drawn. Our examination of the record shows that, from a constitutional perspective, Act 64's contribution limits are not narrowly tailored and are too restrictive to survive First Amendment scrutiny.

- The Act could interfere with political parties and with participation in campaigns through volunteer activities, and it could inhibit effective advocacy by those who seek election. There is a danger of putting challengers to a significant disadvantage compared with incumbents.

Concurrence (Alito, J.). Ds' primary defense of their expenditure limits is that those limits are consistent with *Buckley*. And Ds make only a naked plea for us to reexamine *Buckley*, almost as an afterthought. They do not discuss the doctrine of stare decisis or the Court's cases explaining when it is appropriate to reconsider a prior constitutional decision. Because Ds have not made a case for reexamining *Buckley*, it is unnecessary to reach the issue.

Concurrence (Kennedy, J.). Campaign finance regulation may cause more problems than it solves, but in this case, the limitations Vermont places on campaign expenditures and contributions violate the First Amendment.

Concurrence (Thomas, Scalia, JJ.). The Court erred in *Buckley* by distinguishing between contribution and expenditure limits. *Buckley* should be overruled, and both the contribution and expenditure limits of Act 64 should be subject to strict scrutiny. *Buckley* does not provide any consistent protection to the core of the First Amendment.

Dissent (Stevens, J.). Although stare decisis is a principle of fundamental importance, it is not a command, and the holding of *Buckley* itself upset long-established practice as to expenditure limits. The Framers would have viewed federal statutes limiting the amount of money that congressional candidates may spend in elections as well within the authority of Congress. They would not have expected judges to interfere with the enforcement of expenditure limits that only require candidates to budget their activities and do not impose any restrictions on what they may say. Vermont's limits are constitutional.

Dissent (Souter, Ginsburg, Stevens, JJ.). The court of appeals correctly remanded for further inquiry into the limitations on candidates' expenditures, and the contribution limitations satisfy controlling precedent. The time-protection interest should be considered as a support for expenditure limits, and *Buckley* should be applied to determine whether the evidence here suffices to support the enacted limitations. The findings of Vermont's legislature are significant enough to justify the remand for the decision as to whether Vermont's spending limits are the least restrictive means of accomplishing its worthy objectives. The Vermont legislature responded to the realities of campaigning in that state, and there is no evidence of constitutional miscalculation sufficient to interfere with its judgment.

---

5. **Speech and Association Rights of Government Employees.**

   a. **Introduction.** "Free speech" and "free association" issues may be raised by statutes or rules that limit a government employee's right to engage in political activities. Although such restrictions would be clearly improper if imposed against employees in private industry, the strong public interest in freeing government from graft and political favoritism justifies reasonable restrictions on the political activities of those employed by government.

   b. **Public employee dissension--**

Connick v. Myers,

Facts. Myers (P) worked as Assistant Attorney General under Connick (D), the local district attorney. Despite her objections, P was to be transferred to another section. She prepared a questionnaire intended to solicit her fellow employees' opinions about transfer policy, office morale, the level of confidence in named supervisors, and pressure to work in political campaigns. D fired P for insubordination. P sued, claiming wrongful termination based on her exercise of free speech. The lower courts upheld P's claim, and the Supreme Court granted certiorari.

Issue. Do the First and Fourteenth Amendments prohibit the discharge of a state employee for circulating a questionnaire concerning internal office affairs?

Held. No. Judgment reversed.

- Questions of a public employee's right to free speech involve a balance between the employee's interests as a citizen in commenting on matters of public concern, and the state's interest as an employer in promoting the efficiency of the public services it provides through its employees.

- The focus of P's questionnaire is to gather ammunition for her controversy with D. Such speech dealing with matters of personal interest is normally not the type that federal courts should pass on as to whether the termination was unconstitutional. The matter of pressure to work on political campaigns does touch a public concern, though.

- The state's burden to justify a termination depends on the nature of the employee's speech. Here, P's limited First Amendment interest did not require

D to tolerate disruptive activity. The evidence indicates that P's actions carried the potential to undermine office relations. Therefore, P's dismissal was not unconstitutional.

Dissent (Brennan, Marshall, Blackmun, Stevens, JJ.). P's questionnaire dealt with the manner in which the government is, or should be, operated. Such communication is essential for self-governance, which is a major basis for the First Amendment. The public interest of a statement does not depend on where it is said or why. The district court found that the questionnaire was not disruptive. The deference given by the majority to D's judgment is unjustified. The effect of the decision will be to deter public employees from speaking out.

---

c. **Public employee speech pursuant to official duties--**

Garcetti v. Ceballos,

Facts. Ceballos (P) was a deputy district attorney in Los Angeles County. At the prompting of a defense attorney, P looked into inaccuracies in an affidavit used to obtain a critical search warrant. After he investigated, P concluded that the affidavit contained serious misrepresentations. He told his supervisors of his findings and followed up with a memo recommending that the case be dismissed. A follow-up meeting became heated, and P's supervisor decided to proceed with the case. At a hearing on a defense motion, P was called by the defense, and he described the problems with the affidavit. The trial court rejected the challenge to the warrant. Subsequently, P was transferred to a trial deputy position and denied a promotion. He sued his supervisors, alleging retaliation for his speech in violation of the First and Fourteenth Amendments. The district court granted summary judgment for Ds. The court of appeals reversed. The Supreme Court granted certiorari.

It is well settled that "a State cannot condition public employment on a basis that infringes the employee's constitutionally protected interest in freedom of expression." The question presented by the instant case is whether the First Amendment protects a government employee from discipline based on speech made pursuant to the employee's official duties.

Issue. Does the First Amendment protect a government employee from discipline based on speech made pursuant to the employee's official duties?

Held. No. Judgment reversed.

♦ Under *Pickering v. Board of Education of Township High School District 205, Will County*, 391 U.S. 563 (1968), courts ask two questions to determine the scope of constitutional protections accorded to public employee speech. First, did the employee speak as a citizen on a matter of public concern? If no, the employee has no First Amendment cause of action based on the employer's reaction to the speech. If yes, then a First Amendment claim may arise unless the relevant government entity had an adequate justification for treating the employee differently from any other member of the general public. A government entity acting as employer has broader discretion to restrict speech, but the restrictions must be directed at speech that has some potential to affect the government's operations.

- Like private employers, government employers need substantial control over their employees' words and actions; otherwise, government offices could not function. Furthermore, public employees often have trusted positions in society, and when they speak out, they might express views that go against governmental policies or decrease the performance of governmental functions. Thus, an employee for the government must accept certain limitations on his freedom.

- Still, a government employee is a citizen, and the First Amendment limits a public employer's restriction of the liberties employees enjoy as private citizens. As long as employees are speaking as citizens about matters of public concern, they must face only those speech restrictions that are necessary for their employers to operate efficiently and effectively. This Court has sought both to promote the individual and societal interests that are served when employees speak as citizens on matters of public concern and to respect the needs of government employers performing their important public functions.

- In this case, it is not dispositive that P expressed his views and his recommendation in a memo to his supervisor in the office instead of publicly. Employees sometimes receive First Amendment protection for expressions made at work. It is also nondispositive that P's memo concerned the subject matter of P's employment. The First Amendment protects some expressions related to the speaker's job. Employees must be able to speak out freely on job-related questions without fear of retaliatory dismissal.

- Here, the controlling factor is that P's speech was made pursuant to his duties as a deputy district attorney, a government employee. The fact that P spoke as a prosecutor fulfilling a responsibility to advise his supervisor about a pending case distinguishes P's case from cases in which the First Amendment provides protection against discipline. P's memo led to a heated meeting with employees from the sheriff's department. If Ds determined that P's memo was misguided, they had the authority to take corrective action.

- When public employees make statements pursuant to their official duties, the Constitution does not insulate their communications from employer discipline. Employers have heightened interests in controlling speech made by an employee in his professional capacity. P's proposed contrary rule, adopted by the court of appeals, would mandate judicial oversight of communications between government employees and their superiors in the course of official business, displacing managerial discretion by judicial supervision. Such permanent judicial intervention in the conduct of governmental operations is inconsistent with sound principles of federalism and the separation of powers.

Dissent (Stevens, J.). The First Amendment may sometimes protect a government employee from discipline based on speech made pursuant to his official duties. Public employees are still citizens while they are in the office. It is senseless to let constitutional protection for identical words hinge on whether they fall within a job description and to create a rule that gives employees an incentive to voice their concerns publicly before talking frankly to their superiors.

Dissent (Souter, Stevens, Ginsburg, JJ.).

♦ Private and public interests in addressing official wrongdoing and threats to health and safety can outweigh the government's stake in the efficient implementation of policy, and public employees who speak on these matters in the course of their duties should have First Amendment protection. Just because a speaker is employed by the government does not eliminate the value to the public of receiving the opinions and information that a public employee may disclose, and the value may well be greater when the employee speaks pursuant to his duties.

♦ However, entitlement to protection is not absolute. There must be a balancing between individual and public interests in the speech, on the one hand, and the government's interest in operating efficiently, on the other. The government needs civility in the workplace, consistency in policy, and honesty and competence in public service. Governmental interests can be protected by holding that an employee commenting on subjects in the course of his duties should not prevail on balance unless he speaks on a matter of unusual importance and satisfies high standards of responsibility in the way he speaks.

Dissent (Breyer, J.). Courts should apply the *Pickering* standard even when a government employee speaks on matters of public concern in the course of his ordinary duties. Here, P complained of retaliation, in part, on the basis of speech contained in his memo that he says fell within the scope of his constitutional obligations. The Constitution mandates special protection of employee speech in such circumstances. I agree with much of Justice Souter's analysis, but the constitutional standard he proposes fails to give sufficient weight to the serious managerial and administrative concerns that the majority describes. The First Amendment sometimes authorizes judicial actions based on a government employee's speech that involves a matter of public concern and also takes place in the course of ordinary job-related duties. But it does so only when there is an augmented need for constitutional protection and diminished risk of undue judicial interference with governmental management. Because these conditions are met in this case, *Pickering* balancing is appropriate.

d. Federal employees' participation in political activity--

United States Civil Service Commission v. National Association of Letter Carriers,

Facts. The National Association of Letter Carriers (P) and other interested parties challenged 5 U.S.C. section 7324(a)(2) (section 9(a) of the Hatch Act), which prohibits federal employees from taking "an active part in political management or in political campaigns." The district court held the statute invalid as unconstitutionally vague and fatally overbroad. The United States Civil Service Commission (D) appeals.

Issue. May Congress prevent federal employees from participating in certain forms of partisan political conduct?

Held. Yes. Judgment reversed.

- ♦ Neither the right to associate nor the right to participate in political activity is absolute, and the conduct of political campaigns is manifestly subject to governmental regulation. Congress has balanced the interest of federal employees as citizens against the interest in promoting the efficiency of public services, and no constitutional provision requires that their determination be invalidated.

e. Federal employees' freedom of speech--

United States v. National Treasury Employees Union,

Facts. In response to a Presidential Commission's report finding that honoraria paid to federal officials for appearances, speeches, and writings presented ethics problems, Congress enacted a law prohibiting federal employees from receiving compensation for making speeches or writing articles. The prohibition applied even when neither the subject of the speech or article nor the group compensating the employee had any connection with the employee's official duties. The National Treasury Employees Union and several individual civil servants (Ps) challenged the statute's applicability to executive branch employees. The district court granted summary judgment for Ps, and the court of appeals affirmed. The Supreme Court granted certiorari.

Issue. May Congress prohibit federal employees from earning any compensation for speaking or writing, even where the topics addressed are unrelated to the speaker's or writer's official duties?

Held. No. Judgment affirmed.

- Historical figures who were both federal employees and spare-time authors include Nathaniel Hawthorne, Herman Melville, and Walt Whitman. Like those authors, Ps seek compensation for their expressive activities conducted in their capacity as citizens, not as employees of the government. In most cases, the content of Ps' work and the audiences they address have no relevance to their employment.

- Ps' employment by the government does not deprive them of the First Amendment rights they would otherwise enjoy as citizens to comment on matters of public interest. While Congress may impose restraints on public employees' job-related speech, as the Court held in *Pickering v. Board of Education of Township High School District*, 391 U.S. 563 (1968), Ps' expression in this case falls within the protected category of "citizen comment on matters of public concern."

- Congressional judgments are generally given a strong presumption of validity by the courts, but this statute presents special dangers because it is broad and it chills potential speech rather than responds to illegal speech after it is made. The United States (D) thus has a greater burden of showing "that the interests of both potential audiences and a vast group of present and future employees in a broad range of present and future expression are outweighed by that expression's 'necessary impact on the actual operation' of the [g]overnment."

- The ban was motivated by the actions of a relatively small group of lawmakers who, because of the nature of their work, typically spoke or wrote about matters related to their official responsibilities. Yet the ban reaches far beyond this group to include lower-paid, nonpolicymaking employees who receive invitations to speak mainly because of the market value of their messages. The speculative benefits of the ban are insufficient to justify the burden on Ps' freedom of speech.

- There is no proof that Ps' speech risks workplace disruption as was the case in *Pickering*. D claims that the ban is permissible because Congress determined that honoraria interfered with the efficiency of public service. D notes that the Hatch Act, which prohibits partisan political activity by federal employees, has been upheld. But the Hatch Act is intended to ***protect*** employees' rights to free expression and to protect their morale and liberty. The ban in this case instead ***restricts*** employees' rights to free expression.

- The lower courts enjoined enforcement of the ban as it applied to the entire executive branch; however, only employees below Grade GS-16 are plaintiffs in this case, and the injunction should be limited to them. D may have a different justification for a ban limited to more senior officials, which would present different constitutional issues than this case does. Nor can the courts modify the remedy by creating a nexus requirement for the ban, because determining the nature of such a nexus between speech and official duties would require legislative factfinding and deliberation.

Concurrence and dissent (O'Connor, J.). The ban is unconstitutional, but only to the extent that it bars Ps' class of employees from receiving honoraria for expressive activities that bear no nexus to government employment.

Dissent (Rehnquist, C.J., Scalia, Thomas, JJ.). D's primary interest is prevention of impropriety and the appearance of impropriety. Even employees holding a rank lower than GS-16, such as tax examiners and bank examiners, have substantial power to confer favors. The Hatch Act, which in fact does restrict expressive activity, is relevant by analogy to this case. In fact, the ban on honoraria prohibits no speech and is unrelated to Ps' message or viewpoint. This limited burden on speech is justified by D's interest in preventing impropriety. Even if the ban were unconstitutional, it would be so only as applied to Ps' class of employees who seek honoraria unrelated to their government employment.

---

f. Patronage hiring--

Rutan v. Republican Party of Illinois,

Facts. James Thompson, the Governor of Illinois and a Republican, issued an executive order that imposed a hiring freeze on every government position he controlled. Hiring employees and filling positions was permitted only with the approval of the Governor's office. The Governor created an office to review requests for permission. In practice, participation in the Republican Party of Illinois (D) was a key criterion for hiring and advancement. Rutan (P) challenged the practice after she had been repeatedly denied promotions for which she was qualified because she had not worked for or supported D. Others complained of not being recalled after layoffs or not being hired at all because they did not support D. The district court dismissed the complaint. The court of appeals affirmed, holding that patronage practices violate the First Amendment only when they are the "substantial equivalent of a dismissal." The Supreme Court granted certiorari.

Issue. May a government official refuse to hire or promote people to nonpolicymaking positions solely because of party affiliation?

Held. No. Judgment reversed.

- *Elrod v. Burns*, 427 U.S. 347 (1976), held that a newly elected government official could not replace office staff with members of his own party. Conditioning employment on political activity is tantamount to coerced belief. Patronage dismissals are not the least restrictive means for protecting the government's interest in ensuring that it has effective and efficient employees, because employees whose performance is inadequate can be discharged for that reason, regardless of party affiliation. Patronage impedes the associational and speech freedoms necessary for an effective democratic government.

- In *Branti v. Finkel*, 445 U.S. 507 (1980), the Court applied *Elrod* to prohibit the firing of employees on the basis of their private political beliefs. The policymaking exception created by *Elrod* was limited to those situations in which party affiliation is an appropriate requirement for the effective performance of the public office involved; in all other cases, the knowledge that one must have a sponsor in the dominant party to retain one's job necessarily involves a coercion of belief.

- D claims that patronage dismissals, which are not involved in this case, are different in kind from a failure to promote, transfer, or recall after a layoff. But employees in dead-end positions due to their party affiliation will still feel obligated to support their superiors' political positions in order to advance, obtain a transfer, or be recalled. The *Elrod* and *Branti* concerns therefore apply to these personnel actions.

- Patronage hiring is just another form of patronage practice that allows the government, without sufficient justification, to pressure employees to discontinue the free exercise of their First Amendment rights. If an individual's employment application is set aside because she does not support D, her First Amendment rights have been violated.

Dissent (Scalia, J., Rehnquist, C.J., Kennedy, O'Connor, JJ.). The majority decides that the Constitution forbids consideration of party membership as a factor in dispensing government jobs, except where party affiliation is an "appropriate requirement," a standard that is unclear. If anything, the job of being a judge should not hinge on party affiliation, but in fact even the Justices of the Court are appointed based on the party affiliation of the federal administration. The increasing weaknesses of the major political parties in this country since the *Elrod* and *Branti* decisions is apparent, and the Court should not assume that patronage has no important benefits. The government as a lawmaker is properly restricted from making classifications, but as an employer, the government may properly impose special restrictions on its employees. In fact, political patronage existed when the Bill of Rights was adopted, and the Court should not reject such an unbroken tradition based on an ambiguous constitutional text. Even applying a balancing test, there is evidence that political patronage strengthens the two-party system with its benefits for democracy. There is no right line that the courts can draw; it is a legislative matter.

D. FREEDOM OF THE PRESS

1. **Introduction.** As a general matter, freedom of the press includes no greater rights than the freedom of speech enjoyed by other members of the public.

However, the freedom of the press includes the liberty to broadly disseminate expression. Its inclusion as a separate freedom may simply have been intended to ensure that the government did not single out the media as an object of regulation.

a. **Special tax treatment for the press--**

Minneapolis Star v. Minnesota Commissioner of Revenue,

Facts. Minnesota imposed a general sales tax and a related use tax (for items on which no sales tax had been paid). Publications were exempt from these taxes until 1971, when the state imposed a use tax on the cost of paper and ink products consumed in producing a publication. Three years later, the state exempted the first $100,000 of paper and ink used. As a result, the *Minneapolis Star* (P), one of 11 newspapers (of 388 in the state) that had to pay a use tax, paid nearly two-thirds of all the use tax collected. P sued the Minnesota Commissioner of Revenue (D) for a refund. The state courts upheld the tax and P appeals.

Issue. May the states single out the press for special tax treatment?

Held. No. Judgment reversed.

- Other than the structure of the tax itself, there is no indication that the state imposed the tax with an impermissible or censorial motive. This case therefore differs from *Grosjean v. American Press Co.*, 297 U.S. 233 (1936), in which a publishing tax was held invalid because of improper government motive.

- Differential taxation of the press, unrelated to any special characteristic that requires such treatment, is unconstitutional. Such treatment suggests suppression of expression, a presumptively unconstitutional goal. In the absence of a compelling counterbalancing interest, differential taxation may not be allowed.

- D has no adequate justification for the tax. Even though the tax burden may be lighter than it would be under general application of the regular sales tax, differential treatment of any kind opens the door for more burdensome treatment.

- The tax also targets a small group of large newspapers, presenting an impermissible potential for abuse.

Concurrence and dissent (White, J.). The Court need not reach beyond the unconstitutional targeting of the tax to hold it unconstitutional in all cases.

Dissent (Rehnquist, J.). This tax favors newspapers. It does not abridge the freedom of the press. D's scheme is rational because the large volume of inexpensive items involved (newspapers) makes the regular sales tax impractical.

2. **Restraints on Editorial Judgment.**

a. **Classified ads--**

Pittsburgh Press Co. v. Pittsburgh Commission on Human Relations,

Facts. The Pittsburgh Press Co. (D), a newspaper publisher, carried "help wanted" ads in sex-designated columns, contrary to a local ordinance forbidding such classifications as discriminatory. The Pittsburgh Commission on Human Relations (P) sued to enjoin D's practice, and was granted relief in the lower courts. D appeals.

Issue. Is editorial judgment as to where to place commercial speech in a newspaper immune from government regulation?

Held. No. Judgment affirmed.

- The want ads are clearly commercial speech unprotected by the First Amendment. D's headings and the editorial judgment of location of the ads are not sufficiently severable from the ads themselves to bring them within the First Amendment. D's actions, coupled with the ads, are in effect an integrated commercial statement, and are therefore subject to proper regulation.

- The ordinance is proper in that it is narrowly drawn to prohibit placement in sex-designated columns of advertisements for nonexempt job opportunities. Therefore, D's rights are not infringed on.

b. **Requiring access to the press.**

1) **"Fairness doctrine" in broadcasting.** The Court has upheld FCC orders, under a statutory "fairness doctrine," requiring a radio station to offer free broadcasting time: (i) to opponents of political candidates or views endorsed by the station; and (ii) to any person who has been personally attacked in the course of a broadcast, for reply to the attack. [*See* Red Lion Broadcasting v. FCC, 395 U.S. 367 (1969)]

2) **Newspapers--**

Miami Herald Publishing Co. v. Tornillo,

Facts. Tornillo (P) was a candidate for the Florida state legislature. The Miami Herald Publishing Co. (D), a newspaper publisher, printed editorials critical of P's candidacy.

P sued to force D to publish P's response under a Florida "right of reply" statute. The state supreme court reversed the lower court and held the statute constitutional. D appeals.

Issue. May the state require a newspaper to publish a candidate's reply to criticism made by the newspaper?

Held. No. Judgment reversed.

- ♦ P demonstrates the consolidation of control over the public media, and argues that an enforceable right of access is a necessary remedy to ensure open public debate. However, such a right requires some mechanism, either governmental or consensual. If governmental, as here, the First Amendment protections are invoked.

- ♦ Although a responsible press is desirable, it is not mandated by the Constitution and, like many other virtues, cannot be legislated. P would use governmental coercion to compel D to publish material that D deems improper for publication. Such interference with editorial decisionmaking exceeds constitutional bounds. Additionally, it would motivate editors to avoid controversial subjects, to the detriment of public discussion.

Concurrence (Brennan, Rehnquist, JJ.). I join this opinion only regarding "right of reply" statutes. I express no opinion regarding the right of retraction in defamation cases.

---

3. Prohibition of Publication of Government Information.

a. Sensitive government documents--

New York Times Co. v. United States (The Pentagon Papers Case),

---

Facts. The United States (P) sought to enjoin publication by *The New York Times* (D) and the *Washington Post* of a classified study known as the Pentagon Papers. All federal courts involved, except the court of appeals in the *New York Times* case, held that P had not met its heavy burden of justification. D appeals the judgment of the court of appeals in its case.

Issue. May the executive branch prevent publication of items that it considers to threaten grave and irreparable injury to the public interest?

Held. No. Judgment reversed.

- ♦ The United States has failed to meet its heavy burden of showing justification for the enforcement of such a prior restraint.

Concurrence (Black, Douglas, JJ.). The injunctions should have been vacated and the cases dismissed without oral argument because it would be impossible to find that the President has "inherent power" to halt the publication of news by resort to the courts.

Concurrence (Douglas, Black, JJ.). The only possible power possessed by the government to restrict publication by the press of sensitive material arises from its inherent power to wage war successfully. Congress has not declared war, so the government cannot exercise this power.

Concurrence (Brennan, J.). Courts cannot issue temporary stays and restraining orders to accommodate the government's desire to suppress freedom of the press without adequate proof of a direct, inevitable, and immediate serious adverse effect.

Concurrence (Stewart, White, JJ.). The executive branch has the duty to protect necessary confidentiality through executive regulations. The courts are limited to construing specific regulations and applying specific laws. Since the courts were asked to do neither here, they cannot act.

Concurrence (White, Stewart, JJ.). Some circumstances might justify an injunction as requested, but not these. Congress has relied on criminal sanctions and their deterrent effect to prevent unauthorized disclosures, and the courts should not go beyond the congressional determinations.

Concurrence (Marshall, J.). The Court would violate the concept of separation of powers by using its power to prevent behavior that Congress has specifically declined to prohibit.

Dissent (Harlan, J., Burger, C.J., Blackmun, J.). Judicial review of executive action in foreign affairs is narrow. The Court should inquire only whether the subject matter is within the President's foreign relations power and whether the head of the department concerned has personally made the determination that disclosure would irreparably impair national security.

---

b. **Prior restraints.** There is a strong presumption against prior restraints in the case of injunctions sought against media reporting of criminal proceedings (on the ground of preserving a fair trial for the accused). Before such an injunction may issue, the court must find that: (i) there is a clear and present danger that pretrial publicity would (not merely could) threaten a fair trial; (ii) alternative measures are inadequate; and (iii) an injunction would effectively protect the accused. Furthermore, under no circumstances can the media be prohibited from reporting what occurs at a public hearing.

1) **Pretrial publicity--**

Nebraska Press Association v. Stuart,

Facts. Stuart (D), a state district judge, presided over the criminal trial involving a shocking multiple murder that had occurred in a small Nebraska town. To avoid the dangers that pretrial publicity would present to the fairness of the accused's trial, D entered a restrictive order that prohibited the Nebraska Press Association (P) and others from reporting certain subjects relating to the trial. The order applied only until the jury was impaneled. On appeal, the Nebraska Supreme Court modified D's order to prohibit reporting only of any confessions made by the accused (except to members of the press) and other facts "strongly implicative" of the accused. P appeals.

Issue. Is a prior restraint on pretrial publicity, intended to ensure the fairness of a criminal defendant's trial, subject to a lesser standard of review than prior restraints generally?

Held. No. Judgment reversed.

- ♦ Generally, pretrial publicity does not threaten the right to a trial by an impartial jury because of the trial judge's control over proceedings (*e.g.*, change of venue, continuance, sequestration of jury). However, in certain "sensational" cases, like that described here, the possibility arises that these normal means of preserving fairness are inadequate. Accordingly, resort is sometimes made to a restrictive order such as that used by D.

- ♦ Prior restraints on speech and publication pose the most serious and least tolerable infringement on First Amendment rights. The barriers to prior restraint may not be relaxed even when there is a possible conflict with an equally important constitutional right. The barrier may be breached only where "the gravity of the 'evil,' discounted by its improbability, justifies such invasion of free speech as is necessary to avoid the danger."

- ♦ The "evil" of an unfair trial is clearly great. However, the evidence here is insufficient to show that, except for the prior restraint imposed by D, the accused would certainly have had an unfair trial. Before any prior restraint is permissible, the court must find a clear and present danger that pretrial publicity would (not merely could) threaten a fair trial, that alternative measures would be inadequate, and that the prior restraint would actually protect the accused.

Concurrence (Brennan, Stewart, Marshall, JJ.). Resort to prior restraints on the freedom of the press is a constitutionally impermissible method for enforcing the right to a fair trial.

Concurrence (White, J.). A more general rule on the subject might be necessary.

Concurrence (Powell, J.). Any permissible prior restraint must be specific.

Concurrence (Stevens, J.). A prior restraint is probably impermissible in all cases, but some extreme circumstances might justify its use.

---

c. **Invasion of privacy--**

Florida Star v. B.J.F. *See* *supra*

d. **Confidential proceedings.** A state may have a legitimate interest in maintaining confidentiality about some proceedings (*e.g.*, inquiries into the fitness of judges). The Court has not decided whether a state may punish disclosures about such proceedings by participants or persons who secure the information by illegal means. But criminal sanctions may not be imposed on other persons (including the press) for divulging truthful information regarding such confidential proceedings, absent substantial interests that justify encroachment on freedom of speech and press. [*See* Landmark Communications, Inc. v. Virginia, 435 U.S. 829 (1978)]

4. **Government Demands for Confidential Press Information.** Freedom of the press does not afford news reporters a privilege to refuse to answer relevant and material questions asked during a good faith grand jury investigation. In such proceedings, reporters may be forced to disclose their sources and other information within their possession. However, "official harassment of the press undertaken, not for purposes of law enforcement, but to disrupt a reporter's relationship with his news sources would have no justification."

a. **No reporter's privilege--**

Branzburg v. Hayes,

Facts. Branzburg (D), a reporter, observed illegal drug transactions that he used in a news article. D was subpoenaed to appear before a grand jury; he then sought prohibition and mandamus to avoid having to reveal his confidential information, but the state courts denied his petition. D appeals. (Other cases involving two similarly situated reporters were joined for decision by the Court.)

Issue. Does the First Amendment grant a special testimonial privilege to reporters, protecting them from being forced to divulge confidential information to a grand jury's investigation?

Held. No. Judgment affirmed.

- D claims that forcing reporters to reveal confidences to a grand jury will deter other confidential sources of information, thus curtailing the free flow of information protected by the First Amendment. However, reporters have no constitutional right of access to several types of events (grand jury proceedings, meetings of private organizations and of official bodies gathered in executive session, etc.). Although these exclusions tend to hamper news gathering, they are not unconstitutional.

- All citizens have an obligation to respond to grand jury subpoenas and to answer questions relevant to crime investigation. The only testimonial privilege for unofficial witnesses is in the Fifth Amendment; there is no necessity to create a special privilege for reporters based on the First Amendment. The public interest in pursuing and prosecuting those crimes reported to the press by informants, and thus deterring future commission of those crimes, is ***not*** outweighed by the public interest in possible future news about crime from undisclosed, unverified sources.

- A judicially created reporter's privilege would necessarily involve significant practical and conceptual problems in its administration. However, Congress and the state legislatures are not precluded from fashioning whatever standards and rules they might deem proper if they choose to create a statutory reporter's privilege.

Concurrence (Powell, J.). Reporters are not without remedy in the face of a bad faith investigation. Motions to quash and appropriate protective orders are available where the requested testimony is not within the legitimate hold of law enforcement.

Dissent (Douglas, J.). Reporters have an absolute privilege against appearing before a grand jury, unless personally implicated in a crime, in which case the Fifth Amendment immunity applies.

Dissent (Stewart, Brennan, Marshall, JJ.). The Court undermines the independence of the press by inviting authorities to annex the journalistic provision as an investigative arm of government. Exercise of the power to compel disclosure will lead to "self-censorship" and, as a consequence, significantly impair the free flow of information to the public. To force disclosure, the government must show: (i) probable cause that the reporter has information clearly relevant to a specific probable violation of law; (ii) the absence of any less obtrusive means of obtaining the information; and (iii) a compelling and overriding interest in the information.

---

5. **Press Access to Government Information.**

a. **Prisons.** The First Amendment guarantees neither the public nor the press access to prisoners or prisons (or other information controlled by the government). But if government voluntarily grants such access, the public and the press must be treated equally. Where limitations that might be reasonable as to individual members of the public would impede effective reporting (*e.g.*, prohibition on cameras), such limitations may not—consistent with reasonable prison rules—be used to hamper effective media presentation of what is seen by individual visitors. [*See* Houchins v. KQED, 438 U.S. 1 (1978)]

b. **Exhibits.** Freedom of the press does not extend to physical access to exhibits introduced in a judicial proceeding, where the public has not had such access. [*See* Nixon v. Warner Communications, 435 U.S. 489 (1978)—holding that the press has no First Amendment right to obtain tape recordings played at a criminal trial]

c. **Access to trials--**

Richmond Newspapers, Inc. v. Virginia,

Facts. Early in the fourth criminal trial of the same defendant, the trial judge granted an uncontested closure motion made by the defendant. Later, reporters for Richmond Newspapers, Inc. (P) sought a hearing on a motion to vacate the closure order, which was granted but from which the public was again excluded. The Court denied the motion, considering the defendant's interest paramount. The defendant was acquitted in the closed trial. P appealed from the trial court's closure order, but the state courts affirmed. P appeals.

Issue. Is the right of the public and press to attend criminal trials guaranteed by the Constitution?

Held. Yes. Judgment reversed.

- In *Gannett Co., Inc. v. DePasquale*, 433 U.S. 368 (1979), the Court held that neither the public nor the press had an enforceable right of access to a pretrial suppression hearing.

- Throughout the evolution of the trial procedure, the trial has been open to all persons who cared to observe. However, the Constitution contains no explicit provisions protecting the public from exclusion from the courtroom.

- The First Amendment protects freedom of speech and press, including expression regarding events at trials. These guaranteed rights would be meaningless if access to the trial could be foreclosed arbitrarily. Other constitutional rights, not explicitly established, have been recognized as implied; clearly, the public interest in judicial functions and in freedom of speech requires open trials.

- ♦ In some circumstances, where an overriding interest is articulated in findings, a criminal trial may be closed to the public, but only if the common alternatives are insufficient (*e.g.*, jury sequestration, witness sequestration).

Concurrence (White, J.). If *Gannett* had been decided correctly, this case would not have arisen.

Concurrence (Stevens, J.). The case is especially significant because it holds for the first time that the acquisition of news is entitled to constitutional protection.

Concurrence (Brennan, Marshall, JJ.). Publicity is an important means of ensuring the right to a fair trial. What happens in a courtroom is public property. The First Amendment requires open access.

Concurrence (Stewart, J.). *Gannett* merely held that access to a pretrial hearing was not guaranteed by the Sixth Amendment. At least now we know that the First and Fourteenth Amendments require open trials; maybe the pretrial question will be similarly resolved.

Concurrence (Blackmun, J.). The Sixth Amendment, by itself, requires open public trials.

Dissent (Rehnquist, J.). Neither the First nor Sixth Amendment requires this result, and the Ninth Amendment precludes our review of orders of state trial judges where both the prosecuting attorney and defendant have consented to the order of closure.

E. RELIGION AND THE CONSTITUTION

The First Amendment provides: "Congress shall make no law respecting an establishment of religion, or prohibiting the free exercise thereof." Article VI provides: ". . . no religious Test shall ever be required as a Qualification to any Office or public Trust under the United States."

1. The Establishment Clause.

a. Introduction.

1) **Generally.** The central purpose of the "Establishment of Religion" Clause is to ensure governmental neutrality in matters of religion; *i.e.*, "When government activities touch on the religious sphere, they must be secular in purpose, evenhanded in operation, and

neutral in primary impact." As applied to schools, the state may not enact laws that further the religious training or doctrine of any sect. [Gillette v. United States, 401 U.S. 437 (1971)]

2) **Transportation to parochial schools--**

Everson v. Board of Education,

Facts. A local New Jersey Board of Education (D) authorized reimbursement to parents of the costs of using the public transportation system to send their children to school, whether public or parochial. Everson (P) challenged the scheme as an unconstitutional exercise of state power to support church schools. P appeals adverse lower court decisions.

Issue. May a state use public funds to assist student transportation to parochial as well as to public schools?

Held. Yes. Judgment affirmed.

- The Establishment Clause was intended to erect a wall between church and state. It does not prohibit a state from extending its general benefits to all its citizens without regard to their religious beliefs.

- Reimbursement of transportation is intended solely to help children arrive safely at school, regardless of their religion. It does not support any schools, parochial or public. To invalidate D's system would handicap religion, which is no more permissible than favoring religion.

Dissent (Jackson, Frankfurter, JJ.). The Court's rationale contradicts its conclusion.

Dissent (Rutledge, Frankfurter, Jackson, Burton, JJ.). The Court should be as strict to prohibit use of public funds to aid religious schools as it is to prevent introduction of religious education into public schools.

b. **Government religious exercises, ceremonies, displays, and practices.**

1) **Public school released time program--**

Zorach v. Clauson,

Facts. New York City established a "released time" program pursuant to which students whose parents so requested were permitted to leave school grounds for religious instruction. The Zorachs (Ps), parents whose children attended the New York public schools, challenged the program. The lower courts upheld it, and Ps appeal.

Issue. May a state grant willing students permission to leave public school grounds during school hours in order to receive religious instruction elsewhere?

Held. Yes. Judgment affirmed.

- There is no evidence of coercion on the part of school officials. Only those students whose parents requested their release were permitted to participate.

- Although the First Amendment requires a separation of church and state, that separation is not absolute but well defined. Otherwise, there would be hostility between the two, and religious groups would be unable to benefit from such basic services as fire and police protection.

- Clearly, students may be released from school to attend religious holidays or observances. This release time program is no different in character.

- Religion is an integral part of our society, and although the state may not coerce religious observances, it may make provision for those citizens desiring to retreat to a religious sanctuary for worship or instruction.

Dissent (Black, J.). The state, by manipulating its compulsory education laws to help religious sects get pupils, has combined church and state.

Dissent (Jackson, J.). The wall between church and state is now warped and twisted.

---

2) Prayer at school functions--

Santa Fe Independent School District v. Doe,

Facts. Before 1995, the Santa Fe Independent School District (D) allowed a student elected as Santa Fe High School's student council chaplain to give a prayer over the public address system before each home varsity football game. Two sets of current or former students and their mothers (Ps), one set Mormon and the other Catholic, sued anonymously as Doe for a restraining order to prevent D from violating the Establishment Clause at an upcoming graduation. Ps alleged that D had engaged in several proselytizing activities. The district court ordered that a student chosen by the graduating class could deliver a nondenominational prayer at the graduation. The text of the prayer would also be determined by the students without D's participation. In response, D adopted a policy that authorized two student elections, the first to determine whether "invocations" should be delivered at games, and the second to select the spokesperson to deliver them. D later adopted another policy requiring that invocations and benedictions be nonsectarian and nonproselytizing. The district court enjoined enforcement of the first, open-ended policy. Both parties appealed. The court of appeals agreed with Ps that both of D's policies violated the Establishment Clause. The Supreme Court granted certiorari.

Issue. May a public school district allow student-led, student-initiated prayer at high school football games?

Held. No. Judgment affirmed.

- In *Lee v. Weisman*, 505 U. S. 577 (1992), the Court held that a school could not allow a prayer delivered by a rabbi at a graduation ceremony. The rationale was that the Establishment Clause guarantees that government may not coerce anyone to support or participate in religion or its exercise, or otherwise act in a way that establishes a state religion or religious faith, or tends to do so.

- D claims that *Lee* does not apply here because its policy resulted in messages that were private student speech, not public speech. However, the delivery of a message such as the invocation in this case—on school property, at school-sponsored events, over the school's public address system, by a speaker representing the student body, under the supervision of school faculty, and pursuant to a school policy that explicitly and implicitly encourages public prayer—is not properly characterized as "private" speech.

- D also claims that the school football game is a public forum, but this setting differs from a public forum in several ways. D does not open its ceremony to general use by the student body but only allows one student to give the invocation. The content of the invocation itself is subject to regulations regarding its content and topic. By making these a matter of vote, D guarantees that minority candidates cannot prevail and their views will be effectively silenced.

- D is closely involved with the message by facilitating it, by directing its performance, and by requiring that it be consistent with D's goals of solemnizing the event. The only type of message allowed by D's policy is an "invocation," suggesting a focused religious message. D's policy is obviously intended to preserve its traditional practice of prayer before football games, which is not private speech.

- *Lee* also noted that students could not be coerced into participating in religious observances. Yet the students were not unanimously in favor of the invocation. D was directly involved by holding the elections in the first place. While attendance at a football game may be voluntary for many students, for others, such as cheerleaders, band members, and team members, it may be part of their class requirements. There is also great social pressure on students to attend. Students cannot be forced to decide whether to attend or to risk facing a personally offensive religious ritual.

- ♦ D has subjected the issue of prayer to a majoritarian vote, thereby establishing a governmental mechanism that turns the public school into a forum for religious debate and empowers the majority of students to subject students of minority views to constitutionally improper messages. The award of that power alone violates the Constitution.

Dissent (Rehnquist, C.J., Scalia, Thomas, JJ.). Even if the *Lemon* test (*infra*) is appropriate to this case, it would not mean that D's student-message policy should be invalidated on its face. D's policy might result in a Christian prayer most of the time, and if the policy operates in that fashion, a record would be created that would help determine whether the policy, as applied, violated the Establishment Clause or unduly suppressed minority viewpoints. But possibly the students would vote not to have a pregame speaker, or the election might not focus on prayer. The policy has an expressed secular purpose that the Court does not defer to. The Court should await actual implementation of the policy before finding it unconstitutional.

---

3) **Restrictions on teaching particular subjects.** While the state undoubtedly has the right to prescribe curriculum for the public schools, it does not have the right to forbid the teaching of any scientific theory, doctrine, or other subject merely because it may be contrary to the religious doctrines of various sects.

a) **Ban on teaching of evolution.** The Court held that an Arkansas statute that forbade the teaching of evolution in public schools violated freedom of religion under the First and Fourteenth Amendments. The statute was not "religiously neutral"; it was aimed at one doctrine (evolution) that was offensive to certain fundamentalist religions. [*See* Epperson v. Arkansas, 393 U.S. 97 (1968)]

b) **Teaching of creationism and evolution--**

Edwards v. Aguillard,

Facts. Louisiana enacted a law requiring "balanced treatment" of the theories of creation and evolution if the subject of the origin of man, life, the Earth, or the universe was dealt with in public schools. Neither theory could be taught without the other, although neither had to be taught, and both were statutorily defined as science. The lower courts, including a sharply divided fifth circuit, held that the law was unconstitutional because the theory of creation is a religious belief.

Issue. May a state require its public schools to teach creation science if they teach evolution?

Held. No. Judgment affirmed.

- ♦ The first requirement under *Lemon* (*infra*), is that a statute must have been adopted with a secular purpose. The legislature here purportedly adopted this statute to protect academic freedom, but the public school teachers were not prohibited from teaching any particular scientific theory before the statute was adopted anyway. The legislative history indicates the statute was intended to eliminate the teaching of evolution, and the statute protects creationism and its proponents without protecting evolutionists.

- ♦ There is a well-known antagonism between the teachings of certain religions and the teaching of evolution. The clear purpose of the statute was to advance the religious viewpoint by restructuring the science curriculum. This does not mean that a variety of scientific theories may not be taught, but only that this act violated the Establishment Clause because it was intended to endorse a particular religious doctrine.

Concurrence (Powell, O'Connor, JJ.). The Establishment Clause only prohibits the use of religious teachings in public schools when the purpose of their use is to advance a particular religious belief, not when the purpose is a better understanding of culture, history, and so forth.

Concurrence (White, J.). The lower courts found that the statute was enacted to further a religious belief. I cannot say they are so plainly wrong that they should be reversed.

Dissent (Scalia, J., Rehnquist, C.J.). As long as there was a genuine secular purpose, the Act should not be invalidated. The secular purpose set forth in the Act should not be dismissed. In addition, the *Lemon* test is not based on the language of the Establishment Clause and leads to unpredictable decisions. The purpose test should be abandoned.

---

4) **Limitations on religious displays on government property.**

a) **Introduction.** For many years, governments at many levels allowed religious groups to set up displays such as a crèche at Christmas and a menorah at Chanukah. Such displays have been challenged as violations of the Establishment Clause. In *County of Allegheny v. American Civil Liberties Union*, 492 U.S. 573 (1989), the Court held that the government could not permit a religious group to display a Christmas crèche at a courthouse during the Christmas season. The crèche stood alone, with no other holiday displays, so the Court found that this could give the appearance that the government was promoting or affiliating with a religious doctrine or organization. However, the Court allowed a display at another government building that included a Christmas tree, a Chanukah menorah, and a sign saluting liberty, because this display sent a message of pluralism and did not endorse religious faith.

b) **Display of Ten Commandments held to violate Establishment Clause--**

McCreary County, Kentucky v. American Civil Liberties Union of Kentucky

Facts. McCreary County and another Kentucky county (Ds) posted large framed copies of the King James version of the Ten Commandments on the walls of their courthouses. The ACLU of Kentucky sought a preliminary injunction against maintaining the displays, which the ACLU alleged violated the Establishment Clause. Ds' legislative bodies authorized a second, expanded display and adopted resolutions stating that the Ten Commandments were the precedent legal code upon which the civil and criminal codes of Kentucky were founded. In the second display, the Commandments were surrounded by eight other documents in smaller frames, including the "endowed by their Creator" passage from the Declaration of Independence; the preamble to the Constitution of Kentucky; and the national motto, "In God We Trust." The federal district court ordered the displays to be removed. Ds then installed another display in each courthouse, setting out the Ten Commandments along with the Magna Carta, the Bill of Rights, and other historic documents. The collection was entitled "The Foundations of American Law and Government Display," and each document included a statement about its historical and legal significance. The ACLU moved to supplement the preliminary injunction to enjoin the counties' third display, and the district court supplemented the injunction. The court of appeals affirmed. The Supreme Court granted certiorari.

Issue. May the government display the Ten Commandments as part of a display of historic documents if its purpose is to advance religion?

Held. No. Judgment affirmed.

♦ Under *Lemon*, *infra*, a secular legislative purpose, although seldom dispositive, has been a common element of our cases and serves an important function. When the government acts with the predominant purpose of advancing religion, it violates the central Establishment Clause value of official religious neutrality. Ds assert that the purpose test of *Lemon* should be abandoned, or at least not applied in this case. Ds argue that, because true purpose is unknowable, the purpose test allows courts to act selectively and unpredictably in picking out evidence of subjective intent. But in an Establishment Clause analysis, the courts evaluate official objectives based on readily discoverable facts.

- In *Stone v. Graham*, 449 U.S. 39 (1980), this Court recognized that the Commandments are an "instrument of religion." In the first display in this case, as in the display rejected in *Stone*, the text of the Commandments was not part of a secular display. *Stone* stressed the importance of integrating the Commandments into a secular scheme to avoid an otherwise clearly religious message.

- After they were sued, each D authorized a second display that was accompanied by religious references, showed that Ds were posting the Commandments because of their sectarian content, and included the resolution's claim about the embodiment of ethics in Christ, disclosing an impermissible purpose.

- When Ds put up their third displays, the "Foundations of American Law and Government" exhibit, Ds placed the Commandments along with other documents they considered significant in the historical foundation of American government. However Ds did not repeal nor repudiate the resolutions of the former displays. In fact, the third displays quoted more of the Commandment's purely religious language than the first two displays had done.

- We do not hold that a sacred text can never be integrated constitutionally into a governmental display on the subject of law or American history. But purpose must be taken seriously under the Establishment Clause and must be understood in light of context.

- The framers' views on the Establishment Clause were varied, and there was no common understanding about the limits of the Establishment Clause. But the divisiveness of religion in public life is clear. The government must stay neutral on religious belief.

Concurrence (O'Connor, J.). The goal of the Religion Clauses is to carry out the Founders' plan of preserving religious liberty to the fullest extent possible in a pluralistic society. Religion is a matter for the individual conscience. Our country's regard for constitutional boundaries has protected Americans from the violent consequences of the assumption of religious authority by governments, which can be seen around the world. In the present case, the history of Ds' displays demonstrates that the purpose was religious.

Dissent (Scalia, J., Rehnquist, C.J., Thomas, Kennedy, JJ.).

- Our nation has a tradition of recognizing God, and this country's views on this matter have not significantly changed. Presidents continue to conclude the Presidential oath with "so help me God." This Court and our legislatures continue to open with prayer. Our Pledge of Allegiance acknowledges that we are a nation "under God." Furthermore, the First Amendment does not mandate governmental neutrality between religion and nonreligion.

- The *Lemon* test has been manipulated to fit whatever result the Court has aimed to achieve. Today the Court sets forth an "objective observer" test of intent and focuses its inquiry, not on the actual purpose of government action, but on the "purpose apparent from government action." Thus, even if a government could show that it did not have the purpose of advancing religion, its actions could be held unconstitutional.

- However, even under the Court's *Lemon*-based premises, Ds' displays were constitutional. The Ten Commandments were part of a larger display that showed their contribution to the development of the legal system, and the frame holding the Ten Commandments was of the same size and appearance as that which held each of the other documents.

---

c) Monument of Ten Commandments held not to violate Establishment Clause--

Van Orden v. Perry

Facts. The grounds of the Texas State Capitol contained 17 monuments and 21 historical markers, including a six-feet-high monolith inscribed with the text of the Ten Commandments. The monument was provided by the Fraternal Order of Eagles ("Eagles"), a national social, civic, and patriotic organization. Van Orden (P) sued state officials (Ds), seeking a declaration that the monument's placement on these grounds violated the Establishment Clause and seeking an injunction requiring its removal. The court found that the state had a valid secular purpose in recognizing the Eagles and that a reasonable observer would not conclude that the state endorsed religion by placing the monolith on the grounds. The court of appeals affirmed. The Supreme Court granted certiorari.

Issue. May a state include a monument inscribed with the Ten Commandments on the grounds of its state capitol along with numerous other monuments and markers commemorating the state's heritage?

Held. Yes. Judgment affirmed.

- Our institutions presuppose a Supreme Being, but they cannot press religious observances upon their citizens. Government can look to the past and acknowledge our nation's heritage and also look to the present and demand a separation of church and state. We should not demonstrate hostility toward religion by ignoring our religious heritage.

- The *Lemon* test does not help decide a challenge to a passive monument such as the one in this case. The monolith acknowledges the role played by the Ten Commandments in our nation's heritage. There are similar displays within the Supreme Court building. Moses was a lawgiver as well as a religious leader. In this context, the monolith also has dual significance and does not violate the Establishment Clause.

Concurrence (Scalia, J.). There is nothing unconstitutional about a state favoring religion generally, such as by honoring God through public prayer and acknowledgment or venerating the Ten Commandments in a nonproselytizing manner.

Concurrence (Thomas, J.). The Establishment Clause should not be applied to restrain the states. Even if it is, it should only apply to an actual "establishment" in the sense that it would prohibit legal coercion. Texas does not compel P to do anything.

Concurrence (Breyer, J.). This is a borderline case that turns on the context of the display. The placement of this monument suggests that the state intended the nonreligious aspects of the tablets' message to predominate.

Dissent (Stevens, Ginsburg, JJ.).

- The monument does not refer to any event in the state's history; its sole function is to display one version of the Ten Commandments. The Eagles wanted to curb juvenile delinquency by providing children with a code of conduct, and the Eagles believed that disseminating the message of the Ten Commandments would help young people to observe civilized standards of behavior. Although the Eagles' motive was admirable and secular, achieving that goal through biblical teachings inserts a religious purpose into an otherwise secular endeavor.

- The state may genuinely want to combat juvenile delinquency and honor the Eagles for their efforts, but it cannot do so through an explicitly religious medium. We held 25 years ago that it is indisputable that the Ten Commandments are a sacred text in the Jewish and Christian faiths. The sacred message on the monument is emphasized by the words, "I AM the LORD thy God" in large letters. The message directs us to follow a code of divine law, some of which has been integrated into our secular legal code, but much of which has not.

- The plurality relies heavily on the fact that our nation's founders spoke in religious rhetoric. But those views were not espoused at the Constitutional Convention in 1787 and are not part of the Constitution's text. Furthermore, there is a crucial difference between benign government recognitions of religion and the state's display of the full text of the Ten Commandments. When our public officials deliver speeches today, we realize that their words include the personal views of the speaker. On the other hand, the permanent placement of a display of the Ten Commandments on state property appears to be a collective statement of government approval.

- ♦ The Establishment Clause forbids religious discrimination and prohibits Texas from displaying the Ten Commandments monument. Holding that the Constitution permits governmental displays of sacred religious texts makes a mockery of the constitutional ideal that government must remain neutral between religion and irreligion.

Dissent (O'Connor, J.). My concurrence in *McCreary County* also applies here.

Dissent (Souter, Stevens, Ginsburg, JJ.). The display in this case is obviously religious, and nothing detracts from its religious nature. The presentation of the Ten Commandments is unlike neutral displays where Moses is placed in the framework of a lawgiver. Furthermore, there is no common denominator among the displays on the Texas grounds; each memorial stands on its own terms. The message of this monument is that God is the source of Jewish and Christian morality.

---

d) Unattended religious symbol on public forum--

Capitol Square Review & Advisory Board v. Pinette,

Facts. The Capitol Square Review and Advisory Board (D) managed a state-owned plaza surrounding the statehouse in Columbus, Ohio. The plaza had been used for over a century for public expression. Among other things, D had traditionally permitted a variety of unattended displays during the year, such as a state-sponsored lighted tree during the Christmas season, a privately sponsored menorah during Chanukah, a display showing the progress of a United Way fundraising campaign, and a booth and exhibits during an art festival. D authorized the state to put up its annual Christmas tree. It also granted a rabbi's application to erect a menorah. The same day, D received an application from Pinette and other members of the Ku Klux Klan (Ps) to put a cross on the square during the Christmas season. D denied Ps' application. Ps sued and obtained an injunction ordering D to allow Ps to erect the cross. D then received and granted several additional applications to erect crosses. D appealed. The Sixth Circuit affirmed, and the Supreme Court granted certiorari.

Issue. Does a state violate the Establishment Clause when, pursuant to a religiously neutral state policy, it permits a private party to display an unattended religious symbol in a traditional public forum located next to its seat of government?

Held. No. Judgment affirmed.

- ♦ Compliance with the Establishment Clause is a state interest sufficiently compelling to justify content-based restrictions on speech. However, the state may not violate an applicant's free speech rights by denying it use of public facilities available to other groups solely because of the applicant's religious viewpoint. For example, in *Lamb's Chapel v. Center Moriches Union Free School District*, 508 U.S. 384 (1993), the Court held that since a school permitted the use of school property for social, civic, and recreational meetings, it could not prohibit the use of school property by student Bible clubs. This holding followed *Widmar v. Vincent*, 454 U.S. 263 (1981), which held that a public university could not exclude student religious groups from facilities open to other student groups.

- D claims that this case differs from *Lamb's Chapel* because the forum's proximity to the seat of government may produce the perception that Ps' cross bears the state's approval. They claim that application of the so-called "endorsement test" from *County of Allegheny*, *supra*, would support the content-based restriction. But the cases have equated "endorsement" with "promotion" or "favoritism," and the government does not promote or favor a religious display by giving it the same access to a public forum that all other displays enjoy.

- In *County of Allegheny*, the Court held that the display of a creche in the county courthouse violated the Establishment Clause because the forum was not open to all on an equal basis. In *Lynch v. Donnelly*, *supra*, the Court held that the city's display of a creche did not constitute an endorsement of religion in the specific factual context. Neither case supports the position that government's neutral treatment of private religious expression can be unconstitutional.

- The difference between the endorsement language of *County of Allegheny* and *Lynch* and the approach taken in *Lamb's Chapel* and *Widmar* is the difference between government speech and private speech. That distinction does not disappear just because private speech can be mistaken for government speech, at least where the government has not fostered or encouraged the mistake.

- The Establishment Clause applies only to the words and acts of government. It does not bar purely private speech connected to the state only through its occurrence in a public forum. As long as religious expression is purely private and occurs in a traditional or designated public forum, is publicly announced, and is open to all on equal terms, the government may not prohibit the expression.

Concurrence (O'Connor, Souter, Breyer, JJ.). The Court reaches the correct result on the facts of this case. However, the endorsement test would invalidate any government practice that a reasonable observer would view as an endorsement of religion. The test is based on what an observer similar to the "reasonable person" in tort law would understand from the situation. In this case, for example, a reasonable observer would see Ps' cross display fully aware that the site is a public space in which a multiplicity of groups, secular and religious, participate in expressive conduct. Hence, the observer would not interpret the state's tolerance of the display as an endorsement of religion.

Concurrence (Souter, O'Connor, Breyer, JJ.). The per se rule applied by the plurality instead of the endorsement test is actually a new exception to the endorsement test. If an intelligent observer may mistake private, unattended religious displays in a public forum for government speech endorsing religion, the Court should not uphold the display. In this case, D could have imposed a less restrictive condition, such as requiring that a disclaimer sign be put on the display.

Dissent (Stevens, J.). The Establishment Clause should create a strong presumption against the installation of unattended religious symbols on public property. As long as some reasonable observers would attribute a religious meaning to the state, a religious display on public property violates the Establishment Clause.

Dissent (Ginsburg, J.). This display too closely associates a religious symbol with the state. Whether a more restricted display such as Justice Souter proposes would violate the Establishment Clause is a question not presented in this case.

---

e) After-school use of school building--

Good News Club v. Milford Central School

Facts. The Milford Central School (D) adopted a community use policy that permitted seven uses of its building after school. One use was "instruction in any branch of education, learning or the arts." Another was for "social, civic and recreational meetings . . . and other uses pertaining to the welfare of the community" as long as the meetings would be nonexclusive and open to the general public. The Good News Club (P) was a private Christian children's organization. P sought to use D's facility to sing songs, hear a Bible lesson, and memorize scripture. D declined on the ground that D's policy did not allow use for religious purposes. P sued. The district court granted D's motion for summary judgment. The Second Circuit affirmed. The Supreme Court granted certiorari.

Issue. May the government exclude speech from a limited public forum on the basis of the religious nature of the speech?

Held. No. Judgment reversed.

- The parties agree that D operates a limited public forum. In a limited public forum, the state does not allow persons to engage in every type of speech and is not required to under the Constitution. However, the restriction of speech must not discriminate on the basis of viewpoint and must be reasonable in light of the purpose served by the forum.

- D excluded P solely on the basis of P's religious nature, which is viewpoint discrimination. D permits any group that promotes the moral and character development of children to use its building. P teaches morals and character development to children. This case falls squarely within the *Lamb's Chapel* (*supra*) rule. As a foundation for lessons, there is no difference between invoking Christianity and invoking teamwork, loyalty, or patriotism. The government cannot exclude speech purely because it discusses otherwise permissible subjects from a religious viewpoint.

- Once viewpoint discrimination is established, there is no need to decide whether the restriction is unreasonable.

- D claims that its interest in not violating the Establishment Clause outweighs P's interest in gaining equal access to D's facilities. However, D has no valid Establishment Clause interest. As in *Lamb's Chapel*, D's instruction takes place outside of school hours and is not sponsored by D. There is no coercive pressure on the children because the parents decide whether their children will attend D's meetings. D's instructors are not school teachers. The classroom setting is not like school because D's classes have a wider range of age groups attending. There is no basis for concluding that children would misperceive that D is endorsing religion.

Concurrence (Scalia, J.). Any "coercion" that arises from private activities is one of the attendant consequences of freedom of association that is constitutionally protected. Religious expression that is purely private and occurs in a public forum cannot violate the Establishment Clause. The dissent argues that P's religious speech is aimed at instilling belief in a particular religious faith. However, this does not distinguish P's activities from the other groups' discussions of moral issues. Furthermore, the Court cannot distinguish worship from other religious speech.

Concurrence (Breyer, J.). The Court is merely denying D summary judgment. At trial, both parties will have a chance to fill evidentiary gaps regarding whether allowing P to participate will be perceived as an endorsement of religion by D.

Dissent (Stevens, J.). D specifically excluded "religious purposes" from its allowed uses. There are different levels of religious speech, from mere expression of a religious point of view about a particular topic, to religious worship, and finally to proselytizing. D could reasonably believe that evangelical meetings designed to convert children pose a risk.

Dissent (Souter, Ginsburg, JJ.). The Court's approach would stand for the proposition that any public school opened for civic meetings must be opened for use as a church, synagogue, or mosque. This case is much different from *Lamb's Chapel* since it involves elementary age children, a limited forum, and close proximity in time, location, and format with regular school hours.

c. **Financial aid to church-related schools.**

1) **Tax exemptions.** The Court has upheld the constitutionality of a state's exempting from local property taxes any real or personal property owned by a church and used exclusively for religious purposes. Such tax exemptions do ***not*** constitute attempts to "establish, support, or sponsor" religion, as proscribed by the Establishment Clause. [*See* Walz v. New York City Tax Commission, 397 U.S. 664 (1970)]

2) **Financial aid.**

a) **Basic test.** The Court has promulgated three guidelines for determining the validity of state statutes granting financial aid to church-related schools. To be valid, the statute must: (i) reflect a clearly secular purpose; (ii) have a primary effect that neither advances nor inhibits religion; and (iii) avoid "excessive government entanglement" with religion. [*See* Lemon v. Kurtzman, 403 U.S. 602 (1971)]

b) **Limited grants.** The Court upheld government statutes authorizing monetary grants for construction of buildings to be used exclusively for secular education at church-related colleges. [*See* Tilton v. Richardson, 403 U.S. 672 (1971); Roemer v. Board of Public Works, *infra*] The rationale is that the government program has a "secular purpose" (enlarging available facilities for college education); its primary impact is neither to "enhance nor impede" religion (buildings were for secular education only); and there is no "excessive government entanglement"—the one-time grant of money requiring only minimum contact between the government and the colleges.

c) **Unlimited grants.** Even though a state law has a valid secular purpose and effect, if any other "primary" effect of the law would be to advance or inhibit religion, the law violates the Establishment Clause. (There is no weighing of the effects to determine which is the most "primary.") [*See* Committee for Public Education & Religious Liberty v. Nyquist, 413 U.S. 756 (1973)]

(1) **Maintenance and repair grants.** Thus, a state program for direct money grants to sectarian (as well as nonsectarian) schools "for maintenance and repair of school facilities" has been held to violate the Establishment Clause where there was no restriction on the use of the facilities thus improved. Even though one primary ef-

fect of the program was to foster nonpublic education, another effect advanced religious training—*i.e.*, state funds could be used to subsidize facilities in which religion was taught or practiced. [*See* Committee for Public Education, *supra*]

(2) **Tuition credits.** Furthermore, a state program of "tuition reimbursement grants" paid directly to parents of sectarian school children (or income tax credits to such parents) violates the Establishment Clause. Although such a program may have a valid secular purpose and effect, another primary effect of such program would be to underwrite the financial cost of religious training. [*See* Committee for Public Education, *supra*]

d) **Public employees on parochial school grounds--**

Agostini v. Felton,

Facts. In *Aguilar v. Felton*, 473 U.S. 402 (1985), the Court held that New York City's program to send public school teachers into parochial schools to provide remedial education to disadvantaged children involved an excessive entanglement of church and state contrary to the First Amendment's Establishment Clause. On remand, the district court entered a permanent injunction against the program. Ten years later, Felton and other school officials (Ps) sought relief from the injunction, noting that compliance had cost over $100 million. The district court denied the motion, and the court of appeals affirmed. The Supreme Court granted certiorari.

Issue. Does placement of public employees on parochial school grounds inevitably result in the impermissible effect of state-sponsored indoctrination?

Held. No. Judgment reversed.

- Earlier cases were based on the assumption, since abandoned, that the mere placement of public employees on parochial school grounds inevitably resulted in impermissible state-sponsored indoctrination or a symbolic union between government and religion. In addition, since the *Aguilar* decision, the Court has departed from the rule that all government aid that directly aids the educational function of religious schools is invalid. For example, in *Zobrest v. Catalina Foothills School District*, 509 U.S. 1 (1993), the Court upheld a program to provide an interpreter who did not inculcate any religious messages, noting that her mere presence on private school property should not be presumed to inculcate religion.

- The program in this case directs services toward the eligible students, not the institutions. The same aid is provided whether the services are provided off-campus or on-campus. The aid is allocated on the basis of neutral, secular criteria that neither favor nor disfavor religion.

- ♦ The Court's finding of excessive entanglement in *Aguilar* rested on three grounds, including the requirement for administrative cooperation between the plaintiff and the parochial schools and the possibility of increasing the dangers of political divisiveness. But these two considerations are insufficient to create an excessive entanglement.

- ♦ The program does not result in governmental indoctrination; define its recipients by reference to religion; or create excessive entanglement. Therefore, it is permissible.

Dissent (Souter, Stevens, Ginsburg, Breyer, JJ.). It is impossible to draw a line between "supplemental" and general education. If the state may enter parochial schools to teach, it must in constitutional principle be free to assume, or assume payment for, the entire cost of instruction provided in any ostensibly secular subject in any religious school. The *Aguilar* approach drew a sensible line. The *Zobrest* holding should be limited to situations in which a public employee simply translates for one student the material presented to the class for the benefit of all students.

---

e) Loans to private secular schools--

Mitchell v. Helms,

Facts. Chapter 2 of the Education Consolidation and Improvement Act ("ECIA") provided for federal grants to local educational agencies ("LEAs"), which in turn loaned educational materials and equipment, including library and media materials and computer equipment, to public and private elementary and secondary schools to implement "secular, neutral, and nonideological" programs. In Jefferson Parish, Louisiana, about 30% of these funds were allocated for private schools, most of which were religiously affiliated. The amount of the grant was based solely on enrollment in each school. Helms (P) filed suit claiming that ECIA violated the First Amendment's Establishment Clause. The district court agreed with P. The district court judge was later replaced with another judge, who upheld the statute. During P's appeal, the Supreme Court decided *Agostini v. Felton, supra.* The court of appeals held that *Agostini* had not rejected the distinction between textbooks and other in-kind aid and held that the statute was unconstitutional. The Supreme Court granted certiorari.

Issue. May the federal government provide funds to local educational agencies that loan educational materials, including books and computer equipment, to private secular schools, so long as the purpose is to implement secular, neutral, and nonideological programs?

Held. Yes. Judgment reversed.

- In *Agostini*, *supra*, the Court modified the *Lemon* test (*supra*) by recasting the entanglement inquiry as simply one factor relevant to determining a statute's effect. Under *Agostini*, a court may determine that government aid has the effect of advancing religion if it (i) results in governmental indoctrination, (ii) defines its recipients by reference to religion, or (iii) creates an excessive entanglement. In this case, the district court held that Chapter 2 has a secular purpose and that it did not create an excessive entanglement. This leaves the first two *Agostini* criteria to consider.

- The first criterion is whether any indoctrination that occurs at the school could reasonably be attributed to governmental action. To determine whether indoctrination is attributable to the government, the Court applies the neutrality principle. Aid that is offered to a broad range of groups of persons without regard to their religion is permitted. If the government, seeking to further some legitimate secular purpose, offers aid on the same terms, without regard to religion, to all who adequately further that purpose, then any aid going to a religious recipient only has the effect of furthering that secular purpose.

- One factor that helps assure neutrality is whether any governmental aid that goes to a religious institution does so as a result of the genuinely independent and private choices of individuals. In this case, the grants were based on school enrollment, which reflects the private choices of students and their parents. This process makes it more difficult for a government to grant special favors that might lead to a religious establishment.

- *Agostini*'s second primary criterion—whether an aid program defines its recipients by reference to religion—is closely related to the first. It uses the same facts to answer a different question—whether the criteria for allocating the aid create a financial incentive to undertake religious indoctrination. Such an incentive is not present when the aid is allocated on the basis of neutral, secular criteria that neither favor nor disfavor religion, and is made available to both religious and secular beneficiaries on a nondiscriminatory basis.

- P claims that direct, nonincidental aid to religious schools is always impermissible, but such an approach is inconsistent with the Court's more recent cases. The purpose of the direct/indirect distinction is to prevent "subsidization" of religion, and the Court's more recent cases address this concern through the principle of private choice, as incorporated in the first *Agostini* criterion (*i.e.*, whether any indoctrination could be attributed to the government). If aid to schools, even "direct aid," is neutrally available and, before reaching or benefiting any religious school, first passes through the hands (literally or figuratively) of numerous private citizens who are free to direct the aid elsewhere, the government has not provided any "support of religion."

Concurrence (O'Connor, Breyer, JJ.). The plurality appears to treat neutrality as the most important factor in evaluating Establishment Clause challenges to school-aid programs. While neutrality is an important factor, it is not the only consideration. The per-capital aid program is not the same as the true private choice programs approved in prior cases. The Court should simply apply the *Agostini* criteria. Application of *Agostini* to these facts does demonstrate that the program is not unconstitutional. P would have to prove that the aid actually is, or has been, used for religious purposes. Although there may have been some minor use of government-loaned equipment for religious instruction, it was at best de minimis.

Dissent (Souter, Stevens, Ginsburg, JJ.). The First Amendment prohibits any government act favoring religion, a particular religion, or even irreligion. The Establishment Clause has been consistently applied to prohibit public aid to religion and to the religious mission of sectarian schools. Until now, the question has been whether the benefit was intended to aid in providing the religious element of the education and was likely to do so. The Court today changes this approach by applying an evenhandedness approach. It holds that there is nothing wrong with aiding a school's religious mission, so long as the religious teaching obtains its tax support under a formally evenhanded criterion of distribution.

---

f) Publicly financed school choice--

Zelman v. Simmons-Harris

Facts. The state of Ohio adopted a pilot program that gave financial assistance to families living in any Ohio school district that was under a federal court order to be supervised by the state education superintendent, Zelman (D). The Cleveland City School District, which included 75,000 children, was the only district in that category. The children in the Cleveland district were mostly from low-income and minority families. The pilot program provided tuition aid for students to attend a participating public or private school chosen by their parents instead of the one they would otherwise be assigned to. Any private school, religious or nonreligious, could participate in the program, but the school had to agree not to discriminate on the basis of race, religion, or ethnic background. Forty-six of the fifty-six participating private schools had a religious affiliation, and 96% of the students who participated in the program attended the religious schools. Simmons-Harris and other taxpayers (Ps) sought an injunction against the program. The district court granted Ps summary judgment. The court of appeals affirmed. The Supreme Court granted certiorari.

Issue. May a state provide tuition vouchers that enable students who would otherwise attend public schools to attend private religious schools?

Held. Yes. Judgment reversed.

- The state had a valid secular purpose for adopting the program—to provide educational assistance to poor children in a demonstrably failing public school system. The program would violate the Establishment Clause only if it had the forbidden "effect" of advancing or inhibiting religion.

- There is a clear distinction between government programs that provide aid directly to religious schools and programs that allow, through the exercise of true private choice, for government aid going to religious schools. In previous cases, the Court has upheld neutral government programs that provided aid directly to individuals who, through their own choice, directed the aid to religious schools.

- Funding programs based on choice might lead to the incidental advancement of a religious message, but that advancement is attributable to the individual recipient who makes the choice, not to the government. Ohio's program does not give rise to any reasonable inference that the government is endorsing religious schools in general.

- Unlike the program in *Committee for Public Education & Religious Liberty v. Nyquist*, *supra*, cited by Ps, this program does not provide financial support exclusively to private schools and the parents of private school enrollees. *Nyquist* does not govern neutral educational assistance programs like the program in this case.

Concurrence (O'Connor, J.). The Court's decision today follows precedent. Although a significant portion of the funds appropriated for the program reach religious schools with no restriction on the use of the funds, the total amount of $8.2 million that flows to religious schools in one year is small compared with the amount provided to religious institutions at all levels of government through tax credits and exemptions and other public benefit programs. The main point is that the parents are free to have their children attend either nonreligious or religious private schools.

Concurrence (Thomas, J.). Ohio's program is a response to an educational emergency that deprived the inner-city children of the opportunity for a good education. The Fourteenth Amendment was adopted to guarantee individual liberty and should not be used to prohibit the exercise of educational choice.

Dissent (Stevens, J.). D's educational crisis should not affect the constitutionality of D's program. The issue is simply whether or not public funds may be used to indoctrinate thousands of grammar school children in a particular religious faith.

Dissent (Souter, Stevens, Ginsburg, Breyer, JJ.). Ohio's program allows the government to pay tuition at private religious schools to support the schools' religious missions. In *Everson*, *supra*, the Court held that no tax may be levied to support any religious activities or institutions. Ohio's program allows tax money to be used to teach religious doctrines in these schools. The Court is ignoring *Everson*. The facts that over 96% of the students attending private schools are in religious schools, and that most families did not choose the schools because of the religion taught there, demonstrate that the problem is a lack of sufficient nonreligious schools. Parents' choices are actually restricted to choosing which religious school to send their children to.

3) **Higher education.**

a) **Introduction.** The Court has allowed federal aid for construction of academic facilities at church-related colleges, as long as the facilities were used for nonsectarian instruction only. [Tilton v. Richardson, *supra*]

b) **Noncategorical grants--**

Roemer v. Board of Public Works,

Facts. Maryland provided for annual noncategorical grants to private colleges, subject only to the restrictions that the funds not be used for "sectarian purposes." Roemer (P) challenged the law, but a three-judge district court upheld it. P appeals.

Issue. May a state make annual noncategorical grants to religiously affiliated colleges by restricting the use of the funds to nonsectarian purposes?

Held. Yes. Judgment affirmed.

- The parties agree that there is a valid state purpose behind the statute.
- The question of whether there is a primary effect of advancing religion is satisfied by the finding that the recipient colleges are not pervasively sectarian but that the secular side can be separated and the funds used exclusively for those purposes.
- The question of excessive entanglement is satisfied by finding that the state's aid was reviewed only once a year and that the program applied to all private colleges, not just religious ones.

Concurrence (White, Rehnquist, JJ.). The third prong of the Court's test is redundant. If there is a secular legislative purpose, and the law's effect is neither to advance nor inhibit religion, it is permissible.

Dissent (Brennan, Marshall, JJ.). The act in actuality provides for payment of general subsidies to religious institutions from public funds. This is an impermissible state involvement with religion.

Dissent (Stewart, J.). The act is unconstitutional as applied to those colleges that teach theology to inculcate the religious beliefs of the affiliated church rather than as an academic discipline.

Dissent (Stevens, J.). State subsidies tend to tempt religious schools to compromise their religious mission and should not be permitted.

---

4) Financial assistance--

Rosenberger v. Rector & Visitors of the University of Virginia,

Facts. The Rector and Visitors of the University of Virginia (D), a public university, sponsored student publications by authorizing the payment of outside contractors for the printing costs. A student group became eligible for reimbursement by becoming a Contracted Independent Organization ("CIO"). Reimbursement funds came from a Student Activities Fund ("SAF"), which was funded by mandatory student assessments. CIO activities that are excluded from SAF support include religious and political activities, but these restrictions do not preclude funding of otherwise eligible student organizations that espouse particular viewpoints. Rosenberger and others (Ps) organized Wide Awake Productions ("WAP") and qualified it as a CIO. Although Ps' objective was to publish a magazine of philosophical and religious expression, WAP was not deemed a "religious organization." Ps published a paper that presented a Christian viewpoint on a variety of issues relevant to the student community. Ps applied for reimbursement of printing costs. D denied Ps' request on the ground that the paper promoted a particular belief in, or about, a deity, and thus was a religious activity. Ps sued on the ground that D's refusal to reimburse violated their rights to freedom of speech and press. The lower courts found for D, and the Supreme Court granted certiorari.

Issue. May a public university deny reimbursement to a student newspaper solely on the ground that the newspaper expresses a religious viewpoint?

Held. No. Judgment reversed.

- ♦ The government may not regulate speech based on its substantive content or the message it conveys. Viewpoint discrimination is prohibited even when the limited public forum is one that the state has created. Once a state has opened a limited forum, it must respect the lawful boundaries it has set.

- ♦ A state may use content discrimination to preserve the purposes of a limited forum, but it may not use viewpoint discrimination, which is presumed impermissible when directed against speech otherwise within the forum's limitations.

- The SAF is a forum created by D. D has not excluded religion as a subject matter, but it has selected for disfavored treatment student papers such as Ps' that have religious editorial viewpoints. This obvious viewpoint discrimination is permissible merely because D discriminates against all religious viewpoints. The exclusion of several views on an issue is just as offensive to the First Amendment as the exclusion of only one view.

- Where the state is the speaker, it may make content-based choices in its expression. However, viewpoint-based restrictions are not proper when the state does not itself speak, but instead expends funds to encourage a diversity of views from private speakers.

- D's funding program is neutral toward religion. This neutrality distinguishes the student fees from a tax levied for the direct support of a church. The SAF cannot be used for supporting one religion, but the funds are available to all students with CIO status. Reimbursements are available for the entire spectrum of speech, including religious, antireligious, and other viewpoints. The program respects the critical difference between government speech endorsing religion, which the Establishment Clause prohibits, and private speech endorsing religion, which the Free Speech and Free Exercise Clauses protect.

- The dissent's approach would require D to scrutinize the content of student speech to assure that the speech in question, which is otherwise protected by the Constitution, does not contain too great a religious content. The effect would be government censorship with the objective of assuring that all student writings meet a standard of secular orthodoxy. Such official censorship would be far more inconsistent with the Establishment Clause than is the provision of secular printing services on a religion-blind basis.

Concurrence (O'Connor, J.). On the one hand, not financing Ps' paper could violate the principle of neutrality and sends a message of hostility toward religion. On the other hand, financing Ps' paper could violate the prohibition of direct state funding of religious activities. Under these specific facts, however, D does not endorse Ps' religious perspective. Student organizations are independent of the university. The financial assistance is distributed in a manner that ensures its use only for permissible purposes. The assistance is provided in such a way as to avoid the perception of government endorsement of the religious message. The assistance funds are collected from the students themselves, and are not government resources.

Concurrence (Thomas, J.). It is more likely that the Framers saw the Establishment Clause as a prohibition on governmental preferences for some religious faiths over others than that it was intended to forbid government preferences for religion over irreligion. However, there is no indication that the government must discriminate against religious adherents by excluding them from more generally available financial subsidies.

Dissent (Souter, Stevens, Ginsburg, Breyer, JJ.). The Court has, for the first time, approved direct funding of core religious activities by an arm of the state. The Establishment Clause prohibits the use of public funds to directly subsidize religious preaching. D requires students to pay the SAF, and to use any part of the SAF for the direct support of religious activity clearly establishes religion. The doctrine of limited government forum discussed in *Widmar* and *Lamb's Chapel*, *supra*, does not apply outside the context of a forum for literal speaking. Here, the government is extending economic benefits to Ps beyond the provision of a forum for speech. D has prohibited all religious activities, not just those of a particular faith.

---

2. **The Free Exercise of Religion.** The Free Exercise Clause is designed to protect against governmental compulsion in regard to religious matters. It bars governmental acts that would regulate religious beliefs as such, interfere with the dissemination thereof, impede the observance of religious practices, or discriminate in favor of one religion over another, where such acts are not otherwise justifiable in terms of valid governmental aims. [Gillette v. United States, *supra*]

   a. **Belief, expression, and conduct.**

      1) **The Mormon polygamy cases.** The Mormons, whose leader is sustained as a prophet in the biblical sense, practiced polygamy pursuant to the prophet's teachings. A federal statute made polygamy a crime in federal territories, including Utah. The Supreme Court upheld a conviction under the statute, holding that the First Amendment furnished no defense in any case where a statute of general application punished conduct compelled by religious belief. [Reynolds v. United States, 98 U.S. 145 (1878)] Later, the Court upheld an Idaho territorial statute intended to prevent Mormons from voting. To call advocacy of polygamy "a tenet of religion is to offend the common sense of mankind," according to the Court, despite the fact that the major biblical prophets accepted the practice. [Davis v. Beason, 133 U.S. 333 (1890)]

      2) **Flag saluting.** Several decisions have dealt with the right of various religious faiths (particularly Jehovah's Witnesses) to refuse to participate in flag salute ceremonies in school or other programs, where the faiths claim a violation of their religious tenets.

         a) In one wartime decision, the Court upheld a state regulation requiring the flag salute ceremony in public schools, adopting an attitude of concern only for the general reasonableness of the state law. [*See* Minersville v. Gobitis, 310 U.S. 586 (1940)]

b) The modern position of the Court is that a compulsory flag salute ceremony for all school pupils is a violation of freedom of expression. [*See* West Virginia State Board of Education v. Barnette, *supra*]

b. **Regulation of conduct compelled by religious belief.** The Free Exercise Clause absolutely prohibits any infringement of the freedom to believe a particular religion, but actions taken pursuant to religious beliefs are not absolutely protected.

1) **Disqualification for public benefits--**

Sherbert v. Verner,

Facts. South Carolina, through Verner (D), denied unemployment compensation benefits to workers who failed to accept employment when offered, without good cause. Sherbert (P) was denied benefits because she failed to accept a job that required Saturday work. Her basis for refusal was her membership in the Seventh-Day Adventist Church, which recognized Saturday as the Sabbath day. The state courts upheld the denial of benefits, and P appeals.

Issue. May a state deny benefits to otherwise eligible recipients whose failure to meet all the requirements is based on a religious belief?

Held. No. Judgment reversed.

- Conditioning the availability of benefits on P's willingness to violate a cardinal principle of her religious faith effectively penalizes the free exercise of her constitutional liberties, and can only be justified by a compelling state interest.
- The only state interest lies in discouraging spurious claims, but D has failed to show that this possibility is significant or that no alternative, less damaging regulation exists.
- The result here reflects merely the governmental obligation of neutrality in the face of religious differences and does not promote or favor one religion over the other.

Concurrence (Stewart, J.). The Establishment Clause as previously construed by this Court requires denial of P's claim; otherwise, the government would be establishing P's religion by granting her benefits because of her beliefs, while others, not of P's faith, are denied benefits. The decision proves that the Court has incorrectly construed that clause in prior cases. Additionally, we should specifically overrule *Braunfeld v. Brown*, 366 U.S. 599 (1961), which upheld Sunday closing laws against a Free Exercise Clause challenge.

Dissent (Harlan, White, JJ.). The Court actually overrules *Braunfeld*, since the secular purpose of the statute here is even clearer than the one in that case. The Court goes too far in holding that a state must furnish unemployment benefits to one who is unavailable for work whenever the unavailability arises from the exercise of religious convictions.

---

2) **Denial of unemployment benefits.** In *Thomas v. Review Board*, 450 U.S. 707 (1981), the Court held that a state could not deny unemployment benefits to a person who was transferred to a division that fabricated armaments and who refused to work because his religious beliefs forbade his participation in such production. The basic principle behind the case was that the state may not burden religion by conditioning the receipt of an important benefit upon conduct proscribed by a religious faith, or by denying such a benefit because of conduct mandated by religious belief.

3) **Compulsory education.** A state has a strong interest in the education of its citizenry and may therefore require that all children attend school (public or private) until a specified age. However, the state's interest in compulsory education is not absolute; in appropriate cases, it must be balanced against the interests protected by the Free Exercise Clause.

a) **Exception for Amish students--**

Wisconsin v. Yoder,

Facts. Yoder and other Amish parents (Ds) refused to send their children to school beyond eighth grade despite a Wisconsin law requiring attendance until age 16. Ds claimed further education would violate their religious beliefs because the values taught in public high school contrasted with the Amish values and way of life. Ds were convicted, but the conviction was reversed by the Wisconsin Supreme Court. Wisconsin (P) appeals.

Issue. Must a state make provision in its compulsory education laws for students whose religious beliefs prevent them from attending secondary schools?

Held. Yes. Judgment affirmed.

- The values of parental direction of the religious upbringing and education of their children in their formative years have a high place in our society. Only essential state interests not otherwise served can prevail over legitimate claims to the free exercise of religion.

- The Amish way of life is an essential part of their religious beliefs and practices. Elementary education, given locally, did not subject Ds' children to adverse influences, and is not challenged. D has adequately shown, however, that secondary education would tend to severely infringe on Ds' religious beliefs.

- P's interest in ensuring education is substantially achieved in the elementary grades. Ds' children continue their education through parent-supervised agricultural vocational training. The children are thus fully prepared for responsibility. Because the state's interest in requiring the one or two extra years of education is minimal compared with Ds' religious interests, Ds' interests must prevail.

Concurrence (Stewart, Brennan, JJ.). The case does not involve the right of Amish children to attend public high schools if they so desire.

Concurrence (White, Brennan, Stewart, JJ.). The balancing of these important but conflicting interests favors Ds.

Dissent in part (Douglas, J.). We ought to reserve decision as to the parents of those students who have not affirmatively indicated a desire not to attend public high school.

Comment. In *United States v. Lee*, 455 U.S. 252 (1982), the Court held that an Amish employer may be required to withhold Social Security taxes from his employee's wages and to pay the employer's contribution. Although the Amish oppose payment of such taxes and receipt of the benefits, the infringement of religious liberty was essential to accomplish the overriding governmental interest in having an effective, functioning tax system.

---

4) Standard for law of general applicability--

Employment Division, Department of Human Resources v. Smith,

Facts. The state of Oregon made it a crime to use peyote. Smith (P) was dismissed from his job for using peyote as part of his religious ritual as a member of the Native American Church. P was denied unemployment benefits because his dismissal was due to misconduct. P sued the Employment Division, Department of Human Resources (D), claiming that his use of peyote was inspired by religion and therefore was protected under the Free Exercise Clause of the First Amendment. The Oregon Supreme Court reversed, holding that the criminal sanction was unconstitutional as applied to the religious use of peyote, and ruled that P was entitled to unemployment benefits. The Supreme Court granted certiorari.

Issue. May a state make criminal certain conduct that is part of a religious organization's ritual?

Held. Yes. Judgment reversed.

- ♦ P relies on *Sherbert, supra*, which held that a state could not condition the availability of unemployment insurance on an applicant's willingness to forego conduct required by his religion. In that case, however, the conduct was not prohibited by law; in this case, peyote use was prohibited by law.

- ♦ The states cannot ban acts or abstentions only when they are engaged in for religious reasons, or only because of the religious belief they display, because this would constitute a prohibition on the free exercise of religion. This does not mean that a religious motivation for illegal conduct exempts the actor from the law. If prohibiting the exercise of religion is merely an incidental effect of a generally applicable and otherwise valid law, the First Amendment is not implicated.

- ♦ In some cases, such as *Wisconsin v. Yoder, supra*, the First Amendment may prevent application of a neutral, generally applicable law to religiously motivated action, but these cases involve the Free Exercise Clause in connection with other constitutional protections, such as parents' right to direct the education of their children.

- ♦ P argues that the *Sherbert* test should be applied, but this test has never invalidated governmental action except the denial of unemployment compensation, and should not be extended beyond that field to require exemptions from a generally applicable criminal law. In the unemployment cases, the test is applied to prevent a state from refusing to extend religious hardship cases to a system of individual exemptions.

- ♦ If the compelling interest requirement were applied to religion cases such as this, many laws would not satisfy the test, and the result would approach anarchy, particularly in a society such as ours that contains a diversity of religious beliefs. This alternative would raise a presumption of invalidity, as applied to the religious objector, of every regulation of conduct that does not protect an interest of the highest order. The states are free, as many have, to exempt from their drug laws the use of peyote in sacramental services, but the states are not constitutionally required to do so.

Concurrence in part (O'Connor, Brennan, Marshall, Blackmun, JJ.). A law that prohibits religiously motivated conduct implicates First Amendment concerns, even if it is generally applicable. The First Amendment does not distinguish between laws that are generally applicable and laws that target particular religious practices; it applies to generally applicable laws that have the effect of significantly burdening a religious practice. The balance between the First Amendment and the government's legitimate interest in regulating conduct is struck by applying the compelling interest test. To be sustained, a law that burdens the free exercise of religion must either be essential to accomplish an overriding governmental interest or represent the least restrictive means of achieving some compelling state interest. In this case, the prohibition on use of peyote does satisfy the compelling state interest test.

Dissent (Blackmun, Brennan, Marshall, JJ.). The state's broad interest in fighting the war on drugs is not the interest involved in this case; the interest is the state's refusal to make an exception for the religious, ceremonial use of peyote. There is no evidence that the religious use of peyote ever harmed anyone, and 23 other states have adopted exemptions for the religious use of peyote. The assertion that requiring the state to make an exemption in this case would open the government to anarchy is speculative; such a danger is addressed through the compelling interest test.

Comment. If the purpose of a statute or other governmental action is to single out religion for adverse treatment, it violates the Free Exercise Clause unless it is narrowly tailored to advance a compelling state interest. [*See* Church of the Lukumi Babalu Aye, Inc. v. City of Hialeah, 508 U.S. 520 (1993)—a city ordinance barring ritual animal sacrifice practiced by particular religion violated the Free Exercise Clause because its purpose was to suppress that religion]

---

5) Excluding the study of religion from public scholarships--

Locke v. Davey

Facts. Davey (P) received a Promise Scholarship under a program funded by the state of Washington. Recipients were prohibited from using the scholarship at an institution where they would pursue a degree in devotional theology. P wanted to attend a private Christian college to become a church pastor. When P learned that he could not use his scholarship to pursue his desired degree, he sued Locke (D), the governor of Washington, for damages and injunctive relief. The district court granted D summary judgment. The Ninth Circuit reversed on the ground that D had singled out religion for unfavorable treatment, contrary to *Church of the Lukumi Babalu Aye, Inc. v. City of Hialeah, supra*. The Supreme Court granted certiorari.

Issue. May a state prohibit recipients of state-financed scholarships from using the money to pursue a degree in devotional theology?

Held. Yes. Judgment reversed.

- States may take actions that are permitted by the Establishment Clause but not required by the Free Exercise Clause. In this case, D could have permitted Promise Scholars to pursue a degree in devotional theology without violating the Establishment Clause.

- P claims that, under *Lukumi*, D's program is presumptively unconstitutional because it is not facially neutral with respect to religion. But *Lukumi* involved sanctions on a type of religious service or rite, whereas D's scholarship program merely chooses not to fund a distinct category of instruction.

- Training someone to become a minister is an essentially religious endeavor and is distinct from other academic pursuits. D has a substantial interest in not establishing religion. States have even included provisions in their constitutions to exclude the ministry from receiving state funding. D's scholarship program does allow attendance at religious schools and covers theology courses. It merely denies funding for vocational religious instruction. The difference between the two religion clauses is illustrated by this case.

Dissent (Scalia, Thomas, JJ.). D's exclusion of religion from a public benefit generally available violates the Free Exercise Clause as much as would a special tax on vocational religious instruction. The scholarship program facially discriminates against religion. No field of study but religion is singled out for disfavor. D acted purely from a philosophical preference, and D's rationale could be extended to deny priests and nuns other generally available public benefits, including health benefits.

Dissent (Thomas, J.). The study of theology does not necessarily implicate religious devotion or faith. It can be studied from a secular perspective as well as from a religious one.

---

6) Religious Freedom Restoration Act held unconstitutional--

City of Boerne v. Flores. *See supra*

7) Protecting free exercise of religion in prison--

Cutter v. Wilkinson,

Facts. The Religious Land Use and Institutionalized Persons Act of 2000 ("RLUIPA") prohibited the government from imposing a substantial burden on the religious exercise of a person residing in or confined to an institution unless the burden furthered a compelling governmental interest by the least restrictive means. Current and former inmates in Ohio correctional facilities (Ps) claimed they were adherents of nonmainstream religions, including Wicca and Satanist, and that Ohio prison officials (Ds) failed to accommodate their religious exercise in different ways, including retaliating and discriminating against them for exercising their nontraditional faiths and denying them access to religious literature and group worship granted to adherents of mainstream religions. Ps sued under the statute. Ds responded by challenging RLUIPA as a violation of the Establishment Clause. The district court denied Ds' motion to dismiss, but the court of appeals reversed. The Supreme Court granted certiorari.

Issue. May Congress prevent the imposition of a substantial burden on the religious exercise of inmates held in a state prison?

Held. Yes. Judgment reversed.

- ♦ In *Employment Division v. Smith, supra*, the Court held that the First Amendment does not inhibit enforcement of otherwise valid laws of general application that incidentally burden religious conduct. In response to *Smith*, Congress enacted the Religious Freedom Restoration Act of 1993 ("RFRA"), which was invalidated in *City of Boerne* because the RFRA exceeded Congress's remedial powers under the Fourteenth Amendment. Subsequently, Congress adopted RLUIPA to prevent imposition of substantial burdens on the religious exercise of persons in confinement.

- ♦ RLUIPA's institutionalized-persons provision is compatible with the Establishment Clause; removal of government-imposed burdens on religious exercise is more likely to be perceived as an accommodation of the exercise of religion rather than as a government endorsement of religion. And courts must be satisfied that RLUIPA's prescriptions are administered neutrally among different faiths.

- ♦ RLUIPA applies to state-run institutions, such as mental hospitals and prisons, in which the government exerts a degree of control unparalleled in civilian society. Thus, RLUIPA protects institutionalized persons who are dependent on the government's permission and accommodation for exercise of their religion.

- ♦ According to the understanding of the court of appeals, precedent holds that RLUIPA advanced religion in violation of the Establishment Clause by giving greater protection to religious rights than to other constitutionally protected rights. But if this were true, many religious accommodations would fall. For example, Ohio provides inmates with chaplains but not with political consultants, and Ohio allows prisoners to assemble for worship, but not for political rallies.

- ♦ RLUIPA does not elevate accommodation of religious observances over an institution's need to maintain order and safety; an accommodation must be measured so that it does not override other significant interests. Even with RLUIPA's compelling governmental interest standard, context matters in the application of that standard. Lawmakers supporting RLUIPA were aware of the need for discipline, order, safety, and security in penal institutions.

Concurrence (Thomas, J.). While the Court's opinion is correct, the same conclusion can be reached by viewing the Establishment Clause as a federalism provision.

TABLE OF CASES
(Page numbers of briefed cases in bold)

NOTES

NOTES

NOTES

NOTES

NOTES

NOTES

NOTES

NOTES

NOTES

NOTES